Contrastive Studies in
Morphology and Syntax

Bloomsbury Studies in Theoretical Linguistics

Bloomsbury Studies in Theoretical Linguistics publishes work at the forefront of present-day developments in the field. The series is open to studies from all branches of theoretical linguistics and to the full range of theoretical frameworks. Titles in the series present original research that makes a new and significant contribution and are aimed primarily at scholars in the field, but are clear and accessible, making them useful also to students, to new researchers and to scholars in related disciplines.

Other titles in the series

Agreement, Pronominal Clitics and Negation in Tamazight Berber, Hamid Ouali
A Neural Network Model of Lexical Organisation, Michael Fortescue
Approaches to Predicative Possession, edited by Gréte Dalmi, Jacek Witkoś and
Piotr Cegłowski
Deviational Syntactic Structures, Hans Gotzsche
First Language Acquisition in Spanish, Gilda Socarras
Grammar of Spoken English Discourse, Gerard O'Grady
Pragmatic Syntax, Jieun Kiaer
The Semantic Representation of Natural Language, Michael Levison, Greg Lessard,
Craig Thomas and Matthew Donald
The Syntax and Semantics of Discourse Markers, Miriam Urgelles-Coll
The Syntax of Mauritian Creole, Anand Syea

Contrastive Studies in Morphology and Syntax

Edited by
Michalis Georgiafentis, Giannoula Giannoulopoulou,
Maria Koliopoulou and Angeliki Tsokoglou

BLOOMSBURY ACADEMIC
LONDON • NEW YORK • OXFORD • NEW DELHI • SYDNEY

BLOOMSBURY ACADEMIC
Bloomsbury Publishing Plc
50 Bedford Square, London, WC1B 3DP, UK
1385 Broadway, New York, NY 10018, USA
29 Earlsfort Terrace, Dublin 2, Ireland

BLOOMSBURY, BLOOMSBURY ACADEMIC and the Diana logo are trademarks of
Bloomsbury Publishing Plc

First published in Great Britain 2020
Paperback edition published 2021

A catalogue record for this book is available from the British Library.

A catalog record for this book is available from the Library of Congress.

ISBN: HB: 978-1-3500-7918-2
PB: 978-1-3502-7309-2
ePDF: 978-1-3500-7919-9
eBook: 978-1-3500-7920-5

Series: Bloomsbury Studies in Theoretical Linguistics

Typeset by Deanta Global Publishing Services, Chennai, India

To find out more about our authors and books visit www.bloomsbury.com and
sign up for our newsletters.

Contents

List of contributors   vii

Preface   *Giannoula Giannoulopoulou*   xi

Acknowledgements   xix

Introduction   *Michalis Georgiafentis, Giannoula Giannoulopoulou,*
    Maria Koliopoulou and Angeliki Tsokoglou   1

Part One   Theoretical issues in contrastive linguistics

1   Heuristic dimensions of contrastive linguistics   *Paul J. Hopper*   9

2   English as a bridge: An L3-approach to contrastive linguistics   *Livio Gaeta*   26

3   'Verb-first' in proverbs and slogans: A German-based contrastive view
    Torsten Leuschner   45

Part Two   Morphology

4   Gender marking in English and Polish job titles: Referring to female
    physicians   *Bożena Cetnarowska*   63

5   Congruence and equivalence in adjective-forming suffixation in Spanish
    and English: A contrastive study   *José A. Sánchez Fajardo*   81

6   Linking elements in German compounds: A morphological analysis in
    comparison with Greek   *Maria Koliopoulou*   102

7   Compounding in Albanian as a case of 'structural blending': Evidence
    from the contrastive analysis of Greek and Albanian   *Asimakis Fliatouras*   119

8   Past tense usages in tense-rich and tenseless languages: A contrastive
    study   *Masahiko Nose*   137

Part Three   Syntax

9   A contrastive analysis of interrogative constructions in Romance:
    Microvariation and theory   *Caterina Donati*   155

10   *Wh*-questions at the syntax-discourse interface: German–Swedish
    contrasts   *Valéria Molnár*   174

11 Focus types: A crosslinguistic study of clause and information
structure *Michalis Georgiafentis and Angeliki Tsokoglou*   191

12 Strong pronouns as postverbal subjects in Spanish and Italian
Manuel Leonetti and Victoria Escandell-Vidal   210

13 Cliticization patterns in Greek: A comparative examination with
crosslinguistic remarks *Anthi Revithiadou and Vassilios Spyropoulos*   225

14 Towards a formal model of transfer under contact: Contrasting Asia
Minor Greek to mainland Greek and Turkish in search of syntactic
borrowings *Dimitris Michelioudakis and Ioanna Sitaridou*   245

15 Goal prevalence and situation types: An empirical analysis of
differences in Greek and German motion event descriptions
Thanasis Georgakopoulos and Holden Härtl   262

Index of subjects   281
Index of languages   287

Contributors

Bożena Cetnarowska is the Head of the Department of Contrastive Studies in the Institute of English at the University of Silesia in Katowice (Poland). Her research interests include word-formation, morphosyntax and lexical semantics in English and Slavonic languages, as well as contrastive Polish–English studies. She is the author of three monographs: *The Syntax, Semantics and Derivation of Bare Nominalisations in English* (1993), *Passive Nominals in English and Polish: An Optimality-theoretic Analysis* (2005) and *Compound Nouns and Phrasal Nouns in English and Polish* (2019).

Caterina Donati is a syntactician working primarily on Romance and Sign languages. After her PhD in 1998 in Florence, she was first recruited to work at the University of Urbino and then at Rome Sapienza. Since 2014, she has been a Full Professor at the University Paris Diderot. Her research focuses on movement and labels, the typology of relativization strategies, the grammatical description of Sign languages, the parsing of ambiguous structures, and bilingualism. She is the author of a Linguistic Inquiry Monograph on (re)labelling in 2015 (with C. Cecchetto), of several articles and book chapters, and of two introductions to syntax in Italian.

Victoria Escandell-Vidal is Professor of Linguistics at the National University of Distance Education (UNED), Spain. She is the author of several books: *Introducción a la Pragmática* (1996/2006), *Fundamentos de Semántica composicional* (2004), *La comunicación: lengua, cognición y sociedad* (2014), and has co-edited *Procedural Meaning: Problems and Perspectives* (2011, with M. Leonetti and A. Ahern). She has published papers in journals such as *Language Sciences*, *Lingua*, *Studies in Language*, *Journal of Pragmatics*, *Language and Speech*, *Intercultural Pragmatics* and *International Review of Pragmatics*. She is currently the principal investigator of a project investigating how semantic feature mismatches are inferentially solved in the course of utterance interpretation.

Asimakis Fliatouras is a lecturer in historical linguistics (Department of Greek Philology, Democritus University of Thrace, Greece). He has published three books (in Greek), papers in journals, conference proceedings and collective volumes. His publications focus on the morphological change of the Greek language, the impact of Balkan language contact in morphology, onomastics and the connection between Modern and Ancient Greek.

Livio Gaeta (PhD 1998, University of Rome III) is Full Professor of German Linguistics (Department of Humanistic Studies, University of Turin). Previously, he held tenured positions as Assistant and Associate Professor at the University of Rome III and at the University of Naples 'Federico II' and was awarded a Fellowship of the Alexander von

Humboldt foundation at the Humboldt University of Berlin (2009). His main research interests comprise morphology, language change and grammaticalization, cognitive linguistics, minority languages and language contact.

Thanasis Georgakopoulos is a Marie Curie postdoctoral fellow at the University of Liège. He earned his PhD at the National and Kapodistrian University of Athens in 2011. He held various academic positions at the Aristotle University of Thessaloniki (Greece), the Free University of Berlin, the Humboldt University of Berlin, the University of Münster and the University of Kassel (Germany). His research interests focus on historical linguistics, cognitive semantics, lexical typology, linguistics of space and semantic maps.

Michalis Georgiafentis is Assistant Professor of Linguistics at the National and Kapodistrian University of Athens. He has studied English Language and Literature (specialization Language-Linguistics) at the National and Kapodistrian University of Athens and Linguistics (MA and PhD) at the University of Reading. His main research interests include theoretical linguistics, English and Greek syntax, word order variation, focusing phenomena, information structure and grammar teaching. He has published papers in international journals, in edited volumes and in conference proceedings. He has co-edited six volumes as well as a special issue for the *Journal of Greek Linguistics*.

Giannoula Giannoulopoulou is Professor of Linguistics at the National and Kapodistrian University of Athens and has taught Linguistics and more specifically Contrastive Linguistics since 1999 in several Greek universities. Her main research interests are contrastive morphology between Modern Greek and Italian, the emergence of linguistic structures and the history of linguistic theories. She has published several articles on contrastive linguistic issues. She is a member of the editorial board of *Languages in Contrast*.

Holden Härtl is Full Professor of English Linguistics at the University of Kassel (Germany). He has a doctorate in theoretical linguistics from the University of Leipzig (2001) and held various academic positions in Leipzig and Berlin (Germany). His current research focuses on event conceptualization as well as processes of lexicalization and quotation.

Paul J. Hopper has published books and articles in the areas of language change, historical linguistics and discourse analysis. His interests include Germanic and Indo-European historical linguistics and Austronesian languages. His current work involves studies in the emergent nature of grammar in natural conversation. He has served as the Collitz Memorial Professor at the Linguistic Society of America Linguistics Institute, as Directeur d'Études at the École Pratique des Hautes Études, and as lecturer at the Collège de France. He is the Paul Mellon Distinguished Professor Emeritus of Humanities at Carnegie Mellon University.

Maria Koliopoulou is an assistant professor at the Institute of Translation Studies of Innsbruck University (Austria). She holds a PhD in Linguistics (2013). Her research interests include word-formation, the interaction between morphology and syntax and morphological aspects of translation and terminology. Her contrastive studies focus on Greek and German. She is the author of papers in several journals, such as *Journal of Greek Linguistics*, *Italian Journal of Linguistics* and *Languages in Contrast*, as well as chapters in books published by Peter Lang and de Gruyter.

Manuel Leonetti is Professor of Spanish Linguistics at Complutense University of Madrid. His main research interest is the interaction of syntax, semantics and pragmatics from a formal, synchronic and cognitive perspective; he has worked on topics like information structure and word order, tense and mood, coercion, reference, definiteness and specificity. He has co-edited volumes on *Procedural Meaning* (2011), *60 problemas de gramática* (2011), and *New Perspectives in the Study of* Ser *and* Estar (2015).

Torsten Leuschner has been Professor of German Linguistics at Ghent University since 2011. He studied English, German and History at the Free University of Berlin, where he also wrote his PhD thesis on concessive conditionals in English, German and Dutch (2006). His research interests are in grammaticalization and constructionalization, word-formation, discourse analysis, lexical borrowing, and the contrastive and historical linguistics of Germanic. He is co-editor of the journal *Germanistische Mitteilungen* and of the book series *Linguistik in Empirie und Theorie – Empirical and Theoretical Linguistics*, and national chairman of the *Belgian Association of Teachers and Lecturers of German* (BGDV).

Dimitris Michelioudakis is Assistant Professor at the Aristotle University of Thessaloniki, where he teaches theoretical linguistics and syntax. He holds a BA in Philology from the National and Kapodistrian University of Athens and postgraduate degrees (MPhil and PhD) in Linguistics from the University of Cambridge. His research interests include theoretical, diachronic and comparative syntax, with a focus on the study of Greek dialects, issues at the interface between syntax and semantics (argument and event structure), morphology (case loss and syncretisms, compounding and the content of roots) and pragmatics (discourse particles). He is also interested in syntactic typology and the indigenous languages of South America.

Valéria Molnár has been working at Lund University as a Professor since 1999, after the defence of her doctoral thesis in German linguistics. She received a teachers' diploma in several subjects (Russian, Scandinavian languages, German, English) after studies at ELTE University in Budapest and at Lund University in Sweden. Her research focuses on the interface between grammar and discourse and she is interested in information structure, from both a contrastive and a general theoretical perspective. Her great interest in foreign languages as well as contrastive and typological issues is also manifested in her research concentrating on different verbal categories (aspect and voice).

Masahiko Nose is an associate professor at the Faculty of Economics, Shiga University, Japan. He obtained his PhD in functional linguistics of Finno-Ugric languages from

Tohoku University, Japan in 2003. He has held visiting positions at Max Planck Institute for Evolutionary Anthropology (Germany) and La Trobe University (Australia). His major research interests include the languages in Papua New Guinea and linguistic typology. He has been conducting fieldwork in Papua New Guinea with the Amele and the Bel community since 2006.

Anthi Revithiadou is Professor of Linguistics (Phonology) at the Aristotle University of Thessaloniki and received her PhD from Leiden University/HIL in 1999. Her research interests focus on phonological theory (metrical and prosodic phonology), the morphosyntax–phonology interface, language typology and language contact. She has also a profound interest in contact-induced systems and, especially, in endangered varieties of Greek that have been in long-term contact with Turkish (e.g. Asia Minor Greek and Ofitika Pontic). She has published two books and over sixty-five articles in scientific journals, peer-reviewed volumes and proceedings. She has presented her work in more than 100 international conferences, workshops and colloquia.

José A. Sánchez Fajardo is a lecturer in linguistics at the Department of English Studies, University of Alicante. He has a PhD in Linguistics (2016) and his core research domains are English morphology, pragmatics and lexicology. He has a special interest in lexical borrowing and marginal language in English and Spanish, particularly slang words and hispanicisms.

Ioanna Sitaridou is a reader in Spanish and historical linguistics at the Faculty of Modern and Medieval Languages, University of Cambridge. She is also Fellow and Director of Studies in Linguistics and Modern and Medieval Languages at Queens' College, Cambridge. Her main areas of research are the comparative and diachronic syntax of the Romance languages, especially thirteenth-century Spanish, and dialectal Greek, especially Pontic Greek. She studies the relationship between syntactic change and acquisition, language contact, microvariation and syntactic phylogenies.

Vassilios Spyropoulos is Associate Professor of Linguistics (Generative Syntax) at the National and Kapodistrian University of Athens. He received his PhD from the University of Reading in 1999. His research interests focus on syntactic theory and its interface with morphology and phonology, comparative linguistics and typology with emphasis on morphology and syntax, the grammatical description of Greek, dialectology (documentation and description of Greek dialectal varieties, especially Asia Minor Greek dialects), the diachrony of Greek morphosyntactic structures, and the structural and historical aspects of language contact. He has published three books and over fifty papers in journals, edited volumes and proceedings.

Angeliki Tsokoglou is Associate Professor of Linguistics at the National and Kapodistrian University of Athens. Her research interests (PhD thesis and publications) include theoretical linguistics, contrastive linguistics (specialization on Greek-German syntax) and foreign language teaching (with a specialization on grammar teaching). She has also taught (2000–2015) at the Hellenic Open University and has taken part at research projects in relation to the certification of language knowledge.

Preface

Giannoula Giannoulopoulou

The present volume contains fifteen contributions, which contrastively examine languages and dialects from several parts of the world; in this respect the papers belong to the sub-discipline of Contrastive Linguistics. In this preface, I aim to retrace the steps of Contrastive Linguistics, in order to suggest that the host of questions that Contrastive Linguistics has raised in every phase of its development is dependent on the linguistic paradigms that were dominant in the respective era and, as a result, although the focus changed according to the paradigm involved, the route of Contrastive Linguistics runs parallel to that of the most important theoretical questions raised by Linguistics in general.

I would thus like to propose that knowing the history of Contrastive Linguistics, as well as its relations with other sub-disciplines of Linguistics that are concerned with comparing languages, may have a positive impact on the progress of this sub-discipline. In Koerner's (2004: 11) words, 'This historical knowledge may prevent the practicing linguist from dogmatism in linguistic theory and lead him/her to circumspection with regard to seemingly new ideas offered on the market of ideas and, possibly, the acceptance of diversity of views that hardly can be overvalued in current linguistic debate.' Knowing the history of Contrastive Linguistics and its ancestors could also lead to a 'moderation in linguistic theory', as Paul Garvin (1970) suggested many years ago.

Several authors in current literature (see e.g. Fisiak 1984; Koliopoulou and Leuschner 2014) locate the beginning of Contrastive Linguistics or Contrastive Analysis (CA) in the mid-1950s in the pioneering works of Fries (1945) and Lado (1957). Wardhaugh (1970) in his 'Contrastive Analysis Hypothesis' aptly summarizes these views:

> The claim that the best language teaching materials are based on a contrast of the two competing linguistic systems has long been a popular one in language teaching. It exists in strong and weak versions, the strong one arising from evidence from the availability of some kind of metatheory of Contrastive Analysis and the weak from evidence from language interference.

Ringbom (1994: 738) also assumes Weinreich's (1953) and Lado's (1957) works as pioneering in Contrastive Analysis and explains that 'the main idea behind contrastive analysis was originally that a detailed comparative and contrastive study of the L1 and the L2 might reveal exactly which problems learners with the same L1 have in learning the L2' (1994: 737).

The origins of Contrastive Linguistics in Foreign Language Teaching, as well as the increasingly severe criticism Contrastive Linguistics has faced since 1970 (e.g. Alatis 1968) is a commonplace in the literature on Contrastive Linguistics and can be found in various introductions to the field, especially in European and American contexts. A non-Western point of view, as that of Wenguo and Wai Mun (2007), however, is refreshing in allowing for more general taxonomies. They argue that the beginning of Contrastive Linguistics should be dated back at least 130 years and that Humboldt should be regarded as the founder of the discipline (see, for details, Sun and Rong 2009). Chinese scholars refer to von Humboldt's (1822) work '*Über das vergleichende Sprachstudium in Beziehung auf die verschiedenen Epochen der Sprachentwicklung*' and support that the first scholar to apply Humboldt's contrastive views to the study of language was Jespersen in his *Philosophy of Grammar* (1924), where he employs contrastive methods to compare and contrast more than twenty languages. According to Wenguo and Wai Mun (2007), Western contrastive history can be divided into three phases. In the first phase (1820–1940s) a range of theoretical contrastive issues arose, dominated by such scholars as Humboldt, Jespersen and Whorf. In the second phase (1940s–1970s) the aim of Contrastive Linguistics was to serve language teaching and learning on a micro-level, with Lado and di Pietro as representative scholars. The third phase (after 1980) was a return to a macro-perspective, represented by the works of James, Fisiak and Krzeszowski.

However, despite the fact that such a non-Western point of view could be very useful, and although the comparing element is omnipresent in Linguistics from Historical-Comparative Linguistics through to Sapir's *Language* (1921) up to now, it is better to assume that the birth date of Contrastive Linguistics lies in the 1950s and is associated with the practical needs of teaching languages and translation. This connection with practical needs and goals offers Contrastive Linguistics a different perspective, that of the dialectical connection (and tension) between theory and praxis, whereas such an interrelation is not clearly visible in other sub-disciplines involving the comparison of languages. Every phase and version of this comparison can be seen as intricately linked with the linguistic questions, the research and thought paradigms that were dominant in the respective era.

For instance, Humboldt's philosophical/linguistic thought concerned such issues as: 'Kategorien des Denkens anregt, da das Positive das Negative, der Theil das Ganze, die Einheit die Vielheit, die Wirkung die Ursach, die Wirklichkeit die Möglichkeit und Nothwendigkeit, das Bedingte das Unbedingte' (Categories of thought, as the positive and the negative, the part and the whole, the unity and the plurality, the impact and the cause, the reality, the possibility and the necessity, the conditional and the unconditional).

When in the 1980s generative theory dominated the field, theory-based Contrastive Linguistics discussed theory-internal issues. Van Buren (1980: 94), for example, mentions: 'We have compared three approaches to contrastive analysis, namely a slot-in-frame technique based on a structuralist approach to language, a transformational-generative account following Chomsky (1965) and lastly what may be loosely termed a "notional" view of contrastive analysis.' And although Van Buren is a supporter of the transformational-generative account, he concludes that 'we must allow for the possibility that different jobs may require different tools'. It is interesting that Lipinska (1980: 170), on the other hand, chooses to support generative semantics against the transformational-generative point of view in the field of Contrastive Analysis because, according to her, 'The common syntactic base (in the meaning of Chomsky (1965)) is something which would still have to be proved and, thus, could not be used as a level of reference in the comparison of languages. On the other hand, the possibility of expressing the same meaning in different languages can be reasonably safely assumed.'

Today's Contrastive Linguistics has close or remote relationships with previous phases of comparing languages, although every comparison of languages does not necessarily belong to Contrastive Linguistics. It is helpful at this point to keep in mind the continuity of Contrastive Linguistics research programmes. Hawkins's (1986) 'typological turn' did not emerge *ex nihilo*. As Ringbom (1994: 741–2) informs us, 'Several large-scale contrastive projects with English as one of the languages were started in Europe in the 1960s and 1970s, some of them still continuing in the 1990s. Aspects of Polish, Serbo-Croat, Romanian, Hungarian, Finnish, German, and Swedish were compared and contrasted with English. The Polish project, in particular, has produced an impressive number of theoretically based contrastive studies.' Ringbom then moves to a very interesting conclusion:

> Most of the studies emanating from these projects have, however, made relatively little impact on English linguistics. There are several reasons for this. Since the languages contrasted with English in general are comparatively un-investigated, compared with English, which is the language most analyzed in the world, it is only natural that the flow of the new ideas resulting from these contrastive studies has been in the direction from English into the other languages rather than the other way round. Most of the projects results are published in series not very widely known outside their respective countries, and the number of English-speaking linguists sufficiently familiar especially with East European languages is very limited.

Nowadays the 'typological turn' belongs to the framework of functional typology. Fortunately, the theoretical dialogue is developing and new prospects are emerging, though the questions raised in the recent literature have not been seen for the first time in the discipline of Contrastive Linguistics. In contrast, what is more important in recent literature is the reformulation of the relationship between Contrastive Linguistics and other sub-disciplines in the general field of comparing languages. As König (2012: 4) states:

> Only by relating contrastive linguistics to, and by delimiting it from, other subfields of comparative linguistics will we obtain a clear picture of the agenda, its potential and its limits. What contrastive linguistics shares with these other approaches is its focus on variation between languages and within a language, but it clearly has its own agenda, even if it partly overlaps with these other approaches in certain respects.

In order to delimit Contrastive Linguistics from other subfields of Comparative Linguistics, König (2012: 21–3) formulates the essential components of the Contrastive Linguistics agenda as follows:

1. *Synchronic orientation*: Contrastive Linguistics has a synchronic orientation.
2. *Granularity*: Contrastive Linguistics is also concerned with fine-grained, in-depth analysis of similarities and contrasts that are generally inaccessible to typological generalizations. In that sense, it is a complement to typology rather than a small-scale typology.
3. *Comparison of language pairs*: Contrastive Analysis is mainly concerned with bilateral language comparisons.
4. *Perspective*: Contrastive Analysis describes one language from the perspective of another and will therefore reveal properties of languages that are not easily visible otherwise.
5. *Falsifiability*: Just like the results of any serious scientific inquiry, those of contrastive descriptions are easily falsifiable, if they are expressed with precision and great explicitness.
6. *Theoretical framework*: The challenge for Contrastive Analysis lies in discovering the contrasts and describing them in a maximally general way and not in the choice of a specific theoretical format. Its explanandum is the contrasts between languages.

A similar concern to define the relationship between Contrastive Linguistics, Historical-Comparative Linguistics and Linguistic Typology, with the aim not of delimiting but of integrating different aspects of language comparison, was expressed some decades earlier by Makaev (1969: 42):

La description, la comparaison et l'analyse des faits linguistiques et des langues dans les termes de la théorie des associations de langues ou de grammaire typologique, ne peuvent ni éliminer ni remplacer l'analyse historico-comparative des faits et des langues en question. Il peut s'agir actuellement de savoir de quelle manière et dans quelle mesure la linguistique comparative peut et doit être complétée, précisée, partiellement reformulée du point de vue du niveau atteint maintenant par les méthodes de recherche en linguistique; c'est justement pour cette raison qu'une place adéquate doit être faite à la grammaire typologique. L'interaction entre les méthodes de recherche historico-comparative et les méthodes typologiques s'exprime avec netteté dans la grammaire historico-typologique d'un groupe déterminé de langues.

(The description, the comparison and the analysis of the linguistic facts and the languages in terms of the theory of linguistic associations or typological grammar can neither eliminate nor replace the historic-comparative analysis of the facts and the languages in question. Actually, it would be necessary to know in what way and to what extent Comparative Linguistics can and ought to be complete, precise, partially reformulated under the point of view of the attained level by the research methods of linguistic analysis; it is exactly for this reason that an adequate place should be created for typological grammar. The interaction between the methods of historical-comparative research and the typological methods is expressed clearly in the historical-typological grammar of a specific group of languages.)

This point of view is reminiscent of van der Auwera's (2012) position that Contrastive Linguistics has the role of 'pilot typology', following Hawkins's (1986) 'typological turn'.

In my view, articulating the interrelationships between Contrastive Linguistics, Historical-Comparative Linguistics, Linguistic Typology, Comparative Dialectology (microvariation) and Intercultural Communication is a sign of maturity. Thus, Contrastive Linguistics does not exist without being interconnected with other domains of comparing languages and, consequently, cannot exist outside some theory of language.

The majority of the papers appearing in this volume were originally presented in the 8th International Contrastive Linguistics Conference (ICLC8, Athens 2017).[1] Participants from twenty-nine countries presented in ICLC8 papers that examined thirty-five languages. In the present volume, twelve languages and dialects are contrastively examined, while English, although quite frequent, is not omnipresent. This means that the direction from English to other languages is not always followed and neither is the restriction of the discussion in the Standard Average European linguistic area (Haspelmath 2001). The main reason for this is, first, that Greek, one of the main languages of comparison in this volume, is a language which, although it has a long history and has exercised great influence on the vocabularies of all European languages, is at the moment a non-dominant language in Europe. In addition, opening up the comparison of languages means opening the theoretical questions that arise from it. To restrict Contrastive Linguistics to some European languages only, belonging either to the Charlemagne *Sprachbund* or to the Balkan *Sprachbund*, or to have English as the obligatory member in each pair of languages to be contrasted, would mean narrowing our perspective, that is, to yield to the position that Ringbom discerned in 1994.

A further concern in organizing ICLC8, as well as in preparing this volume, was to broaden the theoretical discussion so as to refer not only to Contrastive Linguistics but to Linguistics as such. In the present volume, functional and formal points of view can be found side-by-side and this is not a coincidence. It is an editorial choice, because we do believe that in the current state of linguistic thought, every point of view is not just legitimate but necessary for an integrated explanation of the contrasts between languages.

Apart from the pluralism in theoretical paradigms and the languages to be contrasted, a number of prerequisites for Contrastive Analysis can be summed up here, as they derive from contrastive research of the recent years and, in particular, from the papers presented in ICLC8 and selected for the present volume.

A general theory of language, either functional or formal. The main conclusion from the study of the different phases of Contrastive Linguistics is that comparing languages is impossible outside the theoretical point of view that each scholar or school of linguistic thought takes, either explicitly or implicitly. There was a general tendency in the initial phases of Contrastive Linguistics to regard contrasting languages as an 'objective' process just for practical purposes, for example, for teaching second or foreign languages or translation. Critical approaches to this tendency were already formulated in the late 1960s, but their impact was keenly felt in Second Language Teaching rather than in Theoretical Contrastive Linguistics. In contrast to König's (2012) claim that 'the challenge for CA lies in discovering the contrasts and describing them in a maximally general way and not in the choice of a specific theoretical format', I would like to suggest that describing and explaining linguistic contrasts already presupposes a theoretical framework. Since almost nothing in contemporary science can be considered 'objective', thinking of contrasting languages as an 'objective' process outside theory is a clear fallacy.

Awareness of the distinction between diachrony and synchrony as a presupposition of their relation. Although Contrastive Linguistics is conceived as synchronic *par excellence*, the diachronic dimension cannot be avoided, especially if our aim is the explanation of linguistic data and their contrasts (cf. Giannoulopoulou 2015). As in many other distinctions in our science, the diachrony versus synchrony distinction is better seen as a continuum rather than a dichotomy.

Awareness of the sociolinguistic status of several phenomena. Many contrasting papers, both in this volume and in general, are in close relationship with sociolinguistic phenomena (e.g. language contact, dialect versus language). The interrelation between linguistic and sociolinguistic concepts and tools could prove fruitful in contrasting languages. At any rate, it is not possible to ignore the sociolinguistic status of the phenomena under investigation and contrast.

And last but not least, a *tertium comparationis*. As Krzeszowski (1984: 301) showed already in 1984, 'tertium comparationis', 'the concept that lies at the heart of any comparison (*eo ipso* at the heart of Contrastive Analysis), remains remarkably neglected'. Almost forty years after Krzeszowski's warning, the need for a detailed and fine-grained formulation of the *tertium comparationis* used in every contrastive analysis persists. The development of corpus linguistics in these intervening forty years has helped with the quantitative dimensions of contrastive analysis, but has not resolved the problem of defining the *tertium comparationis* with precision. Formal, semantic and translational correspondences are often used in contrastive research, many times combined with each other.

The present volume first discusses some theoretical issues on Contrastive Linguistics and then focuses on morphological and syntactic phenomena, something which presupposes formal similarities and differences; in other words, a formal *tertium comparationis* is entailed.

I hope that this volume, although clearly not giving the whole picture of contemporary contrastive research, is representative of the current state of this sub-discipline. It is also my belief that, as I have tried to argue in the previous pages, comparing languages lies in the nucleus of Linguistics. The long journey of comparing languages coincides with the journey of the discipline of Linguistics. Fortunately, in the context of the revival of Contrastive Linguistics in the last twenty years, ICL Conferences have contributed to the realization that Contrastive Linguistics takes centre stage in the discipline of

Linguistics. Krzeszowski's (1984: 301) fear that Contrastive Linguistics 'continues to perform the role of Cinderella of Linguistics' is nowadays clearly unfounded.

Note

1 ICLC8 continued the tradition of Conferences that began in September 1999 at the University of Santiago de Compostela. The four first ICLCs took place at the University of Santiago de Compostela (1999, 2001, 2003, 2005), the 5th at the University of Leuven (2008), the 6th at the Free University of Berlin (2010) and the 7th at Ghent University (2013).

References

Alatis, J., ed. (1968), *Contrastive Linguistics and its Pedagogical Implications*, Monograph Series on Languages and Linguistics, 21. Washington D.C.: Georgetown University Press.

Chomsky, N. (1965), *Aspects of the Theory of Syntax*, Cambridge: The MIT Press.

Fisiak, J. (1984), 'Introduction', in J. Fisiak (ed.), *Contrastive Linguistics: Prospects and Problems*, 1–4, Berlin: Mouton de Gruyter.

Fries, C. C. (1945), *Teaching and Learning English as a Foreign Language*, Ann Arbor, MI: University of Michigan Press.

Garvin, P. L. (1970), 'Moderation in Linguistic Theory', *Language Sciences*, 9: 1–3.

Giannoulopoulou, G. (2015), 'Morphological Contrasts between Modern Greek and Italian: The Case of Compounding', *Languages in Contrast*, 15 (1): 65–80.

Haspelmath, M. (2001), 'The European Linguistic Area: Standard Average European', in M. Haspelmath, E. König, W. Oesterreicher and W. Raible (eds), *Language Typology and Language Universals, Handbücher zur Sprach- und Kommunikationswissenschaft* 20, 1492–510, Berlin: Mouton de Gruyter.

Hawkins, J. A. (1986), *A Comparative Typology of English and German: Unifying the Contrasts*, London: Croom Helm.

Koerner, E. F. K. (2004), 'On the Place of Linguistic Historiography within the Sciences of Language, Again', in E. F. K. Koerner (ed.), *Essays in the History of Linguistics*, 3–17, Amsterdam: Benjamins.

Koliopoulou, M. and T. Leuschner (2014), 'Einleitung: Perspektiven der kontrastiven Linguistik', *Germanistische Mitteilungen. Zeitschrift für deutsche Sprache, Literatur und Kultur*, 40 (1): 5–14.

König, E. (2012), 'Contrastive Linguistics and Language Comparison', *Languages in Contrast*, 12: 3–26.

Krzeszowski, T. P. (1984), 'Tertium Comparationis', in J. Fisiak (ed.), *Contrastive Linguistics. Prospects and Problems*, 301–12, Berlin: Mouton de Gruyter.

Lado, R. (1957), *Linguistics across Cultures: Applied Linguistics for Language Teachers*, Ann Arbor, MI: University of Michigan Press.

Lipinska, M. (1980), 'Contrastive Analysis and the Modern Theory of Language', in J. Fisiak, (ed.), *Theoretical Issues in Contrastive Linguistics*, 127–84, Amsterdam: Benjamins.

Makaev, È. A. (1969), 'Les rapports entre grammaire comparée, grammaire contrastive et grammaire typologique', *Languages*, 15, *La linguistique en URSS*, 32–42.

Ringbom, H. (1994), 'Contrastive Analysis', in R. E. Asher and J. M. Y. Simpson (eds), *The Encyclopedia of Languages and Linguistics*, 737–42, Oxford: Pergamon Press.

Sun, K. and W. Rong (2009), 'Review of Pan Wenguo and Tham Wai Mun (2007) "Contrastive Linguistics: History, Philosophy and Methodology"', *Languages in Contrast*, 9 (2): 291–5.

Van Buren, P. (1980), 'Contrastive Analysis', in J. Fisiak (ed.), *Theoretical Issues in Contrastive Linguistics*, 83–117, Amsterdam: Benjamins.

Van der Auwera, J. (2012), 'From Contrastive Linguistics to Linguistic Typology', *Languages in Contrast*, 1: 69–86.

Von Humboldt, W. (1822), 'Über das vergleichende Sprachstudium in Beziehung auf die verschiedenen Epochen der Sprachentwicklung', *Abhandlungen der Königlichen Akademie der Wissenschaften zu Berlin aus den Jahren* 1820–1, 239–60, Berlin: Reimer.

Wardhaugh, R. (1970), 'The Contrastive Analysis Hypothesis', *TESOL Quarterly*, 4 (2): 123–60.

Weinreich, U. (1953), *Languages in Contact: Findings and Problems*, New York: Linguistic Circle of New York.

Wenguo, P. and T. Wai Mun (2007), *Contrastive Linguistics: History, Philosophy and Methodology*, London: Continuum International Publishing Group.

Acknowledgements

The chapters comprising this volume primarily originate from papers presented at the 8th International Contrastive Linguistics Conference (ICLC8, Athens, May 2017). We would like to take this opportunity to express our sincere thanks to various people and institutions. First of all, we would like to thank our colleagues who organized previous International Contrastive Linguistics Conferences and decided to entrust the organization of the ICLC8 to the National and Kapodistrian University of Athens.

We are also grateful to the authorities of the National and Kapodistrian University of Athens for the financial and technical support they provided us with during the organization of the Conference, as well as to the members of the Scientific Committee, the participants at the Conference and the students who voluntarily offered their assistance and made the Conference successful. Special thanks are due to our fellow colleagues, Angélica Alexopoulou, Rea Delveroudi, Dionysis Goutsos and George K. Mikros who – along with the editors of this volume – were the members of the ICLC8 Organizing Committee.

This volume would not have been possible without the support and assistance of a number of people. We would like to thank the authors who eagerly accepted our invitation to contribute a chapter to the book and all the reviewers who generously offered their expertise by providing constructive comments for the chapters of the book. Finally, we would like to express our gratitude to Bloomsbury Publishing Plc for the acceptance of our book proposal and their decision to include it in *Bloomsbury Studies in Theoretical Linguistics*. In particular, we would like to thank the commissioning editor Andrew Wardell and the editorial assistants Becky Holland and Helen Saunders for their precious help and cooperation throughout the publishing process.

Introduction

Michalis Georgiafentis, Giannoula Giannoulopoulou,
Maria Koliopoulou and Angeliki Tsokoglou

This volume, which brings together fifteen papers on a broad range of themes in Contrastive Linguistics, aims at adding to the discussion about analysing linguistic phenomena from different theoretical perspectives. In particular, the contributors of this volume analyse data from various languages, focusing on the contrastive aspect, on the basis of a given theory, which offers a concrete methodology and is used as a necessary tool. In other words, the majority of the studies in the volume are theoretically driven; that is, the analysis of linguistic data is based on a specific theory, although the explicit mention of the theoretical framework adopted in each case is not always present, while in very few cases the description of the data prevails and no particular theory is adopted.

The authors of this volume address a number of theory-internal as well as morphological and syntactic phenomena such as derivation, compounding and inflection, tense, wh-questions, postverbal subjects, focus, clitics, language contact and event descriptions, using different theoretical approaches and frameworks (including formal and functional points of view). The papers collected here all testify to the same spirit: They compare two or more languages, aiming at contributing to our understanding of language typology and language universals. They highlight the significance of the contrastive perspective for language-specific description, on the one hand, and general interface issues, on the other, shedding light on contrasts between languages at different linguistic levels.

The volume is divided into three parts. Part I comprises three chapters which are concerned with theoretical issues in Contrastive Linguistics. Part II is devoted to Morphology and includes five chapters dealing with different phenomena related to derivation, compounding and inflection. Part III, which consists of seven chapters, focuses on Syntax as well as its interfaces with other levels of linguistic analysis.

The volume starts with **Paul J. Hopper**'s contribution on heuristic dimensions of Contrastive Linguistics, where the author examines the intrinsic comparability of the features that are chosen in comparing and contrasting languages. He suggests a heuristic approach in which the starting point is the linguist's initial assessment of prior discourse and cognitive principles, rather than the objective linguistic structures, which frame the data sets to be compared. Hopper's paper postulates three heuristic levels: the mental-representational, where examples are made up or checked from *a priori* sources; the textual, where monologic discourse (primarily written) texts are analysed; and the social-interactive, whose source is spontaneous dialogues. According to his view, awareness of the heuristic levels is a prerequisite for contrastive research in order for category errors to be avoided, that is, the confusion of data sets that are stateable at different heuristic levels.

In the next chapter **Livio Gaeta** assumes that contrastive analysis has to be understood as a micro-typology able to attain a degree of granularity which is far beyond any macro-typological research. In this regard, Gaeta contrastively examines the tense systems of English, Italian and German. In particular, he proposes that English, given its role as a 'global language', will be fruitful for the purposes of the contrastive analysis and of its didactic implications insofar as it serves as a bridge language for a micro-typology in which it is systematically contrasted in a trilateral comparison with Italian and German.

In the third chapter of Part I, **Torsten Leuschner** discusses the productivity of the verb-first conditional construction as a template for German proverbs in contrast with English Subject-Auxiliary Inversion, which has no corresponding potential. Borrowing Norrick's notion of 'p-grammar' (where 'p' stands for 'proverbial'), Leuschner introduces the concept of 'p-constructicon', and he suggests that the p-constructica of different languages should be treated contrastively in future research under the theoretical framework of Social Construction Grammar.

Part II opens with a chapter by **Bożena Cetnarowska**, who focuses on word-formation phenomena. In particular, in order to investigate gender marking in job titles, the author contrasts English and Polish, two typologically and morphologically different languages. Based on corpus data, she deals with terms denoting female physicians and investigates the interrelation between derivation and compounding in Polish by means of a double gender marking. After a comparison of the sociolinguistic role of the masculine form as well as the possible lexical means of expressing femininity, Cetnarowska shows that speakers of English tend to use gender-neutral occupation terms in order to avoid sexist language, while speakers of Polish employ masculine forms of professions in gender-indefinite contexts.

In the next chapter **José A. Sánchez Fajardo** deals with derivational phenomena examining equivalence and congruence in English and Spanish. In particular, Sánchez Fajardo studies the width of the logico-semantic relations having as a theoretical background the semantic structure of a word-building model. More specifically, he investigates the semantic relations that can be expressed in the selected languages by means of adjectival suffixation. On a dictionary-based analysis, he examines adjectival suffixes and morpho-semantic variants found in both languages. His contrastive analysis shows that English and Spanish share most of the logico-semantic relations used in the formation of adjectives by suffixation, despite the analytic and synthetic nature of the morphology of these two languages, respectively.

Word-formation, and especially compounding, is the topic of the sixth chapter written by **Maria Koliopoulou**. She investigates the occurrence of linking elements in German and Greek, which she claims are morphologically similar languages displaying, though, different characteristics with respect to the linking element. The main aim of this chapter is to define the parameters that influence the characteristics of the linking element in both languages. Contrasting the Greek morphological system with the German one, she shows that in both languages the appearance of the linking element is connected to the semantic relation between the first and the second part of the compound. Taking advantage of this contrastive analysis, she also investigates the function of the various linking elements in German compounds.

Compounding is also investigated by **Asimakis Fliatouras**, who contrasts Albanian with Greek. Based on an overview of the structural characteristics found in Albanian and Greek, he claims that they display two different compounding systems, with the Albanian compounding resembling more that of Romance languages. However, marginal characteristics of the compounds in Albanian share many similarities with the Greek ones. He refers to characteristics concerning coordinative compounds, the appearance of the linking element -*o*-, (de)verbal compounds, the headedness of one-word compounds and, finally, the exocentricity of adjectival compounds. Contrastive analysis has shown that these characteristics can be explained by the phenomenon of language contact and that Albanian is a case of structural blending between Romance and Greek compounding.

The last chapter of Part II written by **Masahiko Nose** investigates how morphologically and typologically different languages express the grammatical category of tense. His analysis focuses on the investigation of past tense features of four languages: two Trans-New Guinea languages, that is, Amele and Ma Manda, an Austronesian language Nguna and Mandarin Chinese. His data have been drawn from descriptive grammars as well as from field research. The study expands to other languages, for example, Japanese and French. The contrastive analysis he performs shows that tense-rich languages concentrate on expressing the difference between the present and the past, while tenseless languages express past tense by means of temporal adverbs or perfective aspect markers express whether the action is completed or not.

Part III opens with **Caterina Donati**'s contribution on interrogative constructions in Romance. In this chapter Donati discusses a very important phenomenon for linguistic theory and particularly for the generative framework, namely wh-questions and their realization across languages. After showing some crosslinguistically stable properties and some parameters of variation that wh-movement displays, she concentrates mainly on different varieties of Romance languages. Within the presentation she addresses wh-movement, wh-*in situ* in French, the use of special complementizers introducing interrogative constructions and the ambiguity between wh-questions and free relatives. For the latter, she proposes a labelling analysis, according to which either C or D projects yielding a CP (wh-question) or a DP (free relative). The contribution clearly supports that, for a study of microvariation, a contrastive analysis is necessary to shed light on differences that appear in Romance varieties which use lexical material stemming from the same Latin sources.

Wh-questions are also the focus of **Valéria Molnár** who investigates information-eliciting wh-questions at the syntax-discourse interface by comparing two closely related Germanic languages, namely German and Swedish. She draws her attention on the differences that this language pair shows in the realization of wh-questions and in their mapping to discourse strategies. More specifically, while clefts are often used in Swedish wh-questions to indicate the need for referential specification of the wh-element, German employs modal particles for marking different discourse-semantic aspects of wh-questions. In order to support her analysis of different strategies used in Swedish and German, she also uses empirical evidence, provided by the comparison of relevant examples taken from Swedish detective novels translated into German.

Focus types (i.e. information and contrastive focus) and the various word order patterns that result from them are taken up by **Michalis Georgiafentis** and **Angeliki Tsokoglou**, who comparatively examine the clause and information structure of English, German, Spanish, Italian and Greek. As they observe, the morphosyntactic characteristics of the languages affect clause structure and the syntactic mechanisms involved. Given that information structure, which comprises focus, is not a purely syntactic phenomenon, the role of intonation is equally important. In the axis of the languages considered, they suggest that there are two poles, namely a very restricted one with respect to morphosyntactic properties, that is, English, where focus is regulated by prosody, and an almost unrestricted one, that is, Greek, where both prosodic and syntactic operations are allowed. They further propose that in between stands German with a restricted clause structure, where *in situ* stressing is available, whereas Spanish and Italian with restricted prosodic properties (absence of *in situ* stress) opt for movement mechanisms.

Manuel Leonetti and **Victoria Escandell-Vidal** are also concerned with word order phenomena. In their contribution they provide a unified account of the differences between Spanish and Italian in the distribution of postverbal subject pronouns. In particular, the authors use three sets of data, namely syntactically induced inversion and 'free' inversion with either 'unmarked' pronouns or special respect pronouns. Their analysis shows that the contrasts follow a systematic pattern, by which Spanish strong pronouns may occur in positions where Italian pronouns are excluded. In particular, whereas Spanish allows for pronouns to occur inside larger informational units without being interpreted as topics or as narrow foci, Italian requires that overt pronouns be singled out as topics or as narrow foci, that is, they must be pushed out from a larger informational constituent through some kind of split (topic/comment or focus/background). The major advantage of such a perspective is that the distribution of postverbal subject pronouns follows from the same principles that explain other additional differences between Spanish and Italian. The authors conclude that the way information structure is expressed in syntax and prosody is the crucial factor behind all examined phenomena.

Anthi Revithiadou and **Vassilios Spyropoulos** address issues related to the dialectal and diachronic variation in the cliticization pattern of weak pronouns, that is, clitics, in Greek. In particular, the authors comparatively examine two cliticization systems of Greek (namely that of Standard Modern Greek and the one existing in the southeastern dialects, as well as in Byzantine and Medieval Greek) with the corresponding adverbal Romance cliticization system and the cliticization system of Slavic languages. This comparison reveals that Greek clitics are neither C- nor v*-related elements, and cliticization involves clitic movement to the T-layer. The authors further argue that the attested variation results from the ways PF processes the syntactic output of this movement. Finally, they show that the two systems are diachronically related to each other by means of a prosodic reanalysis that resulted in the evolution of the non-second position system of Standard Modern Greek from the second position system of Medieval Greek. A welcome result of the proposed account is that it treats the observed patterns of variation in Greek cliticization as a result of the PF-syntax interface.

Dimitris Michelioudakis and **Ioanna Sitaridou**'s contribution falls within the studies of language contact. The authors contrast Asia Minor Greek to older and contemporary mainland Greek and the dominant language of the area, that is, Turkish, with respect to two phenomena, namely multiple wh-fronting and the syntax of NPs/DPs. The analysis, which is based on the generative framework, treats all relevant diachronic and cross-dialectal differences as the result of parametric changes. In particular, the authors propose that, in order for a parameter to change its value in a language La under contact with a language Lb, the 'borrowed' value must already be allowed by the pre-existing grammar of La, that is, prior to contact with Lb.

In the final chapter of the volume **Thanasis Georgakopoulos** and **Holden Härtl** examine the crosslinguistic differences that exist in the encoding of motion events and the distribution of their constituent parts, that is, the manner as well as the path, dealing mainly with the Goal component. With a focus on German and Greek, they analyse verbal descriptions of motion events presented in video clips and link the linguistic characteristics of the different verbalizations to the salience of the Goal point. What they find is that in situations containing highly evident Goals towards which the motion is targeted, German speakers tend to realize Goals more often than Greek speakers. This finding is complemented with a crosslinguistic examination of the inventory for expressing manner and path of motion, as well as by an analysis of the type of information expressed in the verbalizations.

In view of the above, we believe that the chapters comprising this volume will contribute to the current dialogue in Contrastive Linguistics and will be of particular interest to scholars working in theoretical as well as applied linguistic fields.

Part One

Theoretical issues in contrastive linguistics

Heuristic dimensions of contrastive linguistics

Paul J. Hopper

In comparing and contrasting the members of a set of languages, the linguist must at the outset judge the intrinsic comparability of the features that are chosen. Often the standard structural divisions, such as 'vowel system', 'verb morphology' and 'interrogative structures', fall short because the features in question may be relevant at different levels or in different genres across the members of the set. In this chapter, a heuristic approach is suggested in which the starting point is the linguist's initial assessment of the prior discourse and cognitive principles, rather than the objective linguistic structures, that frame the data sets to be compared. The chapter postulates three heuristic levels: mental-representational, where examples are made up or checked from *a priori* sources; textual, where monologic discourse (primarily written) texts are analysed; and social-interactive, whose source is spontaneous dialogues. The heuristics are illustrated with examples from lexicon, morphosyntax, narrative and conversation.

1 Introduction

In an article from 1948, Richard Pittman (1957)[1] described some of the analytic practices of descriptive linguists when confronted with the problem of the ranking of constituent pairs or multiples. These practices were not envisaged as procedural rules but rather as rules of thumb based on observation of practice; that is, they sought to describe what linguists actually did. Pittman noted, for example, that, given a longer form and a shorter form in association, 'it is very likely that the longer [form] will be classified as nuclear and the shorter form as a satellite' (Pittman 1957: 270). Also: 'Substantival and verbal concepts are very strongly associated in the minds of most of us with linguistic nuclei' (Pittman 1957: 277). That is to say, a concept that is noun-like or verb-like is very likely to be analysed linguistically as a nucleus. In his article, Pittman was not concerned with logical definitions. Rather, his method was a probabilistic one that relied on judgement and experience enshrined in a familiarity with a variety of languages, the relevant scientific literature and the possible contributions of adjacent disciplines. In assessing the relative ranking of constituents (a significant issue in linguistics at that time), his goal was 'to codify the criteria which *probably* serve as the basis for *most* judgements of relative rank that have been *tacitly invoked* in linguistic analysis' (Pittman 1957: 278; my italics). Seventy years on, we might characterize his approach as a heuristic one; heuristic, in the general sense of a preliminary approach to data, is perceived not as conforming to an exact definition, but as approximating a profile established on the basis of experience. Martin Joos, in an editorial comment on Pittman's article, wrote: 'This admirable paper has been much misunderstood; hasty readers have thought that Pittman was advocating or proposing what he was simply describing' (Joos 1957: 278).

In the present chapter, I wish to suggest that Pittman's heuristic approach may be extended as a preliminary method that is relevant to the goals of contrastive linguistics. These goals include identifying, explaining and correcting errors made in learning a second language; the discovery of common features such as area or *Sprachbund* phenomena; the exploration of language universals and linguistic typology. In all of these enterprises, a direct isomorphism between the target structures is the exception, and in fact is of limited interest compared to the recognition of contrastive differences. More often, the correspondences between (or among) the data sets are indistinct, for example, when a syntactic construction is matched beside a pragmatic expression (Fillmore 1984).

Viewed from the perspective of Pittman's description, heuristics offers a principled starting point in the enterprise of comparing and contrasting features in a set of target languages. It is a first-order approximation. Heuristics does not proceed directly from data to a hypothesis, but is a preliminary hunch, based on what we suspect might be there. Heuristics does not look for definite results, but rather for promising leads. As much as anything, heuristic methods work to exclude possibilities, some of which might be pursued at a later date. This search is not normally a random one, but is guided by the knowledge and experience brought to the enterprise by the investigator. Heuristics aims to simplify an investigation, beginning by making an initial 'educated guess', or dividing up the territory in intuitive ways. It favours enthymemic rather than syllogistic thinking.

Yet there is nothing unscientific about heuristics in this sense. Indeed, one of the most fundamental discoveries of the modern era, Einstein's quantum theory of the propagation of light, is owed methodologically to heuristics, as Einstein himself noted in the title of his article 'On a Heuristic Point of View about the Creation and Conversion of Light' (Einstein 1905). Einstein's heuristic procedure is to set up hypothetical situations and explore the consequences of assuming them, couching statements in a preliminary, perhaps even tentative, form. Some of the characteristic expressions that he uses are: '*in folgenden Fällen denkbar*' (can be imagined in the following cases), '*lässt sich folgendermassen ... auffassen*' (can be understood in the following way), '*nicht ausgeschlossen, daß*' (not excluded that) and '*wird anzunehman sein, daß*' (it is to be assumed that). Often, a German subjunctive creates a suppositional frame for an assumption: '*Nach der Auffassung, dass das erregende Licht aus Energiequanten ... bestehe*' (Assuming that the stimulating light consists [*subjunctive*] of energy quanta) or '*wir wollen annehmen, daß dies vorkomme*' (we will assume that this occurs [*subjunctive*]). Manjit Kumar comments (2014: 73): 'What [Einstein] was offering physicists was a way to explain the unexplained when it came to light, not a fully worked out theory derived from first principles. His paper was a signpost towards such a theory.'

2 Heuristic levels

Out of the mass of linguistic data, we can establish heuristic divisions that represent starting points for a contrastive comparison of a set of languages. The divisions go from the single isolated speaker's intuitions, to forms in a textual environment, to social space and usage among groups of speakers. They are not self-contained structural modules, but represent the linguist's first-order simplification of undifferentiated data, viewed from the perspective of the source of the judgements being made. The proposed divisions are as follows:

1. mental-representational
2. textual
3. social-interactive

The basic division sets off 1–2, which are monologic, against 3, which is dialogic. Within the first pair, that is, 1 and 2, the first or mental-representational group consists of forms that we can think up as native speakers, or that can be elicited directly from a native speaker, or that can be thought up as a line of inquiry by a linguist familiar with the language. These forms are divorced from performance, and reflect what is commonly called intuition, or introspection. They are linguistic forms that can be adjudged as correct or incorrect without a context. Problematic forms in this group can be marked with an asterisk or a question mark. The second group, the textual, consists of longer discourses in which targeted forms occur within a context, such as in a corpus. The textual heuristic looks for fixed forms presupposing the absence of a listener. Usually, textual means a written text, but there are exceptions, such as lectures and sermons. This second group can be studied with a bird's-eye-view perspective that assumes the text is fully and simultaneously present. The third heuristic looks for a conversation in a casual or informal register or for monologues that are interactive, in that the speaker may be prompted or encouraged to continue by an interlocutor. Structure in these circumstances is volatile and emergent. It moves forward along with the interaction as the speaker adapts his or her grammar to the exigencies of the ongoing interaction.

These heuristic partitions are not definable divisions. Rather, because they are preliminary, the procedure is fuzzy, with loosely defined and overlapping borders. The term 'method' refers to something more precise than what is discussed here, and belongs to a subsequent stage of the inquiry. The more modest goal is to simplify the task of comparing and contrasting structures across a set of languages by introducing at the outset a certain degree of uniformity into how the selected data are perceived. However, what might seem like rather obvious heuristic procedures may have significant implications. One implication is that there is a hierarchy of explanation to which corresponds an investigatory hierarchy. The extremes of this hierarchy are at one end the individual's knowledge accessible by introspection, for example, some kinds of lexical knowledge, and at the other end, the insights about language gained by the empirical study of the most basic communicative activity, which we may take to be dialogic interaction taking place in real time. These hierarchies conform to the following general principle:

The Heuristic Hierarchy

Explanations for linguistic facts go from stronger to weaker in the order:

social interactive > textual > cognitive

This principle acknowledges the contributions to knowledge made by ascertaining mental, social, textual and other kinds of facts, but points up the priority of the study of dialogic interactions when resources are available to do this. It recognizes that explanations can be formulated in more than one way, but postulates a hierarchy within which this is to be accomplished. This hierarchy also corresponds to the degree of difficulty in obtaining relevant contrastive data – the further to the left of the hierarchy, the greater the difficulty. Another facet of approaching linguistic data in this way is that the goals of contrastive linguistics are not confined to the comparison of texts in different languages, but can be expanded to the study of texts that are within the same language, but are at different heuristic levels, such as genres and styles.

2.1 The mental-representational level

In this first heuristic division, we can place the contrastive study of solo lexical items. As one of many examples, there are three words in Malay for which English has only one word, 'rice' – padi (rice on the stalk) or (rice plant), beras (husked grains of rice), and nasi (rice cooked and ready to be eaten). It proceeds from a fixed essential meaning, in English, the botanical entity 'rice', and assumes overlays that link it to context. Padi is associated with fields and planting, the agricultural dimension of rice; beras is typically rice that is being sold, bought or stored; nasi is a culinary item, cooked rice. Behind this first level, there perhaps lurks an ideology that unconsciously derives from dictionaries, written grammars and the millennia-long encounter with the written word. At this level, the native speaker can often make judgements without looking at a text. For example, speakers of English know there is no verb *to aggress corresponding to the noun *aggression,* even though several nouns in *-ession* (*digression,* etc.) have corresponding verbs in *-ess.* Another example of this first heuristic is the English *wounded* versus *injured* compared to the French *blessé. Wounded* implies some kind of visible lesion (i.e. a wound), whereas *injured* is more likely to be accidental. Usually, we are, in effect, abstracting from a mentally summoned context, this context then being reintroduced when we are required to justify the analysis. Thus, an English speaker's intuition about the difference between *wounded* and *injured* could be validated by composing and translating sentences in contexts that reveal the contrast with French:

(1) Le soldat a été *blessé* par un obus.
     The soldier was *wounded* by a shell.

(2) Didier a été *blessé* dans un accident de ski.
Didier was *injured* in a skiing accident.

Often, however, such contrasts are too subtle to be judged reliably from introspection. The German noun *Freund* overlaps semantically with English *friend*, but the correspondence is not exact. English speakers construe their word more broadly than do Germans, who would use *Bekannte(r)* 'acquaintance' in some contexts where English speakers would say 'friend'. A corpus study of the four terms would be needed in order to identify the typical ranges of their use.

2.2 The textual level

In the second division, the textual, where the comparative frequencies of grammatical constructions are studied, corpus investigations play a prominent role. When we compare the members of a set of languages in the domain of grammar, we often find that a construction that is represented robustly in one language exists in a restricted or rudimentary form in another; that is to say, the study of a construction commonly used by speakers of one language can reveal the rudiments of that construction in another language. In this way, constructions may be discovered that are quite fragmentary. Consider Comrie's example of the absolutive in English noun compounds (Comrie 1978: 337). While English does not distinguish transitive and intransitive subjects in active sentences, in certain noun-verb nominalizations, the noun is an absolutive, that is, a transitive object or an intransitive subject:

(3) Bird-hunting < 'they are hunting birds' ('bird' is object)
(4) Bird-chirping < 'birds are chirping' ('bird' is intransitive subject)

In peripheral constructions such as this one, English can be said to have a fragmentary counterpart to a system that exists in a more central form in ergative languages like Basque.

2.3 Syntactic constructions

Wider syntactic constructions that are syntacticized in one language may also show up in another language in a looser, more pragmatic form (Fillmore 1984). In a number of languages, a family of verbs or ex-verbs, one of which is the translation equivalent of *take*, may create case relationships with a following noun. Lord (1993) cites examples of these serial verb constructions from West African languages. In Dagbani, a verb *zang*, historically meaning 'take', marks a following noun as a direct object (Lord 1993: 128):

(5) o zang loori peenti   (Dagbani)
he take lorry paint
'He painted the lorry.'

The equivalent of *show* can create a benefactive relationship in Twi (Lord 1993: 32):

> (6) wó-tòw túo kyèrɛ̨ borɔ̨héne   (Twi)
>   they-fire gun show governor
>   'They fire guns for the governor.'

Instrumental meanings are also common (Lord 1993: 117). In Ga, the object of *kɛ̀* 'take' can function as an instrumental in a following transitive verb phrase:

> (7) è kɛ̀ tsò tswà gbékɛ̀ lɛ̀   (Ga)
>   he take stick hit child the
>   'He hit the child with a stick.'

Comparable examples are possible from a wide variety of languages. Generally, we find that the *take* verb is on a cline of grammaticalization from verb to prepositional case marker, depending on the language. English differs from canonical serial verb languages in that comparable English constructions are formulated as double clauses joined with a conjunction, typically *and*. Moreover, in the English examples usually cited, the first verb is intransitive, such as *try and*, *go and*. However, a corpus study of the English verb *to take* yields numerous examples in which the speaker splits a simple transitive expression into two parts: a clause that includes a lexical noun phrase introduced as the direct object of *take*, and a second clause that includes the transitive verb:

> (8) This test will take national standards and move them down into the classroom.
>   (Barlow 1998)

The meaning of the example is identical to its single clause counterpart:

> (9) This test will move national standards down into the classroom.

Nonetheless, there are some interesting parallels between the English *take NP and* construction and serial verbs (Hopper 2007). One is that, as in some serial verb languages, the *take NP and* construction requires its direct object to be affected; objects that come into being as a result of the verb (that is, effected objects) cannot be construed with *take and*. Thus, a sentence like *they took a fire and lit it* is not possible because the fire comes into being as a result of the action. In other serial verb languages, grammaticalization of the *take* verb has proceeded to the point where it is construed with effected objects. The lexical meaning of *take* is preserved in some serial verb languages, such as Dagbani, in that only objects that can be physically handled are eligible for the object role in a serial verb construction. But this is not true of English, in which it is easy to find examples of an object of *take* that are quite abstract:

> (10) Somehow they took a complicated concept and made it seem so simple.
>   (Google.com)

Another important difference between the English *take and NP* construction and the canonical serial verb construction is that, in the English version, the follow-up clause after *and* is not syntactically integrated with the initial clause. Consider our previous example:

(11)   This test will take national standards and move them down into the classroom. (Barlow 1998)

It is seen that the verb *take* projects a follow-up co-referential transitive verb *move,* and that the noun phrase *national standards* projects a co-referential direct object pronoun *them.* But many examples of *take-and* are not of this kind; that is, they are not followed by a transitive verb and a noun phrase referring back to the clause with *take:*

(12)   Actually, if you look, what I did is *I took the last five years of data by division and by rank and* I saw also where the lowest percentages are for women and it seems to be that at the instructor and assistant professor level proportions are kind of high but when it comes to the associate and full professor level this is bringing people in in the last five years we have the lowest percentages. (Barlow 1998)

What such examples have in common is a tendency to distribute complex structures over adjacent clauses, delivering them one by one rather than letting them accumulate inside a smaller, but more complex, set of sentences. So, *move national standards down into the classroom* is formulated as two clauses: (8) *take national standards* and (9) *and move them down into the classroom.* From a fully syntacticized construction in one language, we can be led to discover the existence of a more rhetorical, pragmatic routine in another.

In another example, a simple canonical construction in English is also possible in French, but in a less used and more circumstantial construction. English allows indirect objects to be passivized, as in *I was offered the job.* A literal translation of the construction in French, **j'ai été offert l'emploi,* is impossible. However, French speakers, or writers, can topicalize an indirect object by using the verb *se voir.* In the following set, the verbs *délivrer, reprocher* and *rendre* require their human objects to be in the dative, and are therefore ineligible to be passive subjects (examples from Price 1971: 236):

(13)   Chaque conducteur étranger d'un véhicule entrant en France se verra délivrer une carte de carburant.
'All foreign drivers of vehicles entering France will be issued a fuel card.'
(cf. 'on lui délivrera')

(14)   Le commissaire Dides se voit reprocher de ne pas avoir rendu compte de ses activités.
'Commissioner Dides was criticized for not having given an account of his activities.' (cf. 'on lui reproche')

(15) André Blanc, qui fut, jusqu' à sa mort en 1966, l'un des animateurs de
      l'architecture en France, se voit rendre un hommage tardif au Musée des
      Arts Décoratifs.
      'André Blanc, who was until his death in 1966, one of the leading lights of
      French architecture, was paid a belated tribute at the Museum of Decorative
      Arts.' (cf. 'on lui rend')

The construction with *se voir* is perhaps exclusively literary. In spoken German, where,
as in French, ordinary dative verbs cannot be passivized and turn the indirect object
into a subject, a similar effect can be obtained using *kriegen* 'to get': *sie hat eine Medaille
verliehen gekriegt* 'she was awarded a medal' (cf. *man verlieh ihr* (Dative) *eine Medaille*).

2.4 Typological issues

Often an analysis will depend on the heuristic rank at which we address the data.
Consider Greenberg's universals of word order, especially regarding the position of
the verb. Greenberg (1963) identified three major word order types, called VSO, SVO
and SOV, according to whether the verb is initial, or comes between the subject and
the object, or follows the object. Malay offers an example. Malay is listed by Greenberg
as an SVO language, and it is therefore aligned with English, Greek and French, as in
the following examples:

(16) Our mechanics (S) are repairing (V) the motorbike (O). (English)
(17) Οι μηχανικοί μας / επισκευάζουν / τη μοτοσικλέτα.   (Greek)
(18) Nos mécaniciens / réparent / la moto.   (French)
(19) mekanik kami / membaiki / motosikal.   (Malay)

However, the status of Malay as an SVO language is confirmed through the first
heuristic, that at which we manufacture simple subject-verb-object sentences. When
sentences within a context are considered, the situation is a little more complicated,
and the question becomes 'What is the *basic* word order?' The regular Malay passive
is quite straightforward and conforms to the Noun-Verb-Noun pattern expected in an
SVO language:

(20) Se-orang banduan mendapati pisau itu
      a   prisoner found   knife the
      'A prisoner found the knife.'

(21) Pisau itu didapati   oleh se-orang banduan.
      knife the was-found by   a   prisoner
      'The knife was found by a prisoner.'

In the active voice, there is an active verb prefix *me(ng)-*. The passive has a third-person
passive agent prefix *di-*, and an agentive preposition *oleh*. In the traditional narrative
text, that is, the data set to which we move in the second or textual heuristic, the use

of the passive diverges sharply from that of English. In this passage, the passive is the dynamic construction, used to report actions and events (Hopper 1983):[2]

(22) Maka satelah dilihat oleh Tuan Farquhar, maka ia sendiri hendak
      then when see:PASS by Mr Farquhar then he himself want
      'When Mr Farquhar saw it, he wanted himself
      menangkap ikan itu dengan tangannya. Maka ditangkapnyalah beberapa ekur dengan
      take:ACT fish the with hand-his. And grasp:PASS-EVENT several of-them with
      to take the fish in his hands. And he grasped several of them in
      tangannya. Maka anaknya perempuan itu pun hendak menangkap ikan itu, maka satelah
      hand-his. And child-his female the also want hold:ACT fish the, and when
      his hands. Then his daughter wanted to hold a fish, too, and when
      ditangkapnya dari ekurnya, maka dikebaskan oleh ikan itu tangannya
      grasp:PASS from tail-its then shock:PASS by fish the hand-her
      she grasped it by its tail, the fish shocked her hand'.

Moreover, the typical word order is VSO, rather than SVO, except that when the intensity of the narrative is slowed, the active reappears, with the verbal prefix *me(ng)-* and SVO word order. In the following, the SVO clauses are indented:

(22') Maka satelah dilihat oleh Tuan Farquhar,
       then when see:PASS by Mr Farquhar
       'When Mr Farquhar saw it,
             maka ia sendiri hendak menangkap ikan itu dengan tangannya.
             then he himself want take:ACT fish the with hand-his.
             he wanted himself to take the fish in his hands.
       Maka ditangkapnyalah beberapa ekur dengan tangannya.
       And grasp:PASS-EVENT several of-them with hand-his.
       And he grasped several of them in his hands.
             Maka anaknya perempuan itu pun hendak menangkap ikan itu,
             And child-his female. the also want hold:ACT fish the,
             Then his daughter wanted to hold a fish, too,
       maka satelah ditangkapnya dari ekurnya,
       and when grasp:PASS from tail-its
       and when she grasped it by its tail,
       maka dikebaskan oleh ikan itu tangannya
       then shock:PASS by fish the hand-her
       the fish shocked her hand'.

The most reasonable analysis is that the 'passive' here is not really a passive at all but an ergative, similar to the one in Basque and many other ergative languages, and that the word order is VSO:

(23)   dikebaskan (V) oleh ikan itu (S) tangannya (O)
        the fish (S) shocked (V) her hand (O)

Is Malay, then, an SVO or a VSO language? And is it nominative-accusative, or ergative-absolutive? The answer is that it depends on whether one is making up new sentences from memory or studying discourse distributions. In other words, it depends on the initial heuristic starting point. There is no basic word order independent of the context for creating the sentence, but rather the narrative context provides for a distinction between foregrounded VSO sentences with ergative morphology in the verb and backgrounded SVO sentences with nominative-accusative structure.

2.5 Pragmatic strategies

A different, but parallel, relationship between heuristic levels is suggested by a direct comparison of texts within the same language, but in different heuristic levels. Consider first the following exchange between a factory employee, 'Fred', and a former employee at the same factory, 'Rich':[3]

(24)

1	FRED	Yeah.
>2		I tell you man,
>3		that factory's the pits man,
4	RICH	What's new.
5	FRED	last night I got into a hassle with James Boyd.
>6		I'm in the cafeteria,
7	RICH	Yeah.
8	FRED	and I took a break,
9		.. that was <VOX just a little bit VOX> too long man.
10		You know.
11	RICH	Yeah,
12	FRED	@@
13	RICH	I can imagine.
14	FRED	@ ha]=lf hou=r brea=k @>,
15	RICH	.. You stretched a fifteen minute break into a half hour break.
16	FRED	@@@@@@
17		to a half hour.
>18		And then he comes into the cafeteria.
19		And I thought he was coming in to chase everybody away.
20	RICH	He was after you.
>21	FRED	But he's coming after me.
>22		.. And he calls me.
>23		And I'm @walking out the door.
>24		Right as he's walking in the other one?

The lines marked with > are 'present tense' clauses, although, as most researchers have pointed out, there is little justification for this term in English. Rather, the 'present tense' forms in spoken narrative work to distinguish foregrounded events from backgrounded material such as commentary, preliminary settings and speaker's thoughts. (Schiffrin 1981). As long as the analysis is limited to spoken narrative, that is, at level 2, English can be compared and contrasted with languages such as French that have a thoroughgoing system of background forms (known in French as *imparfait*) and foreground forms (*parfait* or, if in literary texts, *passé simple*). Weinrich (1964) and Hopper (1979) are two of many studies of these distinctions.

Foregrounding in spoken English narrative is consistently signalled by the use of the so-called present tense. In literary narrative, however, no such morpho-semantic structure is available. Instead, foregrounding and backgrounding are signalled inferentially through such things as semantic aspect and agency. Consider the following passage from James Lee Burke's novel *Jolie Blon's Bounce* (Burke 2002: 230), in which the completed events of the narrative are printed in italics:

(25)   *I awoke before sunrise on Tuesday and walked down the slope through the oaks and the pecan trees to the bait shop.* The fog was a bluish gray in the false dawn, then the sun broke on the horizon and the fog turned the color of cotton candy and I could see snow egrets rising like confetti above the cypress trees in the swamp. *Batist and I scrubbed down the spool tables, popped open the umbrellas above them, picked up the beer cans and bait cups from the boat ramp, and used a boat hook to gather floating trash from the pilings under the dock.* All of this was done under the supervision of Tripod, Alafair's fat, three-legged, silver-ringed pet raccoon. *Then Batist took a break and poured a cup of coffee for himself from a drip pot on the gas burner and dropped a red quarter into the jukebox and played Guitar Slim's 'I Done Got Over It'.* The haunting sounds of Slim's music reverberated across the water and into the trees like electronic echoes inside a stone pipe.

Foregrounding consists of ongoing actions that are largely transitive, humans doing things to other things with props. The background parts are diffuse and consist of scattered observations about sense impressions. Contrasting literary narrative in Written English and Spoken English and Malay, we can say that there are striking functional parallels, but that Written English lacks a dedicated morphology for the distinction. Written English makes up for this lack with a combination of pragmatic strategies:

1. The foregrounded parts have verbs that signify finished events: *awoke, walked down, scrubbed down, popped open, picked up, gather, took, dropped, played*. These verbs are mostly transitive, and several of them also have adverbial complements that add to the idea of completion (*from, into, down, open, up*).
2. The backgrounded parts have verbs that are intransitive (*broke, turned, was, rising*), or modal (*could see*), passive (*was done*), or nominalized (*under the supervision of*), or continuous (*reverberated*).
3. The foregrounded parts have human agents (*I, Batist*), the backgrounded parts have nonhuman subjects (*the sun, the fog, snow egrets, Tripod, sounds*).

4. The foregrounded parts have continuity of subjects *(I, Batist)*, the backgounded parts have a variety of subjects *(fog, sun, snow egrets, Tripod, sounds)*. In the background, there are frequent changes of subject.

It can be seen from this varied and disparate set that there is no specialized structure in English that corresponds to the grammatical distinction of foreground and background that we have in languages such as Malay and French. Users of English can deploy the varied rhetorical resources at their disposal to gain the same effects that users of languages with more dedicated grammar can also achieve.

2.6 The social-interactive level

A final example of heuristic levels concerns an area of contrastive linguistics that may have suffered from excessive attention to the first level: demonstratives. Demonstratives are, surprisingly perhaps, a source of difficulty to learners of English. It is customary to distinguish three degrees of deixis, named proximal, distal and remote. Holger Diessel's book (Diessel 1999) has surveyed in great detail the different possibilities that exist, and shows that the threefold system is the most common. English has only two degrees of deixis: *this, that* and their plurals *these, those*, although a third, based on *yon*, is met with in some dialects and in older writings. At the level of the first heuristic, the mental one, it is uncomplicated: *this* singles out an entity near the speaker, *that* identifies an entity further away from the speaker. *This* is my plate, *that* is your plate. Not all uses of *this/that* can be reduced to 'geographical' location, however. Learners of English often have difficulty grasping when to use *this* and when to use *that*. Clearly, it cannot be reduced to literal nearness to or distance from the speaker. It is also clear that we must move away from the first two levels in which we rely on memory and introspection, and study the deployment of the demonstratives in live discourse. The data source of conversational English here is the Santa Barbara Corpus (Du Bois et al. 2000–5).

In the first example, someone is commenting on a painting that is in front of the two speakers:

(26)   You know I've had that painting for … thirty-five years, I guess.

The speaker uses *that* deictically, to thematize a physical object that is relatively distant from him and the interlocutor. Similarly, in the following example:

(27)

Now=.
… I would like to ask you,
how these three things.
.. Tell me please.
(H) How are they all alike.
… (H) These three things.
This ice here in this pan.
(H) This water in this glass,
and the steam rising from this pot

A lecturer is demonstrating three forms of matter: solid, liquid and gas. The objects with which he is carrying out the demonstration are in his vicinity and close, relative to himself and the audience, so his use of *this* is easily explained. In the next example, we might also at first assume that the lecturer needs to distinguish an object which is close (a container) from an object that is relatively further away (the balloons):

(28) So I can fit all those balloons,
     into this little itty-bitty container.

However, the speaker has previously referred to the same balloons with *these*. Since the container and the balloons are at about the same distance from the speaker, there must be something other than closeness at hand to account for the use of *this*. It is apparent that proximity and distance, even when construed relatively, are secondary uses of the demonstratives once we leave the first level. The crucial fact at this point is that the container is thematic; that is, it is in focus, it is what he is talking about.

The pragmatic features of demonstratives are especially conspicuous when we consider their uses in extended texts, that is, in the second heuristic level. Moving to Level 2, in written texts a demonstrative, which can be either *this* or *that*, refers to an adjacent portion of text rather than to a physical object. *That* is far more common, and has been grammaticalized in English as a relative pronoun and as a complementizer, but discourse uses of *this* do occur. *This* is often used to project and organize a sequence of events. The following passage is from a book about the race between Scott and Amundsen to reach the South Pole, so we see not only the proleptic (projective) use of *this*, but also its very common use to refer to something especially significant. It is in fact the climactic point of the book:

(29) When the navigators cried 'Halt!', and the Norwegians had arrived as close [to the South Pole] as they were provisionally able to decide, this is what happened:
     Without a word they shook hands with each other. Then Amundsen got out the Norwegian flag, which had been bent to a pair of ski sticks lashed together the night before in readiness. (Huntford 1985: 454–5)

At the third heuristic level, forms are deployed across speakers in interactions. In the following excerpt from the Santa Barbara Corpus of Spoken American English (Du Bois et al. 2000–5), *this* and *that* are deployed to thematize and background different elements. Miles is telling Jamie and Harold about his visit to a certain nightclub and the scandalous behaviour of a woman he saw there:[4]

(30)
     MILES:) (H) ... But uh,
         ... she's marrie=d,
         and apparently she's there= .. without her husband.
         ... She has her wedding ring on.
     5   ... And it's like she's with this guy=,

and they're kinda like all over each other (Hx).
.. And I'm thinking,
we=ll,
9   ... I guess that's her husband,
JAMIE: .. Uh-oh [did you] say @something?
MILES: [but I-] --
JAMIE: @@
MILES: but I was thinking,
(H) but the thing is,
... you know she's kind of all sophisticated and everything,
and I'm thinking,
you know,
18   this guy %,
19   %= I can't .. really believe that guy's her husband.
So I don't know what's going on here.
... And of course later on I find out,
22   .. that's not her husband.

The so-called proximal demonstrative series *this/these* are deictic, but at the first level. At the second level, they have forward- and backward-looking functions that are still readily ascertainable in static written texts. In the third level, that of conversational interactions, they are distributed in approximately the following manner. Stated broadly, *this* foregrounds, *that* backgrounds. Although the woman seems to be married, she is making advances to a man she has just met. The man in question is mentioned with *this* in lines 5 and 18, and with *that* in lines 9, 19 and 22. The problem is how to explain Miles's use of *this* versus *that*. Since Miles uses both forms of the demonstrative to refer to the same person, it cannot be a deictic use. Rather, the man in the nightclub is sometimes in focus, that is, thematic, and sometimes not. Now being a theme is not decided in advance of an interaction. It emerges out of the speaker's ongoing assessment of the progression of the narrative and the listener's likely interest. A spectrograph of the adjacent mentions of the man in the nightclub in lines 18 and 19 shows the low thematic profile of *that* (128.4 Hz) as against the high thematicity of *this* (224.3 Hz) as manifested in the intensity of the stream, and shows that the two mentions *this guy* and *that guy* differ in intensity and duration. Functionally, *this guy* is an abandoned topic whose continuation is reduced to two glottal stops and a drawl, while *that guy* is part of a subordinate clause *that guy's her husband* which is the complement of an emphatic verb phrase *I can't..really believe*. Here, it is the verb phrase *I can't really believe* which is in focus; the clause *that guy's her husband* is less important, having been adumbrated by *I guess that's her husband* in line 9.

To what degree can the analysis of the English demonstratives proposed here be extended to other languages? Is there a contrastive dimension to the observations made here? In an earlier work, Peter Auer (1981) showed how the German demonstrative *diese(r)*, like the English *this*, can single out a new participant, and also how the German equivalent of *that*, identical to the definite article, but with stress, can refer analeptically to a discourse participant:

(31)

> Speaker X:
> manche Sachen sin ma in Erinnerung geblieben
> *some things stay in my memory*
> zum Beispiel diese Engländerin:,
> *for example, this Englishwoman*
> die: die Chaplin - Tochter - die da dauernd durch die Szene äh geht,
> *the, the Chaplin daughter who keeps walking across the set*
> Speaker Th:
> Is des die Geraldine Chaplin?
> *Is that Geraldine Chaplin?*

At least in some other languages, then, we may conclude that the proximal demonstrative can be used for a new mention. An interesting contrastive dimension to the discourse uses of demonstratives is provided by *obviation*, a referential category based on focus rather than deixis. In Ojibwa (Bloomfield 1958; Mithun 2001: 76–8), as in other Algonquian languages, noun phrases and verbs index a participant according to whether it is *proximate*, that is, in focus, or *obviative*, that is, out of focus. In the following example from the Ottawa dialect of Ojibwa (cited in Mithun 2001: 78), it can be seen that the distribution of obviative and proximate noun phrases parallels the use of demonstratives in English discourse: *this/these* for foregrounded, in-focus participants, corresponding to Ottawa proximate, *that/those* for backgrounded, out-of-focus participants corresponding to Ottawa obviative:

(32) There towards the woods Nenabozh:PROX turned into a poplar. The
      sun:OBV rose high. He:PROX saw the lake:OBV with ripples circling out.
      First the frog:OBV surfaced, and then various other spirits:OBV. They:OBV
      all came out of the water onto that sandy island:OBV. And some:OBV went
      to sleep there.

The Ottawa word translated as 'that' in 'that sandy island' suggests that in Ottawa, too, as in English, the distal demonstrative favours backgrounded contexts.

3 Conclusion

There are a number of implications of the use of heuristics in contrastive linguistics. One is that in making crosslinguistic comparisons, we should be aware of the heuristic level, or respective levels, at which the data are being examined. To confuse data sets that are stateable at different heuristic levels, for example, by searching for *a priori* sentences in a connected discourse, may be a kind of category error. At the same time, comparisons across different levels, both inter- and intra-language, may have their own interest and be relevant to the study of grammaticalization and language change generally. The notion of different heuristic levels means that we should be cautious about the use of metaphor as an explanatory tool for bridging the gaps between different levels. A usage identified as metaphorical may simply be a question of different kinds of data. The same is true of 'as if' explanations, which are basically metaphorical in nature. The higher levels of the hierarchy are more difficult to process, but bring us closer to the empirical realities of language use. Everyday experience, and especially the ways we talk about it, should precede our theorizing. Heuristics does not constitute a novel method, but reflects the actual practices of linguists in the initial phases of a contrastive study; the present contribution has simply aimed to make these practices explicit.

Notes

1 Page references are to the reprinted article in Joos (1957).
2 From the Malay narrative *Hikayat Abdullah* (Abdullah [1840] 1932).
3 From Du Bois et al. (2002–5). Each numbered line is an Intonation Unit. The symbol @ is a pulse of laughter, .. is a short pause.
4 Numbers are supplied for lines mentioned in the text. The transcriptional symbols used here are:
   ... and .. each dot is a one-fifth second pause
   = a drawled vowel or consonant
   % a glottal stop
   . (full stop) terminal intonation
   , (comma) rising intonation
   H an inhalation
   Hx an exhalation
   @ a pulse of laughter
   [ ] encloses simultaneous talk

References

Abdullah bin Abdul Qadir, 'Munshi' ([1840] 1932), *Hikayat Abdullah*, Singapore: Malay Publishing House.

Auer, P. (1981), 'Zur indexikalitätsmarkierenden Funktion der demonstrativen Artikelform in deutschen Konversationen', in G. Hinderlang (ed.), *Verstehen und Handeln: Akten des 15. linguistischen Kolloquiums*, 301–10, Tübingen: Niemeyer.

Barlow, M. (1998), *Corpus of Spoken Professional American English*, Houston, TX: Athelstan. Available online: http://www.athel.com/cspa.html

Bloomfield, L. (1958), *Eastern Ojibwa: Grammatical Sketch, Texts and Word List*, in C. F. Hockett (ed.), Ann Arbor: University of Michigan Press.

Burke, J. L. (2002), *Joli Blon's Bounce*, New York: Pocket Star Books.

Comrie, B. (1978), 'Ergativity', in W. P. Lehmann (ed.), *Syntactic Typology: Studies in the Phenomenology of Language*, 329–94, Austin, TX: University of Texas Press.

Diessel, H. (1999), *Demonstratives: Form, Function, and Grammaticalization*, Amsterdam: John Benjamins.

Du Bois, J. W., W. L. Chafe, C. Meyer, S. A. Thompson, R. Englebretson and N. Martey (2000–5), *Santa Barbara Corpus of Spoken American English*, Parts 1–4, Philadelphia: Linguistic Data Consortium.

Einstein, A. (1905), 'Über einen die Erzeugung und Verwandlung des Lichtes betreffenden heuristischen Gesichtspunkt' (Concerning an Heuristics Point of View toward the Emission and Transformation of Light), *Annalen der Physik* 17; trans. into English in *American Journal of Physics*, 33 (5): 1–15. Available online: https://einsteinpapers.press. princeton.edu/vol2-trans/100

Fillmore, C. F. (1984), 'Remarks on Contrastive Pragmatics', in J. Fisiak (ed.), *Contrastive Linguistics: Prospects and Problems*, 119–42, Berlin: Mouton de Gruyter.

Greenberg, J. H. (1963), 'Some Universals of Grammar with Particular Reference to the Order of Meaningful Elements', in J. H. Greenberg (ed.), *Universals of Grammar*, 73–113, Cambridge, MA: MIT Press.

Hopper, P. J. (1979), 'Aspect and Foregrounding in Discourse', in T. Givón (ed.), *Discourse and Syntax*, Syntax and Semantics, vol. 12, 213–41, New York: Academic Press.

Hopper, P. J. (1983), 'Ergative, Passive, and Active in Malay Narrative Discourse', in F. Klein-Andreu (ed.), *Discourse Perspectives on Syntax*, 64–87, New York: Academic Press.

Hopper, P. J. (2007), 'Emergent Serialization in English: Pragmatics and Typology', in J. Good (ed.), *Language Universals and Language Change*, 520–54, London: Oxford University Press.

Huntford, R. (1985), *The Last Place on Earth*, New York: Atheneum.

Joos, M. ed. (1957), *Readings in Linguistics: The Development of Descriptive Linguistics in America since 1925*, Washington DC: American Council of Learned Societies.

Kumar, M. (2014), *Quantum: Einstein, Bohr, and the Great Debate about the Nature of Reality*, London: Icon Books.

Lord, C. (1993), *Historical Change in Serial Verb Constructions*, Amsterdam: Benjamins.

Mithun, M. (2001), *The Languages of Native North America*, Cambridge, UK: Cambridge University Press.

Pittman, R. S. (1948), 'Nuclear Structures in Linguistics', *Language*, 24: 287–92, reprinted in Joos (ed.) (1957), *Readings in Linguistics: The Development of Descriptive Linguistics in America since 1925*, 275–8, Washington DC: American Council of Learned Societies.

Price, G. (1971), *The French Language: Present and Past*, London: Arnold.

Schiffrin, D. (1981), 'Tense Variation in Narrative', *Language*, 57 (1): 45–62.

Weinrich, H. (1964), *Tempus: Besprochene und Erzählte Welt*, Stuttgart: W. Kohlhammer.

2

English as a bridge: An L3-approach to contrastive linguistics[1]

Livio Gaeta

Contrastive Analysis has to be understood as a micro-typology able to attain a degree of granularity which is far beyond any macro-typological research. In this regard, given its role as 'global language', English will be fruitful for the purposes of Contrastive Analysis and its didactic implications insofar as it will serve as a bridge language for a micro-typology in which it is systematically contrasted trilaterally with Italian and German. In particular, the chapter will focus on two case studies taken respectively from the temporal-aspectual domain, and the morphosyntax of subjects and objects.

1 Introduction

As is well known, Contrastive Linguistics saw the light as an empirical hypothesis on language acquisition when first Charles Fries, and subsequently Robert Lado, suggested to incorporate the tradition of comparative studies into the discussion for foreign language teaching as the latter emerged in the golden age of Structuralism, with a particular focus on phonological studies. The so-called Contrastive Analysis Hypothesis basically maintains that 'in the comparison between native and foreign language lies the key to ease our difficulty in foreign language learning' (Lado 1957). To find this key, we have to make use of 'effective materials … based upon a scientific description of the language to be learned, carefully compared with a parallel description of the native language of the learner' (Fries 1945). In spite of several attempts to apply this suggestive hypothesis to the method and practice of language teaching, especially in the 1960s and the 1970s, the results were rather scarce, which ultimately led to abandoning this enterprise as a general framework apt for developing methods for language teaching.

Its limits must probably be sought in its scarce degree of elaboration as a language acquisition theory. In particular, it has been objected (cf. Gast 2011, 2013; König 2012a, b) that in order to be taken seriously as an acquisition theory, Contrastive Analysis should essentially be improved with regard to its capacity for differentiating acquisition stages, as well as taking into account important parameters in the acquisition of a second language, such as, for instance, natural (L2) versus mediated acquisition (Foreign Language), sequential or simultaneous acquisition, L2- versus L3-acquisition, and so on (cf. Carrol and Lambert 2006; von Stutterheim and Lambert 2005; Hawkins and Filipović 2011). Furthermore, Contrastive Analysis lacks a solid psychological base providing a general framework suitable for language acquisition, and – from a more practical point of view – it never developed a reliable empirical base which might have supplied a sufficient theoretical elaboration. Finally, since it cannot seriously be credited as a language acquisition theory, Contrastive Analysis turns out to lack a clear epistemological status with regard to other comparative approaches developed in linguistics, and, in the first place, the typological and the historical-comparative school.

2 The typological turn

Recently, the attempt has been made to overcome the deadlock hinted at in the previous section by taking seriously the idea that Contrastive Analysis represents an extreme case of typological comparison carried out on the basis of a small language sample (cf. König 1996).[2] One main advantage of a typological comparison conceived in these terms consists in the high granularity of the structural analysis which has become elusive, especially in recent typological investigations based on very large language samples. Considered from this vantage point, Contrastive Analysis aims to identify structural correlations of a typological nature and – besides attaining explanations of a general order with regard to language structure – has as ultimate goal to 'unify the contrasts' (Hawkins 1986). In this way, Contrastive Analysis can be understood as a 'pilot typology' (van der Auwera 2012; Gaeta 2014) or as a 'micro-typology', and constitutes an autonomous object of investigation which is interesting in itself, independent of any didactic finality and/or application.

In order to carry out this research programme, it is convenient to limit the 'micro-typological' comparison to a small number of languages, generally two, at most, three or four. In the light of the small sample, the comparison is expected to consider highly complex structural aspects involving a high number of linguistic traits with the explicit aim of attaining a granularity which is far beyond any macro-typological research. At any rate, in compliance with this latter goal, the issue of comparability has clearly to be the compass orienting the empirical research. Concretely, this consists of the identification of similarities and differences of two or more language-specific categories along a certain dimension, as, for instance, exemplified by Haspelmath's (2010) definition of what a future tense has to be composed of: 'A future tense is a grammatical marker associated with the verb that has future time reference as one prominent meaning.' In other words, a central tenet of Contrastive Analysis is the comparative method exploiting an onomasiological approach to the Ontological Domain, for example, (future) time reference (see Figure 2.1).

On the other hand, in the light of the quite complex functional space which can be occupied by a morpheme or – in more precise terms – by a grammatical construction, the onomasiological approach has to be combined with a semasiological approach depicting the range of Ontological Categories conveyed

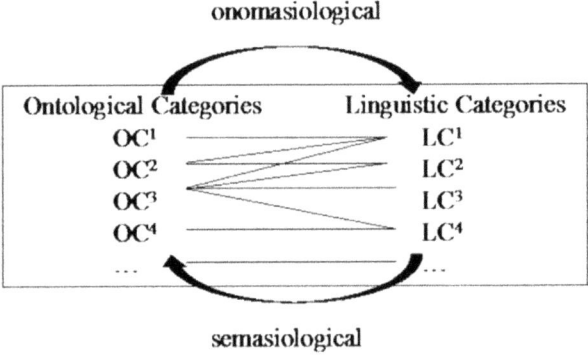

Figure 2.1 Comparative method in Contrastive Analysis.

by or associated with a Linguistic Expression. Although formal and functional properties often stand in manifold relationships as shown in Figure 2.1 above, their relation is not entirely arbitrary and can be represented with the help of semantic maps (cf. van der Auwera 2012).

Moreover, the languages undergoing Contrastive Analysis are likely to have a connection of a socio-cultural type (cf. Gast 2011, 2013). This is given by a significant number of bilingual or multilingual speakers and/or a significant quantity of linguistic performances (texts, discourses, etc.) translated by a language into the other(s) which testify to relations of cultural exchange or contact. The latter are expected hopefully to be structured in (especially parallel) translation and/or learners' corpora. Such a requirement enhances the role of contact phenomena and especially of areality for the contrastive perspective. This has been shown by recent typological enterprises to be one of the main factors shared by most languages in Europe, as witnessed by the debate around Whorf's old idea of a Standard Average European (SAE) and the so-called Charlemagne *Sprachbund* consisting of one or more centres surrounded by several possible peripheries (cf. Ramat 1998; Haspelmath 2001). In this way, single linguistic aspects traditionally considered in a separate manner can be shown to be crucially conjoined by areal features. For instance, one can mention the so-called 'Germanic sandwich' consisting of Dutch contrasted with English and German and clearly influenced by contact with Romance languages to a different extent with regard to its cognate languages (Hüning, Vogl and van der Wouden 2006).

3 English as a bridge language

Comprehended in the wider perspective sketched above in which the SAE is a fundamental vantage point, one can attempt a further challenge involving English in its role of 'global language' (cf. Crystal 2003). In this regard, although more and more speakers master or have access to it – often as a first foreign language – the advantage in didactic terms of the 'global' status reached by English in the last decades has not been seriously exploited yet.[3] This is even more surprising in the light of several contrastive investigations available, for instance, for English and Italian (cf. Iamartino 2001; Vanni 2016), or for Italian and German (cf. Blasco Ferrer 1999; Bosco Coletsos and Costa 2013; Di Meola and Puato 2015), and especially for English and German (cf. Kufner 1962; Moulton 1962; Hawkins 1986; König and Gast 2007). For the latter two languages, the 'micro-typological comparison' is highly significant also from a historical-comparative point of view insofar as their contrasts have to be regarded as the result of a long-standing diachronic development: 'Where the grammars of English and German contrast, the surface forms (morphological and syntactic) of German are in closer correspondence with their associated meanings' (Hawkins 1986: 121).

In addition, at least with respect to the other European languages and in the first place, Italian, English and German form an essential part of the SAE, although their position is more or less peripheral, displaying more or less strict contacts with and influences of Romance or Celtic languages.

In the next sections, I will try to further develop this idea of taking English as a bridge language for a micro-typology in which it is systematically contrasted with Italian and German. In particular, I will focus on two case studies of such a trilateral Contrastive Analysis with regard to the temporal-aspectual domain and to the morphosyntactic properties of subjects and objects. These subjects have been conveniently chosen because of their well-defined Onomasiological and/or Semasiological Domain, which allows us to carve out sets of data which are easily matched within a highly granular trilateral comparison.

3.1 The temporal-aspectual domain

The onomasiological background of future time reference has been already sketched in Section 2. The definition has to be further articulated with regard to the reliability of the prediction entailed in the future time reference. Accordingly, the onomasiological space is carved out in English in the following way (see König and Gast 2007: 84–7 for details).

The reliability of the prediction clearly plays a crucial role in German, as well as in Italian, future time reference, although the picture is essentially less articulated than in English (cf. Tables 2.1 and 2.2)

Both in German and in Italian the forms used to convey present tense, respectively the *Präsens* and the *presente*, are also commonly used for future time reference; in this way, a more reliable prediction is intended by the speaker with respect to what is normally obtained by using the future tense forms, namely the *Futur I* and the *futuro*. This is shown especially by the contrast between their usage in the same context (see Table 2.2, examples 1ii versus 2ii for German, and examples 3ii and 4ii for Italian). On the other hand, when the future time reference is profiled as imminent, either the future tense is inappropriate because the prediction is highly reliable (see Table 2.2, example 4ii) or vice versa: the present tense is odd because it is rather about a supposition (see Table 2.2, example 4iii). It should be stressed that this difference is independent of the time adverbial employed in the sentence. In addition, in Italian, a specific form for the imminential future occurs which stands in competition with the present tense, while the future tense is odd (see Table 2.2, example 3iii). On the other hand, the present tense, the imminential future and a further periphrasis containing

Table 2.1 The Onomasiological Space of English Future Time Reference

1) Complete reliability / Imminential future	+ reliable
a) ***be going to*** **+ infinitive**	
i) It's going to rain.	
ii) Are you going to play tennis today?	
2) Contingent reliability (also in connection with a condition)	
a) **future**	
i) Tomorrow's weather will be cold and cloudy.	
ii) We'll miss the train if we don't hurry up.	
3) Event scheduled by a program	
a) **present**	
i) Mary starts her new job on Tuesday.	
ii) The train leaves at 5 o'clock.	
4) Reliability related to implicatures	
a) **present progressive**	
i) Are you playing tennis today?	
ii) I'm taking Mary to the theatre tonight.	
5) Reliability restricted (by external conditions)	
a) **future progressive**	
i) When will you be paying me back?	
ii) You can come with me. I'll be driving	
through Soho anyway.	– reliable

the verb *andare* 'to go', commonly used with a projective value, cannot be replaced by the progressive form which is also common in Italian (see Table 2.2, examples 3iv–v).

English clearly contrasts with German and Italian with regard to the progressive form, because the latter has to be employed for present time reference with both activities and achievements (1a–b), while the present tense normally expresses a habitual or a scheduled event (1c) (see also Table 2.1, example 3aii):

(1) a. Charlie is working / *works now.
    b. Fred is starving / *starves now.
    c. Usually, Charlie works / *is working three hours a day.

Italian is partially similar to English insofar as a grammaticalized progressive form can be used, which stands, however, as an alternative to the *presente*, although the latter can get a habitual interpretation in contrast to the former:

(2) a. Carlo sta lavorando / lavora ora.
       'Charlie is working (lit. stands working) / works now.'
    b. Fred sta morendo / muore di fame ora.
       'Fred is starving / starves now.'

Table 2.2 The Onomasiological Space of German and Italian Future Time Reference

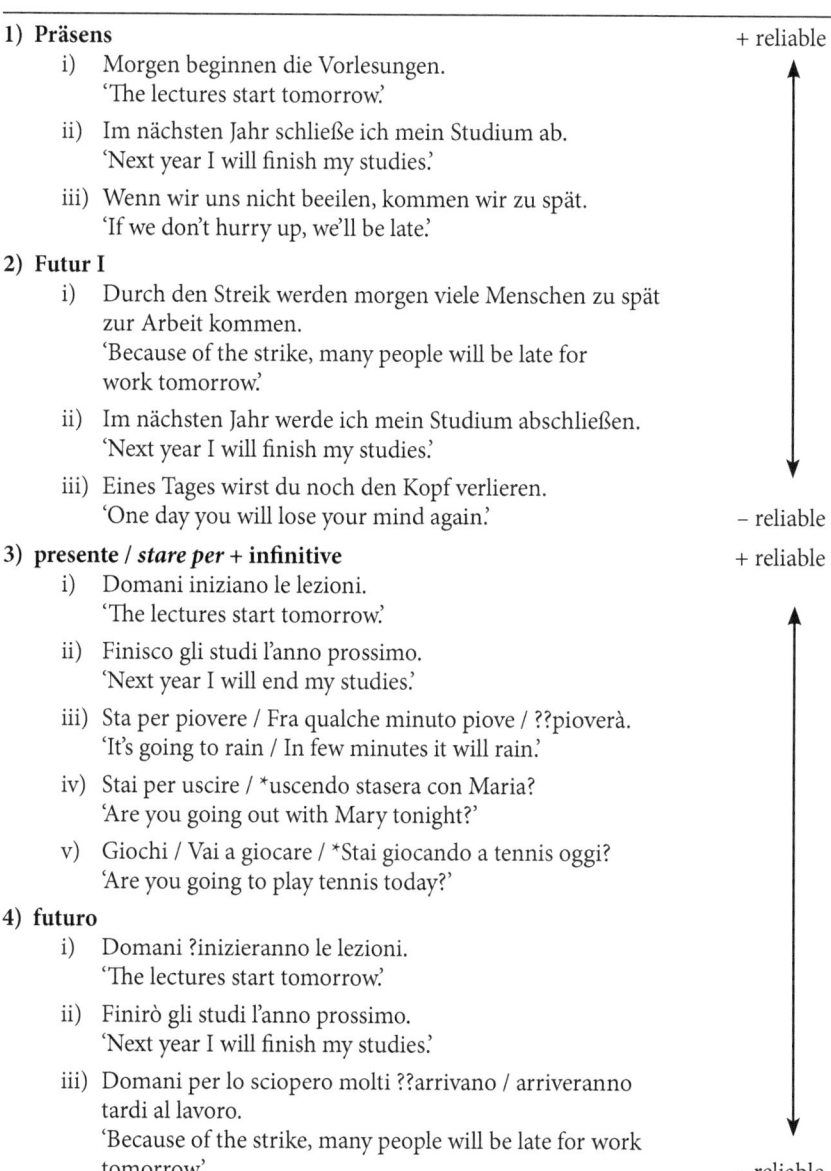

1) **Präsens** + reliable

   i) Morgen beginnen die Vorlesungen.
      'The lectures start tomorrow.'

   ii) Im nächsten Jahr schließe ich mein Studium ab.
      'Next year I will finish my studies.'

   iii) Wenn wir uns nicht beeilen, kommen wir zu spät.
      'If we don't hurry up, we'll be late.'

2) **Futur I**

   i) Durch den Streik werden morgen viele Menschen zu spät
      zur Arbeit kommen.
      'Because of the strike, many people will be late for
      work tomorrow.'

   ii) Im nächsten Jahr werde ich mein Studium abschließen.
      'Next year I will finish my studies.'

   iii) Eines Tages wirst du noch den Kopf verlieren.
      'One day you will lose your mind again.' − reliable

3) **presente / *stare per* + infinitive** + reliable

   i) Domani iniziano le lezioni.
      'The lectures start tomorrow.'

   ii) Finisco gli studi l'anno prossimo.
      'Next year I will end my studies.'

   iii) Sta per piovere / Fra qualche minuto piove / ??pioverà.
      'It's going to rain / In few minutes it will rain.'

   iv) Stai per uscire / *uscendo stasera con Maria?
      'Are you going out with Mary tonight?'

   v) Giochi / Vai a giocare / *Stai giocando a tennis oggi?
      'Are you going to play tennis today?'

4) **futuro**

   i) Domani ?inizieranno le lezioni.
      'The lectures start tomorrow.'

   ii) Finirò gli studi l'anno prossimo.
      'Next year I will finish my studies.'

   iii) Domani per lo sciopero molti ??arrivano / arriveranno
      tardi al lavoro.
      'Because of the strike, many people will be late for work
      tomorrow.' − reliable

In other words, a factor 'Pnin' forcing a strictly habitual interpretation of the present tense is at play in English as hinted at by Nabokov with his usual sense of humour: '"I go now", said Hagen, who, though a lesser addict of the present tense than Pnin, also held it in favour' (Nabokov 1953/1989: 170).

In neat contrast with English and Italian – where it is robustly established – the progressive in German is rather to be conceived as an emergent category because it can be expressed by a number of constructions displaying a growing range of selectivity and/or a decreasing diffusion (cf. König and Gast 2007: 94):

(3) V + gerade > sein + am V_{INF} > sein + dabei + V_{INF} > sein + beim V_{INF} > sein + im V_{INF}
 a. Karl arbeitet gerade.
    'Charlie is working.'
 b. Karl ist am Arbeiten / Verhungern.
    'Charlie is working / starving.'
 c. Karl ist am Äpfelpflücken.
    'Charlie is gathering apples.'
 d. Als du kamst, war ich dabei, meinen Aufsatz abzuschließen / ?Äpfel zu essen.
    'When you came in, I was closing my article / ?eating apples.'
 e. Karl ist beim Arbeiten / *Verhungern.
    'Charlie is working / *starving.'
 f. Karl ist im Kommen / *Arbeiten.
    'Charlie is coming / *working.'
 g. Karl ist arbeiten / einkaufen / schwimmen.
    'Charlie is working / shopping / swimming (elsewhere).'

In this typical example of *layering* (cf. Hopper and Traugott 2003: 124), the commonest construction displays a lower degree of selectivity and a higher diffusion (3a), while the so-called *rheinische Verlaufsform* ('Rhenish progressive form', cf. DUDEN: 434) is diatopically restricted to western varieties (3b). The latter also allows for noun incorporation with unspecified objects (3c). The construction in (3d) preferably selects transitive verbs entailing a clear result state, while the constructions in (3e) and (3f) are limited respectively to agentive and movement verbs (cf. König and Gast 2007: 93). It has to be added that in German an absentive construction also occurs (3g) which – besides displaying a progressive value – also implies that the subject involved in the predication is not physically present in the speech situation (cf. de Groot 2000).

In agreement with the requirement discussed above relating to the occurrence of a significant number of translated texts in the languages involved in the Contrastive Analyses, in the following table, the results of an investigation which looked at the correspondence of expressions with future time reference contained in a collection of German short stories in Italian and English translations are reported (cf. Gaeta 2006 for details):

The *Präsens* is mostly translated by means of the English future tense, while its present tense translation only amounts to one-quarter of the total. This stands in neat contrast with Italian where both the *presente* and the *futuro* are used – although the *presente* slightly stands out – to which the two constructions containing the verbs *stare* 'to stand' and *andare* 'to go' must be added. On the other hand, the *Futur I* is mostly translated by means of the Italian *futuro* and of the English future tense, although in the

Table 2.3 Italian and English Translation of German Future Reference

%	%		Italian	German	English	%	%	%
24	47	38	**presente**		**present**	9	24	11
21	41	33	**futuro**		**future**	28	74	35
6	12	10	stare per + INF andare a + INF	**Präsens**	be going to	1	2	1
1	4	2	stare per + INF		be going to	11	28	14
1	4	2	**presente**	**Futur I**				
31	92	49	**futuro**		**future**	29	72	37
16		25		others		1		1
100		159		tot.		79		100

Source: Hermann, J. (1998), *Sommerhaus, später* (Frankfurt/M.: Fischer); Italian trans: (2001) *Casa estiva, più tardi*, trans. B. Griffini (Roma: edizioni e/o); English trans.: (2002) *The Summer House, Later*, trans. M. Bettauer Dembo (London: Flamingo).

latter language, a significant preference for the construction containing the verb *go* in one-third of the cases is observed. In short, the clear dominance of the correspondence of the English future for the future time reference found in the German original text emphasizes the role of the grammaticalized verb *will* used in the English construction. The latter has even been characterized as a 'grounding predication' insofar as it has the effect of anchoring a certain event to the 'ground' which consists in 'the speech event, its participants, and its immediate circumstances' (cf. Langacker 1991: 318). This results in a subjectification process in which the speaker's subjective perspective remains implicit, offstage, because it is wired into the conceptualization of the scene as a whole. The advanced status of subjectification of *will* is shown by its usage in predictions which are presented as universally valid laws, while in German and Italian respectively, the *Präsens* and the *presente* are strictly required:

(4) a. She will always drink her whiskey straight.
     b. Sie trinkt.PRS ihr Whiskey pur / ??wird ihr Whiskey pur trinken.FUT.
     c. Lei beve.PRS / ??berrà.FUT sempre il suo whisky liscio.

On the other hand, the restricted usage of the *Futur I* with regard to the *futuro* can be accounted for by making an appeal to the former's pronounced degree of subjectivity, which has the effect of presenting a prediction as a purely conjectural evaluation. This emerges quite clearly in the contrast between predictions formulated respectively in objective (5a) and subjective terms (5b) where the Italian translation prefers the *futuro* in both cases, while in the German original text the *Präsens* contrasts with the *Futur I*:

(5) a. Den Efeu schneid.PRS ich, wenn du kommst.PRS, du weißt, du hast die Schlüssel immer noch.

Taglierò.FUT l'edera quando verrai.FUT, le chiavi, lo sai, le hai ancora tu.
I'll cut the ivy when you come. Remember, you still have the keys.

b. 'Wenn [der Hurrikan] kommt.PRS, wirst du dir in die Hosen scheißen.FUT, verdammt noch mal', sagt Kaspar … 'Du wirst flennen.FUT und kreischen.FUT'.
'Quando arriverà.FUT [l'uragano] ti cacherai.FUT sotto, maledizione', dice Kaspar … 'Piangerai.FUT e strillerai.FUT'.
'If [the hurricane] does come, you'll shit in your pants, damn it all, says Kaspar … 'You'll be wailing and blubbering.'

The stronger subjective value of the *futuro* compared to the *Futur I* is confirmed by the high number of cases – about 40 per cent in Table 2.3 – in which it translates a *Präsens* like the following one:

(6) Ich sah aus dem Autofenster und dachte: 'Das ist.PRS es noch fünf Minuten'.
Guardai fuori dal finestrino e pensai: 'Sarà.FUT questa ma per non più di cinque minuti ancora'.
I looked out of the car window and thought, That's it for another five minutes, maybe.

Note that the subjective value is explicitly expressed in English by means of the afterthought *maybe*. Thus, in Italian, the dividing line between subjective and objective predictions is pulled further up towards reliability in the scale seen in Table 2.2, as shown by the following examples in which the *presente* and the progressive form refer respectively to a promise involving the highest personal engagement (7a) and to an event presented as imminent, although in truth it is not (7b):

(7) a. 'Platz genug, verstehst du? Platz genug! Ich mach.PRS euch hier 'nen Salon und 'n Billardzimmer und 'n Rucherzimmer, und jedem seinen eigenen Raum'.
'C'è posto abbastanza, capisci? Posto abbastanza! Io vi faccio.PRS un salone e una sala da biliardo e una sala per fumatori, e a ciascuno la sua camera'.
'Plenty of room, you understand? Plenty of room. I'll build you a salon here, and a billiard room, and a smoking room, and separate rooms for everyone.'
b. 'Stein' rief ich. 'Komm da raus! Es stürzt.PRS zusammen!'.
'Stein!' gridai. 'Vieni fuori! Sta crollando.PROG!'.
'Stein!' I called up. 'Get out of there! It's going to collapse!'

Let us now turn to the past time reference, which offers a more complex picture insofar as at least two different tenses are present in the three languages, namely a present perfect – corresponding respectively to the German *Perfekt* and to the Italian *passato prossimo* – and a simple past – corresponding respectively to the German *Präteritum* and to the Italian *passato remoto*.

Given this complexity, it is convenient to adopt in this case a semasiological perspective, taking as a vantage point the German *Perfekt*, which displays a variety of different values that only partially have correspondences in the other two languages (cf. König and Gast 2007: 87–92):

(8) a. *resultative (hot news)*
    i. Schau mal, es hat geschneit.
       Look, it has snowed.
       Guarda, ha nevicato.
    ii. Die Maschine aus Paris ist gelandet.
       The airplane from Paris has landed.
       L'aereo da Parigi è atterrato.

    b. *narrative*
    i. Gestern sind wir ins Kino gegangen.
       Yesterday we went to the cinema.
       Ieri siamo andati al cinema.
    ii. Anschließend haben wir bei einem Italiener gegessen.
       Then we ate at an Italian restaurant.
       Poi abbiamo mangiato in un ristorante cinese.

    c. *future*
    i. Wenn du das nächste Mal kommst, sind wir schon umgezogen.
       The next time you come, we'll already have relocated.
       La prossima volta che vieni, avremo già traslocato.
    ii. Morgen Abend habe ich dieses Kapitel abgeschlossen.
       I will finish this chapter tomorrow night.
       ?(Entro) domani sera ho finito questo capitolo.

    d. *universal (non-persistent)*
    i. Ich habe seit mehr als zehn Jahren nicht mehr getanzt.
       (Bitte entschuldigen Sie, wenn ich Ihnen auf die Füße trete.)
       I have not been dancing for more than ten years. (I apologize if I step on your foot.)
       Non ballo da più di dieci anni.
    ii. Ich tanze seit mehr als zehn Jahren nicht mehr.
       I have not danced for more than ten years.
       Non ballo da più di dieci anni.

    e. *existential (experiential)*
    i. Ich habe schon mal Tennis gespielt.
       I have already played tennis.
       Ho già giocato a tennis in passato.
    ii. Ich bin Gerhard Schröder erst einmal begegnet.
       I have met Gerhard Schröder only once.
       Ho incontrato Gerhard Schröder solo una volta.

iii. Ich bin Willy Brandt nur einmal begegnet.
I met Willy Brandt only once.
Ho incontrato Willy Brandt solo una volta.

While the resultative value (8a) is expressed in the three languages by the similar construction based on HAVE + past participle, English clearly contrasts with German and Italian with regard to the narrative value because it can only use the simple past (8b) even for events placed in the recent past. On the other hand, while the German *Perfekt* can be used with a resultative value projected into the future (8c), this is impossible in English – as expected in the light of the previous discussion – and only possible to a limited extent in Italian, where, however – as in English – the *future anteriore* or future perfect is largely preferred. Furthermore, the English present perfect can be used with a so-called 'universal value', referring to a state of affairs which has been true in the past and is still persisting at the moment of utterance, as shown in (8dii), while in German and Italian, this has to be conveyed by the *Präsens / presente*. On the other hand, the German *Perfekt* can be used to refer to a non-persistent state of affairs, while in English and Italian, this has to be done by means of the present perfect progressive and of the *presente*. Finally, while the three languages converge in using the perfect for the so-called 'existential value' referring to personal experiences which have been made in the past (8ei), English and German can also distinguish between the possibility of repeating the experience in the future or not, by making use respectively of different tenses (present perfect and simple past) and of different adverbs (8eii–iii).

One important aspect of the contrast between the two different tenses used for referring to past events relates to the expansion – observed in German and in Italian – of the *Perfekt / passato prossimo* towards also covering narrative values in the case of events placed in the distant past besides those seen in (8bi–ii) above:

(9) a. Im letzten Jahr besuchte ich China ~ habe ich China besucht.
L'anno scorso visitai ~ ho visitato la Cina.
Last year I visited China.

  b. L'anno scorso visitai la Cina e vidi anche Sciangai.
L'anno scorso ho visitato ~ ??visitai la Cina e ci rivado ora.
'Last year I visited China and I also saw Shanghai. / Last year I visited China and I'm going there again now.'

  c. Plötzlich ging das Licht aus und es wurde dunkel. / Plötzlich ist das Licht ausgegangen und es ist dunkel geworden.
Improvvisamente si spense la luce e divenne buio. / Improvvisamente si è spenta la luce ed è divenuto buio.
'Suddenly the light turned off and it became dark.'

  d. Deswegen ist er gekommen. Zum Hausarzt ist er nicht gegangen, weil er gestern gearbeitet hat und weil's noch nicht so schlimm war.
Therefore he has come. He didn't go to the doctor because yesterday he worked / *has worked / *has been / was working and it *has been / was not so painful.
Perciò è venuto. Non è andato dal dottore perché ieri ha lavorato / lavorava e non è stato / stava poi così male.

e. Hat Michael Jackson noch gelebt als ihn sein Leibarzt fand?
Was / *Has been Michael Jackson still alive when his physician found him?
Era / *È stato ancora vivo Michael Jackson quando lo trovò il suo medico?

In neat contrast with English which only admits the simple past, in (9a) the *Perfekt* and the *passato prossimo* are largely used for referring to distant past events as an alternative to the *Präteritum* and the *passato remoto* – especially in colloquial speech registers and respectively in the South and in the North of their national territories. For Central and Southern varieties of Italian, however, a further distinction has to be observed in (9b): the usage of the *passato prossimo* for referring to distant past events is sensitive to the topic-relevance of the event for the speech act situation. If the distant past event is topic-relevant, the *passato prossimo* has to be used, while a purely narrative context requires a *passato remoto* with an aoristic value. Furthermore, notice that in the absence of any temporal reference, the usage of the *Perfekt* and of the *passato prossimo* in (9c) remains non-specific with regard to the distance from the utterance time, while the *Präteritum* and the *passato remoto* clearly collocate the event in the distant past – and also adds a certain literary flavour. Finally, in German, the effect of the expansion of the *Perfekt* at the expenses of the *Präteritum* has further consequences on the tempo-aspectual system, insofar as the former also comes to be used in clearly imperfective contexts. In (9d), the German *Perfekt* corresponds to an English simple past – as expected – or to the progressive form, depending on the aspectual nuance that the speaker intends to emphasize, while in Italian – besides the expected *passato prossimo* – the *imperfetto* can be used, again depending on the intended meaning. The imperfective value is the only choice in (9e), where the German *Perfekt* cannot assume any possible perfective nuance. In other words, the systematic replacement of the *Präteritum* – which is not intrinsically specified for perfectivity – by means of the *Perfekt* causes a breach through the perfective/imperfective wall in German, while the distinction remains robustly stable in English and Italian, thanks to the presence of clearly imperfective tenses. Note that the disappearance of the preterital tense in Southern German (also referred to as *Präteritumschwund* in the German-speaking literature, cf. DUDEN: 520) and in Northern Italian is particularly interesting from the viewpoint of the areal perspective advocated previously as a possible dimension relevant for Contrastive Analysis, as well as for the purposes of a micro-typology.

The Table 2.4 summarizes – from an onomasiological viewpoint – the most salient distinctions outlined above, with the addition of the future perfect and of the past perfect which are used in a roughly similar way in the three languages.

Asymmetries and differences are particularly pronounced in the three Onomasiological Categories of [imperfective], [universal/persistent] and [narrative], while in the other cases – in spite of minor differences – the usage of the tenses largely overlaps in the three languages. This complex network of relations is charted in Figure 2.2, in which the semasiological correspondences of the single tenses in the three languages are shown, which are indirectly connected to each other by means of the Onomasiological Categories summarized in Table 2.4.

As can be gathered from the chart, the picture is multi-faceted, in that only in a few cases is the relationship between the two levels bidirectional or at least unidirectional. On the other hand, the Contrastive Analysis is able to show similarities and differences reaching a high degree of detail and complexity.

Table 2.4 The Tempo-Aspectual Domain in the Three Languages Ordered on the Basis of the Onomasiological Categories

Onomasiological Categories	German	English	Italian
- anterior / posterior	**Präsens** Ich schlafe von 12 bis 17. Morgen fahre ich ab. 'I will leave tomorrow.'	**Present** I sleep from 12pm to 7am. → Future	**Presente** Dormo dalle 24 alle 7. Domani parto.
anterior, aoristic	**Präteritum** Ich schlief den ganzen Tag.	**Simple past** I slept the whole day.	**Passato remoto** Dormii tutto il giorno.
anterior, imperfective	→ Verlaufsform, Präteritum, Perfekt	→ Progressive form	**Imperfetto** Dormivo sempre. 'I was always sleeping.'
futural	**Futur I** Ich werde schlafen.	**Future** I will sleep. I am going to sleep.	**Futuro** Dormirò. Sto per dormire.
resultative existential hot news universal (persistent) narrative	**Perfekt** Jemand hat mein Auto gestohlen. Ich habe Tennis gespielt. Schröder ist zurückgetreten. → Präsens Ich bin gestern im Theater gewesen.	**Present perfect** Someone has stolen my car. I have played tennis. Schröder has resigned. I have lived here for two years. → Simple past	**Passato prossimo** Qualcuno mi ha rubato la macchina. Ho giocato a tennis. Schröder si è dimesso. → Presente Ieri sono stato a teatro. 'Yesterday I was at the theatre.'
posterior, resultative	**Futur II** Ich werde das bis morgen gemacht haben.	**Future perfect** I will have done this by tomorrow.	**Futuro anteriore** Entro domani l'avrò finito.
pre-anterior	**Plusquamperfekt** Ich hatte geschlafen.	**Past perfect** I had slept.	**Trapassato prossimo** Avevo dormito.

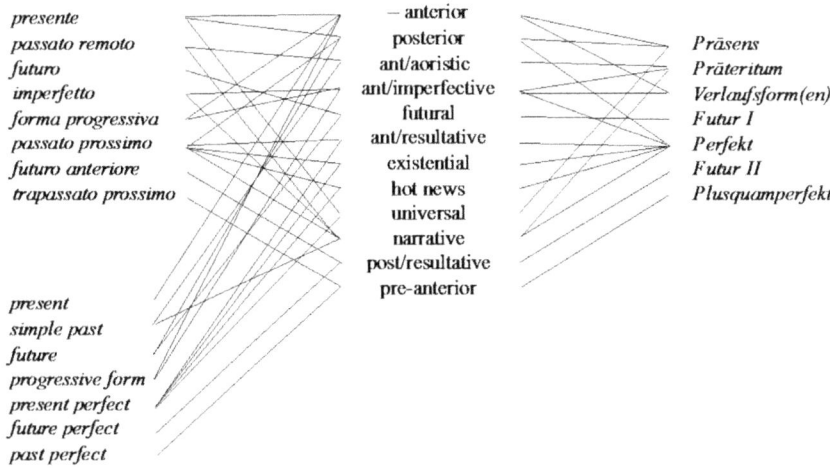

Figure 2.2 Semasiological correspondences in the three languages.

3.2 Properties of subjects and objects

The properties of subjects and objects refer to the morphosyntactic domain and are interesting to the extent that the relations among the three languages are quite varied. On the one hand, English and German – traditionally described as non-pro-drop languages – clearly contrast with Italian with regard to the subject properties:

(10) a. *Dropping*
        *Sleeps the whole day.
        *Schläft den ganzen Tag.
        Dorme tutto il giorno.

      b. *Coreferentiality*
        Mary$_i$ is happy when she$_{i/j}$ is drunk.
        Marie$_i$ ist zufrieden, wenn sie$_{i/j}$ besoffen ist.
        *Maria$_i$ è contenta quando lei.$_{i/j}$ è ubriaca.

      c. *Expletives*
        *(It) is raining.
        *(Es) regnet.
        (*Ciò / *Esso) piove.

      d. *Correlatives*
        Now it$_i$ is clear [that is a good boy]$_i$.
        Jetzt ist es$_i$ klar, [dass Hans ein braver Kerl ist]$_i$.
        Adesso (*esso$_i$ / *ciò$_i$) è chiaro [che Gianni è un bravo ragazzo]$_i$.

      e. *Late-coming*
        *Has spoken Mary.
        *Hat gesprochen Marie.
        Ha parlato Maria.

    f. *Dislocability of the relative sentence*
       A man$_i$ came whom$_i$ I know well.
       Ein Mann$_i$ ist gerade angekommen, den$_i$ ich gut kenne.
       *Un uomo$_i$ è appena arrivato che$_i$ conosco bene.

    g. *Extraction*
       *Who$_i$ do you think that $\_i$ will come?
       *Wer$_i$ glaubst du, dass $\_i$ kommen wird?
       Chi$_i$ credi che $\_i$ verrà?

Besides dropping (10a), English and German also converge with regard to the use of the subject pronoun for referring to the subject of the main clause (10b), of the expletives (10c) and of the correlatives (10d). Moreover, the subject cannot be freely dislocated at the end of the clause (10e), while its initial position does not require a relative clause to be immediately adjacent (10f). Finally, a subject cannot be freely extracted from a dependent clause (10g), although this latter option is partially available in German in dependence of longer clauses which provide more context to justify the extraction (cf. Bayer 2005): *Wer$_i$ glaubst du, dass $\_i$ 1933 Bürgermeister in Hamburg gewesen ist?* (lit.: *Who$_i$ do you think that $\_i$ was the mayor in Hamburg in 1933?*).

    On the other hand, if we turn to the properties of the object, the picture is radically different, insofar as German goes with Italian and clearly contrasts with English. This is especially true of the object extraction from subordinate clauses embedded within an interrogative sentence (cf. König and Gast 2007: 219–21):

(11) a. [– clause-external]
        [$_{+FIN}$ Who$_i$ has Charlie seen $\_i$ in our garden?]
        [$_{+FIN}$ Wen$_i$ hat Karl in unserem Garten $\_i$ gesehen?]
        [$_{+FIN}$ Chi$_i$ ha visto $\_i$ nel nostro giardino Carlo?]

      b. [+ clause-external], [– finite]
        [$_{+FIN}$ Who$_i$ did Charlie believe [$_{-FIN}$ to see $\_i$ in the garden?]]
        [$_{+FIN}$ Wen$_i$ glaubte Karl [$_{-FIN}$ im Garten $\_i$ zu sehen?]]
        [$_{+FIN}$ Chi$_i$ credette [$_{-FIN}$ di vedere $\_i$ in giardino] Carlo?]

      c. [+ clause-external], [+ finite]
        [$_{+FIN}$ Who$_i$ did he believe [$_{+FIN}$ that he saw $\_i$ in the garden?]]
        *[$_{+FIN}$ Wen$_i$ glaubte Karl [$_{+FIN}$ dass er im Garten $\_i$ sah?]]
        *[$_{+FIN}$ Chi$_i$ credette [$_{+FIN}$ che vide $\_i$ in giardino] Carlo?]

      d. [+ clause-external], [– finite], [– argument]
        [$_{+FIN}$ What$_i$ did he come [$_{-FIN}$ in order to pick up $\_i$?]]
        *[$_{+FIN}$ Was$_i$ ist er gekommen, [$_{-FIN}$ um $\_i$ abzuholen?]]
        *[$_{+FIN}$ Cosa$_i$ è venuto qui [$_{-FIN}$ per comprare $\_i$?]]

      e. [+ clause-external], [+ finite], [– argument]
        *[$_{+FIN}$ Which film$_i$ did you go to the movies [$_{+FIN}$ even though you did not want to see $\_i$?]]
        [$_{+FIN}$ You went to the movies [$_{+FIN}$ even though you did not want to see which film?]]

Table 2.5 Object Extraction from Dependent Clauses in the Three Languages

clause-internal	clause-external			
	argument clauses		circumstantial clauses	
	non-finite	finite	non-finite	finite
German / Italian		[– animate O]		
English				

It has to be added that the crucial cut-off point of the implicational hierarchy – which is summarized in Table 2.5 above – consisting of the possibility of extracting an object from a finite dependent argument clause (11c) is partially possible in German and Italian when the object refers to inanimate referents:

(12) $[_{+FIN}$ What$_i$ do you think $[_{+FIN}$ (that) he will say $\_{i}$?]]
$[_{+FIN}$ Was$_i$ denkst du, $[_{+FIN}$ was$_i$ / *dass er $\_{i}$ sagen wird?]]
$[_{+FIN}$ Che$_i$ / Cosa$_i$ pensi $[_{+FIN}$ che / (*cosa$_i$) $\_{i}$ dirà?]]

However, this possibility involves for German the employment of the interrogative pronoun *was* which is co-referent with the object of the embedded clause.

As shown by Table 2.5 German and Italian contrasts with English which is more liberal as to the possibility of object extraction, which, however, does not extend to a finite dependent circumstantial clause (11e).

Finally, this implicational hierarchy – and especially its cut-off point – also holds for the accessibility to an object extracted from a clause embedded within a relative clause, in which German and Italian contrast again with English:

(13) The man$_i$ $[_{+FIN}$ who$_i$ you think $[_{+FIN}$ you saw $\_{i}$]] ...
*Der Mann$_i$, $[_{+FIN}$ welchen$_i$ du glaubst, $[_{+FIN}$ dass du $\_{i}$ sahst]] ...
*L'uomo$_i$ $[_{+FIN}$ che$_i$ pensasti $[_{+FIN}$ che vedesti $\_{i}$]] ...

In other words, the functional domain identified by Table 2.5 above emphasizes a crucial distinction relating to the blocking effect of clausal boundaries on anaphoric chains.

4 Conclusion

To sum up, Contrastive Analysis as a highly granular 'micro-typology' has many insights to offer, not only for typologists. In particular, English as a global language can be used as a tool in the learner's hands to detect relevant generalizations concerning the mother tongue and the second foreign language.

Italian learners of German as L3 can benefit from mastering English as L2 because of similar structural traits (often revealing similar diachronic paths), as, for instance, in the case of the pronominal subject. On the other hand, Italian and German pattern alike in several respects, as, for instance, with regard to object extraction across clauses which are nicely captured in contrast to English. A similar multi-faceted picture is also found for the other domains investigated here: for instance, Italian and English reveal commonalities with regard to the imperfective and imminential periphrases, while German and Italian partially share the (areal) development of the present perfect. In sum, in spite of its privileged status as a global language English is more than a mere *tertium comparationis*, because it is different enough from the other languages to stand alone as a peculiar system illuminating with its difference the other systems involved. Accordingly, it represents an important base on which the speakers can build their further competence in a second foreign language.

Notes

1   Parts of this chapter were presented as paper at the 8th International Contrastive Linguistics Conference (Athens, 25–28 May 2017) as well as in talks given at the University of Naples 'Federico II', Genoa and Milan. I am very grateful to the people present on these occasions for insightful questions and remarks. Needless to say, I am solely responsible for any remaining mistakes.
2   Fries (1983: 4–5) suggested developing a Theoretical Contrastive Linguistics which should be opposed – in compliance with its wider typological orientation – to Applied Theoretical Contrastive Linguistics that was to be thought of as more concerned with a didactic dimension. In this regard, however, Lotz (1968: 10) had already observed: 'The question has often been raised whether contrastive studies belong to pure linguistics or to applied linguistics. I do not see much relevancy in such a compartmentalization, but it reminds me of the saying of the famous mathematician Courant, founder of NYU's Institute for Applied Mathematics: "Pure mathematics is a small and not very significant part of applied mathematics."'
3   In this regard, see also Zuanelli Sonino (1976), which is however only limited to the phonological comparison.

References

Bayer, J. (2005), 'Was beschränkt die Extraktion? Subjekt – Objekt vs Topic – Fokus', in F. J. D'Avis (ed.), *Deutsche Syntax: Empirie und Theorie*, 233–57, Göteborg: Acta Universitatis Gothoburgensis.

Blasco Ferrer, E. (1999), *Italiano e tedesco: un confronto linguistico*, Torino: Paravia.

Bosco Coletsos, S. and M. Costa (2013), *Italiano e tedesco. Questioni di linguistica contrastiva*, Alessandria: dell'Orso.

Carroll, M. and M. Lambert (2006), 'Reorganizing Principles of Information Structure in Advanced L2s: A Study of French and German Learners of English', in H. Byrnes, H. D. Weger-Guntharp and K. A. Sprang (eds), *Educating for Advanced Language Capacities*, 54–73, Georgetown, Washington D.C.: Georgetown University Press.

Crystal, D. (2003), *English as a Global Language*, Cambridge, UK: Cambridge University Press.

de Groot, C. (2000), 'The Absentive', in Ö. Dahl (ed.), *Tense and Aspect in the Languages of Europe*, 693–719, Berlin: Mouton de Gruyter.

Di Meola, C. and D. Puato (2015), *Deutsch kontrastiv aus italienischer Sicht*, Frankfurt/Main: Lang.

DUDEN = *Grammatik der deutschen Gegenwartssprache* (2005), 7th edn, Mannheim: Dudenverlag.

Fries, C. C. (1945), *Teaching and Learning English as a Foreign Language*, Ann Arbor, MI: University of Michigan Press.

Fries, N. (1983), *Syntaktische und semantische Studien zum frei verwendeten Infinitiv und zu verwandten Erscheinungen im Deutschen*, Tübingen: Narr.

Gaeta, L. (2006), 'Il *Futur* tedesco tra temporalità e modalità', in L. Schena, C. Preite and S. Vecchiato (eds), *Gli insegnamenti linguistici dell'area economico-giuridica in Europa. Il concetto di futurità nella codificazione linguistica. XIV Incontro del Centro Linguistico.* Università Bocconi, 26 Novembre 2005, 183–201, Milano: Egea.

Gaeta, L. (2014), 'Kontrastive Linguistik nach der typologischen Wende. Kommentar zu den Beiträgen', *Germanistische Mitteilungen*, 40 (1): 79–82.

Gast, V. (2011), 'Contrastive Linguistics: Theories and Methods', in B. Kortmann and J. Kabatek (eds), *Wörterbücher zur Sprach- und Kommunikationswissenschaft Online: Linguistic Theory and Methodology*, Berlin: de Gruyter.

Gast, V. (2013), 'Contrastive Analysis', in M. Byram and A. Hu (eds), *The Routledge Encyclopedia of Language Teaching and Learning*, 2nd edn, 153–8, London: Routledge.

Haspelmath, M. (2001), 'The European Linguistic Area: Standard Average European', in M. Haspelmath, E. König, W. Oesterreicher and W. Raible (eds), *Language Typology and Language Universals*, vol. 2, 1492–510, Berlin: Mouton de Gruyter.

Haspelmath, M. (2010), 'Comparative Concepts and Descriptive Categories in Cross-linguistic Studies', *Language*, 86: 663–87, 696–9.

Hawkins, J. A. (1986), *A Comparative Typology of English and German: Unifying the Contrasts*, London: Croom Helm.

Hawkins, J. A. and L. Filipović (2011), *Criterial Features in L2 English*, Cambridge, UK: Cambridge University Press.

Hopper, P. and E. C. Traugott (2003), *Grammaticalization*, 2nd edn, Cambridge, UK: Cambridge University Press.

Hüning, M., U. Vogl and T. van der Wouden (eds), (2006), *Nederlands tussen Duits en Engels*, Leiden: Stichting Neerlandistiek.

Iamartino, G. (2001), 'La contrastività italiano-inglese in prospettiva storica', *Rassegna Italiana di Linguistica Applicata*, 33: 7–130.

König, E. (1996), 'Kontrastive Grammatik und Typologie', in E. Lang and G. Zifonun (eds), *Deutsch – typologisch*, 31–54, Berlin: de Gruyter.

König, E. (2012a), 'Zur Standortbestimmung der Kontrastiven Linguistik innerhalb der vergleichenden Sprachwissenschaft', in L. Gunkel and G. Zifonun (eds), *Deutsch im Sprachvergleich. Grammatische Kontraste und Konvergenzen*, 13–40, Berlin: de Gruyter.

König, E. (2012b), 'Contrastive Linguistics and Language Comparison', *Languages in Contrast*, 12: 3–26.

König, E. and V. Gast (2007), *Understanding English-German Contrasts*, 3rd edn, Berlin: Schmidt.

Kufner, H. L. (1962), *The Grammatical Structures of English and German*, Chicago, IL: Chicago University Press.

Lado, R. (1957), *Linguistics across Cultures: Applied Linguistics for Language Teachers*, Ann Arbor, MI: University of Michigan Press.

Langacker, R. (1991), *Concept, Image, Symbol: The Cognitive Basis of Grammar*, Berlin: Mouton de Gruyter.

Lotz, J. (1968), 'Introductory Remarks', in J. E. Alatis (ed.), *Report of the 19th Annual Round Table Meeting: Contrastive Linguistics and its Pedagogical Implications*, 9–10, Washington DC: Georgetown University Press.

Moulton, W. (1962), *The Sounds of English and German*, Chicago, IL: University of Chicago Press.

Nabokov, V. (1953/1989) *Pnin*, New York: Vintage International.

Ramat, P. (1998), 'Typological Comparison and Linguistic Areas: Some Introductory Remarks', *Language Sciences*, 20: 227–40.

van der Auwera, J. (2012), 'From Contrastive Linguistics to Linguistic Typology', *Languages in Contrast*, 12: 69–86.

Vanni, A. M. (2016), *Quaderno di grammatica inglese. Elementi di linguistica contrastiva*, Palermo: Leima.

von Stutterheim, Ch. and M. Lambert (2005), 'Cross-linguistic Analysis of Temporal Perspectives in Text Production', in H. Hendricks (ed.), *The Structure of Learner Varieties*, 203–31, Berlin: Mouton de Gruyter.

Zuanelli Sonino, E. (1976), *Italiano, tedesco, inglese: analisi contrastiva a livello fonico*, Bergamo: Minerva Italica.

3

'Verb-first' in proverbs and slogans: A German-based contrastive view

Torsten Leuschner

The present chapter discusses the productivity of the verb-first (= V1) conditional construction as a template for German proverbs in contrast with English Subject-Auxiliary Inversion (SAI), which has no corresponding potential. Special attention is paid to the 'proverbiality by association' ('scheinbare Sprichwörtlichkeit', Mieder 1975) of certain commercial and political slogans, which rely, inter alia, on the function of V1 word order as a contextualization cue in German. Borrowing Norrick's notion of 'p-grammar' (where 'p' stands for 'proverbial'), the concept of 'p-constructicon' is introduced, and it is suggested that the p-constructica of different languages should be compared in future research under the theoretical framework of Social Construction Grammar.

1 Introduction

Word order holds a special interest for contrastive linguists, not least with regard to closely related Germanic languages, like German and English. But whereas word order is usually discussed from typological, historical, syntactic or information-structural points of view, the present chapter takes a different approach, discussing the productivity of a specific word order pattern, viz. verb-first (= V1), and the resulting variation in a specific domain of German phraseology in contrast with English. Especially in focus are proverbs (broadly speaking) and slogans in the form of V1-conditionals, as in the following examples from the Online-Wortschatz-Informationssystem Deutsch (OWID) proverb dictionary (OWID n.d.):

(1) *Kommt* Zeit, kommt Rat.
    comes time comes advice
    'Given time, things will work themselves out.'
    (cf. English: Time will tell.)

(2) *Ist* die Katze aus dem Haus, tanzen die Mäuse auf dem Tisch.
    is the cat out the house, dance the mice on the table

'If the cat is out of the house, the mice dance on the table.'
(cf. English: When the cat's away, the mice will play.)

For proverbs like these, the V1-construction provides a structural template in which the initial V1-clause functions as a conditional protasis (occasionally shading into the temporal). The more structurally taut the proverb, the more V1 tends to be supplemented and supported by stylistic elements like metre, repetition and parallelism (cf. (1) with its double trochee, *kommt NP* structure), contrasting lexical pairs (*Katze – Mäuse*) and so on to create a composite effect of proverbiality. The V1-template can in turn be emulated by commercial and political slogans in an attempt to project a sheen of proverbiality-by-association ('scheinbare Sprichwörtlichkeit', Mieder 1975: 70, defined as 'Assoziation zum Sprichwort') in order to benefit from the experience, authority and didacticism invested in genuine proverbs. V1 in German proverbs therefore seems to act as a contextualization cue in the sense of Gumperz (1982) – or, as I will occasionally put it, as a 'proverbiality cue' – allowing other V1 small forms such as slogans to benefit from the template in order to project proverbiality-by-association, as appropriate for their function.

Following a long-standing tradition in German paremiology, V1 proverbs and slogans are approached in the present chapter from the complementary perspectives of schematicity and variability (Mieder 1975; Steyer and Hein 2018). Section 2 takes the perspective of schematicity, pointing out the formulaic character of V1-conditionals. Section 3 compares German with English, where 'Subject Auxiliary Inversion' (SAI) puts heavy lexico-semantic restrictions on the V1-position and thus rules out any paremiological V1-template as in German. After Section 4, which discusses the lexico-semantic specification of V1-conditionals as constructions, Section 5 takes the perspective of variability; this includes the proverbiality-by-association of commercial and political slogans such as Angela Merkel's slogan '*Scheitert der Euro, dann scheitert Europa*' (If the Euro fails, Europe fails). Borrowing Norrick's (1985: 81–100) notion of 'p-grammar' (where 'p' stands for 'proverbial'), the concluding section (Section 6) suggests that the set of structures associated with proverbiality in a given language should be defined as the 'p-constructicon' of its language, and in future research be compared with the p-constructica of other languages under the theoretical framework of Social Construction Grammar (Ziem 2015).

2　The V1-conditional as a paremiological template

When Archer Taylor declared that 'rigidity of form constitutes an essential characteristic of proverbs' (1931: 135), the formulaic nature of proverbs was already a well-established topic in paremiology. Seiler (1922: 186–94) lists fourteen productive proverb templates in German, many of them with subtypes, several with conditional meaning; Röhrich and Mieder (1977: 56–63) have twenty-seven. On the semantic side, conditional proverbs assert generalized, open relationships (though a few non-open, counterfactual proverbs are attested; see e.g. Röhrich and Mieder 1977: 58;

Seiler 1922: 189ff). This is shown by (1) and (2) above and also by the examples (3)–(6) below, which are typically encountered in daily life, in proverb encyclopaedias like Eisbrenner and Fritz (2013) and on the internet:

(3) *Hast* du was, bist du was.
  have you something are you something
  'Being rich makes you important/powerful.'
  (cf. English: Money talks.)

(4) *Kommst* du heute nicht, kommst du morgen.
  come you today not come you tomorrow
  'If you don't come today, you (can always) come tomorrow (instead).'

(5) *Ist* der Ruf erst ruiniert, lebt sich's doppelt unbeschwert.
  is the reputation once ruined lives itself-it doubly …
  'Once your reputation is ruined, you can have twice as much fun.'

(6) *Gibt* man dem Teufel den kleinen Finger, nimmt er die ganze Hand.
  gives one to the devil the little finger, takes he the whole hand
  'If you give the devil the little finger, he will take the whole hand.'
  (cf. English: Give the devil your little finger and he will take your whole hand;
  Give somebody an inch and he will take a mile.)

Examples like these illustrate proverbs in a broad sense (cf. Fix 2007 on proverbs as a family of genres; also Lüger 1999; Leuschner 2018). Apart from proverbs proper, as in (6) and also (2) above, whose distinguishing feature is their metaphorical nature, the main subgenres are commonplaces on the one hand and country and weather lore on the other hand. Commonplaces ('Gemeinplätze') are called 'proverbial apothegms' or 'truisms' by Taylor (1931: 10–16) and represented by (3)–(5) and also (1) above; country and weather lore are subsumed by Taylor under 'weather proverbs' (Taylor 1931: 109–20). The German tradition distinguishes between country lore ('Bauernregeln'), which is directly concerned with farming, and weather lore ('Wetterregeln'), which is concerned with the meteorology of farming without mentioning farming explicitly (cf. Eisbrenner and Fritz 2013). As (7) and (8) below suggest, the difference is somewhat artificial, but since we will have occasion to discuss country lore specifically later, it is nonetheless useful:

(7) *Wächst* das Gras im Januar, ist's im Sommer in Gefahr.
  grows the grass in:January is it in-the summer in danger
  'If the grass grows in January, it is under threat during the summer [because the year is unusually warm].'

(8) *Ist* der Oktober warm und fein, kommt ein scharfer Winter drein.
  is the October warm and nice comes a sharp winter behind
  'If October is warm and pleasant, it is followed by a tough winter.'

Other subgenres of proverbs broadly construed are anti-proverbs and the large number of household quotations known in German as 'Geflügelte Worte' (lit. 'winged words', following a metaphor in Homer; Büchmann 2007). Geflügelte Worte have a known author whose identity is no longer treated as significant or has slipped from collective memory. Anti-proverbs, including wellerisms, and Geflügelte Worte, are discussed in Section 3 below.

On the form side, the above examples all display the familiar mix of metre, parallelism, repetition, contrasting lexical pairs and rhyme that is characteristic of the 'style' of proverbs (Taylor 1931: 135–56). Interestingly, schematicity is in an inverse relationship with complexity: the terser the structure, the more schematic and salient the template; the more complex the structure, the more the template remains in the background and the more room is created for lexico-semantic and syntactic variation. As a result, alternation of V1 with the subordinating conjunction *wenn* 'if, when' is more likely in complex, structurally less taut proverbs, as illustrated above in (2), and lexical variation is more likely as in (6') (from the internet), where *nimmt* and *Hand* have been replaced with *will* and *Arm*:

(6')   *Wenn* man dem Teufel den kleinen Finger gibt, will er den ganzen Arm.
       if one to the devil the little finger gives, wants he the whole arm
       'If you give the devil the little finger, he wants the whole arm.'

Conversely, proverbs which preferably occur with *wenn* like (9) may show up with V1 instead:

(9)   *Wenn* zwei sich streiten, freut sich der Dritte.
      if/when two themselves fight rejoices himself the third
      'If/When two fight, the third party will profit.'

(9')   *Streiten* sich zwei, freut sich der Dritte.
       fight themselves two rejoices himself the third
       'If/When two fight, the third party will profit.'

In the terminology of Ptashnyk (2009: 62–5) and Sabban (1991; cf. Sabban 1998: 265–352), recurrent alternate forms like (9') are 'variants' ('Varianten'): specific lexical or structural components differ, but all versions are equally acceptable and express the same overall meaning. Occasional changes, by contrast, are called 'modifications' ('Modifikationen', Ptashnyk 2009), 'variations' ('Variationen', Sabban 1991, 1998) or 'adaptations' ('Adaptationen', Lüger 1999), and they arise when users spontaneously adapt familiar proverbs for purposes of (con)textual embedding, as exemplified in Section 5 below.

3   Comparison with English

In order to highlight the language-specific preconditions for the productivity of the V1-conditional as a paremiological template in German on the one hand, and the potential consequences of productivity restrictions on V1 on the other hand, a comparison with English is instructive. A tendency for English proverbs to encode conditional and related relationships in paratactical, often elliptical, structures rather than prototypical hypotaxis has been suggested in the literature (Henke 1968: 194), and observations from established proverb collections clearly confirm such findings: there are no English proverbs based on V1-conditionals.

Nevertheless, there are paremiological templates in English which express conditional relationships. They include *if*-constructions (*If anything can go wrong, it will*; *If wishes were horses, beggars would ride*), relative clause constructions that are otherwise archaic (*He who pays the piper calls the tune*) and several paratactical, asyndetic constructions (Dancygier and Sweetser 2005: 255–63). The verb forms in the latter are usually nonfinite (*Nothing ventured, nothing gained*; *First come, first served*), but occasionally finite (*You win a few, you lose a few*, also attested without *you*). To the extent that verb-initial paremiological templates occur in English, they do not have inversion but paratactically coordinated imperatives with syndetic linking (*Give the devil your little finger and he will take your whole hand*), asyndetic linking (*Scratch a cynic, find an idealist*) or optionally both (*Ask no questions, hear no lies/Ask no questions and hear no lies*). Finally, we find asyndetically coordinated noun phrases of varying complexity as in *No pain, no gain* and *Rain before seven, fine before eleven*.

The reason why English has no paremiological V1-constructions involving inversion is well-known: it has a special construction called Subject-Auxiliary Inversion (SAI), which is far more restrictive than inversion-based V1 in German (König and Gast 2018: 198). Whereas inversion in German is lexically and semantically unspecified, and the V1-position can therefore be filled by any verb whatsoever, inversion in English is restricted to auxiliaries (König and Gast 2018: 198ff; cf. Diessel 2007; see below on the additional restrictions determining verb forms in SAI-conditionals). This peculiarity, so familiar to learners of English, obviously rules out forms like *'scratch you a cynic'. It did not, however, hold in earlier stages of the language, as shown by non-proverbial examples like (10) from Early Modern English (Leuschner 2016):

(10) *Come* ye not [...], it shal coste you your lyf. (Caxton, late fifteenth century)
      'If you don't come, it will cost you your life.'

The freedom to use a lexical verb in the protasis of a V1-conditional as in (10) is strikingly reminiscent of present-day German and survives in present-day English in residual constructions with specific protasis verbs that deviate from the strict selection rules of SAI. For example, English has several inversion-based formulae with archaic forms of *be* or *come* in the present subjunctive and concessive-conditional semantics (Leuschner 2006):

(11) February fill dyke, *be* it black or *be* it white.

(12) *come* rain or shine – *come* hell or high water – *come* what may

The source construction is a V1-conditional with *come*, which one can still come across in British English on a lucky day, cf. (13). Given the premodern indicative in *-th*, this is clearly a self-conscious archaism:

(13) And I think / *cometh* the hour [of voting] / it may well be the case / not just that the cabinet backs Mrs May / but the parliamentary party could, too. (BBC assistant editor Norman Smith on Radio Four's 'Today' programme, 6 July 2018; podcast)

From the V1-conditional with *come* sprang, not just concessive-conditional formulae as in (12) above, but also a V1-construction in American English involving the subjunctive *come*:

(14) So *come* the new year, what is your resolution going to be? (Google)

(15) Heat up in the winter so I'm cooler *come* the summer (Lloyd Banks song lyrics)

This construction has so far been overlooked in work on V1-constructions in English (such as Chen 2013; Kim 2011; Diessel 2007; Goldberg 2006). Especially when the subordinate clause is sentence-initial, the indicative *comes* may be used instead of *come*. This variant occurs near the beginning of Woody Allen's 2018 feature film *Wonder Wheel* (at c. 1 min. 45s; film available through Amazon Prime) as the male lead, Justin Timberlake, speaks over images of sunbathers on a 1950s Coney Island beach, cf. (16), and it is particularly frequent in jazz lyrics:

(16) Summers I work here [as a lifeguard] on Base 7. *Comes* the fall, I'm a student at New York University, going for my Master's in European Drama.

(17) *Comes* the fall, flocks of birds float away to a warmer land (Beth Duncan song lyrics)

Given the association of the construction with *summer, fall* and so on (18) implies that love comes around as inevitably as the seasons:

(18) *Comes* love, nothing can be done (jazz standard)

The prototypical form, however, remains the subjunctive *come* in combination with expressions of time, as suggested by film or song titles like *Come Sunday, Come Saturday Morning, Come Next Monday, Come January Snow, Come the Summer Days* and others. In some varieties *come* has clearly been reanalysed as a preposition with the temporal-limitative meaning of *by* ('come(s) the summer ~ by the summer'), as suggested especially by (15) above, and the construction has generally carved out popular culture as a functional niche.

    Precisely by virtue of their formulaic character and the fact that they go against the grain of SAI, examples like (11)–(18) demonstrate just how fragmented

V1-constructions in present-day English are. The narrow constraints governing SAI in English are highlighted more indirectly by the V1-slogan (19) which was coined in 2010 by the German Chancellor, Angela Merkel, in defence of her financial policies. English translations on the internet tend to have *if* in the protasis ('If the Euro fails, Europe will fail') or the modal verb *should*:

(19) *Scheitert* der Euro, dann scheitert Europa.
      fails the Euro, then fails Europe
      'If the Euro fails, Europe will fail.'

(19') *Should* the Euro fail, Europe will fail.

The fact that lexical verbs like *fail* are excluded from SAI-protases by definition (*'Fails the Euro, ...') should not in principle prevent SAI-protases with *do*-support or semantically appropriate auxiliary verbs like *will*. These verbs did in fact occur occasionally in V1-protases until the nineteenth century and beyond (Denison 1998: 299), but are no longer attested in corpora today (*'Does the Euro fail, ...', *'Will the Euro fail, ...' and so on; Leuschner and Van den Nest 2015). Instead, SAI-protases are nowadays restricted to exactly three verb forms: *should* (with the special eventuality meaning, distinct from deontic *should = ought to*; Nieuwint 1989), *had* (mostly as an auxiliary, but occasionally as a lexical verb, despite SAI restrictions) and *were* (mostly in the collocation *were to*, largely synonymous with eventuality *should*). Present-day SAI-conditionals are thus clearly distinguished, not only from their more permissive German cousins, but also from the other major SAI-construction of English, polar interrogatives. In becoming increasingly restricted to *should*, *had* and *were*, English SAI-conditionals have marginalized their lexical overlap with polar interrogatives while carving out for themselves a functional niche typical of conditionality (Leuschner and Van den Nest 2015; Leuschner 2016).

4 Constructional specification

With regard to the systemic locus of, respectively, SAI and V1 in English, German and other Germanic languages, the recent literature has largely repudiated the formerly widespread belief that inversion-based V1 subordinate clauses developed directly out of polar interrogatives (e.g. Paul 1920; Jespersen 1940) or V1 declaratives (Hopper 1975). Instead it has begun to focus on verb-initial order in its own right. On this view, V1 was originally motivated pragmatically as a strategy to neutralize topic-comment structure in certain types of discourse relations (Petrova 2018). In the course of a parallel, if asynchronous, process of constructionalization which affected all Germanic languages at different speeds and to different extents, V1 then emerged as a specialized marker for constructions in specific functional domains, such as interrogatives (with additional niches for V1-declaratives in German and elsewhere, but not in English) and conditionality (cf. Leuschner 2016). Driven by the development of English from (unstable) V2 to SVO (Los 2015, inter alia) and the accompanying loss of any productive functional opposition between V2 and V1, present-day English SAI-constructions have taken this process several stages further. Niche constructions with *be* and *come* as in (19)–(26) thus constitute residues of pre-modern, lexically and semantically unspecified V1 as it continues to exist in modern German.

On the form side, the necessary precondition for German V1-schematicity is lexico-semantic under-specification: this allows for a far higher degree of potential productivity (see Baayen 2009 for the terminology and associated statistical techniques) than in English, where present-day SAI-conditionals are now only attested with *should*, *had* and *were* (cf. discussion above; cf. Leuschner and Van den Nest 2015). On the function side, as mentioned earlier, V1-conditionals are conventionally associated with conditionality, more specifically with the generalized (as opposed to singular) type of conditional relationship that is characteristic of proverbs and any related genres that express generalized links between situations (see Dancygier 1998 for the terminology). This is yet another reason why SAI-conditionals cannot form proverbs in English: *should*, *had* and *were* are incompatible with generality readings and force singularity readings instead (Dancygier 1998: 188–94 on *should*, referring to Nieuwint 1989). The same holds for German V1-conditionals with the cognate modals *sollte*, *hätte* and *wäre*, although this does not preclude generalized conditional relationships in German from being realized in V1-format with any other appropriate verb.

A useful test case is the translation of a quasi-proverbial V1-conditional of literary origin (a 'Geflügeltes Wort', Büchmann 2007: 197), the beginning of Heinrich Heine's poem 'Nachtgedanken' from 1843 (Heine 1983: 129):

(20)   *Denk* ich an Deutschland in der Nacht, / Dann bin ich um den Schlaf gebracht.
         think I on Germany in the night / then am I of the sleep bereft
         'If I think of Germany at night, I lose my sleep.'

One might be tempted to translate the first hemistich into English as 'Should I think of Germany in the night', but that would be inadequate because it would suggest a singular coincidence between the subject's thoughts and the resulting inability to sleep, whereas the original describes a generalized relationship between recurrent events. The suggested translation with 'if' or 'whenever' solves this problem, but destroys the metre. The standard English translation (by Hal Draper, Heine 1982: 407, poem 'Night Thoughts') answers both challenges by rendering 'Denk ich' as a free adjunct, 'thinking':

(21)   *Thinking* of Germany in the night, / I lie awake and sleep takes flight.

Although the reader has to supply the missing finite information and inter-clausal relationship, the first foot is now a dactyl ('Thinking of') as in the original ('Denk ich an'), and so is the last ('sleep takes flight'), again as in the original ('Schlaf gebracht'). The decisive semantic strength of 'thinking', however, is that its preferred reading corresponds to the generalized interpretation of the original. By contrast, 'Should I think of Germany in the night' would force a singularity reading, as would its direct German equivalent with 'sollte'.

5 Modifications

When Taylor (1931: 135) declared formal rigidity an essential characteristic of proverbs (cf. above), he was emphasizing not only schematicity but also the traditional image of proverbs as self-sufficient, invariable micro-texts. Modern, corpus-based phraseology and paremiology has taken a much more nuanced view (e.g. Lüger 1999: 110–25), and some proverb dictionaries such as the OWID now systematically list modifications to illustrate (con)textual embedding. The relevant examples often demonstrate nicely the interplay between structure on the one hand and lexical versus structural modification on the other hand. For example, in the two examples given in OWID, the structurally concise commonplace in (4) above, 'Kommt Zeit, kommt Rat' is changed through lexical modification of the second verb into 'Kommt Zeit, kommt Fusion' ('Given time, the merger will work itself out') in a newspaper article on public libraries in Berlin, and into 'Kommt Zeit, kommt Leid' ('Given time, suffering will come along') in an article on the strained relations between marriage partners and their respective in-laws. OWID also has examples of structural expansion, as in (22)–(23), where a complete second apodosis is added asyndetically to the existing one:

(22) *Kommt* Zeit, kommt Rat, kommt Puste!
       comes time, comes advice, comes breath
       'Given time, things will work themselves out and you will be able to catch your breath.'

(23) *Kommt* Zeit, kommt Rat, kommt Attentat.
       comes time, comes advice, comes assassination attempt
       'Given time, things will work themselves out and someone will try to assassinate you.'

Whereas in (22) the original commonplace is expanded so as to fit the context (an article on training for long-distance running) and remains semantically and pragmatically intact, (23) is a classic anti-proverb (also cited in Mieder 1998: 338) in which the structural expansion is emphasized by the rhyme pattern.

Examples like (22)–(23) show just how difficult it is in practice to distinguish between text-related ('textbezogene') and proverb-related ('sprichwortbezogene') modifications as proposed by Sabban (1991, 1998). Instead, different modifications may display different degrees of dependence on their textual surroundings, even resulting in expansion into self-sufficient anti-proverbs. Transitional forms including both text- and proverb-related modifications are displayed by the wellerism in (24) and the book title in (25):

(24)   *Kommt* Zeit, kommt Unrat, sagte der arbeitslose Straßenkehrer.
       comes time comes rubbish said the unemployed road-sweeper
       (Mieder 1998: 338; *Un-rat* 'rubbish' arose from a metaphorical use of NEG+
       'advice', i.e. 'bad advice')
       'Given time, rubbish will come along, said the unemployed road sweeper.'

(25)   *Kommt* Zeit, kommt Mord.
       comes time, comes murder
       (Durbridge 1965; Wehle 2014; the former is the German translation of the
       title of Durbridge's *The Nylon Murders*)
       'Given time, murder will come along.'

Lexical substitution is also put to literary use in a number of poems based on 'Kommt
Zeit, kommt Rat', as reprinted in Mieder (1998), and in popular song lyrics (Leuschner
2018).

6 Association with proverbiality

Depending on the extent of their text-related modification, some proverb variations as
discussed above display proverbiality-by-association ('scheinbare Sprichwörtlichkeit',
Mieder 1975: 70) thanks to the presence of contextualization cues (Gumperz 1982).
Such contextualization cues are only a necessary, not a sufficient, condition; the more
salient the modification, the less likely the association with proverbiality. For obvious
reasons, surprise does not associate well with proverbs. In the wellerism (24) and the
book title (25) above, the words *Unrat* and *Mord* serve as additional contextualization
cues, with *Mord* suggesting the genre of detective thriller, again lending these
modifications an air of ironic parody.
    Yet another type of interplay between modification and contextualization are
parodies of country and weather lore. (26) is from an anonymous list of parodies of
country lore circulating on the Internet (http://slideplayer.org):

(26)   *Liegt* der Bauer tot im Bett, war die Bäuerin wohl zu fett.
       lies the farmer dead in the bed was the farmer's wife probably too fat
       'If the farmer lies dead in his bed, his wife was probably too fat.'

No less than eight of the ten items on the list have V1. Note that (26) is not a direct
parody of some pre-existing original. Rather, *Bauer* ('farmer') contextualizes (26) as a
representative of the genre 'country lore', supported by the metre, the rhyme and the
contrasting lexical pair *Bauer – Bäuerin*. As in other anti-proverbs, the genre-specific
form contrasts with the unexpected content, and the result could be described as anti-
country lore ('Anti-Bauernregel').
    By contrast, classic cases of proverbiality-by-association are commercial slogans
which deliberately rely on existing proverb templates in the hope of projecting the
credibility and authority associated with proverbs onto the product in question

(Röhrich and Mieder 1977: 5; cf. also Röhrich and Mieder 1977: 108–14; on formulaicity in slogans, cf. Polajnar 2011). Commercial slogans in V1-form as in (27)–(28) are examples:

(27) *Hast* du keins/keinen – miet dir eins/einen.
      have.2SG you none.NEUTR/MASC.ACC rent you.DAT one.NEUTR/MASC.
      ACC (rental of motorcycles, construction tools etc., Internet)
      'If you don't have one, rent one.'

(28) *Ist* die Katze gesund, freut sich der Mensch.
      is the cat healthy, rejoices the human
      (Kit-E-Kat cat food, Internet)
      'If the cat is happy, so is the human.'

A telling difference with the examples discussed earlier in this and the previous section (Section 5) is that (27)–(28) fail to contain any lexical contextualization cues. Instead, it is their form alone, viz. the combination of the V1-template with rhyme, metre, parallelism, repetition and lexical contrast, which provides the required proverbiality cues and is thus responsible for the association with proverbiality.

What makes (27)–(28) particularly instructive is that they foreground the 'postulative' nature of slogans, that is, the fact that slogans embody appeals to the addressee (Fix 2007). In (27), this is expressed overtly by the imperative which verbalizes the intended action. By contrast, (28) camouflages its postulative function by pretending to verbalize a 'binding', timeless experience (Fix 2007), hence the association with proverbiality is more straightforward than in (27). Angela Merkel's political slogan (29), cited earlier as (19), shares some features with (28), but differs in other ways:

(29) *Scheitert* der Euro, dann scheitert Europa.
      fails the Euro, then fails Europe
      'If the Euro fails, Europe fails.'

In (29), the V1-template has been adapted for what has become known in German political linguistics as a 'salient political phrase' ('salienter politischer Satz', Klein 2017 and earlier, also Jacob 2016). It is reminiscent of (28) in that the intended appeal to save the Euro is not expressed directly, but has to be inferred by the reader (see Kindt 2007 on the use of inferencing in the interpretation of slogans). In (28), the appeal to buy cat food is only available by inference – multiple inferences, in fact, as 'Ist die Katze gesund' gives rise first to the inference that the cat food in question is good for the animal's health and only secondarily to the inference that it should therefore be bought. What distinguishes (29) from (28), on the other hand, is the singular (rather than generalized) character of the conditional relationship: although (29) contains plenty of proverbiality cues thanks to the V1 word order, the structural parallelism, the metre, the repetition and near-repetition of lexis, and the didactic message, the verb *scheitern* (fail) suggests a singular event and thus a non-proverb-like conditional relationship.

7 Conclusions and directions for future research

Starting from the productivity of V1 word order in German proverbs, broadly construed, the present chapter has argued that V1 functions as a contextualization cue when it appears, often together with other aspects of form, as part of the V1 conditional template. The benefit that V1 commercial and political slogans draw from the association with V1 proverbs in German is unavailable in English because the English V1 is subject to the far stricter rules of SAI. The particularly restrictive fashion in which SAI applies in English conditionals is responsible for additional fragmentation in the English V1-subconstructicon and contrasts sharply with the highly schematic nature of V1-constructions in German. The latter's lexico-semantic under-specification may therefore require creative solutions when German V1-constructions are to be translated into English, as Heine's 'Denk ich an Deutschland' showed.

Two directions for future research suggest themselves from here. One is historical-comparative, encompassing both synchronic and diachronic perspectives. The tendency for English proverbs to encode conditional and related relationships in paratactical, often elliptical structures has been interpreted in the literature as a characteristic trait of English 'p'-grammar, where 'p' stands for 'proverbial' (Norrick 1985: 81–100). In constructionist terminology, any p-grammar can be construed as a 'p-constructicon', that is, as any part of the constructicon of any given language that is specified for proverbiality, including exemplars that are lexico-semantically and/or syntactically irregular. The crosslinguistic comparison of p-constructica can then be defined as a major goal of linguistic paremiology and phraseology, also suggesting a new focus for the comparison of diachronies ('Sprachwandelvergleich', Fleischer and Simon, eds 2013). The rise of SVO word order in English is clearly a divergent development with drastic consequences for the productivity of V1 and hence for the potential form of proverbs. Furthermore, at least some formal preferences in the English p-constructicon are likely to be the result of an 'overarching tendency towards simplification and shortness' in English proverbs (Aurich 2009: 181) which led to the reduction or replacement of finite hypotactical structures and an increasingly nominal style (Aurich 2009: 93).

Another, closely related, direction for future research is the theoretical integration of the different strands of research that have been touched upon. The entrenchment of proverbs and their constructional templates in the speech community at large and the association of commercial and political slogans with proverbs suggest that Social Construction Grammar (Ziem 2015, following, *inter alia*, Croft 2012 and Schmid 2014) could be the framework of choice for this purpose. Whereas classic usage-based Construction Grammar focuses on language-specific constructica and on the cognition of the individual speaker, Social Construction Grammar highlights the linguistic community as the third factor in the conventionalization of linguistic constructions, thus foregrounding the nature of language as a social gestalt ('Sprache als soziale Gestalt', Feilke 1996). Recent theorizing of genre in Construction-Grammatical terms (Hoffmann and Bergs 2018) provides a strong motivation for the inclusion of micro-genres like proverbs and slogans under this approach.

Abbreviations

SAI   subject-auxiliary inversion
SVO   subject-verb-object
V1   verb-first
V2   verb-second

References

Aurich, C. (2009), *Proverb Structure in the History of English: A Corpus-Based Study*, Baltmannsweiler: Schneider Verlag Hohengehren.

Baayen, H. (2009), 'Corpus Linguistics in Morphology: Morphological Productivity', in A. Lüdeling and M. Kytö (eds), *Corpus Linguistics: An International Handbook*, vol. 2, 899–919, Berlin: de Gruyter.

Büchmann, G. (2007), *Geflügelte Worte. Der klassische Zitatenschatz*, unaltered pocket edn of the 43rd newly revised and updated edition by W. Hofmann, Berlin: Ullstein.

Chen, R. (2013), 'Subject-Auxiliary Inversion and Linguistic Generalization: Evidence for Functional/Cognitive Motivation in Language', *Cognitive Linguistics*, 24 (1): 1–32.

Croft, W. (2012), 'Toward a Social Cognitive Linguistics', in V. Evans and S. Pourcel (eds), *New Directions in Cognitive Linguistics*, 395–420, Amsterdam: Benjamins.

Dancygier, B. (1998), *Conditionals and Prediction: Time, Knowledge and Causation in Conditional Constructions*, Cambridge UK: Cambridge University Press.

Dancygier, B. and E. Sweetser (2005), *Mental Spaces in Grammar: Conditional Constructions*, Cambridge, UK: Cambridge University Press.

Denison, D. (1998), 'Syntax', in S. Romaine (ed.), *The Cambridge History of the English Language*, vol. IV: 1776–1997, 92–329. Cambridge, UK: Cambridge University Press.

Diessel, H. (2007), 'Verberstkonstruktionen im Englischen und Deutschen', in P. Gallmann, C. Lehmann and R. Lühr (eds), *Sprachliche Motivation. Zur Interdependenz von Inhalt und Ausdruck*, 27–41, Tübingen: Narr.

Durbridge, F. (1965), *Kommt Zeit, kommt Mord*, Gütersloh: Signum.

Eisbrenner, R. and K. A. Fritz (2013), *Das große Buch der Bauernregeln & Sprichwörter*, Cologne: Anaconda.

Feilke, H. (1996), *Sprache als soziale Gestalt. Ausdruck, Prägung und die Ordnung der sprachlichen Typik*, Frankfurt: Suhrkamp.

Fix, U. (2007), 'Der Spruch – Slogans und andere Spruchtextsorten', in H. Burger, D. Dobrovolskij, P. Kühn and N. R. Norrick (eds), *Phraseologie. Ein internationales Handbuch zeitgenössischer Forschung*, vol. 1, 459–68. Berlin: de Gruyter.

Fleischer, J. and H. J. Simon, eds (2013), *Sprachwandelvergleich – Comparing Diachronies*, Berlin: de Gruyter.

Goldberg, A. (2006), *Constructions at Work: The Nature of Generalization in Language*, Oxford: Oxford University Press.

Gumperz, J. J. (1982), *Discourse Strategies*, Cambridge, UK: Cambridge University Press.

Heine, H. (1982), *The Complete Poems: A Modern English Version by Hal Draper*, Oxford: Oxford University Press.

Heine, H. (1983), *Historisch-kritische Gesamtausgabe der Werke*, M. Windfuhr (ed), vol. 2, Hamburg: Hoffmann & Campe.

Henke, K. (1968), 'Zur Form des englischen Sprichworts', *Literatur in Wissenschaft und Unterricht*, 1 (2): 190–7.

Hoffmann, T. and A. Bergs (2018), A Construction Grammar Approach to Genre, *CogniTextes*, 18. Available online: https://journals.openedition.org/cognitextes/1032

Hopper, P. (1975), *The Syntax of the Simple Sentence in Proto-Germanic*, The Hague: Mouton.

Jacob, K. (2016), 'Das diskurslinguistische Potenzial salienter politischer Sätze', in B. Beßlich and E. Felder (eds), *Geschichte(n) fiktional und faktual. Literarische und diskursive Erinnerungen im 20. und 21. Jahrhundert*, 331–54, Berne: Lang.

Jespersen, O. (1940), *A Modern English Grammar on Historical Principles*. Part V: Syntax, Fourth Volume, Kopenhagen: Munksgaard.

Kim, J.-B. (2011), 'English Conditional Inversion: A Construction-Based Approach', *Language and Information*, 15: 13–29.

Kindt, W. (2007), 'Muster der Alltagsargumentation als Grundlage für Inferenzen', in G. Kreuzbauer, N. Gratzl and E. Hiebl (eds), *Persuasion und Wissenschaft. Aktuelle Fragestellungen von Rhetorik und Argumentationstheorie*, 111–28, Vienna: LIT.

Klein, J. (2017), 'Saliente Sätze', in K. S. Roth, M. Wengeler and A. Ziem (eds), *Handbuch Sprache in Politik und Gesellschaft*, 139–64, Berlin: Mouton de Gruyter.

König, E. and V. Gast (2018), *Understanding English-German Contrasts*, 4th newly revised edn, Berlin: Schmidt.

Leuschner, T. (2006), *Hypotaxis as Building-Site: The Emergence and Grammaticalization of Concessive Conditionals in English, German and Dutch*, Munich: Lincom.

Leuschner, T. (2016), 'Fictive Questions in Conditionals? Synchronic and Diachronic Evidence from German and English', in E. Pascual and S. Sandler (eds), *The Conversation Frame: Forms and Functions of Fictive Interaction*, 193–213, Amsterdam: Benjamins.

Leuschner, T. (2018), 'Das V1-Konditionalgefüge zwischen Phraseologie und Politolinguistik', in S. Stumpf and N. Filatkina (eds), *Formelhafte Sprache in Text und Diskurs*, 85–114, Berlin: de Gruyter.

Leuschner, T. and D. Van den Nest (2015), 'Asynchronous grammaticalization: V1-Conditionals in Present-day English and German', in *Languages in Contrast*, 15 (1): 34–64.

Los, B. (2015), *A Historical Syntax of English*, Edinburgh: Edinburgh University Press.

Lüger, H. H. (1999), *Satzwertige Phraseologismen. Eine pragmalinguistische Untersuchung*, Vienna: Edition Praesens.

Mieder, W. (1975), 'Sprichwörtliche Formelhaftigkeit und Variabilität', in W. Mieder, *Das Sprichwort in unserer Zeit*, 62–71, Frauenfeld: Huber.

Mieder, W. (1998), *Verdrehte Weisheiten. Antisprichwörter aus Literatur und Medien*, Wiesbaden: Quelle & Meyer.

Nieuwint, P. (1989), '*Should* in Conditional Protases', *Linguistics*, 27 (3): 305–18.

Norrick, N. R. (1985), *How Proverbs Mean*, Berlin: Mouton de Gruyter.

Online-Wortschatz-Informationssystem Deutsch (OWID) (n.d.). Instituts für Deutsche Sprache (IDS), Mannheim. Available at: www.owid.de

Paul, H. (1920), *Prinzipien der Sprachgeschichte*, 5th edn, Halle (S.): Niemeyer.

Petrova, S. (2018), 'Verb-Initial Declaratives in Old High German and in Later German', in A. Jäger, G. Ferraresi and H. Weiß (eds), *Clause Structure and Word Order in the History of German*, 48–63, Oxford: Oxford University Press.

Polajnar, J. (2011), 'Da weiß man, was man hat. Wie Formelhaftes zu Werbeslogans wird und Werbeslogans formelhaft werden. Eine korpusbasierte Untersuchung bekannter

Werbeslogans im elektronischen Zeitungskorpus des DeReKo', *Muttersprache*, 121 (4): 248–74.

Ptashnyk, S. (2009), *Phraseologische Modifikationen und ihre Funktionen im Text. Eine Studie am Beispiel der deutschsprachigen Presse*, Baltmannsweiler: Schneider Verlag Hohengehren.

Röhrich, L. and W. Mieder (1977), *Sprichwort*, Stuttgart: Metzler.

Sabban, A. (1991), '"Die dümmsten Bauern haben nicht mehr die dicksten Kartoffeln." Variationen von Sprichwörtern im und als Text', in A. Sabban and J. Wirrer (eds), *Sprichwörter und Redensarten im interkulturellen Vergleich*, 83–108, Wiesbaden: Westdeutscher Verlag.

Sabban, A. (1998), *Okkasionelle Variationen sprachlicher Schematismen. Eine Analyse französischer und deutscher Presse- und Werbetexte*, Tübingen: Narr.

Schmid, H. J. (2014), 'Lexico-grammatical Patterns, Pragmatic Associations and Discourse Frequency', in T. Herbst, H. J. Schmid and S. Faulhaber (eds), *Constructions – Collocations – Patterns*, 239–93. Berlin: Mouton de Gruyter.

Seiler, F. (1922), *Deutsche Sprichwörterkunde*, Munich: Beck.

Steyer, K. (1997), *Reformulierungen. Sprachliche Relationen zwischen Äußerungen und Texten im öffentlichen Diskurs*, Tübingen: Narr.

Steyer, K. and K. Hein (2018), 'Usuelle satzwertige Wortverbindungen und gebrauchsbasierte Muster', in S. Engelberg, H. Lobin, K. Steyer and S. Wolfer (eds), *Wortschätze. Dynamik, Muster, Komplexität* (= IDS Yearbook 2017), 107–29, Berlin: de Gruyter.

Taylor, A. (1931), *The Proverb*, Cambridge, MA: Harvard University Press.

Wehle, P. (2014), *Kommt Zeit, kommt Mord. Ein Wien-Krimi*, Innsbruck: Haymon.

Ziem, A. (2015), 'Desiderata und Perspektiven einer Social Construction Grammar', in A. Ziem and A. Lasch (eds), *Konstruktionsgrammatik IV. Konstruktionen als soziale Konventionen und kognitive Routinen*, 2–22, Tübingen: Stauffenburg.

Part Two

Morphology

4

Gender marking in English and Polish job titles: Referring to female physicians

Bożena Cetnarowska

This chapter compares morphological and morphosyntactic means of forming gender-marked job titles in English and Polish. It focuses on terms denoting female physicians. The relevant data come from electronic corpora and from Google searches. In the case of English, I discuss the usage of Noun + Noun (NN) compounds, comparing those containing the gender-marking element *woman* and *lady*. In the case of data from Polish, the occurrence of suffixal female forms and compound-like NN combinations is analysed. Moreover, the phenomena of double female marking and mixed gender agreement in Polish are investigated. A difference is demonstrated in the acceptability of certain Polish gender-marked forms when they are employed as terms of address and when they occur in the individual referential use.

1 Introduction

The aim of the chapter is to compare morphological or morphosyntactic means available in English and Polish for the creation of female occupation terms. I will limit my attention to terms denoting female physicians. I will use data from the Corpus of Contemporary American English (COCA), the Corpus of Global Web-based English (GloWbE) and the National Corpus of Polish (NKJP).[1] The corpus data will be supplemented by examples from web searches.

The layout of the chapter is as follows: Section 2 explains the difference between notional gender in English and grammatical gender in Polish. Moreover, some comments are given on the strategies employed by English speakers to avoid sexist language, and on the usage of masculine occupation nouns in Polish as 'gender-indefinite' forms. Section 3 is devoted to suffixal female job titles. Restrictions on the creation and usage of such suffixal nouns in Polish will be exemplified. In Section 4, I will look at NN combinations in both languages which contain lexical-gender words as female markers, for example, *woman* or *lady* in English, and *kobieta* 'woman' or *pani* 'madam, lady' in Polish. Section 5 will provide examples of double means of gender marking in Polish, as in the case of *pani dentystka* (madam dentist+SUFF) 'woman dentist'. The occurrence of mixed gender agreement in Polish will be illustrated as well. Attention will be given to the difference between the acceptability of certain female suffixal forms and NN combinations in the individual referential use and as terms of address. Conclusions will be stated in Section 6.

2 Notional versus grammatical gender; avoidance and non-avoidance of sexist language

Gender marking in occupation terms boils down to the marking of nouns as referring to female human beings, as is observed by Doleschal (2015: 1159). This may be achieved, for instance, by means of feminine suffixes attached to words denoting male (or gender-neutral) names of professions, or by means of NN combinations with lexical-gender words as their constituents.

The trend of political correctness, which is particularly strong in English (see Hellinger 2001; Romaine 2001), regards the unjustified usage of the gender-marked nouns as a reflection of sexist language. Sexism, or gender bias, can be illustrated by the formation of job titles that refer exclusively to women, which may imply that male employees constitute the norm, whereas females are substandard employees who show poor work performance and thus need to be referred to by separate occupation terms. Consequently, it is recommended in English to employ gender-neutral occupation terms. For instance, the expression *flight attendant* can be used instead of the gender-marked nouns *steward* and *stewardess*, while the gender-neutral compound *headteacher* can replace the compounds *headmaster* and *headmistress*. This is the strategy of neutralization, mentioned by Hellinger (2001) as one of the ways of avoiding gender bias in language. It can be employed in English, since it is a language with notional (or covert) gender. The sentences *A new dentist came into the room* and *We want to employ a dentist* can equally well refer to either a female or a male person.

Polish, in contrast to English, is an example of a language with grammatical gender (cf. Koniuszaniec and Błaszkowska 2003; Karwatowska and Szpyra-Kozłowska 2005; Łaziński 2006). Nouns are obligatorily marked for gender, verbs show gender (and number) agreement with subjects of sentences, and adjectives agree with head nouns. When rendering the sentence *A young dentist came into the surgery* into Polish, the translator has to choose between one of the sentences given below.

(1) Do gabinetu   wszedł   młody   dentysta
     into surgery.GEN   come.PST.3SG.M young.M.NOM   dentist.M.NOM

(2) Do gabinetu   weszła   młoda   dentystka.
     into surgery.GEN   come.PST.3SG.F young.F.NOM   dentist+SUFF.F.NOM

On the other hand, the phrase *a dentist* in the sentence *We want to employ a dentist* will be translated into Polish (by most interpreters) by means of the masculine noun *dentysta*, as shown in (3).

(3) Chcemy   zatrudnić   dentystę.
    want.PRS.1PL   employ.INF   dentist.M.ACC.SG
    'We want to employ a dentist.'

The masculine form is thus treated in Polish as 'gender-neutral' or 'gender-indefinite' (see Doleschal and Schmid 2001 for a similar observation on Russian). The usage of such 'gender-indefinite' forms is typical of formal register, especially of the language of official documents (as observed by Nowosad-Bakalarczyk 2006). Consequently, it is common in job advertisements in Poland. A search in the (full version of the) NKJP corpus for the string *zatrudni lekarza* (employ.FUT.3SG physician.M.ACC.SG) 'will employ a (male) physician' returns 167 hits, while the search for the string *zatrudni lekarkę* (employ.FUT.3SG physician+SUFF.F.ACC.SG) 'will employ a female physician' – returns 11 hits. There are no examples of the string *lekarza lub lekarkę* (physician.M. ACC.SG or physician+SUFF.F.ACC.SG) 'male physician or female physician' in the NKJP.

Masculine nouns are used in generic statements, as shown in (4) from the NKJP corpus.

(4) Moim   zdaniem,   chirurdzy
    my.INS.SG opinion.INS.SG   surgeon.M.NOM.PL
    są   największymi   cudotwórcami.
    be.PRS.3PL greatest.M.INS.PL miracle_workers.M.INS.PL
    'In my opinion, surgeons are the greatest miracle-workers.'

Masculine forms of occupation terms can occur in the predicative position when the subject noun denotes a female referent. As shown in (5)a, this is acceptable, even though a feminine occupation term is available, that is, *lekarka* 'female physician', as shown in (5)b.

(5) a. Maria   jest   wyjątkowym   lekarzem
       Mary   be.PRS.3SG   exceptional.M.INS.SG physician.M.INS.SG
       i   kobietą   sukcesu
       and   woman.F.INS.SG   success.M.GEN.SG
       'Mary is an exceptional physician and a successful woman.'
    b. Była   dobrą   lekarką.
       be.PST.3SG.F   good.F.INS.SG   physician+SUFF.F.INS.SG
       'She was a good (woman) physician.'

A search in NKJP returns only one example of the phrase *jest dobrą lekarką* (be.PRS.3SG good.F.INS.SG physician+SUFF.F.INS.SG) 'is a good female doctor' and thirteen examples of the phrase *jest dobrym lekarzem* (be.PRS.3SG good.M.INS.SG physician.M.INS.SG) 'is a good doctor' (with the masculine form of the occupation term). The inspection of the sentences with the latter verb phrase reveals that in five of them, *lekarz* 'physician' has a female personal reference; four of them – masculine personal reference; two of them – generic or indefinite reference; and the next two – inanimate reference, as in *Czas jest najlepszym lekarzem* 'Time is the best doctor (i.e. the best healer).' There are 59 occurrences in NKJP of the verb phrase *była lekarzem* 'was a physician', which consists of the past tense form of the verb *być* 'be' bearing female marking and the masculine occupation term. This contrasts with 25 hits for the phrase *była lekarką* 'was a (female) physician'.

Koniuszaniec and Błaszkowska (2003) assert that most speakers of Polish (including professional women) do not object to the usage of masculine forms as 'gender neutral'.[2] As is pointed out by Sczesny, Formanowicz and Moser (2016), in languages with grammatical gender (such as German or Polish), a way of achieving gender-fair language is the usage of female occupation terms next to male occupation terms, for example, *dentysta lub dentystka* '(male) dentist or female dentist', *internista lub internistka* '(male) internist or female internist'.

Suffixal ways of forming female job titles concerning physicians will be discussed in the next section.

3 Suffixal female names of physicians in English and Polish

Both English and Polish word-formation systems contain suffixes whose function is to form female equivalents of male nouns. In English, female occupation terms are formed by means of suffixes such as *-ess, -ette, -trix*. It is pointed out by Hellinger (2001) and Bauer, Lieber and Plag (2013: 243) that job titles terminating in such suffixes are rarely used in present-day English, as they carry negative connotations. The noun *doctoress* (also spelt *doctress*) appears in (6), culled from COCA. As indicated by the Collins Dictionary, this suffixal derivative is both derogatory and dated, having been used mainly in the second half of the nineteenth century and the first half of the twentieth century.

(6)   the first Black woman to receive a medical degree, the 'Doctress of Medicine'

In Polish, the suffix *-k(a)*, as occurring in the form *dentystka* 'female dentist' in (2), is the most common affix[3] which derives female nouns from male occupation terms (where the final vowel *-a* is the NOM.SG case ending). Numerous feminine job titles, such as *lekarka* 'female physicians', *pielęgniarka* 'nurse', *higienistka* 'school nurse or female dental hygienist', *fizjoterapeutka* 'female physiotherapist' and *okulistka* 'female ophthalmologist', are well-established in the Polish lexicon[4] and listed in dictionaries of Polish, for example, in *Słownik języka polskiego PWN*. However, partly due to the fact the suffix *-ka* is also employed in deriving diminutive nouns (e.g. *dziewczynka* 'little girl' derived from *dziewczyna* 'girl'), some speakers of Polish perceive female nouns as carrying negative connotations of insignificance and lack of professionalism. This is reminiscent of the connotations carried by the English suffix *-ette*, which, as pointed out by Hellinger (2001: 109), can function either as a diminutive suffix (in *kitchenette*) or as a feminine marker (in *usherette*). Koniuszaniec and Błaszkowska (2003: 268) and Jadacka (2005: 127) observe that professional women in Poland object to the use of female-marked job titles, regarding them as denigrating and belittling. This feeling may also be supported by the occurrence of gender asymmetry in job titles (mentioned by Koniuszaniec and Błaszkowska 2003 or Łaziński 2006 for Polish, exemplified for

Russian by Doleschal and Schmid 2001 and for English by Hellinger 2001). In English, the pairs *governor/governess, major/majorette* and *mister/mistress* illustrate gender-stereotypical asymmetry. In Polish, the masculine noun *sekretarz* 'secretary' tends to denote a higher administrative position, as in *sekretarz stanu* 'secretary of state, minister of state' or *sekretarz generalny* ONZ 'UN Secretary-General', while its suffixal female equivalent, that is, *sekretarka* (secretary+SUFF), refers to a woman employed to do office work, such as making phone calls, writing letters and arranging meetings. Consequently, female equivalents of occupation terms denoting more prestigious jobs and positions are either not coined or avoided, though forms such as *prezeska* (chairman+SUFF) '(female) chairperson' and *adiunktka* (assistant_professor+SUFF) 'female assistant professor' can be employed by feminist writers (such as Leniarska and Więcka 2016). Moreover, nouns containing the suffix -*ka* often denote objects, for example, *automatyczna sekretarka* 'answering machine', or *marynarka* 'suit' (from *marynarz* 'sailor').

Normative grammars of Polish (e.g. Jadacka 2005) and Polish morphology textbooks (e.g. Grzegorczykowa and Puzynina 1998) mention a series of constraints on the formation of female occupation terms terminating in -*ka*. Apart from the recommendation to avoid homonymy between female forms and existing -*ka* nouns (which are lexicalized as names of objects), these principles include phonological restrictions that dictate the avoidance of female -*ka* nouns containing difficult consonant groups, such as [ktk], [trk], for example, *architektka* (from the masculine noun *architekt* 'architect'). Masculine nouns ending in -*a* (as a marker of the NOM. SG case), for example, *ortopeda* 'orthopaedist', are not expected to form feminine equivalents by means of the suffix -*ka*. There is also a constraint prohibiting the addition of the suffix -*ka* to job titles ending in the sequence -*log* in Polish.[5]

However, there are 286 attestations in the NKJP of the lexeme *psycholożka* 'woman psychologist' (in various case forms), derived from the masculine noun *psycholog* 'psychologist', 113 examples of the lexeme *socjolożka* 'woman sociologist' (from *socjolog* 'sociologist'), forty examples of the lexeme *ginekolożka* 'woman gynaecologist' (from *ginekolog* 'gynaecologist'), and ten instances of the lexeme *dermatolożka* 'woman dermatologist' (from *dermatolog* 'dermatologist'). The SJP PWN (Słownik języka polskiego PWN) dictionary of Polish does not list the above-given feminine formations in -*lożka*, apart from the lexeme *psycholożka* 'woman psychologist', which is provided with the qualifier 'colloquial'.

Some of the sentences (culled from NKJP) containing nouns ending in -*lożka* show the speaker's doubts concerning the well-formedness of the derivatives in question (as in (7)). The feminine forms terminating in -*lożka* seem to be characteristic of (though not restricted to) either colloquial register (in (9), or feminist writings (see (8)).[6]

(7) Forma   'psycholożka'   jest   błędna,
     form.NOM.SG   psychologist+SUFF.F.NOM.SG   be.PRS.3SG   incorrect
     bo   zwykle   ludzie   tak   nie   mówią.
     because   usually   people.NOM.PL   so   not   say.PRS.3PL
     'The form '*psycholożka*' (i.e. woman psychologist) is incorrect because people don't usually say that.'

(8) Amerykańska   psycholożka   Linda Tropp
     American.NOM.SG   psychologist+SUFF.F.NOM.SG   Linda Tropp
     'Linda Tropp, an American woman psychologist'

(9) Znam   dobrą   ginekolożkę.
     know.PRS.1SG   good.F.ACC.SG   gynaecologist+SUFF.F.ACC.SG
     'I know a good female gynaecologist.'

Other feminine forms condemned by prescriptive grammarians can be found in the National Corpus of Polish (NKJP). The lexeme *architektka* (architect+SUFF) has 149 hits in the corpus (in various case forms), in spite of containing the consonant cluster [ktk]. There are 107 examples of *ortodontka* 'female orthodontist' and 146 attestations of the lexeme *internistka* 'female internist', both of them derived from masculine nouns ending in *-a*, that is, *ortodonta* 'orthodontist' and *internista* 'internist'. The noun *ortopedka* 'female orthopaedist' occurs only four times in the NKJP corpus. It violates both the constraint against derivation from masculine occupation terms terminating in *-a* and the homonymy constraint (since the plural form *ortopedki* denotes both female orthopaedists and orthopaedic shoes for children). *Psychiatrka* 'woman psychiatrist' and *pediatrka* 'woman paediatrician', which are predicted to be ill-formed by virtue of being derived from masculine nouns ending in *-a* (i.e. *psychiatra* 'psychiatrist' and *pediatra* 'paediatrician'), as well as by virtue of containing the complex consonant group [trk], are occasionally attested in the NKJP corpus. *Pediatrka* 'woman paediatrician' has seven attestations and *psychiatrka* 'woman psychiatrist' six attestations.

(10) Moja   psychiatrka   też mnie   chce.
      my.F.NOM.SG   psychiatrist+SUFF.F.NOM.SG   also me.ACC want.PRS.3SG
      'My female psychiatrist also wants me.'

The *-ka* female occupation terms in examples (8)–(10) exhibit an individual referential use, that is, they refer to a specific individual (who is a woman sociologist or a woman psychiatrist). As observed in Section 2, in the predicative position, masculine forms are treated as gender-indefinite in Polish. Example (11) shows that a suffixal female occupation term can be used predicatively in coordination with a masculine occupation term[7] to refer to a female physician. In (12), one comes across the predicative usage of the female job title ending in *-lożka,* whose acceptability is disputed by normative grammars (e.g. by Jadacka 2005).

(11) Jest   internistką   i   alergologiem.
      be.PST.3SG   internist+SUFF.F.INS.SG   and   allergist.M.INS.SG
      '(She) is a (female) internist and an allergist.'

(12) Autorka   jest   psycholożką.
      author+SUFF.F.NOM.SG   be.PRS.3SG   psychologist+SUFF.F.INS.SG
      'The (woman) author is a woman psychologist.'

When discussing restrictions on the coining of feminine equivalents of masculine nouns, Koniuszaniec and Błaszkowska (2003: 269) assert that the majority of personal nouns borrowed recently into Polish lack corresponding feminine forms, for example, *inwestor* 'investor', *konsument* 'consumer', *menedżer* 'manager' and *sponsor* 'sponsor'. The current data from the NKJP corpus contradict such a generalization. *Menedżerka* 'female manager' occurs 284 times in NKJP, *konsumentka* 'female consumer' 223 times, *sponsorka* 'female sponsor' 78 times and *inwestorka* 'female investor' 46 times. The above-given feminine nouns (except for *inwestorka* 'female investor') are listed by the SJP PWN dictionary of Polish. The NKJP data support the observations made by Kaproń-Charzyńska (2006) who, having inspected Polish press articles, websites and dictionaries of new words, identifies 140 novel suffixal feminine occupation terms, one-third of them being derived from loanwords. Kaproń-Charzyńska (2006) concludes, contrary to Jadacka (2001: 81) and Koniuszaniec and Błaszkowska (2003), that the suffix -*ka* is used productively in coining feminine equivalents of (masculine) occupation terms in Polish in order to fill 'lexical gaps' in job titles.

4 NN combinations with gender-specific words

Female job titles in English can take the form of NN compounds with the gender-specific lexeme *woman*. As is shown below by sentences taken from COCA, the occurrence of the word *woman* is conditioned either by the overt contrast with the attributive adjective *male* (see examples (13)–(14)) or by the implied contrast between males and females (in (15)).

(13) Women doctors spent less time reading newspapers and more time reading books than male doctors.

(14) And don't assume that women physicians are more empathetic than male doctors.

(15) Geez; why couldn't they have a woman doctor around here? Being female should be a requirement for becoming an OB-GYN.

Occupation terms denoting specific types of physicians can also combine with the noun *woman*,[8] for example, *woman surgeon, woman dentist, women dermatologists*.

The noun *lady* is another lexical-gender word occurring in English nominal compounds denoting female physicians. The usage of the NN combination *lady doctor* in American English is often perceived as condescending or insulting, as is asserted by Lakoff (1973) and as is indicated by example (16) from COCA.

(16) 'That's pretty lame, even for a lady doctor,' he muttered.

When attention is given to the use of gender-marking *lady* in other geographical varieties of English (outside the United States), it can be noticed that NN combinations such as *lady doctors,*[9] *lady general physicians, lady paediatrician* and *lady dentists,* are attested in British English, as well as in 'global' varieties of English, including Pakistani English, Indian English, Bangladesh English and so on This is shown by sentences culled from the GloWbE corpus or taken from various websites.

(17) No nurse or lady doctor may pass a catheter or examine prostate of male patient? (Pakistani English subcorpus)

(18) A lady doctor is now a norm rather than an oddity and teachers are predominantly women. (Indian English subcorpus)

(19) The lady physician never responded to my letter. (Bangladesh English subcorpus)

(20) Lady General Physicians in Delhi - Instant Appointment Booking, View ... https://www.practo.com > Delhi

(21) Lady Paediatricians in Hyderabad - Instant Appointment Booking, View ... https://www.practo.com > Hyderabad

The order of constituents in compounds such as *lady doctor* and *woman physician* is not reversible, as is shown by the unacceptability of the potential units **doctor lady* and **physician woman*. Both constituents of the combinations with the gender-specific lexeme *woman* can be regarded as morphosyntactic heads of compounds (see Masini and Scalise 2013), since they are inflected. This is indicated by the forms *women doctors* and *women physicians* in examples (13)–(14) above. The compounds *Lady Paediatricians* and *Lady General Physicians* in examples (20)–(21) contain one morphosyntactic head, which is their right-hand constituent.

Let us now examine some examples of Polish NN combinations (taken from the NKJP corpus) with the gender-specific word *kobieta* 'woman'.

(22) wywiad   z   kobietą   ginekologiem.
     interview.NOM.SG   with   woman.F.INS.SG   gynaecologist.M.INS.SG
     'an interview with a female gynaecologist'

(23) Nie każda   kobieta   ginekolog
     not every.F.NOM.SG   woman.F.NOM.SG   gynaecologist.M.NOM.SG
     jest   beznadziejna.
     be.PRS.3SG   hopeless.F.NOM.SG
     'Not every female gynaecologist is terrible.'

Such NN combinations, referred to as juxtapositions by Szymanek (2010), consist of fully inflected words. This is particularly clear in example (22), where the inflectional endings *-ą* and *-iem* are overt markers of case, number and gender. Therefore, NN naming units in examples (22)–(23) do not belong to morphological compounds, as defined crosslinguistically by Lieber and Štekauer (2009) and as discussed at length for Greek by Ralli (2013). Kallas (1980) regards juxtapositions such as *kobieta ginekolog* 'woman gynaecologist' as noun phrases in apposition. However, I argue (in Cetnarowska 2018) that Polish juxtapositions should be treated as compound-like phrasal lexemes. NN combinations of a similar type occur in Russian, for example, *ženščina-vrač* 'woman physician' (Doleschal and Schmid 2001: 261), and in Greek, for example, *yineka-psicholoyos* 'woman-psychologist' (Gavriilidou 2016: 103).

Both constituents of juxtapositions are the locus of inflection, hence both can be analysed as morphosyntactic heads. Example (23) indicates that the left-hand constituent determines the grammatical gender of the whole phrasal noun,[10] hence it can be recognized as its morphological head.

The sentences in examples (24)–(25), culled from NKJP, attest to the reversibility of NN combinations with the lexeme *kobieta* 'woman' in Polish.

(24) Oto   kobieta-   lekarz –
here   woman.F.NOM.SG   physician.M.NOM.SG
dzieci,   dom,   mąż,   praca.
child.NOM.PL   house.NOM.SG   husband.NOM.SG   work.NOM.SG
'Here is a woman physician – children, a house, a husband, work.'

(25) Jest   z   nami   lekarz-   kobieta,   ale   co
be.PRS.3SG   with   us   physician.M.NOM.SG   woman.F.NOM.SG   but   what
poradzi   bez   narzędzi,   wody,   światła?
manage.FUT.3SG   without   tool.GEN.PL   water.GEN.SG   light.GEN.SG
'A woman doctor is with us but how can she manage without any tools, water and light?'

One can come across Polish female job titles with the gender-specific lexeme *pani* 'lady, madam, Mrs', as in examples (26)–(27) from the NKJP corpus.

(26) Teraz pani   dermatolog   przepisała
now madam.F.NOM.SG   dermatologist.M.NOM.SG   prescribe.PST.3SG.F
nam   ten   krem.
us.DAT   this.ACC.SG   cream.ACC.SG
'Now the (female) dermatologist prescribed this cream to us.'

(27) Mamy   sprawdzoną   panią   alergolog.
have.PRS.3PL   proven.F.ACC.SG   madam.F.ACC.SG   allergist.M.(NOM.SG)
'We have a trusty (and reliable) female allergist.'

The NN combinations in examples (26)–(27) show a distinct inflectional behaviour to the juxtapositions with the gender-specific lexeme *kobieta*. The constituent denoting profession takes no overt inflectional ending, and it occurs with the covert (i.e. zero) inflectional marker, which is otherwise reserved for M.NOM.SG case. The string *panią alergolog* (ACC.SG) 'female allergist' in (27) can be compared with NN combinations in which both constituents take overt inflectional endings, for example, the string *kobietą ginekologiem* (INS.SG) 'female gynaecologist' in (22) or the string *lekarza dermatologa* (physician.ACC dermatologist.ACC) 'dermatologist' in (28).

(28) Lekarza   dermatologa   zatrudni
   physician.M.ACC.SG dermatologist.M.ACC.SG employ.FUT.3SG
   prywatne   centrum   medyczne.
   private.N.NOM.SG centre.N.NOM.SG medical.N.NOM.SG
   'A private medical centre will employ a dermatologist.'

NN combinations with *pani* 'lady, madam, Mrs' are not reversible, in contrast to juxtapositions with *kobieta* 'woman', cf. *dermatolog pani (dermatologist madam). This may be due to the fact that the word *pani* can be treated as an honorific pronoun (as proposed by Łaziński 2006). English honorific titles exhibit no reversibility either, cf. *Lady Katherine* or *Madam President* and *Katherine Lady or *President Madam.

 Similarly to the English lexeme *madam*, the Polish lexeme *pani* can be used when addressing a woman of a superior rank, for example, *Pani Prezydent* 'Madam President', *Pani Profesor* 'Madam Professor'. It appears in the combination *pani doktor* (madam doctor),[11] which is a socially approved and polite way of addressing a female physician, no matter whether she does or does not hold the degree of doctor of medicine.

(29) Dziękuję   bardzo, pani   doktor.
   thank.PRS.1SG much madam.F.VOC.SG doctor.M
   'Thank you so much, (madam) doctor.'

In contrast to English expressions with the word *madam*, the Polish NN combination *pani doktor* can be used not only as a term of address, but also in the individual referential use.

(30) Która w końcu jest   matką? –   spytała
   which in end be.PRS.3SG mother.F.INS.SG ask.PST.3SG.F
   pani   doktor   w przychodni.
   madam.F.NOM.SG doctor.M in surgery.LOC.SG
   '"Which (of you) is actually the (child's) mother?", asked the lady doctor in the outpatient clinic.'

The individual referential use is illustrated in examples (26)–(27) above for the combinations *pani alergolog* (madam allergist) 'female allergist' and *pani dermatolog* (madam dermatologist).[12]

 It may be worthwhile at the point to compare the frequency[13] of selected suffixal feminine forms, juxtapositions with the word *kobieta* 'woman' and with the honorific lexeme *pani* 'lady' as attested in the NKJP.

(31) ginekolożka (gynaecologist+SUFF)   – 40 hits
     pani ginekolog (madam gynaecologist)   – 184 hits
     ginekolog kobieta (gynaecologist woman) – 3 hits
     kobieta ginekolog (woman gynaecologist) – 9 hits

(32) dermatolożka (dermatologist+SUFF)   – 10 hits
     pani dermatolog (madam dermatologist)   – 48 hits
     dermatolog kobieta (dermatologist woman) – 0 hits
     kobieta dermatolog (woman dermatologist) – 0 hits

(33) stomatolożka (dentist+SUFF)   – 8 hits
     pani stomatolog (madam dentist)   – 86 hits
     kobieta stomatolog (woman dentist)   – 1 hit
     stomatolog kobieta (dentist woman)   – 0 hits

(34) dentystka (dentist+SUFF)   – 970 hits
     pani dentysta (madam dentist)   – 1 hit
     kobieta dentysta (woman dentist)   – 0 hits
     dentysta kobieta (dentist woman)   – 0 hits

The polite forms with the lexeme *pani* 'lady, Mrs.' (followed by the masculine occupation term) prevail over the suffixal derivative in examples (31)–(33). The opposite situation obtains in (34). Since the feminine form *dentystka* 'female dentist' is a well-established lexeme, the expression *pani dentysta* 'lady dentist' is avoided (but see the Section 5 on such combinations as *pani dentystka* (lady dentist+SUFF)).

It is also shown by the data in examples (31)–(34) that juxtapositions with the gender-specific lexeme *kobieta* 'woman' and the name of a profession (in any order) are attested rather rarely (although they are well-formed and fully acceptable).

5 Double gender marking in Polish and mixed forms

As far as English job titles are concerned, one cannot form NN combinations which show double markers of femininity. The hypothetic forms **lady woman physician* or **woman doctress* are not acceptable, and neither would be the expressions **female women physicians* or **female doctresses*.

In Polish, however, one can employ expressions such as *pani dentystka* (madam dentist+SUFF), *pani lekarka* (madam physician+SUFF), *pani okulistka* (madam ophthalmologist+SUFF) and *pani internistka* (madam internist+SUFF), where both constituents show lexical markers of femininity. There are 59 attestations of the NN combination *pani dentystka* (madam dentist+SUFF) in various case forms in the NKJP corpus, 28 hits for *pani lekarka* (madam physician+SUFF), 23 attestations of *pani okulistka* (madam ophthalmologist+SUFF) and 1 hit for *pani internistka* (madam internist+SUFF). It can be argued that the lexeme *pani* 'madam, lady' is not superfluous, and its main function is honorific in the above-mentioned NN units.

(35) Pani   dentystka
      madam.F.NOM.SG   dentist+SUFF.F.NOM.SG
      dokonywała   cudów.
      perform.PST.3SG.F   miracle.GEN.PL
      'The lady dentist performed miracles.'

Suffixal female occupation terms which are criticized by normative grammarians, for example, *dermatolożka* 'female dermatologist', *chirurżka* 'female surgeon' or *psychiatrka* 'female psychiatrist', sound awkward in the combination with *pani* 'madam', since there arises a clash between the honorific status of the pronoun *pani* 'madam, lady' and a colloquial, denigrating or jocular flavour of the above-mentioned non-institutionalized *-ka* derivatives. The expression *pani doktorka* (madam physician+SUFF) is avoided for the same reason. There are 15 attestations (in various case forms) of this NN combination in the NKJP corpus, compared to 4,414 instances of *pani doktor* (madam physician) 'lady doctor', and they either exemplify the colloquial register or come from a novel published in 1938. Here Polish speakers differ from speakers of Czech. As mentioned by Čmejrková (2003), *paní doktorka* is an established (polite) expression used with reference to a female physician in the Czech language. The NN combination *paní doktor* is currently employed only by older speakers of Czech.

One would expect the forms *kobieta lekarka* (woman physician+SUFF) and *lekarka-kobieta* (physician+SUFF woman) to be unacceptable in Polish, since the double marking of female gender appears to be superfluous. However, such examples are attested in the NKJP corpus.

(36) Natomiast trzy   kobiety-   lekarki
      whereas   three.F.NOM.PL   woman.F.NOM.PL physician+SUFF.F.NOM.PL
      sugerowały   mastektomię.
      suggest.PST.3PL   mastectomy.ACC.SG
      'In contrast, three women physicians suggested mastectomy.'

As observed by Kallas (1980), the word-order in Polish NN combinations reflects the order in which new information is introduced. The juxtaposition *kobieta lekarka* (woman physician+SUFF) can be paraphrased as 'a woman who is a (female) physician', and is similar in meaning to the juxtaposition *kobieta lekarz* (woman physician) 'a woman who is a physician'. The NN combination *lekarki kobiety* (physician+SUFF.PL women) is very rare, yet it appears in one sentence in the NKJP corpus in which this expression is contrasted with the NN combination *lekarze mężczyźni* (physicians men) 'male physicians'.[14]

An opposite tendency, which can be contrasted with the use of double markers of femininity, is the usage of mixed gender agreement, where an occupation noun occurs in its non-inflected form (with a zero case marker characteristic of M.NOM.SG forms). The gender of the referent is then signalled by feminine declension markers on the adjective or conjugational markers on the finite verb (see Doleschal and Schmid 2001: 262–3 for similar examples from Russian). In (37) the masculine occupation term *psycholog* 'psychologist' (treated as 'gender neutral') is pre-modified by the adjective *biegły* 'proficient, expert' in its feminine form and is followed by a feminine finite verb form.

(37) Biegła   psycholog   powiedziała …
     proficient.F.NOM.SG psychologist.M.NOM.SG say.PST.3SG.F
     'A proficient psychologist said …'

Let us note that the sentence in (26) above, with *pani dermatolog* in the subject position, can be modified by omitting the honorific pronoun *pani* 'madam'. The inflectional ending *-a* 'PST.3SG.F' (attached to the verb form) is then the only marker of the female gender of the referent of the occupation term in (38).

(38) Teraz   dermatolog   przepisała   nam
     now   dermatologist.M.NOM.SG prescribe.PST.3SG.F   us.DAT
     ten   krem.
     this.ACC.SG cream.ACC.SG
     'Now the (female) dermatologist prescribed this cream to us.'

Forms with mixed gender agreement are not uncommon in the NKJP corpus. For instance, a search for the sequence *dermatolog przepisała* 'dermatologist (m.) prescribed (f.)' returns six hits, compared to two attestations of *pani dermatolog przepisała* 'madam dermatologist (m.) prescribed (f.)'. There are nineteen hits for the string *ginekolog powiedziała* 'gynaecologist (m.) said (f.)', as compared to seven hits for *pani ginekolog powiedziała* 'madam gynaecologist (m.) said (f.)' and two instances of *ginekoložka powiedziała* 'gynaecologist+suff (f.) said (f.)' in NKJP.

6 Conclusions

The word-formation systems of both the Polish and the English language contain suffixes which derive female nouns from masculine occupation terms. While English derivatives with the female suffixes *-ess*, *-trix* or *-ette* have very strong negative connotations, a number of Polish occupation terms with the feminizing suffix *-ka* are well-established and stylistically neutral, for example, *dentystka* 'woman dentist', *okulistka* 'female ophthalmologist' and *lekarka* 'woman physician'. Polish normative grammars condemn the usage of feminine suffixal nouns to denote more prestigious jobs or titles. They also criticize the use of occupation terms with the suffix *-ka* which violate certain phonetic or morphological constraints. Nevertheless, such 'condemned' derivatives are attested in the NKJP corpus (e.g. *dermatoložka* 'woman dermatologist'), and they are characteristic of colloquial register. Gender-marked female forms with the suffix *-ka* are typically found in the individual referential use.

  Another way of forming female occupation terms, employed both by speakers of English and Polish, is a combination of a masculine (or gender-neutral) job title with a lexical-gender word. English speakers form compounds with the word *woman* (e.g. *woman physician*) and with the word *lady*, the latter type of NN combinations (e.g.

lady doctor, lady dentist) being perceived as derogatory in AmE, though accepted by speakers of Pakistani English or Indian English.

In the Polish language Sex+Profession NN combinations contain the lexical-gender word *kobieta* 'woman', for example, *kobieta lekarz* 'woman physician'. Since they consist of two inflected lexemes, they are often treated as noun phrases in apposition (see Kallas 1980). They show properties of coordinate compounds, for example, reversibility. There occur also non-reversible Sex+Profession combination in Polish whose left-hand constituent is the honorific pronoun *pani* 'madam, lady, Mrs.', for example, *pani dermatolog* (madam dermatologist). Their second constituent, that is, the occupation noun in the masculine form, is not inflected. The honorific pronoun can be omitted, which results in the adjacency of a masculine gender (uninflected) occupation noun and of the feminine finite verb form, or of the pre-modifying adjective with feminine agreement markers. The phenomenon of mixed gender agreement testifies to the prevalence of semantic agreement over syntactic agreement in Polish hybrid structures.

While double gender marking is not allowed in English, as indicated by the unacceptability of **women actresses* or **lady doctoresses*, suffixal *-ka* derivatives in Polish can co-occur with gender-indicating lexemes in NN combinations, for example, *pani internistka* (madam internist+SUFF) 'female internist' and *kobiety lekarki* (women physician+SUFF.PL) 'women physicians'.

Speakers of English avoid sexist language by using gender-neutral occupation terms, for example, *flight attendant*, instead of *steward* and *stewardess*. Speakers of Polish employ masculine forms of professions in generic statements or in gender-indefinite contexts and tend to regard nouns such as *psycholog* 'psychologist' or *lekarz* 'physician' as 'gender-neutral', in spite of recent attempts (such as Leniarska and Więcka 2016) to make women more 'visible' linguistically on the job market (also in the medical professions).

Notes

1 The corpora in question are available online at the following addresses: http://corpus.byu.edu/coca, http://corpus.byu.edu/glowbe; http://nkjp.pl.

2 Koniuszaniec and Błaszkowska (2003) conclude that there is low social awareness of the sexist language in Poland. This conclusion does not refer to feminist writers, as mentioned in Endnote 6.

3 Less productive feminizing suffixes include *-ini/-yni* and *-owa* (see Grzegorczykowa and Puzynina 1998; Szymanek 2010).

4 The National Corpus of the Polish Language (NKJP) provides 32,429 hits for the lexeme *pielęgniarka* 'nurse' and 11,007 hits for the lexeme *lekarka* 'female physician'. There are 940 instances of *dentystka* 'female dentist', 188 examples of *fizjoterapeutka* 'female physiotherapist', 595 instances of *higienistka* 'school nurse or dental hygienist' and 468 examples of the lexeme *okulistka* 'female ophthalmologist'.

5 Incidentally, similar phonological constraints are not formulated for Czech, where the feminine forms *psycholožka* 'female psychologist' and *chiruržka* 'female surgeon' are accepted (see Čmejrková 2003).

6   Example (8), found in the NKJP corpus, comes from an article in *Polityka*, which is a centre-left Polish weekly. More examples of novel female occupation terms (formed by means of the suffix *-ka*) occur in Leniarska and Więcka (2016) and in other articles published by *Gazeta Wyborcza*, a liberal Polish daily, in particular in its Saturday women's supplement entitled *Wysokie Obcasy* (lit. high heels).

7   The speaker could have used the feminine form *alergolożka* 'woman allergist', which has 38 hits in the NKJP corpus. However, this feminine noun is not listed in the SJP PWN dictionary of Polish, and the speaker may have been unsure whether such a form is acceptable.

8   A variation may be observed between NN combinations with the element *woman* and the occurrence of the attributive adjective *female* as an indication of the gender of the referent:

   (i) *When she was 12, Kristen Vierregger read a book on the first female surgeon and decided she wanted to become a doctor.*

   (ii) *I had become the first woman surgeon to join the prestigious Six-Liter Club.*

9   The expression *lady doctors* occurs 27 times in the GloWbE corpus, most of the instances coming from Pakistani English (13 hits), from Indian English (5 hits) and British English (4 hits). The NN combination *lady doctor* in the singular form is attested 109 times in the GloWbE corpus, the majority of the attestations coming from the subcorpora from Great Britain (26 hits), Pakistan (20), India (11), Ireland (8), the United States (7), Sri Lanka (5) and Australia (5).

10 The determiner *każdy* 'every', as well as the predicative adjective *beznadziejny* 'hopeless, terrible' in (23) take the feminine declension marker *-a* (F.NOM.SG).

11 We can note the absence of the form **pani lekarz* (madam physician) as a form of address, since the lexeme *lekarz* 'physician', although carrying no negative connotations, is not recognized as polite enough (in such a context). However, the string *pani lekarz* (madam physician) 'female physician' does appear in the individual referential use, as shown by the NKJP corpus.

12 The expressions *pani dermatolog* (madam dermatologist) or *pani alergolog* (madam allergist) are not normally employed as terms of address. They are replaced in such use by the NN combination *pani doktor* (madam doctor).

13 The counts include the attestations of suffixal derivatives or NN combinations in various case and number forms, for example, *ginekolożki* (gynaecologist+SUFF.NOM.PL) and *ginekologów kobiet* (gynaecologist.M.GEN.PL woman.GEN.PL).

14 The NKJP sentence is as follows: *Skoro nie podobali im się lekarze mężczyźni leczący ich kobiety to należałoby się domyślać, że mieli swoje lekarki kobiety by leczyły ich kobiety?* 'Since they didn't like male physicians who treated their women one can suppose that they had their own female physicians who would treat their women?'

Abbreviations

ACC	accusative
COCA	Corpus of Contemporary American English
DAT	dative
F	feminine
FUT	future

GEN	genitive
GLoWbE	Corpus of Global Web-based English
INS	instrumental
LOC	locative
M	masculine
N	neuter
NOM	nominative
NN	Noun+Noun (combination)
NKJP	National Corpus of Polish
PL	plural
PRS	present
PST	past
SG	singular
SJP PWN	Słownik języka polskiego PWN (PWN Dictionary of the Polish Language)
SUFF	suffix
VOC	vocative

References

Bauer, L., R. Lieber and I. Plag (2013), *The Oxford Reference Guide to English Morphology*, Oxford: Oxford University Press.

Cetnarowska, B. (2018), 'Phrasal Names in Polish: A+N, N+A and N+N Units', in G. Booij (ed.), *The Construction of Words. Advances in Construction Morphology* (Studies in Morphology Series), 287–313, Cham: Springer.

Čmejrková, S. (2003), 'Communicating Gender in Czech', in M. Hellinger and H. Bussmann (eds), *Gender across Languages: The Linguistic Representation of Women and Men*, vol. 3, 27–58, Amsterdam: Benjamins.

Doleschal, U. (2015), 'Gender Marking', in P. O. Müller, I. Ohnheiser, S. Olsen and F. Rainer (eds), *Word-Formation: An International Handbook of the Languages of Europe*, 1159–71, Berlin: Mouton de Gruyter.

Doleschal, U. and S. Schmid (2001), 'Doing Gender in Russian. Structure and Perspective', in M. Hellinger and H. Bussmann (eds), *Gender across Languages: The Linguistic Representation of Women and Men*, vol. 1, 253–82, Amsterdam: Benjamins.

Gavriilidou, Z. (2016), 'The Semantics of NN Combinations in Greek', in P. ten Hacken (ed.), *The Semantics of Compounding*, 94–109, Cambridge: Cambridge University Press.

Grzegorczykowa, R. and J. Puzynina (1998), 'Rzeczownik' (Noun) [in Polish], in R. Grzegorczykowa, R. Laskowski and H. Wróbel (eds), *Gramatyka współczesnego języka polskiego. Morfologia* (A Grammar of Contemporary Polish. Morphology), 389–468, Warszawa: Wydawnictwo Naukowe PWN.

Hellinger, M. (2001), 'English: Gender in a Global Language', in M. Hellinger and H. Bussmann (eds), *Gender across Languages: The Linguistic Representation of Women and Men*, vol. 1, 105–14, Amsterdam: Benjamins.

Jadacka, H. (2001), *System słowotwórczy polszczyzny* (*1945–2000*) (The Word-Formation System of Polish (1945–2000)) [in Polish], Warszawa: Wydawnictwo Naukowe PWN.

Jadacka, H. (2005), *Kultura języka polskiego: fleksja, słowotwórstwo, składnia* (The Culture of the Polish Language: Inflection, Word-formation, Syntax) [in Polish], Warszawa: Wydawnictwo Naukowe PWN.

Kallas, K. (1980), *Grupy apozycyjne we współczesnym języku polskim* (Appositional Groups in Contemporary Polish) [in Polish], Toruń: Uniwersytet Mikołaja Kopernika.

Kaproń-Charzyńska, I. (2006), 'Żeńskie neologizmy osobowe z formantem *-ka* we współczesnej polszczyźnie' (Novel Feminine Personal Nouns with the Suffix *-ka* in Contemporary Polish) [in Polish], *Język Polski* (The Polish Language), LXXXVI (4): 260–70.

Karwatowska, M. and J. Szpyra-Kozłowska (2005), *Lingwistyka płci. Ona i on w języku polskim* (*Gender Linguistics. He and she in the Polish Language*) [in Polish], Lublin: Wydawnictwo Uniwersytetu Marii Curie-Skłodowskiej.

Koniuszaniec, G. and H. Błaszkowska (2003), 'Language and Gender in Polish', in M. Hellinger and H. Bussmann (eds), *Gender across Languages: The Linguistic Representation of Women and Men*, vol. 3, 259–85, Amsterdam: Benjamins.

Lakoff, R. (1973), 'Language and Woman's Place', *Language in Society*, 2 (1): 45–80.

Łaziński, M. (2006), *O panach i paniach. Polskie rzeczowniki tytularne i ich asymetria rodzajowo-płciowa* (*About Gentlemen and Ladies: Polish Titles and their Gender-Sex Asymmetry*) [in Polish], Warszawa: Wyd. PWN.

Leniarska, Z. and A. Więcka (2016), '50 najbardziej wpływowych kobiet w Polsce' (Fifty most influential women in Poland) [in Polish], *Wysokie Obcasy* (December). Available online: www.wysokieobcasy.pl/wysokie-obcasy/0,114019.html?tag=grudzie%F1+2016

Lieber R. and P. Štekauer (2009), 'Introduction: Status and Definition of Compounding', in R. Lieber and P. Štekauer (eds), *The Oxford Handbook of Compounding*, 3–18, Oxford: Oxford University Press.

Masini, F. and S. Scalise (2013), 'The Notion of Head in Morphology', *Round Table: Prominences in Linguistics, Viterbo*, 13 December 2013. Available online: http://www.academia.edu/9941055/The_notion_of_head_in_morphology (accessed 28 January 2016).

Nowosad-Bakalarczyk, M. (2006), 'Tendencje w sposobie wyrażania żeńskości we współczesnej polszczyźnie' (Tendencies in the Ways of Expressing Feminity in Contemporary Polish) [in Polish], *Język Polski* [The Polish Language], LXXXVI (4): 126–36.

Ralli, A. (2013), *Compounding in Modern Greek*, Dordrecht: Springer.

Romaine, S. (2001), 'A Corpus-based View of Gender in British and American English', in M. Hellinger and H. Bussmann (eds), *Gender across Languages: The Linguistic Representation of Women and Men*, vol. 1, 153–75, Amsterdam: Benjamins.

Sczesny S., M. Formanowicz and F. Moser (2016), 'Can Gender-fair Language Reduce Gender Stereotyping and Discrimination?', *Frontiers in Psychology*, 7, Article 25. doi: 10.3389/fpsyg.2016.00025. Available online: http://journal.frontiersin.org/journal/psychology

Szymanek, B. (2010), *A Panorama of Polish Word-formation*, Lublin: Wydawnictwo Katolickiego Uniwersytetu Lubelskiego.

Corpora

COCA= Corpus of Contemporary American English
Available online: http://corpus.byu.edu/coca

GloWbE = Corpus of Global Web-based English
    Available online: http://corpus.byu.edu/glowbe
NKJP = National Corpus of Polish
    Available online: http://nkjp.pl

Dictionaries

Collins = Collins English Dictionary
    Available online: https://www.collinsdictionary.com/dictionary/english
Słownik języka polskiego PWN (PWN Dictionary of the Polish Language)
    Available online: http://sjp.pwn.pl

5

Congruence and equivalence in adjective-forming suffixation in Spanish and English: A contrastive study

José A. Sánchez Fajardo

This study examines the phenomena of equivalence and congruence of English and Spanish suffixes through the implementation of a word-building modelling process (cf. Dunn 2000). The resulting models are useful for grouping the suffixes as regards their underlying logico-semantic relation (LSR) and the word class of bases. The morphological and semantic depiction of their constituents allows for a better understanding of a crosslinguistic analysis of adjectival suffixation in these two languages. The examination of sixty-four suffixes (forty-one in Spanish and twenty-three in English), and 123 morpho-semantic variants (MSVs), or models (sixty-five in Spanish and fifty-eight in English), has indicated that these two languages coincide in most of the logico-semantic relations (fourteen out of twenty-one) expressed through suffixation. However, there also exist some LSRs that are not suffixation-based and whose semantic structures are conveyed through 'native' syntactic means.

1 Introduction

A number of dia-synchronic studies have shown the importance of affixation in English word-building processes (Marchand 1969; Spencer 1994; Lipka 2002; Plag 2003; Bauer 2004, 2008, 2015; Booij 2010, 2012) and in Spanish ones (Casado 1985; Lang 1992; Hallebeek 1992; Alvar 1993; Rainer 1993, 1999; Guerrero 1995; Almela 1999; Varela 2005; Gutiérrez-Rubio 2014; Cifuentes and Rodríguez 2011). The elaboration of a research procedure that allows for a crosslinguistic analysis of affixed words, particularly adjectives, involves the examination of word-formation schemas and segmented constituents.

Thus, this chapter is aimed at carrying out a contrastive study of Spanish and English adjective-forming suffixation systems, particularly the logico-semantic relation as expressed in the semantic structure of a word-building model (Dunn 2000) as the 'tertio comparationis'. This descriptive bilateral unit is used to describe morphologically motivated words in Modern English, and the application of these semantic patterns is evidenced by the common logic underlying the formation of motivated suffixed adjectives despite the analytic or synthetic nature of each language.

To fulfil this objective, the research has been divided into two major stages: (i) data collection, and (ii) data processing (see Section 2). This dictionary-based analytical procedure, based on immediate constituents (ICs) mechanism and word bilaterality, sets the groundwork for further congruence and equivalence contrast. The description of congruent and equivalent adjective-forming suffixes leads to a better understanding of how potentially significant affixation is in the expression of certain LSRs. In fact, these relations correspond to the 'uniform metalanguage' that is meaningful in any contrastive study, provided 'the forms compared have a comparable function' (Williems et al. 2004: 2).

The complexity of adjectives lies in their appreciative and metaphorical extension of meaning. Only 'encyclopaedic', or dictionary-based, meanings are taken into consideration in the present study. Those senses that are acquired through contextual variability, for example, *rocky* meaning 'insensitive', are not examined because the dictionary entries of the suffix -*y* do not show this sense. Therefore, to guarantee the consistency of the study, only examples that correspond to the dictionary-based senses of suffixes have been attested.

2 Methodology

The primary sources of information are English and Spanish dictionaries (MWD11 2003; TAHD5 2011; DLE23 2014; DUE3 2013), which have provided a quantitative and qualitative understanding of adjective-forming morphemes in these two languages. The use of corpora (*News on the Web Corpus (NOW n.d.)*, *Corpus de referencia del español actual (CREA n.d.)*) has contributed to the attestation of senses in various contexts, which has also shed more light on the syntactic and paradigmatic values of these suffixed adjectives. However, the extraction of suffixes is entirely based on the aforementioned dictionaries, which might result in unbalanced, but authentic, data as to the number of suffixes and lexico-semantic variants in Spanish and English. It could, in fact, be of interest to have a comprehensive depiction of 'prescriptive', or normative, adjectival suffixation. The compilation of data involved a revision and annotation of every single adjective-forming suffix in both languages and its corresponding senses.

The data-processing stage includes (a) the modelling of English and Spanish adjective-forming suffixes, (b) the arrangement of the resulting models according to the logico-semantic relations and (c) the elaboration of conclusive remarks based on the contrast of Spanish and English LSRs. Not only does this information add more clarity on homonymic and synonymic groups, but it also shows other crosslinguistic features, such as congruence and equivalence.

The concepts of congruence and equivalence are key aspects in this crosslinguistic study. While congruent units are those regarded as morphologically alike, 'equivalent constructions are those constructions which, at least sometimes, are mutually translatable' (Krzeszowski 1971: 37). Most specialists have centred their research studies on congruent sentences or phrases resulting from a transformational framework that entails a clear distinction of similar and identical patterns (cf. Fisiak 1980; Marton 1981; Krzeszowski 1990; Altenberg and Granger 2002). This examination in particular focuses on congruent suffixes, that is, etymologically related (*-oso* and *-ous*), and equivalent ones, that is, conveying the same LSR (*-y* as in *sandy* and *-oso* as in *rocoso*; LSR: 'containment').

A fundamental definition in our study is what we understand by a 'lexical base'. Morphologically speaking, it is the part of the word that remains once inflectional morphemes and the rightmost derivational suffix are extracted (Curbeira 2004). For instance, in Spanish *novelística*, the lexical base is *novelist-* after *-ic* (derivational morpheme) and *-a* (inflectional suffix) are removed (Curbeira 2004: 56).

An expected finding in the present research is related to the morphological availability and profitability in two different linguistic systems, and this is also connected with the concept of morphological productivity and its gradient perception (Bauer 2001: 15–20). The distinction of these two terms, that is, profitability and availability, is crucial in any contrastive study: the former describes its 'utilization in performance' whereas the latter refers to the 'scope of the rule' (Kastovsky 1986: 586, as cited in Bauer 2001: 49). However, this chapter, in general, is not intended to delve into the category of productivity in English and Spanish adjective-forming suffixation. Its research scope is restricted to a normative description of these morphemes, and the exploration of congruence/equivalence between both codes.

2.1 The modelling of English and Spanish adjective-forming suffixes

The word-building model (see Figure 5.1) is a dictionary-based bilateral unit that indicates how groups of words are formed. It consists of a morphological structure and a semantic structure (cf. Dunn 2000), and it is based on the segmentation of affixed words through the Immediate Constituents (ICs) process (Kastovsky 1982; Tournier 1985).

Its morphological structure (MS) shows the two types of morphological elements that are combined in the formation of the word (base and suffix), while its semantic structure describes the logical meaning generated when these two units are combined. In other words, the semantic structure (SS) is a representation of the sense activated in the model, which corresponds to a specific word-form. The following example shows how the model is used:

$$\text{MODEL} = \frac{\text{N} - + - y}{\text{having N in abundance}}.$$

e.g. *fatty*, *sandy*

$$\text{MODEL} = \frac{\text{MORPHOLOGICAL STRUCTURE (MS)}}{\text{SEMANTIC STRUCTURE (SS)}}$$

Figure 5.1 The bilateral word-building model used in the study.

The modelling process, as it stands, allows for a better visualization of word-building mechanisms, and for a clear-cut connection of the resulting semantic relations. Also, the use of bilateral models makes it possible to establish semantic relations within a group of motivated complex words that are formed the same way. For example,

(1) Synonymic

$$\text{MODEL} = \frac{N - + - ful}{\text{having N in abundance}}.$$

e.g. *graceful*

$$\text{MODEL} = \frac{N - + - y}{\text{having N in abundance}}.$$

e.g. *starry*

(2) Partially synonymic

$$\text{MODEL} = \frac{N - + - ed}{\text{having N}}.$$

e.g. *feathered*

(3) Antonymic

$$\text{MODEL} = \frac{N - + - less}{\text{not having N}}.$$

e.g. *pointless*

(4) Homonymic

$$\text{MODEL} = \frac{N - + - y}{\text{having N in abundance}}.$$

e.g. *rocky*

$$\text{MODEL} = \frac{N - + - y}{\text{having negative characteristics of N}}.$$

e.g. *beachy*

One important feature inferred from the data-processing stage is the existence of two types of models:

1. Full models describe patterns of word-formation for a group of words. In each case, two examples of MSVs formed according to the model are provided, as in -*ful*[1.1] (as in *graceful* or *shameful*), -*able*[1.1] (as in *sustainable* and *understandable*).

2. Potential models describe the formation of one word, and are therefore illustrated with only one example. Since no regularity is observed in these cases, only the resulting LSV is modelled. For example, *-ish*[1.2] (as in *stylish*), *-less*[2.2] (as in *harmless*).

As noticed, the suffixes used in the study are characterized by having superscript numerals, for example, *-y*[1.1], *-y*[1.2], *-y*[1.3], *-y*[2.1]. The first number stands for the grammatical typology of bases (1 → NOMINAL, 2 → VERBAL, 3 → ADJECTIVAL, 4 → ADVERB, 5 → NUMERAL) and the second one represents the number of appearances of its corresponding model. This numerical order is entirely based on dictionary senses, and it is not linked to etymological cues or lexical frequency:

-y[1.1] having (the characteristics of) N in abundance, e.g. *fatty*
-y[1.2] causing N, e.g. *risky*
-y[1.3] that likes N, e.g. *horsey*
-y[2.1] that Vs or tends to V, e.g. *dreamy*

Another feature that is illustrated through these models is the presence of allomorphs. This could be relevant to distinguish the existence of paronyms or 'congruent' units (Marton 1981; Cruse 1986), which reveals the identity of structures between the two languages. Morphological congruence, which in this study is restricted to the morphological level, can be significant to explain the processes of false friend and semantic borrowing. Evidently, the oft-quoted 'identity' is not entirely true, as the majority of the congruent adjective-forming suffixes have undergone orthographic and phonemic disparities, owing to the intrinsic linguistic rules: *-esco/-esque*; *-ous/-oso* (but *-able* in both languages).

3 Models of adjective-forming suffixes in English

Twenty-four adjective-forming suffixes have been extracted from MWD11 and TAHD5 (see Table 5.1). These suffixes have been modelled through the analytical tool proposed, totalling fifty-eight word-building models, of which forty-five are proper, six are potential and seven are neoclassical ones.

The neoclassical model springs from their common feature of forming neoclassical adjectival terms by adding an adjective-forming suffix to a classical base. Their formation is distinguished from ordinary Modern English suffixation in the sense that the suffix is added not to a free base, but to a bound base. It is then a case of neoclassical suffixation. Some prior studies point out that neoclassical elements are lexemes of Latin or Greek origin, but 'their combinations are of modern origin' (Plag 2003: 74).

The study of these neoclassical adjectival terms requires an etymological search to determine whether these neoclassical words were formed in the language or whether they entered as linguistic borrowings. The classical adjective-forming suffixes found in the sources consulted, also confirmed in OED3, are: *-ant*[2.2] (*expectorant*), *-ar*[1.1]

Table 5.1 English Adjective-Forming Suffixes and Their Corresponding Semantic Structure

Semantic Structure	Suffix
Having characteristics of N	$^{1.2}$-*ar*, $^{1.1}$-*ate*, $^{1.2}$-*ine*, $^{1.1}$-*ose*, $^{1.2}$-*ular*, $^{1.1}$-*ly*, $^{1.1}$-*y*, $^{1.2}$-*ish*, $^{1.2}$-*esque*, $^{1.2}$-*en*, $^{1.2}$-*ous*, $^{1.2}$-*an*, $^{1.2}$-*ic*, $^{1.1}$-*ical*
Having N (in abundance)	$^{1.1}$-*ulent*, $^{1.1}$-*ose*, $^{1.1}$-*y*, $^{1.1}$-*ous*, $^{1.1}$-*ed*, $^{1.1}$-*able*, $^{1.1}$-*ate*, $^{1.1}$-*ful*
Causing N	$^{1.2}$-*ful*, $^{1.1}$-*some*, $^{1.3}$-*ous*
Related to N	$^{1.1}$-*ar*, $^{1.1}$-*ine*, $^{1.3}$-*ose*, $^{1.1}$-*ular*, $^{1.1}$-*al*, $^{1.1}$-*ary*, $^{1.3}$-*ic*, $^{1.2}$-*ical*
Made of N	$^{1.3}$-*ine*, $^{1.1}$-*en*
Not having N	$^{1.1}$-*less*
Being from N	$^{1.1}$-*an*, $^{1.1}$-*ic*, $^{1.1}$-*ish*, $^{1.1}$-*ese*
Recurring every N	$^{1.2}$-*ly*
Resembling N	$^{1.1}$-*esque*, $^{1.2}$-*an*
That likes N	$^{1.3}$-*y*, $^{1.4}$-*ose*
That Vs (or tends to V)	$^{2.1}$-*ant*, $^{2.1}$-*ory*, $^{2.1}$-*some*, $^{2.1}$-*ent*, $^{2.1}$-*ful*, $^{2.1}$-*ive*, $^{2.1}$-*ative*, $^{2.1}$-*y*
Unable to V (or to be Ved)	$^{2.1}$-*less*
Able to V (or to be Ved)	$^{2.1}$-*able*, $^{2.1}$-*ile*
Somewhat A	$^{3.1}$-*ish*
Going loc. Adv.	$^{4.1}$-*ward*
Near Num	$^{5.1}$-*ish*
Being Num. in a series	$^{5.2}$-*(e)th*

(*nuclear*), -*ar*$^{1.2}$ (*oracular*), -*ate*$^{1.2}$ (*Latinate*), -*ile*$^{2.2}$ (*contractile*), -*ine*$^{1.1}$ (*estuarine*), -*ine*$^{1.2}$ (*sapphirine*), -*ose*$^{1.1}$ (*verbose*), -*ose*$^{1.2}$ (*cymose*), -*ose*$^{1.3}$ (*comatose*).

It is also relevant to make a brief distinction between combining forms and suffixes. One of the earliest researchers who delved into this domain was Marchand (1969). In his book, combining forms are considered prepositive elements that derive from Latin or Greek origins, but a terminological gap is found when he discusses the morpho-semantic and combinatory traits of prefixes: 'He himself [Marchand] distinguishes between prefixes (bound morphemes that are prefixed to full English words) and prepositive elements which occur in compounding on a Neo-Latin basis, such as *astro-, electro-, galato-, hepato-, osteo-* (...)' (Warren 1999: 113). This gap is not new: various studies show that this confusion is reflected in the lexicographic description of these units (cf. Prćić 2008) and the heterogeneity of lexical meaning and word-building processes involved (Bauer 1998; Iacobini 2009; Kastovsky 2008). For practical reasons, combining forms, such as -*androus* or -*cephalic*, are not units under study in this research. As mentioned earlier, the dictionaries (particularly MWD11; OED3; TAHD5) have been used to attest the nature of suffixes.

Following the descriptive analysis of bases, five types have been found according to word class: nominal (as in *fatty*), verbal (as in *forgetful*), adjectival (as in *thinnish*), adverbial (as in *outward*), numeral (as in *thirtyish*). The study confirms the premise that nominal bases are more abundant in the formation of adjectives by suffixation in Modern English.

As to the degree of independence, two types of bases are described: free (as in *grace*ful), and bound (as in *nucle*ar). The descriptive study shows that free bases are far more frequent in the models described than bound bases. Bound bases are relatively frequent in neoclassical models, for example, *cym*ose, *macul*ar. Regarding the inner make-up of the base, four kinds are perceived: simple, as in *feather*ed; complex (compound), as in *pothol*ed; complex (derived), as in *reus*able; phrasal (as in *Jack-of-all-trad*ey); acronymic (as in *FM*-ish). However, almost all the models described are formed by simple bases.

One of the most noticeable features of these English suffixes is the high degree of polysemy or homonymy that exists in the formation of adjectives by adding *-y* and *-ish* in Modern English. For example, *-y* is observed in three denominal adjective-forming models ('having characteristics of N', 'that likes N', 'having N in abundance'), and in one deverbal adjective-forming model ('that Vs or tends to V'). In the case of *-ish*, three denominal models ('having negative characteristics of N', 'being from N', 'having N in abundance'), one deadjectival model ('somewhat A') and one denumeral model ('approximately Num').

4 Models of adjective-forming suffixes in Spanish

Forty-two adjective-forming suffixes in Spanish have been identified (see Table 5.2). The modelling of these suffixes has revealed the existence of sixty-five models: fifty-four are proper and eleven are potential ones. As explained above, most bases are bound and most suffixes are of Latin origin, which explains why the distinction of neoclassical models is not relevant in the analysis of Spanish word-formation models.

According to the word class of bases, and similarly to English, five types have been identified: nominal (*perruno*), verbal (*olvidadizo*), adjectival (*asperiego*), adverbial (*cercano*) and numeral (*onceno*), being the nominal bases that are most frequent in Spanish. As expected, regarding the degree of boundness of morphemes, two types have been confirmed: free (*revolucionario*) and bound (*resbaloso*). The collection of a database for the syntagmatic description of these units has corroborated the premise that bound-suffixed adjectives are far more frequent in Spanish than the free units. As for the internal constituents of bases, simple forms (*sedoso*) exceed the number of acronymic ones (*pesoísta* 'PSOE member or supporter').

Earlier studies seem to agree on the fact that *-able* and *-oso* are by far the most productive adjective-forming suffixes in Spanish (Lang 1992; Seco 1995). The analytical procedure has also revealed that the most polysemic suffixes are: *-oso* ('having characteristics of N', 'that Vs or tends to V'), *-able* ('that Vs or can be Ved', 'able to become N'), *-esco* ('having characteristics of N', 'being similar to N', 'somewhat A').

5 Contrastive Analysis

This part of the analysis involves the arrangement of models and morpho-semantic variants into the type of semantic structure conveyed and the typology of base

Table 5.2 Spanish Adjective-Forming Suffixes and Their Corresponding Semantic Structure

Semantic Structure	Suffix
Having characteristics of N	-áceo[1.1], -aco[1.1], -ado[1.2], -eno[1.3], -eo[1.2], -esco[1.1], -ico[1.1], -oso[1.2]
Having N (in abundance)	-ado[1.1], -ento[1.1], -oso[1.1], -udo[1.1], -able[1.1]
Related to N	-al[1.1], -áneo[1.1], -ario[1.1], -ático[1.1], -co[1.1], -ego[1.2], -engo[1.1], -ense[1.2], -eño[1.1], -uno[1.1], -estre[1.1], -il[1.1], -ístico[1.1]
Made of N	-izo[1.3], -ño[1.3], -eo[1.1]
Being from N.	-ita[1.1], -és[1.1], -eño[1.2], -ense[1.1], -eno[1.1], -ego[1.1], -co[1.1], -ano[1.1], -án[1.1], -aico[1.1], -aco[1.2]
Recurring every N	-al[1.2], -ario[1.2]
Causing N	-ático[1.2]
Resembling N	-ano[1.2], -esco[1.2], -ista[1.2]
Suffering from N	-aco[1.3], -ático[1.1]
Having negative characteristics of N	-uno[1.2]
Able to become N	-able[1.2]
That Vs (or tends to V)	-ante[2.1], -ego[2.1], -orio[2.1], -oso[2.1], -ticio[2.1], -ivo[2.1], -dizo[2.1]
Able to V (or to be Ved)	-dizo[2.2], -il[2.1], -ble (able, ible)[2.1]
Somewhat A	-esco[3.1], -ecino[3.1], -ego[3.1]
That is located Adv.	-ano[4.1]
Being Num. in a series	-eno[5.2]

(nominal, verbal, adjectival, adverbial and numeral), which is key to examining the data as 'a finite set of semantic components' (Lyons 1968: 472).

Thus, the connection of those morphological structures conveying the same logico-semantic relation is guaranteed, which leads to synonymic and antonymic grouping, and as expected, the extraction of congruent and equivalent units between these two languages. The analysis of polysemy in derivation (cf. Rainer 2014) is entirely crosslinguistic, as the present research is not exactly aimed at exploring the semantic cues and nuances that characterize equivalent suffixes in each language. However, the study of the degree of polysemy and/or equivalence of suffixes under the same LSR could be of interest to establishing a degree of predictability and combinability of suffixes and bases in Spanish and English. Affixes are considered units that are 'subject to polysemy and meaning extensions of various sorts' (Bauer, Lieber and Plag 2013: 641), and '[their] recurrent semantic modification brought about by the derivational process represents a plausible semantic load for an affix' (Cruse 1986: 130).

Potential models have been left out at this stage of the research due to their lack of regularity, but their contribution to polysemy has been pointed out in form of additional remarks in the description of LSR groups.

The following sections show a practical allocation and tagging of the underlying logico-semantic relations, which have been grouped following the word class of the bases these suffixes are attached to. The so-called 'parallel description' (James 1986: 63) denotes more clarity in the description of both systems, in particular equivalent and congruent structures being scrutinized. These models are grouped according to a hierarchical order of classification tags: typology of bases, logico-semantic relation (LSR), semantic structure and morphological structure in both languages. This convenient parallelism results in a global mapping of coincidental and differentiating macrostructural categorization of suffixes. Each LSR is also accompanied by observations, or partial conclusions, which might help readers in their understanding of how these suffixes are interconnected.

5.1 Denominal adjectives

5.1.1 LSR: material ('made of N')

Underlying logico-semantic relation: **material**	
Semantic Structure: 'made of N'	
Morphological Structure (English)	Morphological Structure (Spanish)
N- + -ine$^{1.3}$ (opaline)	N- + -izo$^{1.3}$ (cobrizo)
N- + -en$^{1.1}$ (wooden)	N- + -ño $^{1.3}$ (barreño)
	N- + -eo$^{1.1}$ (lácteo)

Interestingly, no congruent morphological structure has been found. Both languages resort to syntactic means to express a similar meaning. Logically, pre-modification prevails in English (*a gold watch, a silver spoon*), and postmodification with *de* (prepositional phrases) is more common in Spanish (*un reloj de oro, una cuchara de plata*), which corroborates previous studies on prepositional clauses (cf. Jiménez Juliá and Lübke 2013).

5.1.2 LSR: characterizing ('having characteristics of N')

Underlying logico-semantic relation: **characterizing**	
Semantic Structure: 'having characteristics of N'	
Morphological Structure (English)	Morphological Structure (Spanish)
N- + -ar$^{1.2}$ (oracular)	N- + -áceo$^{1.1}$ (acantáceo)
N- + -ate$^{1.2}$ (Latinate)	N- + -aco$^{1.1}$ (paradisíaco)
N- + -ine$^{1.2}$ (crystalline)	N- + -ado$^{1.2}$ (nacarado)
N- + -ose$^{1.2}$ (cymose)	N- + -eno$^{1.3}$ (moreno)
N- + -ular$^{1.2}$ (tubular)	N- + -eo$^{1.2}$ (marmóreo)

N-	+	-ly[1.2] (*friendly*)	N-	+	-esco[1.1] (*bufonesco*)
N-	+	-en[1.2] (*golden*)	N-	+	-ico[1.1] (*atmosférico*)
N-	+	-y[1.2] (*bushy*)	N-	+	-ío[1.2] (*sombrío*)
N-	+	-esque[1.2] (*picturesque*)	N-	+	-oso[1.2] (*esponjoso*)
N-	+	-ous[1.2] (*indigenous*)			
N-	+	-an[1.2] (*Edwardian*)			
N-	+	-ic[1.2] (*idyllic*)			
N-	+	-ical[1.1] (*quizzical*)			

A noticeable feature of this category is that the variety of suffixes conveying this logico-semantic meaning is abundant in both languages. The following group of congruent pairs of suffixes is identified: *-esque/-esco, -ous/-oso, -ic/-ico*.

It is interesting to point out that *-eo* and *-en* are, in spite of their incongruent nature, similar with regard to the logico-semantic relations established both in MSV[1.1] (made of N) and MSV[1.2] (having characteristics of N). This might lead to a possible gradation of equivalence between the models under study. In other words, some suffixes might be classed as 'partially' or 'fully' equivalent forms, depending on the number of MSVs conveyed.

5.1.3 LSR: containment ('having N (in abundance)')

Underlying logico-semantic relation: **containment**					
Semantic Structure: 'having N (in abundance)'					
Morphological Structure (English)			Morphological Structure (Spanish)		
N-	+	-ate[1.1] (*affectionate*)	N-	+	-ado[1.1] (*barbado*)
N-	+	-ose[1.1] (*verbose*)	N-	+	-ento[1.1] (*sangriento*)
N-	+	-ulent[1.1] (*flatulent*)	N-	+	-oso[1.1] (*espumoso*)
N-	+	-able[1.1] (*knowledgeable*)	N-	+	-udo[1.1] (*barbudo*)
N-	+	-y[1.1] (*sandy*)	N-	+	-able[1.1] (*saludable*)
N-	+	-ous[1.1] (*poisonous*)			
N-	+	-ed[1.1] (*feathered*)			
N-	+	-ful[1.1] (*prideful*)			

One group of congruent forms can be noticed: *-ose, -ous/-oso*. The suffix *-y*, having a high degree of availability, shows two MSVs ('having characteristics of N' and 'having N (in abundance)').

The Spanish suffix *-able*, as in *saludable*, is comparable to the MSV of the English suffix *-able* 'having N (in abundance)', as in *knowledgeable*. Spanish *-able* is one of the few congruent suffixes whose morpho-semantic structure coincides fully with its English equivalent counterpart (*-able*).

5.1.4 LSR: cause ('causing N')

Underlying logico-semantic relation: **cause**	
Semantic Structure: 'causing N'	
Morphological Structure (English)	Morphological Structure (Spanish)
N- + -ful[1.2] (shameful)	N- + -ático[1.2] (problemático)
N- + -some[1.1] (troublesome)	N- + -oso[1.3] (peligroso)
N- + -ous[1.3] (dangerous)	

This causative trait does not seem to be very common in Spanish. This explains why the suffixes -some[1.1] and -ático[1.2], besides appearing in synonymic models, form an equivalent and synonymic pair of words, as in *troublesome* and *problemático*. The congruent forms -oso and -ous, as expected, indicate a fully synonymic relation as three of the MSVs are expressed: characterizing, containment and cause.

5.1.5 LSR: association ('related to N')

Underlying logico-semantic relation: **association**	
Semantic Structure: 'related to N'	
Morphological Structure (English)	Morphological Structure (Spanish)
N- + -ar[1.1] (nuclear)	N- + -al[1.1] (esferoidal)
N- + -ine[1.1] (estuarine)	N- + -áneo[1.1] (sucedáneo)
N- + -al[1.2] (autobiographical)	N- + -ario[1.1] (alimentario)
N- + -ular[1.1] (valvular)	N- + -ático[1.1] (lunático)
N- + -al[1.1] (secretarial)	N- + -co[1.1] (selvático)
N- + -ary[1.1] (budgetary)	N- + -ego[1.2] (veraniego)
N- + -ic[1.3] (democratic)	N- + -engo[1.1] (frailengo)
	N- + -eño[1.1] (abrileño)
	N- + -uno[1.1] (gatuno)
	N- + -estre[1.1] (campestre)
	N- + -il[1.1] (estudiantil)
	N- + -ístico[1.1] (periodístico)
	N- + -ario[1.1] (mortuario)

This cluster of MSVs is especially abundant in both languages, but the number of Spanish suffixes clearly exceeds that of English. Congruence can be observed in the following groups: -ary/ario, -al/-al, -ic/-co. Also, like in the LSR 'characterizing', these suffixes convey a gradable level of synonymy due to sociolinguistic features, that is, -ego and -estre are mostly used by high-status speakers. Note that diaphasic information or diastratic markedness are not taken into consideration in the arrangement or classification of suffixes. However, their wide-ranging variability or synonymy is also affected by these sociolinguistic factors.

5.1.6 LSR: absence ('not having N')

Underlying logico-semantic relation: **absence**	
Semantic Structure: 'not having N'	
Morphological Structure (English)	Morphological Structure (Spanish)
N- + -less[1.1](*bottomless*)	Ø

No Spanish adjectival suffix was found that expresses this logico-semantic relation. Instead, Spanish can resort to the use of a prepositional phrase headed by the preposition *sin*. For instance, *a hairless animal – un animal sin pelos*.

5.1.7 LSR: recurrence ('recurring every N')

Underlying logico-semantic relation: **recurrence**	
Semantic Structure: 'recurring every N'	
Morphological Structure (English)	Morphological Structure (Spanish)
N- + -ly[1.2] (*weekly*)	N- + -al[1.2] (*semanal*)
	N- + -ario[1.2] (*diario*)

According to the Spanish dictionaries consulted, there is no suffix in Spanish conveying this given logico-semantic relation ('recurrence'), as opposed to English ones. By finding a Spanish lexical equivalence for each English *-ly*-derived word processed (*daily–diario, weekly–semanal, monthly–mensual*), we may infer that *-al* and *-ario*, but especially *-al*, are Spanish adjective-forming suffixes corresponding to the logico-semantic relation in question.

5.1.8 LSR: origin ('being from N')

Underlying logico-semantic relation: **origin**	
Semantic Structure: 'being from N'	
Morphological Structure (English)	Morphological Structure (Spanish)
N- + -an[1.1] (*American*)	N- + -ita[1.1] (*israelita*)
N- + -ic[1.1] (*Hispanic*)	N- + -és[1.1](*aragonés*)
N- + -ish[1.1] (*English*)	N- + -eño[1.2] (*madrileño*)
N- + -ese[1.1] (*Japanese*)	N- + -ense[1.1] (*gerundense*)
	N- + -eno[1.1] (*nazareno*)
	N- + -ego[1.1] (*manchego*)

$$N- \quad + \quad -co^{1.1} \text{ (flamenco)}$$
$$N- \quad + \quad -ano^{1.1} \text{ (boliviano)}$$
$$N- \quad + \quad -aico^{1.1} \text{ (galaico)}$$
$$N- \quad + \quad -aco^{1.2} \text{ (austríaco)}$$

As to this logico-semantic relation, the Spanish suffixes listed are far more abundant than their English equivalents. The suffixes *-ese/-és* and *-an/-ano* may be paired as possible congruent forms.

5.1.9 LSR: likeness ('resembling N')

Underlying logico-semantic relation: **likeness**	
Semantic Structure: 'resembling N (eponym)'	
Morphological Structure (English)	Morphological Structure (Spanish)
N- + $-an^{1.2}$ (Shakespearean)	N- + $-ano^{1.2}$ (volteriano)
N- + $-esque^{1.1}$ (Dantesque)	N- + $-esco^{1.2}$ (dantesco)

The suffixes *-esque/-esco* and *-an/-ano* are congruent structures. It is significant how both languages resort to a metaphorical transference of features from the eponymic base to a pre-modified noun by means of adjectival suffixation. This LSR ('likeness') constitutes one of the few showing a fully equivalent and congruent correspondence of the models.

5.1.10 LSR: ailment ('suffering from N')

Underlying logico-semantic relation: **ailment**	
Semantic Structure: 'suffering from N'	
Morphological Structure (English)	Morphological Structure (Spanish)
Ø	N- + $-aco^{1.3}$ (cardiaco)
	N- + $-ático^{1.1}$ (perlático)

No English adjective-forming suffix expressing this logico-semantic relation was found.

5.1.11 LSR: negative characterizing ('having negative characteristics of N')

Underlying logico-semantic relation: **negative characterizing**	
Semantic Structure: 'having negative characteristics of N'	
Morphological Structure (English)	Morphological Structure (Spanish)
N- + $-ish^{1.2}$ (sheepish)	N- + $-uno^{1.2}$ (perruno)

Only two negative-meaning suffixes have been found in dictionaries. Interestingly, most of the 'pejorative' suffixes are noun-forming, and they are usually attached to nominal bases (cf. Lázaro 1999).

5.1.12 LSR: preference ('that likes N')

Underlying logico-semantic relation: **preference**	
Semantic Structure: 'that likes N'	
Morphological Structure (English)	Morphological Structure (Spanish)
N- + -$y^{1.3}$ (*beachy*)	Ó

No equivalent counterpart was found in Spanish. In English, the low availability of this model calls for contextual cues.

5.1.13 LSR: likelihood ('able to become N')

Underlying logico-semantic relation: **likelihood**	
Semantic Structure: 'able to become N'	
Morphological Structure (English)	Morphological Structure (Spanish)
Ó	N- + -$able^{1.2}$ (*papable*)

This seems to be an infrequent logico-semantic relation in Spanish, only two examples are provided. However, Lang (1992: 205) considers this suffix highly productive. No English adjective-forming suffix was found which conveyed such a logico-semantic relation.

5.2 Deverbal adjectives

5.2.1 LSR: inability ('unable to V (or to be Ved)')

Underlying logico-semantic relation: **inability**	
Semantic Structure: 'unable to V (or to be Ved)'	
Morphological Structure (English)	Morphological Structure (Spanish)
V- + -$less^{2.1}$ (*harmless*)	Ó

No corresponding adjective-forming suffix was found in Spanish.

5.2.2 LSR: ability ('that can V (or be Ved)')

Underlying logico-semantic relation: **ability**	
Semantic Structure: 'that can V (or be Ved)'	
Morphological Structure (English)	Morphological Structure (Spanish)
V- + -able$^{2.1}$ (*understandable*)	V- + -dizo$^{1.1}$ (*rompedizo*)
V- + -ile$^{2.1}$ (*contractile*)	V- + -il$^{2.1}$ (*contractil*)
	V- + -ble (*able, ible*)$^{2.1}$ (*elegible*)

Two congruent pairs were found: *-able/-able(-ible)*; *-ile/-il*. As commented above, the English suffix *-able* and the Spanish suffix *-able* are both regarded as very productive. Besides, there is a high degree of correspondence between adjectives that are formed with these suffixes both in English and Spanish, for example, *razonable – reasonable, comprehensible – understandable*.

5.2.3 LSR: habit ('that Vs (or tends to V)')

Underlying logico-semantic relation: **habit**	
Semantic Structure: 'that Vs (or tends to V)'	
Morphological Structure (English)	Morphological Structure (Spanish)
V- + -ant$^{2.1}$ (*defiant*)	V- + -ante$^{2.1}$ (*andante*)
V- + -ory$^{2.1}$ (*congratulatory*)	V- + -ego$^{2.1}$ (*andariego*)
V- + -some$^{2.1}$ (*tiresome*)	V- + -orio$^{2.1}$(*cobratorio*)
V- + -ent$^{2.1}$ (*absorbent*)	V- + -oso$^{2.1}$ (*rizoso*)
V- + -ful$^{2.1}$ (*forgetful*)	V- + -ticio$^{2.1}$ (*alimenticio*)
V- + -ive$^{2.1}$ (*creative*)	V- + -ivo$^{2.1}$ (*combativo*)
V- + -ative$^{2.1}$ (*talkative*)	V- + -dizo$^{2.1}$ (*huidizo*)
V- + -y$^{2.1}$ (*catchy*)	

This logico-semantic relation, in which verbal bases are involved, is conveyed through a variety of suffixes in both languages. Some congruent forms are: *-ant,-ent/-ant*; *-ory/-orio*; *-ive/-ivo*. The expression of 'tendency' is a frequent LSR in both languages, which is indicated through the high number of suffixes gathered.

5.2.4 LSR: cause ('causing (someone) to V')

Underlying logico-semantic relation: **cause**	
Semantic Structure: 'causing (someone) to V'	
Morphological Structure (English)	Morphological Structure (Spanish)
V- + -ery$^{2.1}$ (*slippery*)	V- + -dizo$^{2.2}$ (*resbaladizo*)
V- + -ant$^{2.1}$ (*expectorant*)	V- + -ante$^{2.1}$ (*expectorante*)

This is an infrequent logico-semantic relation. *Piso resbaladizo* is, precisely, a floor that causes someone to slip; whereas *droga expectorante* is a drug that causes someone to expectorate. The latter fully coincides with the English adjective *expectorant* whose one MSV also includes a causative trait of this kind.

5.3 Deadjectival adjectives

5.3.1 LSR: similarity ('somewhat A')

Underlying logico-semantic relation: **similarity**	
Semantic Structure: 'somewhat A'	
Morphological Structure (English)	Morphological Structure (Spanish)
A- + -ish$^{3.1}$ (*greenish*)	A- + -esco$^{3.1}$ (*pardusco*) A- + -ecino$^{3.1}$ (*blanquecino*) A- + -ego$^{3.1}$ (*asperiego*)

The number of Spanish adjective-forming suffixes conveying this meaning seems to be far superior to those used in English. Congruence is not perceived, probably due to the etymology of English *-ish* in comparison with the Spanish suffixes. The case of *-ish* is of interest due to the acquisition of lexical properties as a free unit: *ish* is commonly found in English as an independent word meaning 'approximately' (nearly 2,000 hits on NOW).

There are other adjectives that are 'rare' in Spanish, and they belong to this logico-semantic relation; for example, *friolengo, asperiego*. In cases such as these, Spanish may resort to syntactic means, using *algo* to pre-modify the noun, as in *algo frío, algo áspero*.

5.4 Deadverbial adjectives

5.4.1 LSR: location ('that is located Adv.')

Underlying logico-semantic relation: **location**	
Semantic Structure: 'that is located Adv.'	
Morphological Structure (English)	Morphological Structure (Spanish)
Ø	Adv.- + -ano$^{4.1}$ (*lejano*)

No adjective-forming suffixes corresponding to this specific logico-semantic relation were found. English resorts to zero derivation to convey this meaning through some morphological means. For example, the adjective *far* is zero-derived from the adverb *far*.

5.4.2 LSR: direction ('going loc. Adv.')

Underlying logico-semantic relation: **direction**	
Semantic Structure: 'going loc. Adv.'	
Morphological Structure (English)	Morphological Structure (Spanish)
Adv.- + -*ward*[4.1] (*outward*)	Ø

As shown, no Spanish equivalent was found to convey this logico-semantic relation. Various authors agree on the nomenclature of -*ward* as a suffix, as opposed to other suffixoids or semi-suffixes, such as -*bound*, which possess a greater level of complexity due to their lexical meaning and combinability (cf. Marchand 1969; Plag 2003).

5.5 Denumeral adjectives

5.5.1 LSR: approximation ('approximately Num.')

Underlying logico-semantic relation: **approximation**	
Semantic Structure: 'approximately Num.'	
Morphological Structure (English)	Morphological Structure (Spanish)
Num.- + -*ish*[5.1] (*thirtyish*)	Ø

No Spanish form was found. For example, Spanish uses lexico-syntactic means such as *cerca de*, *alrededor de* pre-modifying the numeral (*eightish-alrededor de/cerca de las ocho*).

5.5.2 LSR: order ('being Num. in a series')

Underlying logico-semantic relation: **order**	
Semantic Structure: 'being Num. in a series'	
Morphological Structure (English)	Morphological Structure (Spanish)
Num.- + -*(e)th*[5.1] (*tenth*)	Num.- + -*eno*[5.1] (*onceno*)

These suffixes, used in forming ordinal numbers, coexist with irregularities: *first*, *second* and *third* in English; and *primero*, *segundo* and *tercero* in Spanish. Note that the suffix -*imo* as in *séptimo*, *décimo*, and so on is not used in the research, as the full word was imported from Latin: *septĭmus*, *decĭmus*.

6 Conclusions

The IC-based modelling of suffixed adjectives has been a useful tool in the elaboration of a lexical contrastive study that is aimed at deciphering how adjectival affixation is involved in the expression of logico-semantic relations. The arrangement of the SSs constitutes a significant opportunity to have a clear representation of how these senses are expressed, or not, through affixation in any of the given languages.

The elaboration of these models in the contrastive analysis has shown the existence of twenty-one logico-semantic relations underlying the formation of adjectives by suffixation in English and/or Spanish: 'material', 'characterization', 'containment', 'cause', 'relation', 'absence', 'recurrence', 'origin', 'likeness', 'negative characterization', 'ailment', 'merit', 'preference', 'capacity', 'incapacity', 'habit', 'similarity', 'approximation', 'location', 'direction' and 'order'.

In spite of the different nature (analytic/syntactic) of these two languages, the contrastive analysis shows that English and Spanish share most (fourteen out of twenty-one) of the logico-semantic relations used in the formation of adjectives by suffixation. This shows that although suffixation constitutes a productive word-building mechanism in both languages, various differences exist. In Spanish, four of the logico-semantic relations are not found: 'direction', 'incapacity', 'preference' and 'absence'. Other linguistic means can be used to convey the logico-semantic relations in question: *cerca de* + Num, *alrededor de* + Num (proximity), *sin* + N (absence). In English, three of the logico-semantic relations do not exist: 'location', 'merit' and 'ailment'. In both languages, 'characterization', 'containment', 'relation' and 'habit' were the logico-semantic relations that were expressed with the greatest number of suffixes.

A striking observation is made in relation to the existence of 'fully' or 'partially' equivalent and congruent suffixes within the same LSR. This denomination is based on the number of models or MSVs shared by their contrasted suffixes. The LSR 'likeness' is the only case in which all the suffixes found are fully congruent and equivalent: *-an/-ano* (*Shakespearean/almodovariano*) and *-esque/-esco* (*dantesque/quijotesco*). Partially congruent and equivalent suffixes are therefore more abundant: *-able* is found in the same LSRs in Spanish and English, except for 'likelihood' (as in *papable*), which is only present in the former one.

Abbreviations

A	adjective
Adv.	adverbial
CREA	*Corpus de referencia del español actual*
DEL	*Diccionario de lengua española*
DUE	*Diccionario de uso del español*
IC	immediate constituent
LSR	logico-semantic relations
MSV	morpho-semantic variant
MWD	*Merriam Webster's Dictionary*

MS morphological structure
N noun
NOW *News on the Web Corpus*
Num. numeral
OED *Oxford English Dictionary*
SS semantic structure
TAHD *The American Heritage Dictionary*
V verb

References

Almela Pérez, R. (1999), *Procedimientos de formación de palabras en español*, Barcelona: Ariel.

Altenberg, B. and S. Granger (2002), 'Recent Trends in Cross-Linguistic Lexical Studies', in B. Altenberg and S. Granger (eds), *Lexis in Contrast: Corpus-Based Approaches*, 3–48, Amsterdam: Benjamins.

Alvar Ezquerra, M. (1993), *La formación de palabras en español*, Madrid: Arco/Libros.

Bauer, L. (1998), 'Is There a Class of Neoclassical Compounds, and If So Is It Productive?', *Linguistics*, 36: 403–22.

Bauer, L. (2001), *Morphological Productivity*, Cambridge, UK: Cambridge University Press.

Bauer, L. (2004), 'The Function of Word-Formation and the Inflection-Derivation Distinction', in H. Aertsen, M. Hannay and R. Lyall (eds), *Words in their Places: A Festschrift for J. Lachlan Mackenzie*, 283–92, Amsterdam: Vrije Universiteit.

Bauer, L. (2008), 'Derivational Morphology', *Language and Linguistics Compass*, 2 (1): 196–210.

Bauer, L., R. Lieber and I. Plag (2013), *The Oxford Reference Guide to English Morphology*, Oxford: Oxford University Press.

Booij, G. (2010), *Construction Morphology*, Oxford: Oxford University Press.

Booij, G. (2012), *The Grammar of Words: An Introduction to Morphology*, Oxford: Oxford University Press.

Casado Velarde, M. (1985), *Tendencias en el léxico español actual*, Madrid: Coloquio.

Cifuentes Honrubia, J. L. and S. Rodríguez Rosique, eds (2011), *Spanish Word Formation and Lexical Creation*, Amsterdam: Benjamins.

CREA (Real Academia Española) (n.d.), *Corpus de referencia del español actual (CREA)*. Available online: http://corpus.rae.es/creanet.html (accessed 15 June 2017).

Cruse, A. (1986), *Lexical Semantics*, Cambridge, UK: Cambridge University Press.

Curbeira Cancela, A. (2004), *Semántica léxica*, La Habana: Félix Varela.

Davies, M., ed. (n.d.), *News on the Web Corpus*, Brigham Young University. Available online: https://corpus.byu.edu/now/ (accessed 5 June 2017). (cited as NOW n.d.)

DLE23 (Real Academia Española) (2014), *Diccionario de la lengua española*, 23rd edn, Madrid: Espasa.

Moliner, M., ed. (2013), *Diccionario de uso del español*, 3rd edn, Madrid: Gredos. (cited as DUE3 2013)

Dunn, S. (2000), 'La modelación de la sufijación, de la derivación cero, de la composición y de su combinación parasintética en sustantivos subordinados deverbales concretos del inglés moderno', PhD diss., Universidad de La Habana, Havana, Cuba.

Fisiak, J., ed. (1980), *Theoretical Issues in Contrastive Linguistics*, Amsterdam: Benjamins.

Guerrero Ramos, G. (1995), *Neologismos en el español actual*, Madrid: Arco/Libros.

Gutiérrez-Rubio, E. (2014), *Metonimia y derivación sufijal en español: Estudio multidimensional de los mecanismos conceptuales que rigen la formación de palabras mediante sufijación en español*, Madrid: Liceus.

Hallebeek, J. (1992), *A Formal Approach to Spanish Syntax*, Amsterdam/Atlanta: Rodopi.

Iacobini, C. (2009), 'Composizione con elementi neoclassici', in M. Grossmann and F. Rainer (eds), *La formazione delle parole in italiano*, 69–95, Tübingen: Max Niemeyer.

James, C. (1986), *Contrastive Analysis*, London: Longman.

Jiménez Juliá, T. and B. Lübke (2013), 'Los contextos preposicionales en español y en alemán. Aproximación contrastiva', *Verba*, 40: 203–52.

Kastovsky, D. (1982), *Wortbildung und Semantik*, Tübingen: Francke/Bagel.

Kastovsky, D. (1986), 'The Problem of Productivity in Word Formation', *Linguistics*, 24: 585–600.

Kastovsky, D. (2008), 'Astronaut, Astrology, Astrophysics: About Combining Forms, Classical Compounds and Affixoids', in R. McConchie et al. (eds), *Selected Proceedings of the 2008 Symposium on New Approaches in English Historical Lexis* (HEL-LEX 2), 1–3, Somerville: Cascadilla Proceedings Projects.

Krzeszowski, T. P. (1971), 'Equivalence, Congruence and Deep Structure', in G. Nickel (ed.), *Papers in Contrastive Linguistics*, 37–48, Cambridge: Cambridge University Press.

Krzeszowski, T. P. (1990), *Contrasting Languages: The Scope of Contrastive Linguistics*, Berlin: Mouton de Gruyter.

Lang, M. (1992), *Formación de palabras en español*, Madrid: Cátedra.

Lázaro Mora, F. A. (1999), 'La derivación apreciativa', in I. Bosque and V. Demonte (eds), *Gramática descriptiva de la lengua española*, Madrid: Real Academia Española/ Espasa Calpe.

Lipka, L. (2002), *English Lexicology*, Tübingen: Gunter Narr Verlag.

Lyons, J. (1968), *Introduction to Theoretical Linguistics*, Cambridge, UK: Cambridge University Press.

Marchand, H. (1969), *The Categories and Types of Present-day English Word-Formation*, Munich: Verlag C. H. Beck.

Marton, W. (1981), 'Equivalence and Congruence in Transformational Contrastive Linguistics', in J. Fisiak (ed.), *Theoretical Issues in Contrastive Linguistics*, 19–29, Amsterdam: Benjamins.

Merriam-Webster Dictionary Online (2003), 11th edn, Merriam-Webster. Available online: www.merriam-webster.com (accessed 10 March 2017). (cited as MWD11 2003)

OED3 (*Oxford English Dictionary*) (2000–), 3rd edn, Oxford University Press. Available online: http://www.oed.com (accessed 10 July 2017).

Plag, I. (2003), *Word-Formation in English*, Cambridge: Cambridge University Press.

Prćić, T. (2008), 'Suffixes vs Final Combining Forms in English. A Lexicographic Perspective', *International Journal of Lexicography*, 21 (1): 1–22.

Rainer, F. (1993), *Spanische Wortbildungslehre*, Tübingen: Max Niemeyer Verlag.

Rainer, F. (1999), 'La derivación adjectival', in I. Bosque and V. Demonte (eds), *Gramática Descriptiva de la Lengua Española*, vol. III, Madrid: Espasa.

Rainer, F. (2014), 'Polysemy in Derivation', in R. Lieber and P. Stekauer (eds), *The Oxford Handbook of Derivational Morphology*, 338–53, Oxford: Oxford University Press.

Seco, M. (1995), *Gramática esencial del español*, 3rd edn, Madrid: Espasa Libros.

Spencer, M. (1994), 'Morphological Theory and English', Links & Letters, 1: 71–84.

TAHD5 (2011), *The American Heritage Dictionary Online*, 5th edn, Houghton Mifflin Company. Available online: https://ahdictionary.com (accessed 25 March 2017).

Tournier, J. (1985), *Introduction descriptive à la lexicogénétique de l'anglais contemporain*, Paris-Genève: Champion-Slatkine.

Varela Ortega, S. (2005), *Morfología léxica: la formación de palabras*, Madrid: Gredos.

Warren, B. (1999), 'The Importance of Combing Forms', in W. Dressler et al. (eds), *Contemporary Morphology*, 111–32, Berlin: Mouton de Gruyter.

Williems, D., B. Defrancq, T. Colleman and D. Noël, eds (2004), *Contrastive Analysis in Language*, New York: Palgrave Macmillan.

6

Linking elements in German compounds: A morphological analysis in comparison with Greek

Maria Koliopoulou

The present study investigates the occurrence of linking elements in German and Modern Greek compounds. The main aim is to define common criteria that influence the characteristics of the linking element in both languages. Apart from its primary contrastive perspective, this chapter also focuses on a survey of problems surrounding the function of linking elements in German compounds. It investigates whether linking elements which are distinct in surface form may have distinct functions, and examines why some compounds contain a linking element while others do not. As a result, in part, of divergent background assumptions, it is not even clear whether there really are different linking elements in German synchronically or whether they should not rather be treated as instantiations of a single linking element which shows up in different surface forms. This analysis will benefit from a contrast with compounds in Greek, focusing on the form, the systematicity and the function of this element.

1 Introduction

Traditionally, compounding has been considered to be the word-formation process of combining two – or even more – lexemes to create a new complex word. The present study elaborates on one of the main formal characteristics of compounds, namely the occurrence of linking elements (LEs). An LE is an element that links the two parts of a compound. This study will build on a contrastive analysis of the LE in German and Modern Greek[1] compounds.

The selection of these two languages is not arbitrary; rather, it is based on their morphological similarities (Koliopoulou 2013, 2014a). They belong typologically to the category of fusional languages, since in both languages the formation of words is based on morphemes, which carry a great deal of morphosyntactic information. Furthermore, they display a very high productivity in compounding.[2] German and Greek compounds are both right-headed. Nominal compounds consisting of two nouns as in (1) and (2) are the most productive in both languages.

(1) [NN] compounds in German

    a. Liebe-s-geschichte ←   Liebe   Geschichte
       love story   love   story/history

    b. Bühne-n-haus   ←   Bühne   Haus
       stage area   stage   house

    c. Bild-Ø-band   ←   Bild   Band
       illustrated book   picture   volume

(2) [NN] compounds in Greek[3]

    a. λεμον-ό-φυλλο   ←   λεμόν(ι)$_{MASC}$ φύλλ(ο)$_{NEU}$
       lemon-o-filo   lemon(i)   fil(o)
       lemon leaf   lemon   leaf

    b. θαλασσ-ό-λυκος ←   θάλασσ(α)$_{FEM}$ λύκ(ος)$_{MASC}$
       sea dog (experienced sailor) sea   wolf

    c. ανεμ-ό-μυλος   ←   άνεμ(ος)$_{MASC}$ μύλ(ος)$_{MASC}$
       anem-o-milos   anem(os)   mil(os)
       windmill   wind   mill

The present study will focus on the analysis of noun-noun compounds. The appearance of an LE is a characteristic aspect of compounding in both languages.

However, contrastive analysis has proven that there are some striking differences in German and Greek compounds concerning the occurrence of an LE (Koliopoulou 2014b). From a formal standpoint, the most important differences are the following:

1. Form variation displayed by the LEs in German (1), compared to the stable form of the LE in Greek (2);
2. Non-obligatory appearance of an LE in German compounds ((1)c), contrary to its systematic presence in Greek compounds.

Since there are different forms of LEs in German compounds, while its absence is also possible, the main question that arises is whether there are synchronically different elements or if they should rather be treated as instantiations of a single LE which shows up in different surface forms. This question could find an answer by elaborating on the most important aspect, namely, the LE's function. Considering this matter, it is still not clear whether there are different functions for each form of LE, or if its appearance in German compounds fulfils just one function.

The purpose of this study is two-fold. Firstly, common criteria that influence the characteristics of the LE will be defined between the comparable selected languages. Secondly, taking advantage of the contrastive analysis, I will address the issues presented above in greater detail, in an attempt to make the picture concerning the function of the German LE clearer. This study is placed in a functional framework, avoiding the constraints of a theoretical framework with strict rules. The analysis focuses on the investigation of a rather complicated phenomenon, whose interpretation requires different explanations that in combination can account for the multidimensionality of the phenomenon.

The rest of this chapter is structured as follows: Section 2 provides a contrastive analysis of LEs in German and Greek, focusing on the characteristics of their form (Section 2.1) and the systematicity of appearance (Section 2.2). In Section 3, I discuss in detail its function in the selected languages. Finally, in Section 4, I draw a number of conclusions.

2 Linking elements in German and Greek nominal compounds

A common characteristic of compounding in German and Greek is the occurrence of an LE between the first and the second constituent of the structure, referred to in the German literature as '*Fugenelement*' (Fuhrhop 1996, 1998; Ramers 1997; Fleischer and Barz 2012). This word-internal position is explained by their diachronic origin. The LE in German compounds comes from inflectional suffixes[4] of a preposed genitive, singular or plural (Becker 1992: 10; Fuhrhop 1998: 195–6, 2000: 203–4). As it still keeps some of its diachronic characteristics, there are signs of dependency on the first compound constituent, as I will explain in detail in the following. The origin of the Greek LE lies in the Ancient Greek thematic vowel short -ŏ-, which was combined with the root in order to give the stem of a noun or a verb (e.g. ἄνθρωπος (anthropos) 'man': $[[[\text{anthrop}_{\text{root}}]$ $[\text{-o}_{\text{thematic vowel}}]]_{\text{stem}}$ $\text{-s}_{\text{infl.suffix}}]_{\text{word}})$ (Anastassiadis-Symeonidis 1983; Ralli and Raftopoulou 1999; Crocco Galèas 2002: 151; Ralli 2008: 34). However, the LE in Greek compounds gives no sign of dependency on the first or the second constituent (cf. Section 2.1).

In order to come to a clear judgement regarding the complicated issue of the function of the German LE, and to provide a parallel contrastive analysis of German and Greek data, I will first address the issues of the form (Section 2.1) and the systematicity of appearance (Section 2.2).

2.1 Form

Compounds in German come from syntactic constructions bearing diachronically a genitive suffix between the two constituents, as mentioned by, for example, Fuhrhop (2000). Although these syntactic formations have become the object of morphological analysis, the element that links the two parts of the compound still bears some of its diachronic features, as shown by its dependency on the first constituent, revealed in different aspects:

First of all, the LE is coordinated to the first constituent (cf. Ramers 1997: 34–5; Fuhrhop 1998: 187), as in the following example:

(3) Prüfung-s- und Studi-en-abteilung
     examination and studies department

In (3), the head of the first compound (-*abteilung* 'department') is omitted, since it is the same as the head of the coordinated compound. Despite the fact that the first compound is reduced on the first constituent, the LE still appears attached to it.

Moreover, the possible appearance of the LE and its form variation is related to the lexical category of the first constituent, independently of the lexical category of the head (Wellmann 1991; Becker 1992; Neef 2009; Fleischer and Barz 2012). Specifically, nominal first constituents can be combined with all possible forms of elements: *-e-*, *-s-*, *-es-*, *-n-*, *-en-*, *-er-* and *-ens-*. Productivity plays a central role in the selection of the proper form of nominal first constituents. Primarily *-s-* and secondarily *-n-* are regarded as the most productive among the as Dressler et al. (2001: 190–1) refer to 'interfixed compounds', as for example, in *Liebe-s-geschichte* ((1)a) and in *Bühne-n-haus* ((1)b). On the contrary, after verbal first constituents, the selection is limited only to the *-e-* (schwa) element (e.g. *Zeig$_V$-e-finger$_N$* 'forefinger') or to the interfixless formations (e.g. *Ess$_V$-Ø-zimmer$_N$* 'dining room') (Fuhrhop 1996: 529, 539, 1998: 205–6). Compounds without LE are very common: about seventy per cent of all German compounds, as argued by Fuhrhop and Kürschner (2015: 569).

Another aspect that reveals the dependency of the LE on the first constituent is the fact that its appearance is sometimes related to the inflectional paradigm of the first constituent. Specifically, it has been argued that the choice of the LE in a compound with a nominal first constituent may be determined by the paradigmatic relations between the element and the inflectional suffixes. For instance, in the example *Meeresboden* ('sea bottom', (4)a), the *-es-* element displays a possessive meaning, as does the homophonous genitive suffix of the first constituent. Similarly, in *Bildergalerie* ('picture gallery', (4)b) the element *-er-*, which is homophonous to the plural suffix of the noun *Bild*, displays a plural meaning, indicating that the gallery includes more than one picture.

(4) a. Meer-es-boden   ←   Meer$_{NOM.SG}$, Meeres$_{GEN.SG}$ Boden
         sea bottom   sea   bottom

     b. Bild-er-galerie   ←   Bild$_{NOM.SG}$, Bilder$_{NOM.PL}$ Galerie
         picture gallery   picture   gallery

However, counterexamples reveal that the form of LEs is not necessarily related to a specific meaning. In particular, the element *-er-* does not always indicate a plural meaning, even in cases of nominal first constituents having a homophonous plural suffix. For instance, *Kinderbett* ((5)a) does not mean 'bed for more than one child'. Likewise, the *-es-* in *Freundeskreis* ((5)b) does not bear any possessive meaning, although a homophonous *-es-* suffix appears in the genitive singular of the noun *Freund* ('friend') (cf. Eisenberg 2004: 236–7).

(5) a. Kind-er-bett   ←   Kind$_{NOM.SG}$, Kinder$_{NOM.PL}$ Bett
         crib   child   bed

     b. Freund-es-kreis   ←   Freund$_{NOM.SG}$, Freundes$_{GEN.SG}$ Kreis
         circle of friends   friend   circle

Furthermore, the appearance of the same nominal first constituent in several compounds does not presuppose that the same form of LE also appears. For example, in *Meerjungfrau* ((6)a) an -*es*- would be expected, since both structures in (5)a and (6)a display the same first constituent (*Meer* 'sea'), as well as a possessive meaning. However, *Meerjungfrau* is an interfixless compound. Similarly, *Bildarchiv* ((6)b) having the same first constituent as (4)b and clearly indicating a plural meaning, since there is no picture library including just one picture, is nevertheless a non-interfixed structure.

(6) a. Meer-Ø-jungfrau ← Meer$_{NOM.SG}$, Meeres$_{GEN.SG}$ Jungfrau
         mermaid   sea   virgin

     b. Bild-Ø-archiv ← Bild$_{NOM.SG}$, Bilder$_{NOM.PL}$ Archiv
         picture library   picture   archive

Minimal pairs as in (4) and (6) reveal various characteristics of the LE in German. Firstly, it is demonstrated that the occurrence of an element is not obligatory. Secondly, a certain form of LE does not necessarily make a specific semantic contribution to the compound structure. Thirdly, nominal first constituents are not exclusively related to a certain form of element. Moreover, there are cases of nominal first constituents presenting a variable choice of LEs, for example, the noun *Land* ('country'), as shown in (7).

(7) a. Länd-er-ebene ← Land Ebene
         land (Federal State) level country level

     b. Land-es-amt ← Land Amt
         regional authorities country office/department/agency

     c. Land-s-leute ← Land Leute
         fellow countrymen country people

     d. Land-Ø-sitz ← Land Sitz
         country estate country seat/place

Any kind of paradigmatic relation observed between a specific form of the LE and a first constituent cannot be interpreted as the result of a selection rule, according to which the appearance of this specific form can be predicted. Therefore, despite the detection of some correlations, mostly based on paradigmatic relations or on analogical structures, there are no firmly established criteria concerning the selection of the proper form of the LE.

So far, it has been shown that the different forms of LE, despite being paradigmatically related to the first constituents, reveal no sign of strong formal or semantic dependency. Thus, there is still discussion among scholars about the (un)paradigmatic relation of these various forms to the inflectional suffixes of the first constituent (e.g. Gallmann 1998; Libben et al. 2009). Recently, it has also been also argued that LEs in German compounds should be regarded as being linked equally to both constituents and not dependent on the first part of the structure (Elsen 2014: 34). This claim is based on various arguments,[5] among them the fact that not all LEs are paradigmatically related to the first constituent. However, this does not invalidate the signs of dependency on the preceding constituent presented above.

Despite the various arguments, there is a clear agreement that in most cases, the element -s-, the most productive form,[6] does not show any dependency on the inflectional paradigm of the first compound constituent (Becker 1992: 12–13; Fuhrhop 1996: 529, 545, 1998: 191–7; Eisenberg 2004: 240–1). This can be demonstrated in two ways. Firstly, the -s- element appears in cases in which there is no homophonous suffix in the inflectional paradigm of the first constituent, as in (8).

(8) a. Arbeit-s-platz   ←   Arbeit (*Arbeits)   Platz
         job/workplace   work   place

     b. Universität-s-klinik ←   Universität (*Universitäts) Klinik
         university clinic   university   clinic

Conversely, there are formations in which an -s- element would be expected, but it does not occur. Specifically, in the examples given in (9), -s- does not occur, although the first constituent's paradigm includes an -s- as a genitive suffix ((9)a, b) or a plural suffix ((9)c). Moreover, there is a possessive or a plural meaning associated with the first constituent, and yet, the appearance of an -s- element in these compounds would be ungrammatical ((9)a', b', c').

(9) a. Schrank-Ø-bein   ←   Schrank, Schranks$_{\text{GEN.SG}}$ Bein
         cupboard leg   cupboard   leg
     a'. *Schrank-s-bein

     b. Kloster-Ø-garten   ←   Kloster, Klosters$_{\text{GEN.SG}}$ Garten
         monastery garden   monastery   garden
     b'. *Kloster-s-garten

     c. Auto-Ø-bahn   ←   Auto, Autos$_{\text{NOM.PL}}$ Bahn
         motorway (expressway)   car   railway
     c'. *Auto-s-bahn

As opposed to the considerable formal variation displayed by the interfixed German compounds, Greek compounds display only one productive form of LE[7], -o-. It is a widely known LE, since it appears in the neoclassical compounds of many European languages.[8] The -o- gives no sign of dependency on the first or the second constituent. It can be combined with all lexical categories of the first or the second constituent and is independent of the inflectional properties of either constituent[9] (cf. (2)).

Moreover, coordination between compounds, as shown in (3) for German, is ungrammatical in Greek. For instance, a comparable construction to German such as *αχιν-ο- και καβουρ-ο-σαλάτα (achin-o- ke kavur-o-salata 'sea urchin and crab salad') is not possible, since the omission of part of a compound is ungrammatical. Therefore, it can be argued that -o- needs both parts of the compounds to be linked to it and that it is equally linked to both of them.

2.2 Systematicity of appearance

The differences between German and Greek LEs are not restricted to the form; they are rather obvious in further aspects, too. The occurrence of the Greek element -o- displays an obvious regularity. It is systematic, while its exceptional absence depends on either phonological or morphological word-formation rules (Ralli 2013). Specifically, a second compound constituent beginning with a vowel stronger than /o/ in the Greek vowel hierarchy (e.g. /a/) prevents the occurrence of the element -o-, as in (10)a. Compare, for instance, (10)a with *λεμον-ό-φυλλο* in (2)a. Both structures have the same first constituent. However, (2)a displays an LE, while the structure in (10)a does not.

(10) a. λεμον-Ø-ανθός   ←   λεμόν(ι)   ανθ(ός)
          lemon-Ø-anthos   lemon(i)   anthos
          lemon flower   lemon   flower

Moreover, the element -o- is also missing when the first constituent of a compound structure is an independent word, and not a stem, as in (10)b.

(10) b. επτά-Ø-γωνο   ←   επτά$_{WORD}$ γων(ία)
          epta-Ø-jono   epta   jon(ia)
          heptagon   seven   corner/vertex

Contrary to this, the LE in German compounds is not obligatory. Thus, the existence of non-interfixed compounds is a very common phenomenon, as already shown in several examples ((1)c, (6)a,b, (7)d, (9)a,b). The lack of obligatoriness, in addition to its unsystematic appearance, is still a subject of discussion, since there are no firmly established criteria to predict whether a compound should be interfixed or not.

With regard to the existence of interfixless compounds, I have argued that the non-appearance of an LE in German compounds depends on the tightness of the semantic relation between the constituents (Koliopoulou 2013: 260–2, 2014b: 63–5). On this basis, I argue that there are two basic compound types: compounds with tight semantic relation and compounds with loose semantic relation, as shown in Table 6.1.

Compounds of the first type are characterized by the non-systematic appearance of an LE. This type of structure includes determinative compounds, such as those mentioned so far, in which the head is modified by the non-head, namely the first

Table 6.1 Compounds with Tight and Loose Semantic Relation

Compounds with tight semantic relation		Compounds with loose semantic relation
Determinative compounds	*Copulative compounds with additive relation*	*Copulative compounds with appositive relation*
Arbeit-s-platz ((8)a)	Hose-n-rock ((11)a)	Dichter-Ø-komponist ((12)a)

constituent. Copulative compounds with additive relation, such as those given under (11), also belong to the same class of compounds.

(11) a. Hose-n-rock   ←   Hose   Rock
          baggy pants   trousers skirt

      b. Bluse-n-kleid   ←   Bluse   Kleid
          short dress   blouse   dress

      c. Jacke-n-kleid   ←   Jacke   Kleid
          two-piece dress   jacket   dress

According to Arcodia, Grandi and Montermini (2009: 18–19), in case of a copulative compound with additive relation, the semantic outcome of the whole compound is a hyponym of its constituents. Specifically, the two meanings are blended together ($[[_{N1}] [_{N2}]_{N1/2}]$). However, the type of blending is not identical for all the examples belonging to this category, as revealed in (11).

In contrast, compounds of the second type displaying a rather loose semantic relation are characterized by the systematic non-appearance of an LE. This type of structure includes copulative compounds with an appositive relation,[10] for example, the [*noun-noun*] compounds in (12).

(12) a. Dichter-Ø-komponist   ←   Dichter   Komponist
          poet-composer   poet   composer

      b. Fürst-Ø-bischof   ←   Fürst   Bischof
          prince-bishop   prince   bishop

In this type of structure, the semantic outcome is rather transparent, bearing two separate identities that are not merged into one ($[[_{N1}][_{N2}]_{N1,2}]$). Thus, a copulative compound with an appositive relation could be regarded as a hyperonym of both constituents (Arcodia, Grandi and Montermini 2009: 18–19).

If we compare the examples in (12) with possible compounds composed of the same constituents and displaying an LE, we would come up with determinative compounds. For instance, a *Dichter-s-komponist* would indicate a composer of a specific poet. Similarly, *Fürst-en-bischof* would mean 'prince's bishop'. The occurrence of an LE in those possible determinative structures strengthens the argument that its non-appearance in the copulative compounds of (12) is determined by the loose semantic structure of the constituents (see also Koliopoulou 2014b: 62–5).

Consequently, I argue that its occurrence depends on the compound type determined by the semantic relation of the constituents. On one hand, the appearance of LE is possible, but not systematic in determinative compounds and in copulative ones with additive relations, whose morphological structure display a rather tight semantic relation. On the other hand, the LE is systematically absent in copulative compounds with an apposition relation. In this case, its non-appearance is motivated by the loose structure of these compounds.

With regard to the Greek LE -*o*-, it has been claimed that its obligatory appearance in almost all compound structures strengthens the boundaries between stem constituents (Ralli 2008), since compounds in Greek are mainly formed out of stems (cf. (2)). A major argument is that the -*o*- appears in copulative compounds, which are regarded as displaying a loose structure, in contrast to the determinative ones. Its occurrence in copulative compounds reinforces the relation between the stem constituents in (13).

(13) a. αλατ-ο-πίπερο   ←   αλάτ(ι)   πιπέρ(ι)
         alat-o-pipero   alat(i)   piper(i)
         salt and pepper   salt   pepper

      b. λαδ-ό-ξυδο   ←   λάδ(ι)   ξύδ(ι)
         ladh-o-ksidho   ladh(i)   ksidh(i)
         sauce of oil and vinegar   oil   vinegar

The appearance of the -*o*- in this loose type of compounds is obligatory, even in cases where there is a phonological restriction; namely, when the second constituent begins with a vowel stronger than /o/ in the vowel hierarchy, for example, /a/ in *μαυρ-ό-ασπρος* (*mavr-o-aspros* 'black and white').

Summing up, the Greek LE is a semantically empty element displaying a stable form and a certain systematicity of appearance, since the cases of its absence are determined by word-formation rules. In contrast, the occurrence of an LE in German compounds is characterized by form variation and a certain unsystematic appearance. However, in both languages, the type of semantic relation between the two components influences the (un)systematicity of appearance of the LE.

3 Function of the linking element

The systematicity of appearance of the LE and, moreover, its obligatory presence in specific compound types are strongly related to the question of what kind of function it fulfils. With regard to the Greek element -*o*-, its systematic appearance in all compound structures, and particularly its obligatoriness in the copulative compounds, supports the claim that -*o*- constitutes a compound marker, namely, a marker of the word-formation process of compounding (Ralli 2008). Its occurrence intends to reinforce the boundaries between the stem constituents, specifically in structures with loose semantic relations, such as in copulative compounds.

As far as the German LE is concerned, the difficulty of developing selection criteria for the appearance of a specific form, added to the fact that its non-appearance is also possible, complicates the main question, namely, what kind of function its appearance fulfils. In particular, it cannot be claimed that there is an identical function for all different realizations, since some of them still show signs of dependency on the inflectional paradigm of the first constituent. For instance, the LE -*er*-, usually combined with the umlaut, is, in many cases, paradigmatically related to the plural suffix of the preceding constituent. This means that the -*er*- shows up between two compound constituents, in case the first constituent forms the plural with an -*er*-suffix, as also shown in *Bildergalerie* in (4)b. However, there are cases in which the element -*er*- shows formal but not semantic dependency on the preceding constituent. For instance, *Kinderbett* ((5)a) does not indicate a bed for more than one child, showing that in this case the element -*er*- does not bear the semantic properties of the homophonous plural suffix.

With regard to the possibility of a plural interpretation of the LE, Schäfer and Pankratz (2018) have proven that the relation between plural form and plural meaning is synchronically attested. Their empirical study focuses on determinative compounds of written German and investigates the selection and the interpretation of LEs in a production-oriented decision task. Despite the high form variation reinforced by individual preferences, they argue that a plural interpretation of some LEs is possible, as in *Bildergalerie* ((4)b). Their research supports Fuhrhop and Kürscher's (2015: 577) view on this issue and reinforces the argument that there is not an identical function for all different LEs.

Moreover, taking into consideration cases of compounds displaying the same first constituent, but various forms of LEs, as presented for *Land* ('country') in (7), it has been argued that the first constituent and the LE construct allomorphic stems that participate in the compounding process (Fuhrhop 1996, 1998, 2000: 'Kompositionsstammformen'). It has also been argued that the element selected for the formation of compound neologisms is often based on analogy (Becker 1992). This claim actually suggests that the LE in German has no special morphological function; rather, it has a phonotactic one, namely, to join the two constituents. Nevertheless, the same researchers do not deny the existence of an exception regarding the element -*s*-, the most productive form of LE.

The element -*s*- does not display a paradigmatic relation to the first constituent, since it usually shows up after feminine simple (e.g. *Arbeit-s-platz* in (8)a) or derived words (*Prüfung-s-abteilung* in (3)). According to Aronoff and Fuhrhop (2002: 451–66), the appearance of the -*s*- is related to the existence of a derivational closing suffix attached to the first constituent. A derivational closing suffix, namely -*heit*, -*keit*, -*igkeit*, -*ling* and -*ung*, prevents the stem to which it attaches from participating in further word-formation processes. Thus, Aronoff and Fuhrhop's (2002) claim is that the appearance of the -*s*- overrides this 'closure' and enables the stem to participate further in processes like derivation or compounding.

Moreover, it has been claimed that the element -*s*- shows up after morphologically complex first constituents,[11] that is, a prefixed ((14)a) or a suffixed noun (15) (Žepić 1970; Fuhrhop 1996, 1998; Nübling and Szczepaniak 2009; Kürschner 2010). Comparing (14)a with (14)b, it becomes obvious that -*s*- appears due to the morphological complexity of the noun *Ausland*.

(14) a. [[[Aus-[land]]-s-[bewohner]]   ←   Ausland   Bewohner
          resident of a foreign country   abroad   resident

      b. Land-Ø-bewohner   ←   Land   Bewohner
          countryman   country   resident

(15) [[[Sicher][-ung]]-s-[abrede]]   ←   Sicherung   Abrede
      security arrangement   security   arrangement

A morphologically complex first constituent may also be a compound word, as shown
in examples (16)a and (17)a. In this case, the appearance of the element -*s*- signifies the
boundary between the two constituents. This kind of morphological function becomes
clearer when we see the minimal pairs in (16) and (17). In the examples in (a), the first
constituents are compound words and thus are followed by the element -*s*-. On the
contrary, the first constituents of the examples in (b) are simple words. In (16)b, no LE
appears, while in (17)b, there is an LE other than -*s*-.

(16) a. [[[Bahn]-[hof]]-s-[beamter]]   ←   Bahnhof   Beamter
          railway station official railway   station   official

      b. [[Hof]-Ø-[beamter]]   ←   Hof   Beamter
          court official   court   official

(17) a. [[[Geburt]-s-[tag]]-s-[karte]]   ←   Geburtstag   Karte
          birthday card   birthday   card

      b. [[Tag]-es-[karte]]   ←   Tag   Karte
          day card   day   card

Consequently, it has been claimed that the -*s*- signifies the morphological complexity
of the first constituent. Specifically, its appearance marks the boundary between the
two constituents.

Moreover, the element -*s*- fulfils the same function, even in cases of a monosyllable
left-handed constituent, as in *Land-s-leute* 'fellow countrymen' ((7)c) and *Amt-s-eid*
'official oath'. Kürschner (2010: 851) notes that the frequency of appearance of -*s*- is
particularly high after specific left-handed constituents, for example, *Volk-s-* ('nation'),
Land-s- ('country'), *Staat-s-* ('state'), *Amt-s-* ('agency'). As argued by Wegener
(2005: 180), Kürschner (2010: 849–51) and Nübling and Szczepaniak (2013: 63),
the -*s*- appears even after phonologically simple first constituents in order to mark
the boundaries between the two components and to prevent false syllabifications.
Therefore, it has been concluded that the element -*s*- supports both the morphological
and phonological linking of the two components by indicating their boundaries (cf.
Fuhrhop and Kürschner 2015: 574).

Taking these statements into consideration, I would like to propose that the LE
-*s*- can be considered as a compound marker, a semantically empty element which
serves a morphological function,[12] namely, to indicate the word-formation process of
compounding by marking the boundary between the two constituents. Apart from
the -*s*-, I would like to suggest that the function of the less productive forms of the LE
in German vary according to paradigmatic relations to the first constituent that they
display.

Considering that some forms are still paradigmatically related to the first constituent,
whereas -*s*- can be considered as an independent element, it has been argued that

the different forms of the LE in German have participated in a grammaticalization process (Wegener 2008; Nübling and Szczepaniak 2013). In this respect, I argue that the various forms of element in German have been involved in a morphologization process, in terms of Joseph (2003), in order to move gradually from the status of an inflectional suffix to the status of a semantically empty element (Koliopoulou 2013: 249–50). The linear scale in (18) represents the result of this morphologization process, namely, how close to the status of a compound marker the different forms of LE have come, taking as an example the elements *-es-* and *-s-*.

(18) *Inflectional suffix* (-) → → → (+) *Compound marker*
    -es-   …   -s-

According to this scalar classification, the element *-s-*, which is synchronically the most productive form, has reached the status of a compound marker. The fact that *-s-* has completed this morphologization process is shown not only by its independent occurrence between the components but also by its increasing productivity. Nübling and Szczepaniak (2013) argue that *-s-* appears in 'doubtful cases', in terms of Klein (2003), where *-s-* is gradually replacing the non-appearance of an LE. Specifically, it is argued that, for instance, the compound *Antrag-Ø-steller* ('applicant'), where no LE is to be found, can also be formed with the element *-s-*, as in *Antrag-s-steller*. This is a sign of language change, particularly dominant in communication purposes where forms of oral speech are used. In contrast, the element *-es-* is placed at the right edge of this scale. *-es-* is fully paradigmatically related to the first constituent and rather unproductive, since it appears in a restricted number of fixed formations, as in *Freund-es-kreis* ((5)b). Therefore, it could be considered as a lexicalized element.

Regarding the other forms of LE in German, there are indications that they are spread in between *-s-* and *-es-*. The place of the different forms in this morphologization process is strongly related to the degree of productivity that they synchronically display. For instance, it could be argued that the element *-n-*, which is a very productive form, is placed near *-s-*. This argument is based on the fact that *-n-* is, in many cases, semantically independent from the inflectional paradigm of the first constituent. Neither in the example *Bühne-n-haus* ((1)b) nor in the structures given under (11) is the appearance of the element *-n-* associated with any plural meaning of the preceding constituent, although its inflectional paradigm includes a homophonous plural suffix[13] (e.g. *Bühne*$_{NOM.SG}$, *Bühnen*$_{NOM.PL}$).

In contrast, the element *-er-*, a form with a relatively low productivity, is still paradigmatically related to the first constituent, as it usually indicates a plural meaning, as in *Bild-er-galerie* ((4)b). However, there are exceptions, such as the one discussed earlier on the basis of the structure *Kind-er-bett* ((5)a), in which the *-er-* does not bear a plural meaning. With regard to these remarks, it could be argued that *-er-* is placed not far away from the starting point of the morphologization process.

To summarize, the LEs in German and Greek display different functional properties. Starting with the clearer case, the Greek element *-o-* is regarded as a compound marker, as it has a purely morphological role, namely, to strengthen the boundaries between stem constituents. The role of the compound marker is also assumed for the most productive German LE, -*s*-, since its occurrence is motivated by the morphological complexity of the first constituent. Thus, the -*s*- indicates the boundaries between the compound constituents contributing to the morphological and semantic parsing of the structure, especially in the case of a complex first part. Therefore, -*s*- it can also be considered as an independent element.

Taking into consideration that LEs in German compounds have participated in a morphologization process, it can be argued that the element -*s*- has completed this process, since it displays a new morphological function. With regard to the other forms showing signs of dependency on the first constituent, it is claimed that they are also in the process of morphologization. Their position on the morphologization scale is also determined by the degree of productivity that they display synchronically. Thus, it cannot be argued that the different forms of the LE in German compounds have an identical function.

4 Synopsis and conclusions

The present study has investigated the occurrence of LEs in German and Greek nominal compounds consisting of two nouns. Its primary aim was to define common criteria that influence the characteristics of the LE in both languages. A secondary aim was to analyze the complicated properties of the LEs in German, contrasting them with the characteristics of the LE in Greek.

The systematic contrastive analysis of the LE has revealed a new parameter that determines its (non-)appearance in both selected languages. It has been argued that the compound type and, more precisely, the type of the semantic relationship between the two compound components determines the (non-)appearance of an LE in the two languages. Specifically, its systematic non-appearance in German is motivated by the loose structure of copulative compounds displaying an appositive relation between the constituents. The same parameter, namely the tightness of the semantic relation of the components also determines the appearance of the Greek LE -*o*-, but in the opposite direction. The obligatory appearance of the -*o*- is triggered by the loose compounds, such as the copulative ones.

Moreover, the contrastive analysis between the clearly morphologically motivated occurrence of the Greek LE and the rather opaque character of the LE in German has offered new theoretical insights with regard to the function of the second. Specifically, it has been concluded that there is not just one identical function for all the different forms. In accordance with the Greek element -*o*- displaying the role of a compound marker in order to indicate the word-formation process of compounding, it has been argued that the German element -*s*-, the most productive form, is also a compound marker. In particular, -*s*- has the morphological function of signifying the complexity of the first constituent and consequently of marking the boundary between the constituents. Regarding the other forms of the LE, it has been claimed that they are in a morphologization process, since they still display dependency on the preceding constituents, although not to the same degree. Their position in the morphologization scale is determined by the productivity that they synchronically display. However, the definition of the exact position of each form of LE in the morphologization scale and the specification of its current status require further investigation, as well as an empirical foundation.

Notes

1 Modern Greek will be referred to in the following simply as Greek. Any reference to Ancient Greek will be specified.

2 See, for example, Gaeta and Schlücker (2012), Ralli (2013) for the two languages respectively. Specifically, as far as German is concerned, it has been characterized as a 'compounding-friendly' language ('kompositionsfreundlich', Coseriu 1977).

3 With regard to the examples presented in this study, hyphens are used to signify the LE in each compound structure. The use of the arrow indicates that the structure is composed of the following two constituents. Inflectional suffixes given in parentheses indicate that the compound constituent is a stem and not a word. Moreover, as the phonological representation is not central for the purposes of this study, I will use an orthographic representation for the examples in both languages and a broad phonetic transcription just for those in Greek.

4 It has been argued that some forms of LE (particularly *-er-, -e-* and *-(e)n-*) diachronically derive from stem suffixes, reanalysed into LEs (Wegener 2005: 175–7).

5 Elsen (2014: 34) names four arguments to support this view: (a) the form variation, as also illustrated in (7); (b) non-paradigmatically related appearance of LEs; (c) phonologically motivated instances of appearance of the LE; (d) the fact that the appearance of the loan element *-o-* found in neoclassical compounds (cf. endnote 8) is also related to the right-hand constituent. The degree of paradigmatic relation between LE and first constituent has been discussed in this chapter too and I would agree that there are cases of (b). However, in my view, the first and the third argument do not indicate that the appearance of LEs is not paradigmatically related to the preceding constituent. With regard to the fourth argument, it is clear that the appearance of *-o-* in neoclassical compounds is strongly determined by the characteristics of compounding in Greek.

6 The high productivity of the element *-s-* is determined by the productivity of the first constituents it attaches to, namely to feminine nouns, simple or derived, and more specifically by the high productivity of the feminine derivational suffixes (e.g. *-ung*, *-heit*, *-keit*) of the preceding constituent.

7 There is another form of LE, the *-ι-*, which appears in a small number of lexicalized compounds (e.g. *ταξ-ι-θέτης* 'usher') originating from Ancient Greek (cf. Ralli 2013: 50–2).

8 See for example, Lüdeling, Schmid and Kiokpasoglou (2002) and Fleischer and Barz (2012) with regard to neoclassical compounds in German. The LEs *-o-* (*Elektro-gerät* 'electric appliance') and the unproductive *-i-* from Latin (*Strati-grafie* 'stratigraphy') differ from the native ones, since they are regarded as being synchronically part of the first constituent. Therefore, I will exclude them from this analysis.

9 For detailed information on this argument see Koliopoulou (2014b: 60).

10 One-word nominal copulative compounds are rare in German (for further examples cf. Koliopoulou 2014b: 63), since this type of semantic relation between nouns is usually expressed with the so-called 'Bindestrichkomposita' ('hyphen compounds').

11 Nübling and Szczepaniak (2009, 2011) argue that -*s*- also marks phonologically complex first constituents. A phonological complex word is a word that includes more than one foot, as, for example, the case of the suffixed word in (14)b and especially of the borrowed one, as in *nationalität-s-bezogen* ('referring to the nationality'). For further claims on a phonologically motivated appearance of the element -*s*- cf. also Eisenberg (2004: 240–1) and Wegener (2005).

12 Elsen (2014: 33) has recently argued in favour of the semantically empty character of all forms of LE, supporting their morphological role in a compound structure. This claim offers a consistent analysis of all the various forms. Nevertheless, it cannot be argued that all the different forms of LE are not paradigmatically related to the first constituent and display a pure morphological role, as the element -*s*- does.

13 The fact that the element -*n*- does not indicate a plural meaning despite the existence of a homophonous plural suffix in the inflectional paradigm of the first constituent is determined by the fact that -*n*- is an old genitive suffix that has survived only in compound structures as in *Sonne-n-schein* ('sunshine').

References

Anastassiadis-Symeonidis, A. (1983), 'La composition en grec moderne d'un point de vue diachronique', *LALIES*, 2: 77–90.

Arcodia, G. F., N. Grandi and F. Montermini (2009), 'Hierarchical NN compounds in a cross-linguistic perspective', *Rivista di Linguistica*, 21 (1): 11–33.

Aronoff, M. and N. Fuhrhop (2002), 'Restricting Suffix Combinations in German and English: Closing Suffixes and the Monosuffix Constraint', *Natural Language & Linguistic Theory*, 20: 451–90.

Becker, T. (1992), 'Compounding in German', *Rivista di Linguistica*, 4 (1): 5–36.

Coseriu, E. (1977), 'Inhaltliche Wortbildungslehre (am Beispiel des Typs "coupe-papier")', in H. E. Brekle and D. Kastovsky (eds), *Perspektiven der Wortbildungsforschung*, 48–61, Bonn: Bouvier Verlag Herbert Grundmann.

Crocco Galèas, G. (2002), 'The interradical interfix in Modern Greek compounding', *Studies in Greek Linguistics*, 22: 150–8.

Dressler, W. U., G. Libben, J. Stark, C. Pons and G. Jarema (2001), 'The Processing of Interfixed German Compounds', in G. Booij and J. v. Marle (eds), *Yearbook of Morphology* 1999, 185–220, Dordrecht, The Netherlands: Foris.

Eisenberg, P. (2004), *Grundriß der deutschen Grammatik. Band 1: Das Wort*, 2. überarbeitete und aktualisierte Auflage, Stuttgart: J. B. Metzler.

Elsen, H. (2014), *Grundzüge der Morphologie des Deutschen*, 2. Auflage, Berlin: Walter de Gruyter.

Fleischer, W. and I. Barz (2012), *Wortbildung der deutschen Gegenwartssprache*, 4. völlig neu bearb, Auflage, Berlin: Walter de Gruyter.

Fuhrhop, N. (1996), 'Fugenelement', in E. Lang and G. Zifonun (eds), *Deutsch - Typologisch. Institut für deutsche Sprache. Jahrbuch* 1995, 525–50, Berlin: Mouton de Gruyter.

Fuhrhop, N. (1998), *Grenzfälle morphologischer Einheiten*, Tübingen: Stauffenburg.

Fuhrhop, N. (2000), 'Zeigen Fugenelemente die Morphologisierung von Komposita an?', in T. Rorf, M. Tamrat, N. Fuhrhop and O. Teuber (eds), *Deutsche Grammatik in Theorie und Praxis*, 201–13, Tübingen: Niemeyer.

Fuhrhop, N. and S. Kürschner (2015), 'Linking Elements in Germanic', in P. O. Müller, I. Ohnheiser, S. Olsen and F. Rainer (eds), *Word-Formation: An International Handbook of the Languages of Europe*, vol. 1, 568–82, Berlin: de Gruyter.

Gaeta, L. and B. Schlücker, eds (2012), *Das Deutsche als kompositionsfreudige Sprache. Strukturelle Eigenschaften und systembezogene Aspekte*, Berlin: de Gruyter.

Gallmann, P. (1998), 'Fugenmorpheme als Nicht-Kasus-Morpheme', in M. Butt and N. Fuhrhop (eds), *Variation und Stabilität in der Wortstruktur*, 177–90, Hildesheim: Olms.

Joseph, B. D. (2003), 'Morphologization from Syntax', in B. D. Joseph and R. Janda (eds), *The Handbook of Historical Linguistics*, 472–92, Oxford: Blackwell.

Klein, W. P. (2003), 'Sprachliche Zweifelsfälle als linguistischer Gegenstand. Zur Einführung in ein vergessenes Thema der Sprachwissenschaft', *Linguistik Online*, 16 (4): 1–26.

Koliopoulou, M. (2013), 'Θέματα Σύνθεσης της Ελληνικής και της Γερμανικής: Συγκριτική Προσέγγιση' ('Issues of Modern Greek and German Compounding: A Contrastive Approach') [in Greek], PhD diss., University of Patras, Patras, Greece. Available online: http://nemertes.lis.upatras.gr/jspui/handle/10889/5962?locale=en

Koliopoulou, M. (2014a), 'Issues of Modern Greek and German Compounding: A Contrastive Approach', *Journal of Greek Linguistics*, 14 (1): 117–25.

Koliopoulou, M. (2014b), 'How Close to Syntax are Compounds? Evidence from the Linking Element in German and Modern Greek Compounds', *Rivista di Linguistica*, 26 (2): 51–70.

Kürschner, S. (2010), 'Fuge-n-kitt, voeg-en-mes, fuge-masse und fog-e-ord - Fugenelemente im Deutschen, Niederländischen, Schwedischen und Dänischen. Ein Grenzfall der Morphologie im Sprachkontrast', in A. Dammel, S. Kürschner and D. Nübling (eds), *Kontrastive Germanistische Linguistik, Germanistische Linguistik 206–9*, Band 2, 827–62, Hildesheim: Olms.

Libben, G., M. Boniecki, M. Marlies, K. Mittermann, K. Korecky-Kröll and W. U. Dressler (2009), 'Interfixation in German Compounds: What Factors Govern Acceptability Judgements?', *Rivista di Linguistica*, 21 (1): 149–80.

Lüdeling, A., T. Schmid and S. Kiokpasoglou (2002), 'Neoclassical word formation in German', in G. Booij and J. v. Marle (eds), *Yearbook of Morphology 2001*, 253–83, Dordrecht: Kluwer.

Neef, M. (2009), 'IE, Germanic: German', in R. Lieber and P. Štekauer (eds), *The Oxford Handbook of Compounding*, 386–99, Oxford: Oxford University Press.

Nübling, D. and R. Szczepaniak (2009), 'Religion+s+freiheit, Stabilität+s+pakt und Subjekt(+s+)pronomen: Fugenelemente als Marker phonologischer Wortgrenzen', in P. O. Müller (ed.), *Studien zur Fremdwortbildung*, Germanistische Linguistik 197–8, 195–222, Hildesheim: Olms

Nübling, D. and R. Szczepaniak (2011), 'Merkmal(s?)analyse, Seminar(s?)arbeit und Essen(s?)ausgabe: Zweifelsfälle der Verfugung als Indikatoren für Sprachwandel', *Zeitschrift für Sprachwissenschaft*, 30 (1): 45–74.

Nübling, D. and R. Szczepaniak (2013), 'Linking elements in German Origin, Change, Functionalization', *Morphology*, 23: 67–89.

Ralli, A. (2008), 'Compound Markers and Parametric Variation', *Language Typology and Universals (STUF)*, 61: 19–38.

Ralli, A. (2013), *Compounding in Modern Greek*, Dordrecht, The Netherlands: Springer.

Ralli A. and M. Raftopoulou (1999), 'Η Σύνθεση στην Ελληνική ως διαχρονικό φαινόμενο σχηματισμού λέξεων' ('Compounding in Greek as a Diachronic Phenomenon of Word Formation') [in Greek], *Studies in Greek Linguistics*, 19: 389–403.

Ramers, K. H. (1997), 'Die Kunst der Fuge: Zum morphologischen Status von Verbindungselementen in Nominalkomposita', in C. Dürscheid, K. H. Ramers and M. Schwarz (eds), *Sprache im Fokus. Festschrift für Heinz Vater zum 65. Geburtstag*, 33–45, Tübingen: Niemeyer.

Schäfer, R. and E. Pankratz (2018), 'The Plural Interpretability of German Linking Elements', *Morphology*, 28: 325–58.

Wegener, H. (2005), 'Das Hühnerei vor der Hundehütte. Von der Notwendigkeit historischen Wissens in der Grammatikographie des Deutschen', in E. Berner, M. Böhm and A. Voeste (eds), *Ein groß und narhafft haffen. Festschrift für Joachim Gessinger*, 175–87, Potsdam: Universitätsverlag.

Wegener, H. (2008), 'The Regrammaticalization of Linking Elements in German', in E. Seoane and M. J. López-Couso (eds), *Theoretical and Empirical Issues in Grammaticalization*, 333–54, Amsterdam: Benjamins.

Wellmann, H. (1991), 'Morphologie der Substantivkomposita', in Institut für Deutsche Sprache (ed.), *Deutsche Wortbildung: Typen und Tendenzen in der Gegenwartssprache. Substantivkomposita*, 3–124, Berlin: Walter de Gruyter.

Žepić, S. (1970), *Morphologie und Semantik der deutschen Nominalkomposita*, Zagreb: Philosophische Fakultät der Universität Zagreb, Abteilung für Germanistik.

7

Compounding in Albanian as a case of 'structural blending': Evidence from the contrastive analysis of Greek and Albanian

Asimakis Fliatouras

The aim of this chapter is to discuss Albanian compounding as a possible case of structural blending which involves both inherent and non-inherent schemas working in parallel. The marginal/peripheral variety of Albanian compounding concerning coordinative compounds, linking element -*o*-, (de)verbal compounds, headedness of one-word compounds and exocentricity of adjectival compounds could possibly be interpreted as a result of language contact with Greek. Specifically, each prototypical/inherent structure is connected to a non-inherent Greek-based structure which is marginal/peripheral. Calquing is a highly possible 'path' for influence from Greek, due to historical and political reasons associated with language contact, Albanian bilingualism and the role of Greek as the language of culture and science in the Balkan *Sprachbund*.

1 Aim of the chapter[1]

It is common knowledge that languages possess morphological schemas – not only inherent schemas, but also non-inherent ones, generated through analogy and borrowing (see Scalise and Vogel 2010, among others). Contrastive morphological analysis usually focuses on identifying both categories. The 'contrastive game' seems to follow one fundamental tendency: Canonization involves inherency, whereas marginality/peripherality is derived from analogy or borrowing. Furthermore, language contact may lead to morphological and structural borrowing (see, among others, McMahon 1994; Thomason and Kaufman 1988; Thomason 2001; for Greek, Ralli 2016). For instance, although the characteristics of compounding are fixed and language-dependent – for example, there is a canonical position of the head depending on the language – it is possible that compounding has been influenced by other languages and thus has developed new construction schemas (see Scalise and Fábregas 2010, among others).

Against this theoretical background, the aim of the chapter is to compare Greek and Albanian compounding in order to show the structural, categorical and segmental differences, similarities and correspondences, which may lead to a hypothesis of influence between them as a result of language contact. In fact, we will prove that Albanian compounding is a case of structural blending which involves both inherent and non-inherent schemas working in parallel, and we will interpret the marginal variety of Albanian compounding as a result of language contact with the Greek language. The research is restricted to five cases:

1. Coordinative compounds
2. Linking element -*o*-
3. (De)verbal compounds
4. Headedness of one-word compounds
5. Headedness and exocentricity of adjectival compounds.

2 Methodology

The material involves 100 Greek and Albanian compounds, which have been collected from dictionaries, grammars and linguistic research. We should note that the collection of Albanian compounds is a 'fuzzy' process. The sources are usually contradictory, many words are not confirmed as substantial/actual/frequent by native speakers and etymology is not adequate. An additional research problem of both languages involves the low incorporation of compounds in dictionaries.

Furthermore, the morphological analysis of compounding relies on modern linguistic theory. Greek and Albanian compounding have been sufficiently analysed (for Greek, see Anastassiadis-Symeonidis 1983, 1986, 1996; Ralli 1992, 2013b; Revithiadou 1997; for Albanian, see Newmark, Hubbard and Prifti 1982; Campbell 2000; Revithiadou and Spyropoulos 2013) and a continuum-based contrastive analysis of Greek and Albanian compounding has been proposed by Fliatouras (forthcoming) which serves as a tool for identifying the similarities and differences between the two languages (see Section 4 for more details).

3 Parameters of proximity and differentiation

The similarities between the Albanian and Greek language can be attributed to three major parameters: (a) universal tendencies, (b) inherent/endogenous proximity, as they share structural and morphological characteristics of their common Indo-European origin[2] and (c) external/exogenous proximity due to 'strong' language contact. The latter parameter is justified by their participation in the Balkan *Sprachbund* (see, among others, Sandfeld 1930; Hock 1986; Joseph 1999; Hock and Joseph 2009), geographical proximity, co-existence of populations and cultural/historical interaction and, finally, by the immigration of populations from Albania to Greece throughout history (Medieval period, Ottoman Greece, recent decades), a historical fact that explains the bilingualism of many Albanians.

On the other hand, differentiation is connected to endogenous and exogenous factors. The endogenous parameters involve mostly structural divergence; for example, the Albanian language has a postponed article and two additional cases (dative, ablative). The exogenous parameters refer to both different cases of language contact – for example, the Albanian language has been structurally influenced by Romance and Slavic languages (see Orel 2000) – and the different extent of diachrony – for example, the Greek language has a more extended history which 'feeds' synchrony with a lexicological and structural substratum (see Anastassiadis-Symeonidis and Fliatouras 2004, 2018). Specifically, there is a peripheral[3] type of compounding found in Modern Greek, the so-called learned compounding, which involves compounds or constituents inherited from Ancient Greek or compounds constructed according to Ancient Greek construction patterns (for more details, see Anastassiadis-Symeonidis 1996; Ralli 2005). Most learned compounds are lexicalized and morpho-semantically non-transparent to average speakers of Modern Greek. Many learned compound elements belong to *confixes*, namely productive stem-based affixoids of terminology (for Greek, see, among others, Anastassiadis-Symeonidis 1986; Giannoulopoulou 1999).

4 Albanian versus Greek compounding: how similar or how different?

We will compare Greek and Albanian compounding as far as their basic characteristics, such as headedness, internal structure and categorization are concerned. We will focus on cases of double-structured categories which comprise a prototypical and a marginal/peripheral[4] structure and could possibly involve both an inherent and a non-inherent schema of compounding, respectively. The non-inherent schema may be explained via influence from one language to another. Moreover, such a contrast will lead to conclusions concerning the hypothesis of structural blending. The contrastive process will be Albanian-driven, as the most possible donor language is Greek due to sociolinguistic and historical reasons: Greek, besides being the majority contact language, is also the 'prestigious language' in the Balkan *Sprachbund*, as well as in the generation of terminology (for a plethora of loanwords, see Kyriazis 2001).

4.1 Construction template

Scalise and Vogel (2010: 4–5) show that there is no agreement on whether a compound is formed in morphology or syntax. Along the lines of the morphology-syntax interface, Ralli (2013a,b) shows that on the basis of their structural properties, compounds can be distinguished into two categories, depending on the language one deals with and the data used for illustrating various working hypotheses: (a) Morphological constructions: compounds resulting from morphological rules or templates and as such, sharing properties with other morphological objects, for example, derived words (see also Booij 2010) and (b) Syntactic constructions: phrasal compounds, which are derived from syntax but their structure is semi-visible to syntax and their meaning may be non-compositional (see also Ralli and Stavrou 1998). In particular, both languages bear one-word ((1)a) and phrasal compounds ((1)b):[5]

(1)a One-word compounds: Gr *κουκλόσπιτο < κούκλα + σπίτι*
                  (doll house)   (doll)   (house)
            Al *vajgúri*[6]   < *váj*   *gúri*
              (petroleum) (oil)   (rock)

(1)b Phrasal compounds: Gr *τρίτος κόσμος < τρίτος + κόσμος*
                (third world) (third) (world)
           Al *lúftë e ftóhtë* < *lúftë* + *e ftóhtë*
             (cold war)   (war)   (cold)

In fact, the same phonological, morphological, semantic and syntactic criteria apply to both categories, which account for the processes (for Greek, see Anastassiadis-Symeonidis 1986; Ralli 1992, 2013a; Gavriilidou 1997; Revithiadou 1997; Koliopoulou 2009). Specifically, one-word compounds bear one basic stress and a possible secondary stress in the first syllable (for Albanian, see Revithiadou and Spyropoulos 2013) and they show lexical integrity/word atomicity, absence of word-internal atomicity, presence of morphological categories, involvement of functional categories and strict order of constituents, for example, Gr *πατατοκεφτές* (*pàtatokeftés*) (croquette with potato) versus Al *krÿeqytét* (capital of country). On the other hand, the phrasal compounds show non-visibility to most syntactic operations, such as inversion of constituents ((2)a), ability of the non-head to become definite ((2)b), separate modifiability or coordination ((2)c) as well as semantic noncompositionality, namely idiosyncratic and opaque meaning (metaphoric etc.) which cannot be predicted by the meaning of the constituents:

(2)a Gr **πόλεμος ψυχρός, *ασφαλείας ζώνη* versus *ψυχρός πόλεμος, ζώνη ασφαλείας*
     war   cold   safe   belt   cold   war   belt safe
                               (cold war)   (safe-belt)
    Al **e ftohtë luftë,*   **sigurimi rrip* versus *luftë e ftohtë, rrip sigurimi*
     cold   war   safe   belt   war cold   belt safe
                              (cold war)   (safe-belt)

(2)b Gr **o   πόλεμος είναι ψυχρός* versus *είναι o ψυχρός   πόλεμος*
     the war   is   cold   is   the cold   war
                   (it is the cold war)
    Al **luftë është e*   *ftohtë* versus *është luftë e*   *ftohtë*
     war is   the.FEM cold   is   war   the.FEM cold
                   (it is the cold war)

(2)c Gr **ψυχρός και μεγάλος πόλεμος* versus *μεγάλος ψυχρός πόλεμος*
     cold   and big   war   big   cold   war
                   (big cold war)

4.2 Internal structure

The constituents of compounds comprise stems and words. The criteria to determine their morphological hypostasis in languages with rich inflection and stress rules variation (mainly of the second constituent) such as Albanian and Greek, are both phonological and morphological. Words are free non-inflected lexemes (adverbs etc.) or fully inflected nouns/adjectives/verbs, which preserve their stress, whereas stems are independent from the external inflection and stress of the compounds (for Greek, see Ralli 1992, 2013b). For example, in Greek, the compound *παλιόσπιτ(o)* (bad house) is [Stem + Stem], whereas the equivalent compound *παλιοσπίτι* (bad house) is [Stem + Word]. In the former, the inflection and stress of the second constituent is different from the inflection and stress of the compound, whereas in the latter, the second constituent *σπίτι* (house) preserves both its inflection and stress.

Greek one-word compounds are mostly stem-based. The first constituent is usually stem, whereas the second constituent may be either stem or word (see Ralli 1992, 2013b). There are four combinations identified. The most productive structures, though, are [Stem + Stem] and [Stem + Word]:

(3)a Stem + Stem: *κουκλόσπιτ(o)* (doll house) < *κούκλ(α)* (doll) + *σπίτι* (house)

(3)b Stem + Word: *τυροσαλάτα* (cheese salad) < *τυρ(ί)* (cheese) + *σαλάτα* (salad)

(3)c Word + Stem: *πανωσέντον(o)* (top sheet) < *πάνω* (top)   + *σεντόνι* (sheet)

(3)d Word + Word: *ξαναγράφω* (write again) < *ξανά* (again) + *γράφω* (write)

On the other hand, Albanian compounding is mostly word-based (see also Revithiadou and Spyropoulos 2013). The second constituent is usually word ((4)a, (4)b) and the structures [Stem + Stem] and [Word + Stem] are non-productive and can be found especially in parasynthetic structures ((4)c):

(4)a Stem + Word: *hekurudhë* (railway) < *hekur* (rail) + *udhë* (way)

(4)b Word + Word: *bashkë-bisedim* (conversation) < *bashkë* (con-) + *bidesim* (speech)

(4)c Stem/Word + Stem: *dyrrokësh-e* (two-syllable) < *dy* (two) + *rrok(je)* (syllable) + *-ësh*SUF (cf. **rrokësh-e*)

Furthermore, in both languages, the structure [Inflected Word + Word] is rare. In Greek, it is associated with learned compounding, as it consists of fossils from Ancient Greek where the pattern was more productive or of words generated through analogical patterns from Ancient Greek (see Ralli 1992, 2013b). In Albanian, the inflected word is mostly plural and involves exceptional plurals via root allomorphy:[7]

(5)a Gr *νουνεχής* (prudent) < *νουν* (mind) [accusative] + *εχ-* (have) + *-ή*SUF + -ç INF

(5)b Al *duar-trokitje* (applause) < *duar* (hands) [plural] + *trokitje* (beating)

As far as the internal structure of phrasal compounds is concerned, some structural differences can be identified between the two languages. Specifically, the order of constituents in attributive adjectival compounds is reversed, namely [A + N] in Modern Greek and [N + A] in Albanian ((6)a). Furthermore, the category of [N + N] attributive compounds is common for both languages, even though the case is different: genitive in Greek and ablative in Albanian ((6)b). The case functions as a complement which denotes various semantic roles (possession, use, goal etc.).[8] The difference of case selection can be explained by the fact that the ablative is not one of the cases of Modern Greek. The [N + N] coordinative compounds are common in both languages ((6)c) and do not seem to show any difference in structure:

(6)a Gr A + N: *ψυχρός πόλεμος*   versus   Al N + A: *luftë   e ftohtë*
         cold   war   war   cold
         (cold war)   (cold war)

(6)b Gr N + N(GEN): *ζώνη ασφαλείας*   versus   Al N + N(ABL): *rrip   sigurimi*
                  belt   safe.GEN   belt   safe.ABL
                  (safe-belt)   (safe-belt)

(6)c Gr N + N: *νόμος-πλαίσιο*   versus   Al N + N: *inxhinjer-mekanik*
         law   frame   engineer mechanic
         (law-frame)   (engineer-mechanic)

Finally, it is possible that artificial compounds may be found in both languages, generated by lexicalization processes. In particular, lexicalization leads to agglutination and conversion of phrases into phonological words with one primary stress:

(7)a Gr *καλή μέρα* [*καλή* (good) + *μέρα* (day)] > *καλημέρα* (good morning)

(7)b Al *lule lakër* [*lule* (flower) + *lakër* (grass)] > *lulelakër* (cauliflower)

4.3 Linking elements

Compounding is crosslinguistically prone to linking elements, mainly vowels, between the constituents. These elements serve as phonological segments which allow the connection of the constituents according to the phonotactic constraints, and/or constitute morphological segments, namely compound markers (see Ralli 2008a).

Both languages use linking elements in compounding. In Modern Greek, the basic linking element is -*o*-[9] (Anastassiadis-Symeonidis 1983; Ralli 1992) which is a systematic compound marker (Ralli 2007, 2008a, 2013b) ((8)a) and can be optionally omitted in cases of vowel sequence (see Nikolou 2003) ((8)b):

(8)a *τυρ-ο-σαλάτα* (cheese salad)

(8)b *παλι-ο-άνθρωπος* versus *παλιάνθρωπος* (bad man)

In Albanian, it is possible to find linking elements, such as *-o-* and *-a-* (Newmark, Hubbard and Prifti 1982; Revithiadou and Spyropoulos 2013). They should not be treated, however, as compound markers, since:

1. They are sporadic, not systematic, and in many cases optional: *gusht(o)vjeshtë* (July and August).
2. They are basically phonologically driven, as they are epenthetic vowels in consonant clusters (mostly two-part and three-part clusters with *-sh-*) in order to satisfy phonological constraints or phonotactic restrictions: *dash-a-keq* (bad-wisher).
3. They are not added in cases of vowel sequence since the last vowel of the first constituent is omitted: **vetëadministrim → vetadministrim* (self-administration).

4.4 Categorical structures

One-word compounds of both languages have more or less the same categorical structures (for Greek, see Ralli 1992, 2007, 2013b; Anastassiadis-Symeonidis 1996; for Albanian, see Newmark, Hubbard and Prifti 1982; Campbell 2000; Revithiadou and Spyropoulos 2013). Only some difference in productivity, however, may be properly identified (see Section 5). Table 7.1 shows clearly the similar categorical structures.

We should note, though, that the Albanian language does not have V + V compounds (verbal coordinative compounds), in contrast to the Greek language, for

Table 7.1 Contrastive Categorical Structures

N + N > N:	Gr *πευκοδάσος* (pine forest)	<	*πεύκο* (pine) + *δάσος* (forest)
	Al *bregdet* (coastline)	<	*breg* (coast) + *det* (sea)
A + A > A:	Gr *ασπρόμαυρος* (black and white)	<	*άσπρος* (white) + *μαύρος* (black)
	Al *bardhëzi* (white and black)	<	(*i*) *bardhë* (white) + (*i*) *zi* (black)
N + N > A	Gr *γουρουνοκέφαλος* (pig-headed)	<	*γουρούνι* (pig) + *κεφάλι* (head)
	Al *kokëderr* (headstrong)	<	*kokë* (head) + *derr* (pig)
ADV + V > V	Gr *καλοβλέπω* (see well)	<	*καλά* (well) + *βλέπω* (see)
	Al *keqkuptoj* (misunderstand)	<	*keq* (bad) + *kuptoj* (understand)
ADV + N > N	Gr *ξαναγράψιμο* (writing again)	<	*ξανά* (again) + *γράψιμο* (writing)
	Al *bashkëbisedim* (conversation)	<	*bashkë* (con-) + *bisedim* (speech)
PRO + N > N:	Gr *αλλόγλωσσος* (non-native speaker)	<	*άλλος* (other) + *γλώσσα* (language)
	Al *vetëmbrojtje* (self-defense)	<	*vetë* (self) + *mbrojtje* (defense)

example, Gr μπαινοβγαίνω (come in and out) < μπαίν(ω) (come in) + βγαίνω (come out).[10] Furthermore, the structure of adjectival compounds is reversible, namely [A + N] in Greek ((9)a) and [N + A] in Albanian ((9)b):

(9)a Gr A + N > A: ασπρομάλλης (white-haired) < άσπρος (white) + μαλλί (hair)

(9)b Al N + A > A: *flokbardhë* (white-haired) < *flok* (hair) + *bardhë* (white)

Furthermore, both languages show the same distribution between structures and semantic/syntactic relation of constituents following mostly universal tendencies: [A + N] compounds are attributive, one-word compounds with constituents of the same grammatical and semantic category are coordinative and all other types of compounds are head-complement. The differences between the two languages solely involve productivity. Specifically, in Albanian, attributive compounds are less productive and the coordinative compounds are non-productive (Revithiadou and Spyropoulos 2013). For example, the semantic categories that are prototypically coordinative compounds in Greek usually correspond to syntactic phrases 'X and Z' in Albanian (see Fliatouras forthcoming):

(10)a Colours: Gr ασπρόμαυρος versus Al *bardhë e zi* (white and black)

(10)b Origin: Gr Ισπανοϊταλός versus Al *Spanjoll dhe Italjan* (Hispanian and Italian)

(10)c Energies: Gr τρωγοπίνω versus Al *ha dhe pi* (eat and drink)

(10)d Tastes: Gr γλυκόξινος versus Al *i embël dhe i thart* (sweet and crabbed)

(10)e Dimensions: Gr μακρόστενος versus Al *i gjatë dhe i ngusthë* (long and narrow)

(10)f Food: Gr λαδόξιδο versus Al *vaj e uthull* (oil and vinegar)

4.5 Headedness

Head is the constituent which is responsible for the morphological characteristics of compounds (grammatical category, gender etc.); for example, in the Greek [A + N] compound ασπρόρουχα (linens), the head is ρούχα (clothes), as the grammatical category (noun), the gender (neuter) and the number (plural) percolate from the second constituent (see Scalise 1992, among others). In cases of ambiguity, for example, in many [N + N] compounds, headedness is defined by semantic criteria, such as hyponymity, pragmatic factors (see Ralli 2013b; Andreou 2014, among others). For example, in the Greek compound τυροσαλάτα (cheese salad), the semantic head σαλάτα (salad) equalizes with the morphological head, whereas the complement τυρί (cheese) of σαλάτα is the non-head. Headedness determines exo- and endocentricity: in endocentric compounds, the head is located inside the compound structure, as we show in the Greek compounds ασπρόρουχα and τυροσαλάτα above, whereas in exocentric compounds, the head is located out of the compound structure; for example, the head of the Greek adjectival [A + N] compound κοκκινομάλλ-η-ς (red-haired) is the adjectival suffix *-η* which is attached to the noun compound stem *κοκκινομαλλ-* (red hair) (see Ralli 2013b).

Greek compounding is prototypically right-headed, since it is mainly right-headed in one-word compounds (Ralli 2007, 2013b) and phrasal [A + N] compounds ((11)a) and left-headed in phrasal [N + N] compounds ((11)b):

(11)a Gr *χαρτοπαίζω*V (play cards) < *χαρτ(ιά)*N (cards) + *παίζω*V (play).
         Gr *τρίτος κόσμος*N (third world) < *τρίτος*ADJ (third) + *κόσμος*N (world)

(11)b Gr *ζώνη ασφαλείας* < *ζώνη*N (belt) + *ασφαλείας*N.GEN (safe)
         Gr *νόμος-πλαίσιο*N (law frame) < *νόμος*N (law) + *πλαίσιο*N (frame)

On the other hand, Albanian compounding is prototypically left-headed, as it is mainly left-headed in most categories of one-word and phrasal compounds (12)a with the exception of adjectival compounds which are right-headed (12)b:

(12)a Al *vargmal*N (mountain range) < *varg*N (range) + *mal*N (mountain)
         Al *luftë e ftohtë*N (cold war) < *luftë*N (war) + *ftohtë*ADJ (cold)

(12)b Al *flokbardhë*A (white-haired) < *flok*N (hair) + *bardhë*A (white)

Furthermore, Albanian has fewer exocentric compounds than the Greek language. This can be justified by the following parameters:

1. The productive structure of adjectival compounds A + N A in Greek is endocentric in Albanian, since the adjective in the right position is the head of the structure:

(13)a Gr A + N > A: *ασπρομάλλης* (white-haired) < *άσπρος* (white) + *μαλλί* (hair)

(13)b Al N + A > A: *flokbardhë* (white-haired) < *flok* (hair) + *bardhë* (white)

2. The structure N + N A is not so productive in the Albanian language (Revithiadou and Spyropoulos 2013):

(14)   Al *kokëderr* (pig-headed) < *kokë* (head) + *derr* (pig)

3. The deverbal adjectival compounds with structure V + N/A N/A are rare in both languages and belong to a marginal category (for Greek, see Ralli 2013b; Andreou 2014):

(15)a Gr *χασοδίκης* (one who loses the trial) < *χασ-* (lose) + *δίκ(η)* (trial)

(15)b Al *daskakeq* (bad-wisher) < *dash-* (wish) + *keq* (bad)

4. The adjectival compounds with verbal bound stem as a second constituent are very rare in the Albanian language. In Modern Greek, they are mostly productive in learned compounding:[11]

(16)   Gr *-βόρος* versus Al *-pirës*: *αιμοβόρος* versus *gjakpirës* (blood-thirsty)

4.6 (De)verbal compounds

(De)verbal head-complement compounds with internal theta-role saturation[12] are productive in both languages. The vast majority have internal structure [Stem + Word], categorical structure [N/A N(<V)]N and they are endocentric (for Greek, see Ralli 1992, 2013b; for Albanian, Revithiadou and Spyropoulos 2013):

(17)a Gr *κατσικοκλέφτης* (goat-thief) < *κατσίκ(ι)* (goat) + *κλέφτης* (thief)

(17)b Al *bukëbërës* (bread-maker) < *bukë* (bread) + *bërës* (maker)

Verbal head-complement compounds with structure [ADV/N V]V and coordinative [V V] compounds are not productive in the Albanian language, which is characterized by syntactic structures:

(18)a Gr *χαρτοπαίζω* versus Al *luaj me letra* (play with cards)

(18)b Gr *αδικοχαμένος* versus Al *i shkuar dëm* (die prematurately)

Compounds with verbal bound stems are not productive in the Albanian language, since the second constituent is usually an actual deverbal word. In Modern Greek, it is associated with learned compounding:

(19)a Gr *ωρολογοποιός* (watch-maker) < *ωρολόγ(ιον)* (watch) + *-ποιός* (maker)

(19)b Al *orëndreqës* (watch-maker) < *orë* (watch) + *ndreqës* (maker)

4.7 Conclusions of contrast

An overview of the comparison between Greek and Albanian compounding shall lead to the conclusion that they are two distinct compound systems, as illustrated in Table 7.2. Furthermore, we may conclude that Albanian compounding bears a closer resemblance to Romance compounding, such as French, Italian, Spanish and so on (see, among others, Zwanenburg 1992; Scalise 1992; Rainer and Varela 1992; Giannoulopoulou 2015) and it is possibly part of the Romance compounding group, as it seems to share basic structural characteristics (left-headedness, word-based structures, absence or non-productivity of (de)verbal compounds etc.).

5 Language contact?

If we look closer at the contrastive data between the two languages, we will discover an intriguing clue for further discussion: apart from prototypical tendencies and structures, there seems to be plenty of marginal/peripheral compounds in Albanian that are totally different in structure and resemble to Greek compounding. As a result, it may be possible to interpret these similarities under the scope of language contact

Table 7.2 Structural Differences between Greek and Albanian Compounding

Greek	Albanian
stem-based	word-based
right-headed	left-headed
compound marker	sporadic linking elements
more coordinative/attributive	less coordinative/attributive
more (de)verbal compounds	fewer verbal compounds
more exocentric	more endocentric
bound stems	no bound stems

influence which leads to structural borrowing and, consequently, to structural blending in Albanian compounding.

Fliatouras (forthcoming) has proposed an eight-stage continuum of proximity between Greek and Albanian compounds based on structural, categorical and semantic criteria, as illustrated in Table 7.3. Furthermore, he shows that proximity is systematic, since specific categories of compounds apply to the same level and most categories (especially the marginal/exceptional ones) apply to the higher levels of proximity. This conclusion strengthens the suspicion that there may be a kind of word-borrowing from Greek to Albanian compounding.

Consequently, additional data will show that there is not only borrowing of lexical units, but also some kind of structural influence from Greek compounding due to word-borrowing. Once more, our analysis will heavily rely on the above continuum:

1. We start with the linking vowel *-o-* which is mostly found in southern Albania and/or in a huge group of Greek loans (see Kyriazis 2001), either direct or calques (20)a and Greek-originated internationalisms in scientific terminology[13] (20)b:

(20)a Al *stenohori* < Gr στενοχώρια (worry)

(20)b Al *hipn-o-terapi* < Gr υπνοθεραπεία (hypnotherapy)

As a result, it is possible that *-o-* is a loan linking element from Greek compounding, which begins with lexical loans, for example, Al *stavr-o-drom* < Gr σταυρ-ο-δρόμι (cross-road), and expands to Albanian structures Al *gusht-o-vjeshtë* (July and August).

2. Coordinative one-word compounds are productive only in Level 1 ((21)a) and Level 2 of proximity. The latter involves words that belong to specific lexical categories, for example, wind directions ((21)b), or marginal morphological constructions which compete with syntactic phrases ((21)c):

(21)a Gr Αγγλοαμερικάνος versus Al *Anglo-amerikan* (English-American)

(21)b Gr βορειοανατολικός versus Al *verilindor* (northwestern)

(21)c Gr ασπρόμαυρος versus Al *bardhëzi* (white and black) (cf. also *bardhë e zi*)

Table 7.3 Continuum of Proximity between Albanian and Greek Compounds

Level 1:	totally the same (direct loans)
Level 2:	+constituents, +meaning, +categorical structure
Level 3:	+constituents, +meaning, +categorical structure, -order of constituents
Level 4:	+constituents, +meaning, +categorical structure, -construction template
Level 5:	+constituents, +meaning, -categorical structure, -construction template
Level 6:	+constituents, +meaning, -lexical integrity
Level 7:	+constituents, +/-structure, -meaning
Level 8:	-compounds (non-correspondence)

Source: Fliatouras (forthcoming).

As a result, most coordinative compounds could be interpreted as either, direct loans (Level 1) or calques (Level 2) from the Greek language; it is equally possible that coordination is either a loan or an expanded structure from Greek compounding, where it is more prototypical, in contrast to other Indo-European languages.

3. Non-coordinative [N + N] compounds are prototypically left-headed, since the semantic head is on the left:

(22)a Al *vargmal* (mountain range) < *varg* (range) + *mal* (mountain)

(22)b Al *fjalëkryq* (crossword) < *fjalë* (word) + *kryq* (cross)

However, there are some exceptional cases of right-headed compounds, which apply to Level 2 of proximity (+constituents, +structure):

(23)a Gr *σιδηρόδρομος* (railway) < *σίδηρ(ος)* (iron) + *δρόμος* (way)

(23)b Al *hekurudhë* (railway) < *hekur* (iron) + *udhë* (way)

Taking into account that the inherent schema is left-headed, we could suppose again that the right-headed compounds are calques from the Greek language and that right-headedness in this category is a loan structure from Greek compounding, which constitutes an analogical pattern in parallel to the prototypical one.

4. As we show in Section 4.5, the attributive adjectival compounds correspond systematically to Level 3 (+constituents, -constituent order), namely, they are reversible structures: Greek adjectival compounds are exocentric [A N]A structures and suffix-headed (full or zero affixation) ((24)a), whereas the Albanian adjectival compounds are endocentric [N A]A structures and right-headed ((24)b):

(24)a Gr *κοκκινομάλλ-η-ς* (red-haired) < *κόκκιν(ο)* (red) +*μαλλ(ί)* (hair) + -*η*SUF + -*ç*INF

(24)b Al *flokbardhë* (white-haired) < *flok* (hair) + *bardhë* (white)

There is, however, a category of exocentric suffix-headed adjectival compounds with structure [PRE/AD/A N]A, which apply to Level 2 (+constituents, +structure):

(25)a Gr *πολύχρωμ-ø-ος* < *πολύ* (much) + *χρώμ(α)* (colour) + *-ø*SUF + *-ος*INF

(25)b Al *shumëngjyrshëm* < *shumë* (much) + *ngjur(ë)* (colour) + *-shëm*SUF

The prototypical endocentric structure in (24)b resembles Romance compounding and it is either an inherent structure or a loan structure from Romance languages, since it is contrary to the left-headedness tendency. The marginal exocentric structure in (25)a, b is possibly a loan structure from Greek compounding, possibly via calques, as it is contrary both to the endocentricity of adjectival compounds and to the left-headedness tendency.

5. Verbal compounds are non-productive in Albanian. There is, however, a marginal category of rare verbal compounds with [ADV/N V] structure, which applies to Level 2 (+structure, +constituents) of proximity. They represent a more stylistic and/or formal register, they cannot be found in all dictionaries[14] and, very often, native speakers are not acquainted with them:

(26)a Gr *κακομεταχειρίζομαι* (handle badly) < *κακ(ά)* (badly) + *μεταχειρίζομαι* (handle)

(26)b Al *keqbërdor* (behave badly) < *keq* (badly) + *bërdor* (handle)

In this case, a similar conclusion could be drawn: verbal compounds are calques from the Greek language and the schema is probably a loan structure from Greek as well.[15]

To sum up, the Albanian language seems to bear a parallel template of compound formation or a group of compounds that are possibly influenced or borrowed by Greek compounding. Each prototypical/inherent structure is connected to a non-inherent Greek-based structure which is marginal/peripheral. The criteria to determine such borrowing are mainly structural (e.g. headedness and categorial structure). That 'reflecting' prototypical-marginal picture allows us to suppose that Albanian compounding is a case of structural blending.

Furthermore, the etymology of Albanian compounds sheds more light on the possible explanation of language contact. For example, calquing is a highly possible 'path' for influence from Greek compounding. It must be noted that if we compare the compounds of older and newer Albanian dictionaries, we will find out that there are more left-headed compounds in older dictionaries and a huge group of right-headed neologisms in recent dictionaries which correspond to Level 1 and 2 of proximity and, in many cases, are explained as calques. The Albanian language tends to borrow Greek words as calques due to historical and political reasons associated with language contact, the Albanians' bilingualism and the role of Greek as the language of culture and science in the Balkan *Sprachbund* (for more details, see Krimpas 2007, 2017). The Greek words are either inherent or calques from some European languages, which means that many Albanian calques originate from European languages via the Greek language. The morphological structure is, again, indicative of such a conclusion. For example, if we suppose that the Albanian *hekurudhë* (railway) is a calque from French *chemin de fer*, then it should be adapted to the prototypical left-headed structure as **udhëhekur*. It is obvious that the Albanian *hekurudhë* copies the right-headed structure of the Greek compound *σιδηρόδρομος*, which is a French- or Italian-originated calque in Modern Greek.

6 Conclusions

The inherent Albanian compounding seems to be closer to Romance compounding, which is prototypically left-headed in most categories of compounds and right-headed in adjectival [N A] compounds. Right-headedness is indicative of non-inherent compounding structures in the Albanian language and supports the idea that structural variety, namely variety of headedness, is indicative of word or structural borrowing (see Scalise and Fabrégas 2010 for Italian).

Albanian compounding shows structural blending as a result of language contact mainly with the Greek language. The basic criteria by which influence from Greek can be traced are headedness and the semantic/syntactic relation of the constituents and the basic path of structural borrowing are calques. Specifically, the linking vowel -*o*-, the one-word coordinative compounds, the verbal compounds and right-headed [N N] compounds are loan or expanded structures from Greek compounding, which work in parallel with the inherent elements/structures. The adjectival endocentric compounds are either an inherent structure or a loan structure from Romance languages. The vast majority of calques from Greek tend to be structurally adapted to the Albanian compounding system as far as left-headedness is concerned. There is a category of calques, though, which preserve their structure from the Greek language.

Finally, the etymology of Albanian compounds is a key point that we should take into consideration for further research. Etymological data should be extracted from research and dictionaries, not only in order to support the structure-based suspicion for structural borrowing due to calquing, but also to provide a more efficient, case-by-case and glottochronological interpretation.

Notes

1 I would like to give many thanks to Christopher Lees and Lena Kontakou-Pavlidis for their proof-reading.
2 We should note that this parameter is only a possible explanation and mainly involves the languages of the same 'branch' and perhaps some universal Indo-European tendencies. For example, Greek compounding is totally different from the compounding observed in Romance languages. In the case examined in this chapter, the Indo-European theory cannot be used as an explanation for similarities between Greek and Albanian. It is possible, though, that the similarities between Albanian and Romance languages (see Section 4) could be explained under this scope.

3 Learned compounding usually represents the high register.
4 Henceforth marginal/peripheral compounding refers to units and structures which do not represent the norm of language. They are not productive or frequent and they involve either dialectal/colloquial or mainly formal elements such as terminology or compounds that are used or recognized only by bilinguals (Greek and Albanian speakers).
5 We should note that majority of Greek and Albanian phrasal compounds are calques from European languages, since they refer to terminology and so on. Furthermore, the generation template of phrasal compounds seems to be artificial (maybe loaned) and not productive for both languages, especially as far as inherent multi-word items are concerned. Despite the fact that there is no direct structural influence identified from the Greek language, the contrast between Greek and Albanian phrasal compounding serves only theoretical purposes.
6 Henceforth the Albanian nouns will be presented with their postponed article.
7 The prototypical plurals in Albanian are constructed only by plural inflection, for example, *lul-e*INF (flower), *lul-e*INF (flowers).
8 For more information see Anastassiadis-Symeonidis (1986).
9 Cf. also the learned and less frequent linking element -ι-, for example ταξ-ι-θέτης (usher).
10 As Ralli (2009) has shown, this is an innovative category in the history of the Indo-European languages which is not productive.
11 There are many bound stems in Modern Greek which are of Ancient Greek origin and are not easily connected to verbal lexemes in synchrony, for example -φόρος (who carries/bears < AG φέρω (carry/bear). For more information see Ralli (2008b).
12 In (de)verbal compounds the first constituent is the complement of the verbal element of the second constituent and represents the semantic/syntactic role of object, subject, goal and so on; for example, in Greek χαρτοπαίζω (play cards) the first constituent χαρτ(ιά) (cards) is the object of the verb παίζω (play). For more information see Di Sciullo and Ralli (1999).
13 This category involves mostly the so-called neoclassical compounds.
14 They are neologisms, namely words constructed during the last decades.
15 We should note that the verbal compounds in Greek constitute an analogical diachronic innovation (Ralli 2009).

Abbreviations

A   adjective
ABL   ablative
ADV   adverb
AG   Ancient Greek
Al   Albanian
FEM   feminine
GEN   genitive
Gr   Greek
INF   inflection
N   noun
PRP   pronoun
SUF   suffix
V   verb

References

Anastassiadis-Syméonidis, A. (1983), 'La Composition en Grec Moderne d'un Point de Vue Diachronique', *Lalies*, 2: 77–90.

Anastassiadis-Symeonidis, A. (1986), *Η Νεολογία στην Κοινή Νεοελληνική* (*The Neology in Standard Greek*) [in Greek], Thessaloniki: Annual of the Faculty of Philosophy of the Aristotle University of Thessaloniki 65.

Anastassiadis-Symeonidis, A. (1996), 'Η Νεοελληνική Σύνθεση' ('The Modern Greek Compounding') [in Greek], in G. Katsimalis and F. Kavoukopoulos (eds), *Ζητήματα Νεοελληνικής Γλώσσας: Διδακτική Προσέγγιση* (*Aspects of Modern Greek Language: A Teaching Approach*), 97–120, Rethymno: University of Crete.

Anastassiadis-Symeonidis, A. and A. Fliatouras (2004), 'Η Διάκριση *Λόγιο* και *Λαϊκό* στην Ελληνική Γλώσσα: Ορισμός και Ταξινόμηση' ('The Distinction *Learned* and *Colloquial* in Modern Greek: Definition and Classification') [in Greek], *Proceedings of the 6th International Conference on Greek Linguistics* (ICGL6), Rethymno: Department of Philology of the University of Crete. Available online: www.philology.uoc.gr/conferences/6thICGL/gr.htm (accessed 30 May 2018).

Anastassiadis-Symeonidis, A. and A. Fliatouras (2018), 'Από το Λόγιο Επίπεδο της Νέας Ελληνικής στην Αρχαία Ελληνική: Εφαρμογή και Διδακτικές Προοπτικές' ('From the Learned Register of Modern Greek to Ancient Greek: Research Proposals and Educational Perspectives') [in Greek], *Studies in Greek Linguistics*, 38: 37–50. Available online: http://ins.web.auth.gr/images/MEG_PLIRI/MEG_38_37_50.pdf (accessed 30 May 2018).

Andreou, M. (2014), 'Headedness in Word Formation and Lexical Semantics: Evidence from Italiot and Cypriot', PhD Diss., University of Patras, Greece.

Booij, G. (2010), *Construction Morphology*, Oxford: Oxford University Press.

Campbell, G. L. (2000), 'Albanian', in G. Campbell (ed.), *Compendium of the World's Languages, Vol.1: Abaza to Kurdish*, 2nd edn, 50–7, London: Routledge.

Di Sciullo, A. M. and A. Ralli (1999), 'Theta-role Saturation in Greek Deverbal Compounds', in A. Alexiadou, G. Horrocks and M. Stavrou (eds), *Studies in Greek Syntax*, 185–200, Amsterdam: Kluwer.

Fliatouras, A. (Forthcoming), 'Η Συγκριτική Ανάλυση της Ελληνικής και της Αλβανικής Σύνθεσης ως Μέσο Διδασκαλίας της Ελληνικής ως Δεύτερης/Ξένης' ('The Contrastive Analysis of Greek and Albanian Compounding as a Means of Teaching Greek as a Second/Foreign Language') [in Greek], *Proceedings of the International Conference on The Greek Language in Black Sea and the Balkans*, Komotini: DUTh.

Gavriilidou, Z. (1997), *Etude Comparée des Suites NN en Français et en Grec. Elaboration d'un Lexique Bilingue*, Lille: Presses Universitaires du Septentrion.

Giannoulopoulou, G. (1999), 'Μορφοσημασιολογική Σύγκριση Παραθημάτων και Συμφυμάτων στην Ελληνική και την Ιταλική' ('Morphosemantic Comparison of Affixes and Confixes between Greek and Italian') [in Greek], PhD diss., Aristotle University of Thessaloniki, Greece.

Giannoulopoulou, G. (2015), 'Morphological Contrasts between Modern Greek and Italian: The Case of Compounding', *Languages in Contrast*, 15 (1): 65–80.

Hock, H. (1986), *Principles of Historical Linguistics*, Berlin: Mouton de Gruyter.

Hock, H. and B. D. Joseph (2009), *Language History, Language Change and Language Relationship: An Introduction to Historical and Comparative Linguistics*, 2nd revised edn, Berlin: Mouton de Gruyter.

Joseph, B. D. (1999), 'Romanian and the Balkans: Some Comparative Perspectives', in S. Embleton, J. Joseph and H.-J. Niederehe (eds), *The Emergence of the Modern Language Sciences. Studies on the Transition from Historical-Comparative to Structural Linguistics in Honour of E.F.K. Koerner*. Vol. 2, 218–35, Amsterdam: John Benjamins.

Koliopoulou, M. (2009), 'Loose Multi-Word Compounds and Noun Constructs within a Construction Grammar Framework', *Patras Working Papers in Linguistics*, 1: 59–71.

Krimpas, P. G. (2007), *Επιδράσεις της Νεότερης Ελληνικής στις Βαλκανικές Γλώσσες (Influences of Modern Greek on the Balkan Languages)* [in Greek], Athens: Grigoris.

Krimpas, P. G. (2017), 'Albanian', in G. Kanarakis (ed.), *The Legacy of the Greek Language*, 425–59, New York/Boston: Peridot.

Kyriazis, D. (2001), 'Ελληνικές Επιδράσεις στην Αλβανική. Μέρος I, Μέρος II' ('Greek Influences on the Albanian Language. Part I, Part II') [in Greek], PhD diss., Aristotle University of Thessaloniki, Greece.

McMahon, A. (1994), *Understanding Language Change*, Cambridge, UK: Cambridge University Press.

Newmark, L., P. Hubbard and P. Prifti (1982), *Standard Albanian: A Reference Grammar for Students*, Stanford, CA: Stanford University Press.

Nikolou, K. (2003). 'Μορφολογική και Φιλολογική Ανάλυση των Μονολεκτικών Συνθέτων Λέξεων της Νεοελληνικής' ('Morphological and Philological Analysis of Modern Greek One-Word' Compounds) [in Greek], MA diss., University of the Aegean, Greece.

Orel, V. (2000), *A Concise Historical Grammar of Albanian*, Leiden: Brill.

Rainer, F. and S. Varela (1992), 'Compounding in Spanish', *Rivista di Linguistica*, 4 (1): 117–42.

Ralli, A. (1992), 'Compounds in Modern Greek', *Rivista di Linguistica* 4 (1): 143–74.

Ralli, A. (2005), *Μορφολογία (Morphology)* [in Greek], Athens: Patakis.

Ralli, A. (2007), *Η Σύνθεση Λέξεων: Διαγλωσσική Μορφολογική Προσέγγιση (Compounding: A Cross-linguistic Morphological Approach)* [in Greek], Athens: Patakis.

Ralli, A. (2008a), 'Compound Markers and Parametric Variation', *Linguistic Typology and Universals*, 61: 19–38.

Ralli, A. (2008b), 'Greek Deverbal Compounds with Bound Stems', *Southern Journal of Linguistics*, 29 (1–2): 150–73.

Ralli, A. (2009), 'Modern Greek VV Dvandva Compounds: A Linguistic Innovation in the History of the Indo–European Languages', *Word Structure*, 1: 48–67.

Ralli, A. (2013a), 'Compounding and its Locus of Realization: Evidence from Greek and Turkish', *Word Structure*, 6 (2): 181–200.

Ralli, A. (2013b), *Compounding in Modern Greek*, Dordrecht, The Netherlands: Springer.

Ralli, A., ed. (2016), *Contact Morphology in Modern Greek Dialects*, Newcastle-upon-Tyne: Cambridge Scholars Publishing.

Ralli, A. and M. Stavrou (1998), 'Morphology-Syntax Interface: A-N Compounds vs A-N Constructs in Modern Greek', *Yearbook of Morphology* 1: 229–45.

Revithiadou, A. (1997), 'Stress Patterns and Morphological Structures in Greek (Nominal) Prefixation', *Studies in Greek Linguistics*, 17: 85–99.

Revithiadou, A. and V. Spyropoulos, eds (2013), *Αντιπαραβολική Μελέτη Γραμματικών Δομών Αλβανικής - Ελληνικής (Contrastive Research on the Grammatical Structures of Albanian–Greek)* [in Greek], Thessaloniki, Greece: Aristotle University of Thessaloniki. Available online: www.diapolis.auth.gr/diapolis_files/drasi5/Drasi5_website/Drasi5_Ypodrasi_5_2/Ebook_Alb_Gr.pdf (accessed 30 May 2018).

Sandfeld, K. (1930), *Linguistique Balkanique*, Paris: Klincksieck [First published in Danish in 1926].

Scalise, S. (1992), 'Compounding in Italian', *Rivista di Linguistica*, 4 (1): 175–200.

Scalise, S. and A. Fábregas (2010), 'The Head in Compounding', in S. Scalise and I. Vogel (eds), *Cross-disciplinary Issues in Compounding*, 109–26, Amsterdam: Benjamins.

Scalise, S. and I. Vogel, eds (2010), *Cross-Disciplinary Issues in Compounding* (Current Issues in Linguistic Theory 311), Amsterdam: Benjamins.

Thomason, S. (2001), *Language Contact: An Introduction*, Edinburgh: Edinburgh University Press.

Thomason, S. G. and T. Kaufman (1988), *Language Contact, Creolization and Genetic Linguistics*, Berkeley: University of California Press.

Zwanenburg, W. (1992), 'Compounding in French', *Rivista di Linguistica*, 4 (1): 221–38.

8

Past tense usages in tense-rich and tenseless languages: A contrastive study

Masahiko Nose

The chapter seeks to contrast languages with a rich tense system and those without tenses. In particular, this study focuses on the past tense forms in the four sample languages – Amele, Ma Manda, Nguna from the South Pacific and Mandarin Chinese. Amele and Ma Manda have rich tense systems with remoteness distinctions, while Nguna and Chinese are well known for their tenselessness. This study examines the four languages and their past tense features, and discusses the links between formal tense markers and the meaning.

This study claims that Amele and Ma Manda have a remoteness distinction between the near and remote past, because they focus on the difference between the present and past. In contrast, Nguna and Chinese, the tenseless languages, express the past tense with the help of temporal adverbs or perfective aspect markers, and thus express whether or not the action is completed. These findings indicate that the difference between tense-rich and tenseless languages can be explained by each morphological burden.

1 Introduction

This study seeks to contrast languages with rich tense systems and those without tenses (tenseless). The languages with rich tense systems have many kinds of tenses, such as near past and remote past tenses. In contrast, the tenseless languages lack any tense marking in the grammar (cf. Comrie 1985). Their differences can be explained in terms of morphological marking of tenses (cf. Lin 2012; Smith 2005).

As frequently observed in European languages, the past tense is one of the most basic tense markings, and most languages have at least one present and past tense each (Binnick 2012; Velupillai 2016). This study focuses on the past tense functions in the following four sample languages – Amele, Ma Manda, Nguna from the South Pacific, and Mandarin Chinese. Amele and Ma Manda have rich tense systems with remoteness distinctions (Foley 2000), whereas Nguna and Chinese are well known for their tenselessness (Lin 2012).

Tense, particularly the past tense, is one of the necessary grammatical categories. The past tense is more marked than the unmarked present tense – 'verb+past marker':

study–studied, *run–ran*, *go–went* – in English. Temporal references (such as present, past and future) are necessary in grammar, and all languages have grammatical or lexical means of specifying such temporal references. However, there are languages that are tenseless, and this study makes an effort to clarify the effect of tenselessness by contrasting tenseless languages with tense-rich languages. Moreover, this study considers how to interpret temporal adverbs vis-à-vis the past tense. Almost all languages have temporal adverbs, such as *today*, *yesterday*, and *tomorrow*. Such temporal adverbs are crucial when making temporal references. However, many languages tend to grammaticalize tense and aspect markers.[1]

Thus, this study examines these four languages and their past tense features (their forms and meanings), and discusses the functional basis of the features in the grammars (cf. Aikhenvald 2014; Bybee and Dahl 1989; Smith 2005; the term 'functional' indicates that grammars have a natural tendency to regulate themselves). In particular, this study tries to clarify the functional effects of a rich tense and tenseless system, and ultimately argues that the effects are related to the participants of the event. The tense meaning in languages with rich tense systems is deeply linked to person and number, while tenseless languages are only interested in actions in the past (cf. Smith 1997, 2005; Sinha et al. 2011).

Section 2 provides an introduction to previous general studies on tense and language descriptions in Papua New Guinea, and then sets out the aims of this contrastive study. Section 3 provides the data on the past tense or related phenomena in the sample languages. Section 4 contains a discussion of rich tense and tenseless features, and Section 5 concludes the chapter.

2   General remarks on the past tense

In this section, we review several previous studies on the past tense and introduce basic assumptions about rich tense and tenseless languages.

First, Dahl and Velupillai (2005) conducted a typological survey of past tenses. Figure 8.1 shows that the most frequent type is languages with the present tense and no remoteness distinctions (grey triangles), as observed in most European languages, and that the next most frequent type is tenseless languages (white circles). These tenseless languages are observed in Central Africa, South East Asia and North and Central Africa.[2]

In contrast, there are forty languages that use remoteness distinctions as part of the past tenses (black circles). For example, Amele (Trans-New Guinea, Papua New Guinea) has three basic remoteness distinctions, as shown in (1). These tense-rich languages are observed in New Guinea Island and South America. This study specifically examines data from the New Guinea area.

(1) Amele (Roberts 1987):

    Present:
    Ija   fri-*diga.*
    I   surprise-1SG (1st person singular)/present
    'I am surprised.'

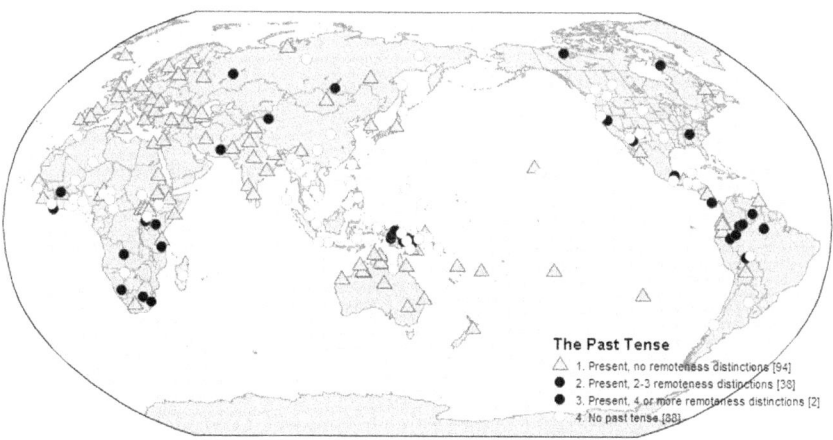

Figure 8.1 WALS map of the past tense by Dahl and Velupillai (2005).

Today's past:
Ija   fri-iti-*ga.*
I   surprise-1SG/today's past
'I was surprised (today).'

Yesterday's past:
Ija   fri-iti-*gan.*
I   surprise-1SG/yesterday's past
'I was surprised (yesterday).'

Remote past:
Ija   fri-it-*en.*
I   surprise-1SG/remote past
'I was surprised (before yesterday).'

Such remoteness distinctions in the past tense in (1) are not observed in English and other European languages. Amele (and other tense-rich languages) have functional reasons for such distinctions, because the speakers want to specify the temporal information more than other languages. On the other hand, there are eighty-eight languages that are tenseless. These languages also have their own reasons for being so. This study aims to find the effects of tense-richness or tenselessness in the grammar and demonstrate that there are reasons for this grammatical behaviour.

We also review the use of the past tense in other languages. First, Japanese has a simple past tense system (one past tense only), as shown in the following (2).

(2) Japanese: yomu (to read) – present: yo-mu (I read)

1st person singular (1SG): *yon-da*   1st person plural (1PL): *yon*-da
2SG: yon-*da*   2PL: yon-*da*
3SG: yon-*da*   3PL: yon-*da*

Japanese does not have a formal perfective and, moreover, it does not have a tense inflection for person and number. This system is almost as simple as tenseless languages.

Second, French involves more complicated past tense usage, as shown in (3).

(3) French: aimer (to love) – present: j'aime (I love)
   a. passé composé (avoir/être + past participle): j'ai aimé. 'I loved.'
   b. imparfait: j'aimais. 'I loved.'
   c. habitual past: quand j'étais petit, j'allais souvent à la piscine. 'when I was little, I often went to the pool.'
   d. plus-que-parfait (avoir/être (imparfait) + past participle): j'avais aimé. 'I loved.'
   e. passé simple (written use): j'aimai. 'I loved.'
   f. passé antérieur (avoir/être (imparfait) + past participle): j'eus aimé. 'I loved.'

French has a mixed system of past and perfect, as shown in (3), and while the semantics of past usages in French is still under discussion. However, Dahl and Velupillai (2005) classified French as a language with no remoteness distinction in the past, and this study will consider the perfective meaning of the sample languages associated with the past usages.

Other typological and descriptive studies, such as Aikhenvald (2014), Bybee and Dahl (1989), Comrie (1976, 1985) and Smith (1997) have already demonstrated that there are a variety of tense-aspect systems around the world, and that some languages are tensedependent, while others are aspect-dependent. Otherwise, modal meanings are more or less related in tense-aspect systems. Dahl and Velupillai (2005) show that only forty languages have past tenses with two or more remoteness distinctions, but that eighty-eight languages have no tenses at all. This means that languages do not in fact necessarily need a tense system, typologically; indeed, it is more unusual to have a high number of remoteness distinctions. This study supposes that there is certain reason or effect of tense-richness or tenselessness to explain their usages (cf. Lin 2012; Velupillai 2016).

3 Data: A contrastive study

This section sets out the examples of the sample languages. This study is a contrastive study, and it will clarify the past tense usages by checking remoteness distinctions, verbal morphology, and grammatical means of perfective implications. The contrastive study methodology used by Aikhenvald (2014), König and Gast (2009) and Nose (2016) will be followed. This study consists of field-based data and descriptive grammars.

Data sources:

1. Amele: Roberts (1987, 2016), author's own data (Nose 2016)
2. Ma Manda: Pennington (2015)[3]
3. Nguna: Schütz (1969), author's own data (Nose 2007)
4. Chinese: Koshimizu and Shimada (2009), Po-Ching and Rimmingston (2004), Setoguchi (2003), Yamashita (2003), author's own data

Generally, Trans-New Guinea languages like Amele and Ma Manada are considered to have more complicated tense/aspect systems than the other Austronesian languages,

Nguna and Sino-Tibetan Chinese (Roberts 1987; Lin 2012). The choice of the sample languages is not wide enough to provide a complete typology, but this contrastive study aims to look at the grammatical possibilities and functional effects of the languages by examining unusual tense features, specifically those that are not found in English and European languages. Additionally, this study aims to identify a better explanation for different tense systems by contrasting these four languages.

The data were collected through the descriptive grammars and the interviews mentioned above. Primarily, this study found that Amele (Trans-New Guinea, Papua New Guinea) has three kinds of past tenses as shown in examples (1) and (4). Moreover, Amele has the habitual past and negative past forms as shown in (5). As shown in Table 8.1, the tense forms are included in verbal inflections. Verbal inflections in Amele are quite complicated and the word-formations of person, number and tense morphemes are portmanteau forms, and cannot be clearly divided. The past form implies a perfective meaning as shown in (6). The verb form is today's past tense and the adverb 'wele' (already) was added as shown in (6). In other words, Amele needs lexical means (i.e. the adverb 'already') to imply the perfective meaning.

(4) Amele (Roberts 1987): three kinds of basic past tenses
   Today's past: Ija (I) hu-*g-a* (come-today's past/1SG). 'I came (today).'
   Yesterday's past: Ija hu-*g-an* (come-yesterday's past/1SG). 'I came (yesterday).'
   Remote past: Ija ho-*om* (come-remote past/1SG). 'I came (before yesterday).'

(5) Amele: other additional past tenses
   Habitual past: Ija ho-*l-ig* (come-habitual past/1SG). 'I used to come.'
   Negative past: Ija qee (not) ho-*l-om* (come-negative past/1SG). 'I did not come.'

(6) Uqa   wele   nui-*a*.
    He/she   already   go-3SG/today's past
    'He has already gone.' (Roberts 1987: 232)

The observation mentioned from examples (4), (5) and (6) (and also (1)) and Table 8.1 together indicate that Amele is tense-rich language, but it is poor in aspect usage (Roberts 1987: 224). Many aspect meanings are realized in other tenses, such as the habitual tense or today's past tense (Roberts states that the perfective aspect is inherent in the today's past tense) or via lexical means, such as the adverb used for the perfective as shown in (6).

Table 8.1 Forms: Verbal Inflections: *huga* 'Come'

	Present	Today's past	Yesterday's past	Remote	Habitual	Negative past	Future
1sg	hu-gu-na	hu-ga	hu-gan	ho-om	ho-l-ig	holo-im	hug-en
2sg	ho-ga	ho-ga	ho-gan	ho-om	ho-l-og	holo-m	hog-en
3sg	ho-na	ho-ya	ho-yan	ho-n	ho-l-oi	hol	hugi-en
1pl	ho-wo-na	ho-wa	ho-qan	ho-m	o-l-ob	hol-um	hoq-en
2/3pl	ho-si-na	hoi-ga	hoi-gan	hoi-n	ho-lo-ig	ho-lo-in	hoqaig-en

Table 8.2 Tense (Realis) Paradigm in Ma Manda (Pennington 2015: 317)

	Singular	Non-singular
Remote past	-go	-gû
Near past	-nga	-ngaa
Present	-la	-waa
Future	-taa	-ntaa

Table 8.3 Subject-Agreement Paradigm (Realis) in Ma Manda (Pennington 2015: 318)

	Singular	Dual	Plural
1st person	-t	-mot	-m
2nd person	-ng	-mok	-ng
3rd person	-k		

Next, Ma Manda (Trans-New Guinea, Papua New Guinea) has two remoteness distinctions between the near past (the form *-a-*) and the remote past (*-ga-*) as shown in (7).⁴ Ma Manda uses tense suffixes through verbal inflections as shown in Table 8.2 and Table 8.3. Thus, the verbal paradigms in Ma Manda are a combination of tense and subject agreement.

(7) Ma Manda (Pennington 2015: 366–9):
Near past:
taamengsùla   membû   tem   laal-*a*-k.
morning   head   hair   scrape-near past-3sɢ
'(This) morning he shaved his head.'
Remote past:
kep   bûsenang   aatûkugu   ba-*go*-t.
yesterday jungle   be-go-durative   come-remote past-1sɢ
'Yesterday going around in the bush, I came (back).'

The negative past in Ma Manda can be expressed using the negator 'dom' (not), but the verbal form is the remote past as shown in (8), and it is not a negative past form, as in (5) of Amele (Pennington 2015: 365). Pennington (2015) explains that the near past is seldom negated. If negated, it seems to carry the implication that the action is still expected to occur. Moreover, there is no perfective aspect marker in Ma Manda (Pennington 2015: 379), but perfective meaning can be expressed with the help of the adverb 'mo' (already) as shown in (9).

(8) nolû   wa   *dom* (not)   nûng-go(remote past)-k (3sɢ).
Brother   that   not   tell-remote past-3sɢ
'He did not tell his brother.'

(9) mi   *mo*   (already)   wi-nga (near past)-t (1SG).
     Water   already   bathe-near past-1SG
     'I've already bathed (today).' (Pennington 2015: 399)

Next, this study gives the examples of tenseless languages. First, Nguna (Austronesian, Vanuatu) has a simple verbal structure and no independent tense and aspect markers as shown in (10)a. When Nguna prefers to clarify the past meaning, it needs temporal adverbs, like 'yesterday' or 'last night', as shown in (10)b. The sentence shown in (10)a expresses the present or neutral situation of 'I eat fish'; it can also express the past situation ('I ate fish' if other contexts help), but it is more accurate to add a temporal adverb indicating the past to specify the past situation as shown in (10)b. On the other hand, the verb form 'a gani' does not have any tense marking.

(10) Nguna (Nose 2007)
      a. Kinau a   gani   naika.
         I   1SG   eat   fish
         'I eat fish.'

      b. Kinau a   gani   naika   *nanofa.*
         I   1SG   eat   fish   yesterday
         'I ate fish yesterday.'

Negation is expressed using a negative particle in Nguna. The negative marker 'taa' (not) expresses the negative past (Schütz 1969: 28), as shown in examples (11) and (12). However, these sentences do not have any tense marking, and hearers need to use clues from the context or temporal adverbs such as 'nanofa' (yesterday) or 'tuai' (before) (Schütz 1969: 62–3).

(11) e   *taa*   munu.
      3SG   not   drink
      'He did not drink.'

(12) eu   *taa*   atae   te   na-vatuuna.
      3PL   not   know   any   thing
      'They did not know anything.'

In Nguna, some tense, aspect and mood (TAM) categories are marked in one form, a so-called TAM marker. The TAM markers carry the meanings of tense, aspect and mood altogether. These TAM markers are inserted between the subject and the verb. Several TAM markers are as shown in (13). This TAM system is a property of Austronesian languages.

(13) Some TAM markers in Nguna:
      Kinau a *do.*   'I used to' (habitual)
      Kinau a *gawo.*   'I will, I must' (necessity)
      Kinau a *masau.*   'I want' (optative)

One TAM marker is the perfective 'poo', as shown in examples (14) and (15). In (14), the adverb 'sua' (already) also helps to give a perfective implication.

Nguna perfective (Schütz 1969: 27):
(14) E   *poo*   munu *sua*.
      3SG   perfective   drink already
      'He has drunk already.'

(15) A   *poo*   punusi a.
      1SG   perfective   see   3SG
      'I have seen him.'

Therefore, Nguna depends on temporal adverbs to specify past tense meaning, but it also has the perfective marker 'poo' and it is important in Nguna to know whether the action has been completed or not.

Second, Chinese (Sino-Tibetan, China) is famous for its tenselessness (Lin 2012). It does not need a past tense marker. Instead, it can use both temporal adverbs, such as 'yesterday' or 'last month', and, at the same time, aspect markers like 'le', which can indicate past meaning, as shown in (16)a–c.

(16) Chinese (Lin 2012: 673):
      a. Lisi   *dapo*   huaping.
         Lisi   break(-perfective)   vase
         'Lisi broke a vase.'

      b. Lisi   *zuotian*   dapo   huaping.
         Lisi   yesterday   break   vase
         'Lisi broke a vase yesterday.'

      c. Lisi   dapo-*le*   huaping.
         Lisi   break-aspect marker   vase
         'Lisi broke a vase.'

In (16)a, the verb 'dapo' (break) does not have any marker, nor any temporal adverb, but it can indicate a past meaning. Because the verb form 'dapo' contains a perfective meaning lexically (break-perf), it can imply that the action happened in the past. The mechanism of the sentence in (16)b is almost the same in Nguna ((10)b). The temporal adverb 'zuotian' (yesterday) in (16)b is used to indicate that the action happened yesterday. In (16)c, the perfective marker 'le' is used to express that the action is already done and this usage is frequently observed to imply a past meaning. According to my Chinese consultant, the sentences in (16) are semantically different from each other, but Chinese speakers prefer to use (16)c to translate the Japanese 'yon-da' (I read; past tense) or the English 'I read' (past tense). Thus, some studies claim that the aspect marker 'le' in practice implies the past. However, the marker 'le' has an aspect meaning, and so, Chinese is considered not to have a formal means of generating past tense and is thus a tenseless language.

In the negative past in Chinese, the aspect marker 'le' cannot appear, as shown in (17)a–c.

(17)   Negative past (Setoguchi 2003: 122–4):
    a. Wo   mai   shuiguo *le.*
       I   buy   fruit   perfective marker
      'I bought a fruit.'

    b. Ta mei(-you)   mai   shuiguo.
      he not   buy   fruit
      'He did not buy a fruit.'

    c. *Ta   mei(-you)   mai shuiguo   *le.*
      He   not   buy fruit   perfective marker
      'He did not buy a fruit.'

Example (17)a is a perfective affirmative sentence using the marker 'le'. Example (17)b is the negative past; note that the perfective maker 'le' disappears, because the marker 'le' cannot be allowed in the negative past situation, as shown in (17)c. The negative past meaning implies that the action is not completed and therefore the perfective marker 'le' cannot be allowed.

The experiential marker 'guo' can also imply the past tense (18)a, but it does have an experiential meaning. The marker 'guo' can appear even in a negative past sentence, as shown in (18)b, because of its experiential meaning, as 'non-experience' can also be a kind of 'experience'.

(18)   Perfective: 'guo' (Setoguchi 2003: 130):
    a. women   chi-*guo*   Zhongguocai.
      we   eat-perfective marker   Chinese food
      'We have eaten Chinese food.'

    b. women   mei(-you) chi-*guo*   Zhongguocai.
      we   not   eat-perfective marker   Chinese food
      'We have not eaten Chinese food.'

Overall, Chinese does not have any tense marker; instead, the aspect markers 'le' and 'guo' imply a past meaning, and temporal adverbs are also used to indicate the past meaning. The aspect markers 'le' and 'guo' differ slightly in terms of whether they can be used in the negative past: the marker 'le' disappears in the negative past, whereas 'guo' remains. This is because the marker 'le' with negation indicates 'the action is not completed', while the marker 'guo' with negation indicates 'the uncompleted action is completed'.

4 Discussion

This section discusses the past tense usages in contrastive terms. The languages in Papua New Guinea have quite different grammars from typical European languages, in that they have rich tense systems (Foley 2000), and in contrast, it is also remarkable that tenseless languages nevertheless do have a way of expressing past meaning. Thus, these two types of languages (tense-rich and tenseless) indicate that there is a wide range of grammatical possibilities for expressing the past tense. This study aims to find the functional characteristics of past tenses (or, how to regulate grammatical systems) by looking at tense-rich and tenseless languages and explaining each mechanism.

The data of the sample languages is summarized in Table 8.4. In this section, we will discuss how temporal adverbs function in the past tense and what kinds of effects tense-rich/tenseless languages have (in particular, we measure morphological burden of past tense marking).

In Table 8.4, we can see that the tense-rich languages have remoteness distinctions in the past tense, generally formed via verbal morphology.[5] However, the perfective meaning is realized lexically using the temporal adverb 'already' (exception: the perfective tense in Kobon (Trans-New Guinea, Papua New Guinea), Davies 1989). In contrast, tenseless languages have no past tense marker and their verbal inflections are not complicated, as shown in examples (13)–(15) for Nguna and in (16) for Chinese. Instead, they have perfective marker(s) and their forms are independent from the verbal morphology.

First, this study considers the roles of temporal adverbs. Theoretically, the tenseless languages can specify the past using temporal adverbs and thus can express past meaning without any tense marker. For example, Nguna needs the temporal adverb 'nanofa' (yesterday) to specify the past meaning, as shown in (19).

(19)   Nguna   (Nose 2007):
      Kinau   a   gani   naika   *nanofa.*
      I   1SG   eat   fish   yesterday
      'I ate fish yesterday.'

In Chinese, the marker 'le' is necessary, as shown in (20)a; the sentence indicates a perfective meaning and partly carries a past tense meaning. The sentence (20)b, without 'le', is not acceptable, even though the temporal adverb 'yesterday' indicates the past. Thus, the temporal adverbs are not sufficient to express the past meaning in Chinese, and the aspect marker '*le*' co-occurs with the temporal adverb in the past.

(20)   Chinese:
      a. *Zuotian*   wo   mai-*le*   taozi
           Yesterday   I   buy-perfective   a peach
           'I bought a peach yesterday.'

      b. *Zuotian wo mai taozi.

In Amele, the verbal morphology of 'yesterday's past' cannot co-occur with the temporal adverb 'the day before yesterday', as shown in (21)b. This is because the verbal structure has already specified the 'yesterday's past' tense and a conflict arises from the tense difference between 'yesterday's past' in the verb and the temporal adverb 'the day before yesterday'. The basic rule in Amele is that the verbal tense marker has priority in terms of indicating tense information and thus, that the temporal adverb should match the past reference in the verb.

(21) Amele:

    a. Ija   hu-*g-an*   *cum.*
        I   come-yesterday's past/1SG yesterday
        'I came yesterday.'

    b. *Ija   hu-*g-an*   *eren.*
        I   come-yesterday's past/1SG the day before yesterday
        'I came (*yesterday/*the day before yesterday).'

Temporal adverbs can help indicate the exact time of the action – 'yesterday' or 'a week ago'. However, if the verb contains the remote past tense marker, the temporal adverbs ('yaar osona' (last year), 'week osol hedocob' (a week ago) become key to specifying the exact time in the past that is being referred to (see Table 8.4).

Next, we discuss the effect(s) of tense-richness/tenselessness. This study found that many languages differ from the English system of one present and one past tense. This study has shown extreme examples of tense-rich and tenseless languages.

This section considers the effects of rich tenses. Amele and Ma Manda, the tense-rich languages, have complicated verbal morphology and they do not need to use temporal adverbs because the verb forms have already indicated the time in the past that has been referred to (the near or remote past meanings of the verb). In contrast, they have poor grammar in aspect (generally, tense and aspect meanings are related to each

Table 8.4 Summary of the Four Languages

	Amele	Ma Manda	Nguna	Chinese
Tense system (particularly, past usages)	Remoteness: Today, yesterday, remote; habitual past and negative past	Remoteness: Near and remote	No (By using temporal adverbs like 'yesterday')	No (By using temporal adverbs like 'yesterday')
Verbal morphology	Incorporated with tense/person/number	Incorporated with tense/person/number	Person/number, but no tense marker	No marker
Negative past	Negator and negative past form	Negator and remote past	Negator only	Negator (particle 'le' cannot co-occur)
Perfective aspect	Lexical (adverb 'wele' (already))	Lexical (adverb 'mo' (already))	Perfective particles 'poo'/adverb 'sua' (already)	Particles 'le' and 'guo'

other and their distributions are balanced). Furthermore, Amele makes a distinction between the positive and the negative in the past and future tenses through verbal morphology (Roberts 1987: 223–7). Because these languages put tense information in the verb, verbs are thus heavier in functional terms (cf. type 2 in (22)).

Instead, Nguna and Chinese, the tenseless languages, lack a complicated verbal morphology (or many grammatical markings on verbs) and they have simple verb forms. These verbs do not carry tense information. Typologically, these tenseless languages are more common (Figure 8.1; eighty-eight languages in Dahl and Velupillai 2005) than tense-rich languages. This study considers that light verbal morphology (or few or no marking on verbs) is the preferred means to indicate past tense information (cf. type 3 in (22)).

The functional frameworks for how the sample languages construct the past tense are summarized in (22). Speakers of different languages look at past events through different lenses and the grammars of their languages reflect these lenses.

(22) Functional frameworks of the past tense:
      Type 1:   English and Japanese: 'study–studied'; non-past and one past
                (happened or not)
      Type 2:   Amele and Ma Manda: 'study–studied (today; yesterday; remote)';
                several past points should be specified (when happened)
      Type 3:   Nguna and Chinese: 'study–study (tenseless)'; realis or irrealis
                (completed or not); Type 3 languages make a clear distinction
                between realis (past, present) and irrealis (future) (Nose 2017).

When tense information is incorporated into verbal morphology,[6] as shown in Amele and Ma Manda, verbal inflections for person number and for tense forms are fused. These word-formations imply that tense information is related to person and number, that is, the participants. Moreover, Amele and Ma Manda distinguish between the near past and the remote past, a distinction that is realized in the grammar, because speakers of the languages want to be able to express whether the action happened today/yesterday or previously. Thus, the tense-rich languages carry the morphological burden of specifying these past meanings.

In contrast, Chinese and Nguna, the tenseless languages, do not indicate how or what people did; instead they concern themselves with the action only and whether the action is completed or not or whether the action really happened. Temporal adverbs are one key to identifying the time reference, but they are still outside of argument structure and they can keep their verb forms simpler.

5 Conclusion

This study argues that Amele and Ma Manda have a remoteness distinction between the near and remote past, because they have grammatical markers of each tense in verbal morphology. Additionally, Amele has an interest in distinguishing between positive and negative situations, as well as between positive and negative past tenses (as in (5) and Table 8.1). These tense-rich languages incorporate the past event into the verbal morphology, which means the participants and the past event are closely interlinked. These types of languages are found in New Guinea and other areas, but they are rarer than tenseless languages.

In contrast, Nguna and Chinese, the tenseless languages, express the past tense with the help of temporal adverbs such as 'yesterday' and 'already' and thus they express whether the action is completed or not. They do not focus on the relationship between the participants and the past event. Instead, these languages are interested in perfective/imperfective actions. To specify such perfective meaning, they may use an aspect marker. Tenselessness is found in Sino-Tibetan and Austronesian languages, and moreover, such languages are typologically not rare (tenseless languages can be found even in New Guinea).

These findings indicate that there are many type 1 languages, such as English (one past tense only), as shown in (22), but that there are other grammatical possibilities for expressing the past tense, namely tense-rich (type 2) and tenseless (type 3) languages. Dahl and Velupillai (2005) show that the major grammatical tendency is for tenseless languages or for languages with one past tense, meaning that complicated tense morphology (type 2) is 'over-grammaticalized' or an 'extra system'.

Acknowledgements

I would like to thank Neret Tamo and the villagers in Sein, Madang Province, Papua New Guinea for their data and kindness. I claim sole responsibility for any errors. This work was supported by JSPS KAKENHI Grant Number 15K02478. An earlier version of this chapter was in a paper presented at the 8th International Contrastive Linguistics Conference, National Kapodistrian University of Athens, Greece (25–28 May 2017). I am grateful to the audience and anonymous reviewers for their comments and criticisms of earlier versions of the chapter.

Notes

1   Dahl (2001) claimed that there is an exception, Maybrat, Papua New Guinea, which does not have any tense or aspect marker.
2   There are two languages that have the present tense and four or more remoteness distinctions. These languages are Chácobo and Yagua, which are spoken in South America.
3   It might be better to conduct a field interview with the Ma Manda people on the spot, but the descriptive grammar of Pennington (2015) is comprehensive and reliable for this study.
4   Tense markers -a-/-ga- in Amele and -a-/-ga- in Ma Manda are accidentally similar, but their origins cannot be common. Although these languages are belonging to the

Trans-New Guinea genera (Papua New Guinea), there is no evidence of any contact or historical relationship between them.

5 There is another possibility for past tense morphology. Lecard (2012) showed the nominal tense in Somali, as shown in (i). It is a characteristic of this language that the past tense marker is added to the noun.

(i) Somali (Lecard 2012: 706):
     Madaxweyni-hii   wuu   dhintay.
     President-past   focus   die-past
     'The president died.'

6 The morphological origins (Bybee, Perkins and Pagliuca 1994: 55–6) of the near/ remote past tenses in Amele and Ma Manda are uncertain. We consider the tense forms in Amele, as shown in Table 8.5.

Table 8.5 Past Usages 'Come' in Amele

Today's past	Yesterday's past	Remote past
hu-ga	hu-gan	ho-om

Today's past and yesterday's past have the same origin '-ga-', but the remote past has another origin, 'om'. Nevertheless, although their original meanings are unclear, the past meanings can be divided into near (today and yesterday) versus far (remote).

References

Aikhenvald, A. Y. (2014), *The Art of Grammar: A Practical Guide*, Oxford: Oxford University Press.

Binnick, R. I. (2012), *The Oxford Handbook of Tense and Aspect*, Oxford: Oxford University Press.

Bybee, J. and Ö. Dahl (1989), 'The Creation of Tense and Aspect Systems', *Studies in Language*, 13: 51–103.

Bybee, J., R. Perkins and W. Pagliuca (1994), *The Evolution of Grammar: Tense, Aspect, and Modality in the Languages of the World*, Chicago, IL: University of Chicago Press.

Comrie, B. (1976), *Aspect*. Cambridge, UK: Cambridge University Press.

Comrie, B. (1985), *Tense*. Cambridge, UK: Cambridge University Press.

Dahl, Ö. (2001), 'Languages without Tense and Aspect', in K. H. Ebert and F. Zúñiga (eds), *Akitionsart and Aspectotemporality in non-European Languages*, 159–72, Seminar für Allgemeine Sprachwissenschaft, Zürich: Universität Zürich.

Dahl, Ö. and V. Velupillai (2005), 'The Past Tense', in M. Haspelmath et al. (eds), *The World Atlas of Language Structures*, WALS #66: 270–3, Oxford: Oxford University Press.

Davies, J. (1989), *Kobon*, London: Routledge.

Foley, W. A. (2000), 'The Languages of New Guinea', *Annual Review of Anthropology*, Vol. 29, 357–404.

König, E. and V. Gast (2009), *Understanding English-German Contrasts*, Berlin: Erich Schmit.

Koshimizu, M and T. Shimada (2009), *Chuugokugo, wakaru bunnpou (Chinese, Understanding Grammar)*, Tokyo: Taishuukan [in Chinese].

Lecard, J. (2012), 'Nominal Tense', in R. Binnick (ed.), *The Oxford Handbook of Tense and Aspect*, 696–718, Oxford: Oxford University Press.

Lin, J. W. (2012), 'Tenselessness', in R. Binnick (ed.), *The Oxford Handbook of Tense and Aspect*, 669–95, Oxford: Oxford University Press.

Nose, M. (2007), 'Nguna: A Brief Grammar Sketch', *Tohoku Journal of Linguistics*, 16: 87–95.

Nose, M. (2016), 'The Forms and Meanings of Past Tense: A Contrastive Study of Papua New Guinea', *The Hikone Ronso (Working Papers of Shiga University)*, 409: 6–14.

Nose, M. (2017), 'A Contrastive Study of Future Tenses in the Languages of Papua New Guinea', *Hikone Ronso (Working Papers of Shiga University)*, 413: 4–14.

Pennington, R. (2015), 'A Grammar of Ma Manda: A Papuan Language of Morobe Province, Papua New Guinea', PhD diss., James Cook University, Queensland, Australia.

Po-Ching, Y. and D. Rimmingston (2004), *Chinese: A Comprehensive Grammar*. London: Routledge.

Roberts, J. R. (1987), *Amele*, London: Croom Helm.

Roberts, J. (2016), *Amele RRG Grammatical Sketch*. Available online: http://linguistics. buffalo.edu/people/faculty/vanvalin/rrg/amelerrg.pdf (accessed 17 February 2017).

Schütz, A. J. (1969), 'Nguna grammar', *Oceanic Linguistics Special Publications*, 5: 1–88.

Setoguchi, R. (2003), *Kanzen master Chinese Grammar (Comprehensive Chinese Grammar)*. Goken.

Sinha, Ch. et al. (2011), 'When Time is not Space: The Social and Linguistic Construction of Time Intervals and Temporal Event Relations in an Amazonian Culture', *Language and Cognition*, 3: 137–69.

Smith, C. S. (1997), *The Parameter of Aspect*, 2nd edn, Dordrecht, The Netherlands: Kluwer.

Smith, C. S. (2005), 'Time with and without Tense', Paper presented at the International Round Table on Tense, Aspect and Modality. Universités Paris 7 and Paris 3, Paris, December 2005. Available online: https://pdfs.semanticscholar.org/56d9/7430df0b8110 e3601c62c18cd64476b38a9e.pdf (accessed 7 April 2019).

Velupillai, V. (2016), 'Partitioning the Timeline: A Cross-linguistic Survey of Tense', *Studies in Language*, 40 (1): 93–136.

Yamashita, T. (2003), *Chuugoku-go no nyuumon (Introduction to Chinese)* [in Chinese], Tokyo: Hakusuisha.

Part Three

Syntax

9

A contrastive analysis of interrogative constructions in Romance: Microvariation and theory[1]

Caterina Donati

This chapter is a brief survey of what we know about wh-questions across languages, and an introduction to the specific contribution of Romance languages within a contrastive analysis. Wh-movement displays some crosslinguistically stable properties and some parameters of variation, which we have briefly reviewed. As for Romance, the phenomenon of wh-*in situ* in French, of the ongoing grammaticalization of special complementizers, and of the systematic ambiguity of free relatives and light-headed relatives are briefly addressed.

1 Introduction: Interrogative clauses, stable and variable properties

Interrogative clauses have been traditionally at the centre of formal syntax inquiries, and for good reasons: they involve typically a long-distance dependency, and represent, as such, a challenge for a purely structuralist/configurational grammar of natural languages.

(1) What will Nikos talk about _?

The example above involves a gap, a position that is not filled and cannot be filled by any lexical material, and that is interpreted as corresponding to *what* at the left periphery of the clause. Whether this long-distance dependency is achieved through actual movement of *what* from its gap position, where it leaves a trace, to its derived position, or whether it is achieved through inserting a copy of *what* to the left periphery and then deleting the lower one, or through some other mechanism, is still open to debate and largely depends on the choice of formalism.[2] In what follows, I will use 'movement' as a descriptive term for long-distance dependency, without necessarily committing to a specific analysis.

The present chapter is a brief survey of the state of the art about wh-movement across languages, and an introduction to the specific contribution of Romance languages within a contrastive analysis. Wh-movement does indeed display some crosslinguistically stable properties and some parameters of variation, which we will briefly review in the following sections (Sections 1 and 2). We will then turn to Romance, and examine some interesting questions that arise with respect to wh-constructions (Sections 3 and 4). A conclusion closes the chapter.

1.1 Stable properties of wh-constructions

Wh-movement is, of course, not the only kind of longdistance dependency that is available across languages. Other clear instances of dislocations involve topicalizations and focalizations of various kinds, both at the left and at the right periphery. A clear advantage of wh-movement, at least in European languages, is that dislocation goes with a clear morphological marking, which makes it easy to identify. From the very beginning of generative grammar, great advances were made in our understanding of human syntax by observing some of the stable properties exhibited by this construction. Let us briefly review these properties that appear not to vary across languages.

First of all, wh-movement appears to be unbounded. By this, I mean that there is no obvious limit in the number of words or syntactic boundaries that can be crossed by the long-distance dependency involving wh-elements. This classical property is illustrated in (2).

(2) a. What do you think [Nikos will talk about _]?
     b. What do you think [Eleni will say [Nikos will talk about _]]?
     c. What do you think [we believe that [Eleni will say [Nikos will talk about _]]]?

Example (2)a contains a dependency crossing one sentential boundary. The addition of an extra sentential boundary in (2)b, or of two such boundaries in (2)c, might make the sentence long and perhaps hard to process, but does not affect its grammaticality. This property has historically played a central role in shedding light on the universal properties of human syntax, because it is not immediately relevant to or explainable by communication needs. By definition, it is also a property that is not easy to test on existing corpora (being a negative property, it is, by definition, not attested), and its role in the development of syntactic theory partly explains the focus on elicited data and on grammaticality judgements data that have traditionally driven the field. Unboundedness is also a property that might be difficult to test in oral languages, where face-to-face communication might tend to avoid complex sentences involving a lot of subordination.

A second important property of wh-movement that has played a central role in syntactic theorizing is sensitivity to islands. Starting from Ross's (1967) seminal work on English, it was observed that some syntactic configurations, such as adverbial clauses (3), relative clauses (4), coordinated clauses (5), among others, appear to block movement: using the movement metaphor, they act as islands, blocking wh-movement. Sensitivity to some islands is illustrated in the following examples.

(3) *What do you cry [when Nikos talks about _]?   *adjunct island*
(4) *What do you know [a person who talks about _]?   *CNPC*
(5) *What do you think [Eleni does all the work and Nikos
     talk about _]?   *Coordinate island*

The crosslinguistic validity of this other property is more controversial: while some islands appear to be very robust across languages (this is true in particular for adjunct islands), other appear to be more subject to variation (see e.g. Stepanov 2007). A lot of literature of the last forty years has been devoted to explaining islands with either purely syntactic theories (Huang 1982; Chomsky 1986; Rizzi 1990; Takahashi 1994; Uriagereka 1999, among many others), or in semantic terms (Beck 2006; Szabolcsi 2006), or grounding the account in processing terms (Hofmeister and Sag 2010; Phillips 2011 among others).[3]

A third property that is worth mentioning here is subject-object asymmetry: both in acquisition and in processing (measured in terms of reading time, accuracy and other measures), wh-movement displays a neat asymmetry between subject dependencies, which are easy, acquired early and more frequent in production ((6) is an example of a subject question in English), and object dependencies, which are instead acquired much later by children, slower to process and less frequent ((7) are examples of object questions in English).

(6) Which professor _ will talk about this topic?
(7) Which topic will the professor talk about _?
(7') Which topic will she talk about _?

The best account to be given to this asymmetry in processing dependencies is again subject to much debate, with pure linear accounts (e.g. Gibson 1998) opposed to structural ones (O'Grady 1997, among others). Facts like those opposing ((7) and (7')), by which a simple change in the nature of the subject (a full NP versus a pronominal) makes the object dependency easier, suggest that an intervention account (Rizzi 1990) is needed: in object dependencies, the relation between the gap and the filler (the wh-element) is disrupted by the intervening subject. The more the subject is similar to the filler, the more severe is this disruption, ranging from simple processing load, as in the case of (7), to unacceptability, as in (8).

(8) *Which topic did who talk about?

Be that as it may, this asymmetry has proven to be very robust crosslinguistically, and to provide as such an excellent diagnostic for language impairments of various kinds (Friedmann, Belletti and Rizzi 2009).

There are other properties that might go with wh-movement in many languages, but we can be content with these for this introduction (see Cheng 2001 for a classical reference on wh-typology). Before moving to variable properties, let us underline that wh-movement is by no means a universal, or not even a common property of languages. In many languages of the world, interrogative elements simply do not move at all: they sit in the position where they are interpreted in the clause, as any other expression. As standard, we refer to these languages as wh-*in situ* languages. Mandarin is an example: in (9), the interrogative element *shenme* sits in the object position, which is postverbal, as any other NP would.

(9) Húfēi mǎi-le shénme.   (Mandarin)
     Hufei buy-PERF what
     'What did Hufey buy?'

An obvious question that arises at the light of this variation, is whether wh-movement and wh-*in situ* are just two radically different phenomena, or rather they have something in common: while this is still in part open to debate, there seems to be good reasons to suppose that they are indeed only superficially different, and that wh-constructions always display some kind of movement, be it overt (as in wh-movement languages) or covert (in wh-*in situ*).[4]

And finally, some variation can be observed across languages displaying wh-movement.

1.2 Variable properties of wh-constructions

Setting apart the issue of wh-*in situ* and its exact status with respect to wh-movement, and only focusing on languages that exhibit this movement, we observe a number of variations that are worth commenting here briefly.

First of all, some languages, but not others, differentiate between direct and indirect wh-questions. This is illustrated, for example, in English.

(10) I wonder what Nikos will talk about _.
(11) *What Nikos will talk about _?
(12) *I wonder what will Nikos talk about _.

In English T to C is obligatory in root questions and forbidden in embedded ones. Similar, word order asymmetries are observed in many languages. Another example might come from French, where the question marker *est-ce que* is only compatible with root questions, at least in standard varieties (13):

(13) a. Qu'est-ce que tu veux?
             what *esk* you want

      b. *Je me demande qu'est-ce que tu veux.
             I wonder what *esk* you want

In other languages no distinction is made between direct and indirect questions.

A second variable property concerns the complementizer: some languages associate (wh-) questions to a special complementizer. This is, for example, the case in Kannada, as illustrated below (14):

(14) a. Tande [$_{CP}$[$_Q$[$_{IP}$ makkalu bandar]-aa] *anta/*annoo-du*] keeLidaru.
          father children come.past.3PL-Q *anta* asked
          'The father asked if the children had come.'

      b. [$_{CP}$[$_{IP}$ Raama geddanu] *annoo-du/*anta*] barii apavaada.
          Rama won *annoo du* only rumour
          'It is only a rumour that Rama won.'

(adapted from Amritavalli 2014)

The phenomenon of doubly-filled Comp filter observed in many European examples (e.g. in Standard English), by which a wh-element and a complementizer can never co-occur, can be interpreted as a property of this kind: wh-questions are introduced by a different complementizer than declaratives or yes/no questions, which actually takes the form of a silent element.

(15) a. I know that Nikos will talk about music.
      b. I wonder if Nikos will talk about music.
      c. *I wonder what that/if Nikos will talk about _.

(16) On va voir comment qu'on va faire ça.
      3SG go see how that 3SG go do this
      'Let's see how to do this.'

Another important parameter of variation has to do with multiple questions. In some languages, multiple questions are constrained, with only one wh-element allowed to sit at the periphery, the other(s) being *in situ*, as in English.

(17) Who do you think saw what?

In other languages, there is no constraint against multiple wh-movement. This is the case in particular in some Slavic languages, like Bulgarian, as illustrated in (18). Still, as (18)b shows, multiple wh-movement appears to be subject to the same kind of intervention effects constraining wh-movement *per se*.

(18) a. Koj kakvo pravi?   (Rudin 1988: 481)
          who what does
          'Who is doing what?'
      b. *Kakvo koj pravi?   (Rudin 1988: 482)
          what who does
          'What is who doing?'

Other dimensions of variation can be cited briefly: German, for example, but also Albanian, Czech and many non-European languages, allow what is usually referred to as partial movement: movement of a wh-phrase to an embedded Spec CP which is not interrogative, and realization of the wh-expletive *was* ('what'), as in (19), in the Spec CP position of the higher clause corresponding to the scope of the interrogative.

(19) [$_{CP1}$Was meinst du [$_{CP2}$ wen Peter Hans _ vorgestellt hat]?
      What think you who Peter Hans introduced has
      'Who do you think Peter has introduced to Hans?'

We shall not go back to such an interesting phenomenon, rather turning now to Romance, and to what wh-questions in Romance varieties can contribute to the picture of crosslinguistic variation around this phenomenon. Before *going Romance*, let me mention one last parameter of variation that appears to be puzzling: in all the languages that have been investigated up to now, wh-elements are either moved to the left periphery, or remain *in situ*. There are no known spoken languages displaying wh-movement to the right. This generalization, which might have called for an explanation in terms of some universal constraint, has been recently confronted with a puzzling observation. If we turn our attention to sign languages, we see that most of them tend to display either wh-*in situ* or wh-movement to the right. Why modality should affect the 'direction' of movement is still largely to be understood.[5]

2 Wh-questions in Romance

Wh-questions in Romance are particularly interesting, because they employ virtually the same lexical material (k-words) stemming from the same Latin source, but they display intricate variation on virtually every single parameter. Observing the subtle and not so subtle variation between different Romance varieties concerning the distribution and syntactic behaviour of words as minimally different as *que* in French, *che* in Italian and the like, makes a good illustration of the independence of syntax from the lexicon, and of the width of syntactic variation within a family of tightly related languages.

I will take advantage of this brief survey of wh-questions in Romance to remind that there is surprisingly a lot that is yet to be understood even at a descriptive level, and even in main Romance varieties such as French. This in turns reminds us that while it is always underlined that it is difficult to work on underdescribed and unwritten languages (and it certainly is), it is also very difficult to work on overdescribed languages, where the weight of prescriptivism is so strong that it makes virtually impossible to elicit naive acceptability judgements from speakers.

2.1 Wh-*in situ* in French versus many other Romance languages

French is quite peculiar among other Romance languages for it allows wh-*in situ* as a systematic alternative to wh-movement.[6] This phenomenon is illustrated in (20).

(20) a. Tu vois *qui* ce soir?
          you see who tonight

      b. Tu fais *quoi*?
          you do what

    c. Tu vas *où*?
        you go where

Contrary to what might happen in other languages, the wh-*in situ* questions displayed in (20) do not require any special pragmatics, nor do they have any echo-flavour: they are simple run-off-the-mill content questions, analogous in all respects to the *est-ce que* questions displayed in (21).

(21) a. Qui est-ce que tu vois ce soir?
         who esk you see tonight

      b. Qu'est-ce que tu fais?
         what esk you do

      c. Où est-ce que tu vas?
         where esk you go

Still, wh-*in situ* questions in French are poorly known as far as their distribution and their underlining syntactic structure are concerned.

As for their distribution, they have been traditionally described as a root phenomenon (Chang 1997; Bošković 1998; Boeckx 1999; Cheng and Rooryck 2000, among others), but it is not at all clear that they are. At least in contemporary French, they are indeed possible under some restricted conditions, yet to be fully understood.

They are reported to be possible as long-distance root questions (Starke 2001; Adli 2006; Baunaz 2011; Shlonsky 2012; Dagnac 2013), as illustrated in (22).

(22) a. Tu crois qu'il va où?   (Baunaz 2011: 44)
         you think that he goes where

      b. Il a décidé de faire quoi?   (Baunaz 2011: 44)
         he has decided to do what

While the examples in (22) are root questions, they differ from the examples in (20) because the wh-*in situ* sits in an embedded clause, and is interpreted as having scope over the main clause. But wh-*in situ* has also been reported to be possible in indirect questions, as in (23) and (24).

(23) a. Je sais pas c'est quoi.   (GGF[7]: 11–12, to appear)
         I know not it is what

      b. On se demande on part quand.
         we wonder we leave where

(24) Elle m'a demandé tu étais avec quel prof.   (ESLO2[8])
      she me asked you were with which professor

In (23)–(24) the wh-element *in situ* does not only sit in an embedded position; it is also interpreted in that clause: the sentences in these examples are not questions, but they contain an indirect question.

As for they underlining syntactic properties, wh-*in situ* constructions in French seem to display some properties associated with wh-movement. In particular, they appear to obey weak islands, namely those islands that selectively block adjunct movement, but not argument movement. The example in (25) below shows that the same wh-*in situ* involving an adjunct (*quand*, 'when') is acceptable under a bridge verb, but gets ungrammatical under a factive verb; this suggests that the dependency relating the in situ wh-element to its scope position in the main clause is blocked by the factive island (Rouveret 1980; Rooryck 1992).

(25) a. Tu penses qu'elle est partie quand?
     you think that she is left when

     b. *Tu regrettes qu'elle est partie quand?   *factive island*
        you regret that she is left when

In (26) below, we see that negation makes an adjunct wh-*in situ* unacceptable.

(26) a. Il est parti quand?
     he is left when

     b. *Il n'est pas parti quand.   *negative island*[9]
        he isn't left when

On the other hand, wh-*in situ* in French does *not* behave like a proper movement structure because it does not obey strong islands, that is, those islands that appear to block unselectively any constituent from moving. This is illustrated in (27) and in (28), with a Complex NP Constraint (*CNPC*, here a relative clause) and with an adjunct island.

(27) Il a construit une machine qui sert à quoi?   (GGF)   *CNPC*
     he has built a machine that serves to what

(28) a. Il était là quand son fils passait quel examen?   (GGF)   *adjunct*
     he was there when his son passed which exam

     b. Bon, il acceptera de venir avec nous si on va où?   (Dagnac 2013)
        well, he will accept to come with us if we go where

This very quick description is sufficient to show how intricate is the phenomenon, and how much still needs to be investigated.[10] It provides a good example of how difficult it is to study the (real) grammar of written and normed languages. Standard acceptability judgement tasks, relying on metalinguistic awareness, are particularly inadequate for investigating this kind of stigmatized phenomena, in that they are prone to prescriptivism interferences. Corpus studies cannot do very much either, if one is interested in exploring the boundaries of the construction, and in particular its possibility for embedding, which is going to be very infrequent, or negative evidence (such as sensitivity to islands).

2.2 Special complementizers for questions: Québec French

Remaining on French, another interesting phenomenon that is observed in some varieties, and notably in Québec French, concerns the development of special complementizers for questions. Consider the following examples.

(29) a. Vous avez-tu peur?   Y/N questions
          you.2PL have-Q fear
          'Are you scared?'

      b. Ta mère est-tu là?
          your mother is-Q here
          'Is your mother here?'

(30) a. Où est-ce que tu étais?   wh-questions
          where *esk* you were
          'Where were you?'

      b. Donc, où ce qu'elle était?
          so, where *sek* she was
          'So, where was she?'

      c. Où qu'il est?
          where *ke* he is
          'Where is he?'

      d. Où ce ça va, après?
          Where *se* it goes, then
          'Where does it go, afterwards?'[11]

The data in (29)–(30) show the *emergence* of a new syntactic distinction that was not known to main Romance varieties up to now, namely a distinction between two specialized complementizers: one for polar questions (29), and one for wh-questions, stemming from the *est-ce-que* we have already discussed, coming in various more or less reduced variants (30). On the other hand, these data seem to display also *the loss* of a distinction which is in place in most standard Romance varieties, namely the ban on wh-filled Comp that we have just discussed (Section 1.1): in all the variants in (30) the wh-element is followed by a filled complementizer taking various forms.

As for polar questions, the exact analysis to be given to the question particle *tu*, which is homophonous to the second person singular pronoun, is not clear, and neither is its exact distribution. Some facts are known, though, and point once again towards an asymmetry between root and embedded questions contexts: the particle is only possible in root contexts as in (29), and ungrammatical in indirect questions (31):

(31) *Je me demande si vous avez-tu peur.
       I me wonder if you.PL have-Q fear
       'I wonder if you are scared.'

This restriction to root contexts is clearly reminiscent of Standard French AUX inversion, from which it clearly originates (see e.g. Picard 1992; Vinet 2001). But other properties, such as the loss of agreement features (*tu* is compatible with any subject) or its incompatibility with negation (32), are peculiar to its functioning as a question particle, and cannot be explained by its origin.

(32) a. *Vous avez-tu pas peur?
          you.2PL have-Q not fear
          'Aren't you scared?'

      b. N'avez-vous pas peur?
          Neg have-you.2PL NEG fear
          'Aren't you scared?'

As for the analysis, its postverbal position calls for placing *tu* in the inflection area (Noonan 1992; Rowlett 2007; Elsig 2009), while its incompatibility with embedding and its function as a clause type (e.g. a question particle) would rather push for analysis as a complementizer (Vinet 2001; Morin 2009). Be that as it may, these data reveal an area of innovation and evolution processes that partly escape from descriptive radars.

Mainland French is not extraneous from the same kind of process: the loss of a distinction, and the emergence of a new one. As we mentioned in the preceding section, French is supposed to be a language making a clear distinction between direct and indirect questions, with AUX inversion and esk-questions forbidden from embedded positions.

(33) *Je me demande quelle heure est-il.
      I wonder what time is it

(34) ?Je me demande qu'est-ce qu'on va faire.
      I wonder kesk we're gonna do

But the form *esk,* which is in French compatible with both polar and wh-questions, is more and more frequently used in embedded contexts (supposed to be ungrammatical in Standard). Interestingly, once again, this new usage goes with the development of a new grammatical feature that is completely absent from the grammar of standard French: embedded *esk* is only possible with wh-questions, not Y/N questions (Munaro and Pollock 2005). There is a contrast between (34), which is supposed to be ungrammatical but is indeed very much used in relaxed conversation, and (35), which is just impossible.

(35) *Je ne sais plus est-ce que la police a arrêté un escroc.
      I not know more esk the police has arrested a crook

This very quick and partial visit into the complementizer system of two varieties of French and its interaction with questions both show the same tendency, in different modes: both in Québec French and in spoken Mainland French, there is a tendency towards reducing the distinction between direct and indirect questions and towards introducing brand new differences between polar and wh-questions. In both cases, these developments escape the radar of official language descriptions and are at odds with prescriptivist attitudes, and are thus extremely difficult to study at least with the traditional methods of elicited acceptability judgements and corpus studies.

3 Wh-structures ambiguity: Free relatives

I will focus in the rest of the chapter on another often-neglected aspect of wh-structures, namely their systematic ambiguity.

In many languages wh-structures are ambiguous. This is the case, for example, of English: the wh-clause in (36) has in fact two interpretations and two distributions: that of a question (36)a and that of a free relative (36)b. What is the source of this ambiguity?

(36)   What Nikos wrote _
    a. I wonder what Nikos wrote _.
    b. I read what Nikos wrote _.

3.1 Analyses

There are at least two possible analyses. One, which has been proposed in particular by myself (Donati 2006) and in joint work with Carlo Cecchetto (Cecchetto and Donati 2015), claims that there is no structural difference between the two interpretations, but only a difference in label, or in category if you like. This can be represented in (37).

(37)   The labelling analysis

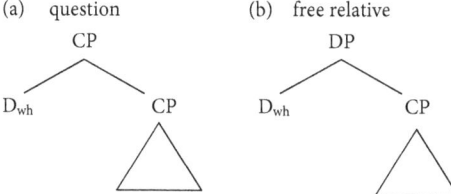

There is only one structure with two labelling possibilities: either the wh-element, which is a Determiner-like element, labels the structure, which is thus a DP (37)b; or the probing C, that is, the complementizer hosting the wh-element in its spec, labels the structure, and it is a (interrogative) CP (37)a.

An alternative analysis presupposes, in more traditional terms, a difference in structure between the two constructions. We shall call this the embedding analysis, since it claims that the free relative is embedded under a null DP stratum (38):

(38)   The embedding analysis

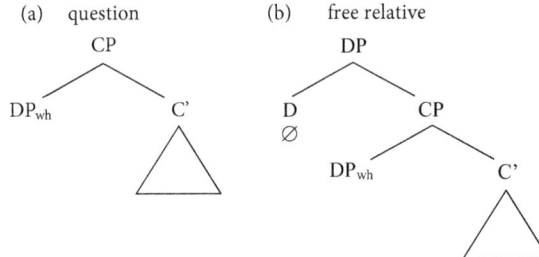

The structures are only superficially identical: in FR there is an extra DP layer embedding the CP. The two analyses can be compared on pure conceptual grounds. From this point of view, the labelling analysis is more parsimonious since it avoids the postulation of an empty D: there is nothing in (37) that doesn't meet the eye. The embedding implies on the other hand a simpler (more traditional) notion of labelling, where labelling ambiguities are simply not possible. The two analyses can also be compared on empirical grounds, to see if one accounts for the facts better than the other. This is what we shall look at in the next and final section.

3.2 Empirical evidence

The first empirical evidence in favour of labelling comes from the observation that the phrase status of the wh-element counts. If instead of a bare wh-element we have a more complex wh-phrase, the ambiguity disappears and the free relative reading is not available. This is illustrated in (39) for English:

(39)   a.   I wonder [[what books] Nikos wrote _.
       b.   *I read [[what books] Nikos wrote _.

This can be explained by the labelling analysis; if only heads (i.e. words) can label structures, not phrases.
     A second type of empirical evidence comes from adverbial clauses, which exhibit the same kind of systematic ambiguity: as shown in (40)–(41), the same wh-clause can be embedded either as an indirect question (a) or as an adverbial clause (b).

(40)   a.   I wonder [when Nikos started writing his book.]
       b.   I left [when Nikos started writing his book.]

(41)   a.   I wonder [where Nikos had told me to go.]
       b.   I went [where Nikos had told me to go.]

Here the embedding analysis would be forced to postulate the presence of some other embedding element, say a preposition, to explain the adverbial reading of the clause. But the phenomenon seems just the same: a wh-structure can give rise to a relative structure reading.[12]

Turning back to Romance, Italian can also provide another piece of evidence going in the same direction. There is an interesting asymmetry in Italian, not observable in English: while wh-clauses introduced by *chi* ('who') are ambiguous with free relatives, wh-clauses introduced by *che* ('what') are never so. This is illustrated in (42) versus (43).

(42)   a.   Seguo sempre chi li ama.
            follow.1SG always who me loves
            'I always follow (those) who love me.'

       b.   Mi chiedo chi mi ama.
            me wonder who me loves
            'I wonder who loves me.'

(43)   a.   Ho letto che ha scritto _.
            have.1SG read what has written
            'I read what he wrote.'

       b.   Mi chiedo che ha scritto.
            me wonder what has written
            'I wonder what he wrote.'

This asymmetry again follows from the labelling account: if *che* really belongs to a complex phrase with *cosa* ('thing'), which can be silent, *che* would then not qualify as a bare element, and thus would not be able as a head to label the structure.

Turning to French, however, consider (44).

(44)   J'ai lu [$_{DP}$ ce [$_{CP}$ que Nikos a écrit _]].
       I have written D *que* Nikos has written
       'I read what Nikos wrote.'

In (44), a CP is preceded by a determiner-like element, the light demonstrative *ce*, in what really looks like the overt counterpart of the abstract embedding postulated under the embedding analysis. As recently discussed in Konrad (2019), the very existence of this kind of 'light-headed' relatives (Citko 2004) seems *prima facie* to provide an important confirmation of the embedding analysis, as schematized in (45).

(45)

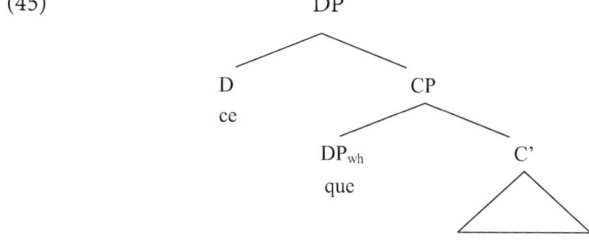

Things are not so simple however. Surprisingly, *ce que* structures are also ambiguous (46):

(46)   Je me demande [_DP_ ce [_CP_ que Nikos a écrit _]].
        I me wonder D *que* Nikos has written
        'I wonder what Nikos wrote.'

Example (46) is an example of an indirect question: surprisingly, here as well the interrogative CP appears to be embedded under a determiner head. This is of course puzzling for the embedding analysis and its related rigid labelling algorithm: a DP-embedded structure should have a DP label and a nominal distribution, not that of a question. See (47) for a representation.

(47)   Embedding analysis

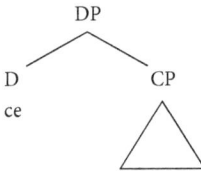

Example (46) is on the other hand somehow predicted under the labelling account, where either the D element or the probing C can label the same structure. A possible analysis is given in (48).

(48)   Labelling analysis

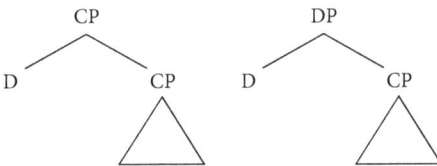

As pointed out in Konrad (2019), there is however an alternative analysis, that makes *ce que* relatives less relevant and less crucial for the understanding of the phenomenon.

It could be the case that *ce que* (*seke*) has been reanalysed as a (new) wh-element, a strong version of *que*_wh_, which is a clitic and has a very restricted distribution, as such (Obenauer 1976). After all, *ce que* needs to always be adjacent, and similar reanalyses are well attested in this domain (cf. *esk*).

(49)   Je me demande [*seke* Nikos a écrit _].
        I me wonder *seke* Nikos has written
        J'ai lu [*seke* Nikos a écrit _].
        I have read seke Nikos has written

If this were the right analysis, then *seke* structures would be yet another case of a wh-structure that is ambiguous between a question reading and a free relative reading, not providing any new argument in favour of one analysis or the other.

The phenomenon of D incorporation into a question word is indeed attested in many Romance varieties. An example is Portuguese, or my dialect (Florentine).[13]

(50) O que dice?
      D que says
      'What does he say?'

(51) Icché la vole?
      D-que she wants
      'What does she want?'

There are some differences however between the French case and these other Romance varieties (Konrad 2019). First of all, *seke* is not possible in root questions, as opposed to what was just illustrated for its equivalents in Portuguese and Florentine in (50) and (51).

(52) *Ce que tu veux _?
      Ske you want

Second, *seke* does not behave like the wh-element *que* (equivalent of 'what', but rather as the complementizer *que* (corresponding to 'that'): in particular, it is incompatible with infinitival clauses: (53), while the wh-element *que* is not (54). This is not true of the authentic D-WH forms attested in Portuguese (55) and in Florentine (56).

(53) *Je me demande ce que faire _.
      I me wonder *ske* do.INF
      'I wonder what to do.'

(54) Que faire _?
      what do.INF
      'What to do?'

(55) Não sabe o que fazer _ da vida.
      not knows o que make.INF of life
      'He doesn't know what to do with his life.'

(56) Non so icché si deve fare.
      not know icché we must do
      'I don't know what we should do.'

This seems to suggest that light-headed relative clauses in French are indeed what they look like: relative clause structures that are ambiguous with questions. They represent as such a missing link for the labelling analysis: just as you can have a question structure that can be interpreted as a relative clause, you can have a relative clause that can be interpreted as a question. Why this is possible in French, but not in other Romance languages using very similar lexical material, such as Italian (see (57)) is yet to be understood.

(57) a. *Mi chiedo quello che Nico ha scritto.
          me wonder DEM that Nico has written

      b. Ho letto quello che Nico ha scritto.
          have.1SG read DEM that Nico has written
          'I read what Nico wrote.'

4 Some conclusions on the importance of micro-contrastive analysis

I hope that these modest pages can assist in reminding us that any superficial lexical similarity is not sufficient to draw conclusions on a syntactic phenomenon, and that rather a fine-grained micro-contrastive analysis is necessary: Romance varieties are currently going in different directions, doing different things with more or less the same lexical material inherited from Latin.

Notes

1 This chapter is a revised version of the plenary talk I gave in beautiful Athens at the 8th International Conference on Contrastive Linguistics. I want to thank again Giannoula Giannoulopoulou and the other organizers for giving me this opportunity by inviting me, and in particular Angeliki Tsokoglou, with whom I shared the first steps into advanced syntax in late 1996 and whom I never forgot. Thanks also to the two anonymous reviewers of the manuscript, who helped improve this modest contribution.
2 See Borsley (2012) for an introduction to syntactic theory comparing a classical transformational approach (including traces) and categorial grammar approach, where long-distance dependencies are directly represented in the lexical specification of the verb.
3 For an introduction to the various accounts of islands, comparing them with a critical view, I recommend the excellent Boeckx (2012).
4 This idea of a substantial similarity of wh-constructions at LF stems from Huang's (1982) seminal work on Chinese.
5 See Cecchetto, Geraci and Zucchi (2009) for some possible answers.
6 Other Romance varieties display wh-*in situ* as well. See Munaro and Poletto (2002) for this phenomenon in some Northern Italian dialects and a comparison with French. See also Manzini and Savoia (2011).
7 GGF = *Grande Grammaire du français*.
8 ESLO2 = *Enquête Sociolinguistique d'Orléans 2*.

9   These data are based on an online experiment whose results are discussed in Métairy (2016).
10 We are abstracting away here from the variation dimension, which is massive; all we said here about locality restrictions in wh-*in situ* in French does not hold elsewhere. See, for example, Vlachos (2014) on Greek.
11 Data taken and adapted from Picard (1991).
12 On the fact that adverbial clauses are indeed free relatives, see Bhatt and Pancheva (2006).
13 See Munaro (2011) for a similar phenomenon in many other Northern Italian dialects.

References

Adli, A. (2006), 'French Wh-in-Situ Questions and Syntactic Optionality: Evidence from Three Data Types', *Zeitschrift Für Sprachwissenschaft*, 25 (2): 163–203.

Amritavalli, R. (2014), 'Separating Tense and Finiteness: Anchoring in Dravidian', *Natural Language & Linguistic Theory*, 32: 283–306.

Baunaz, L. (2011), *The Grammar of French Quantification*, Dordrecht: Springer Science & Business Media.

Beck, S. (2006), 'Intervention Effects Follow from Focus Interpretation', *Natural Language Semantics*, 14: 1–56.

Bhatt, R. and R. Pancheva (2006), 'Conditionals', in M. Everaert and H. van Riemsdijk (eds), *The Blackwell Companion to Syntax*, vol. 1, 638–87, Oxford: Blackwell.

Boeckx, C. (1999), 'Decomposing French Questions', *University of Pennsylvania Working Papers in Linguistics*, 6 (1): 69–80.

Boeckx, C. (2012), *Syntactic Islands*, Cambridge, UK: Cambridge University Press.

Borsley, R. D. (2012), 'Don't Move!', *Iberia: An International Journal of Theoretical Linguistics*, 4 (1): 110–39.

Bošković, Ž. (1998), 'LF Movement and the Minimalist Program', *Proceedings of NELS*, 28: 43–57.

Cecchetto, C. and C. Donati (2015), *(Re)labeling*, Cambridge, MA: MIT Press.

Cecchetto, C., C. Geraci and S. Zucchi (2009), 'Another Way to Mark Syntactic Dependencies: The Case for Right Peripheral Specifiers in Sign Languages', *Language*, 85 (2): 278–320.

Chang, L. (1997), 'Wh-in-Situ Phenomena in French', MA diss., University of British Columbia, Vancouver. Available online: https://open.library.ubc.ca/cIRcle/collections/ubctheses/831/items/1.0087736.

Cheng, L. (2001), *On the Typology of Wh-Questions*, New York: Garland.

Cheng, L. and J. Rooryck (2000), 'Licensing Wh-in-Situ', *Syntax*, 3 (1): 1–19.

Chomsky, N. (1986), *Barriers*, Cambridge, MA: MIT Press.

Citko, B. (2004), 'On Headed, Headless, and Light-Headed Relatives', *Natural Language & Linguistic Theory*, 22 (1): 95–126.

Dagnac, A. (2013), 'La variation des interrogatives en français', MS, Université Toulouse, France. Available online: https://www.researchgate.net/publication/278828491_La_variation_des_interrogatives_en_francais

Donati, C. (2006), 'On Wh-Head Movement', in L. Cheng and N. Corver (eds), *Wh-Movement Moving on*, 21–46. Cambridge, MA: MIT Press.

Elsig, M. (2009), *Grammatical Variation across Space and Time: The French Interrogative System*, Amsterdam: Benjamins.

Friedmann, N., A. Belletti and L. Rizzi (2009), 'Relativized Relatives: Types of Intervention in the Acquisition of A-bar Dependencies', *Lingua*, 119 (1): 67–88.

Gibson, E. (1998), 'Linguistic Complexity: Locality of Syntactic Dependencies', *Cognition*, 68 (1): 1–76.

Hofmeister, P. and I. Sag (2010), 'Cognitive Constraints and Island Effects', *Language*, 86: 366–415.

Huang, J. (1982), 'Logical Relations in Chinese and the Theory of Grammar', PhD diss., MIT, Cambridge, MA.

Konrad, I. (2019), 'At the Crossroads between (Semi-)free Relatives and Indirect Questions in French', in I. Feldhausen, M. Elsig, I. Kuchenbrandt and M. Neuhaus (eds), *Romance Languages and Linguistic Theory 15: Selected Papers from 'Going Romance' 30*, Frankfurt, Amsterdam: Benjamins.

Manzini, M. R. and L. M. Savoia (2011), 'Wh-in Situ & Wh-Doubling in Northern Italian Varieties: Against Remnant Movement', *Linguistic Analysis*, 37: 79–114.

Métairy, J. (2016), 'Le wh- in situ dans les phrases enchâssées en français', MA diss., Université de Paris Diderot.

Morin, A. (2009), 'On the Quebec French Interrogative Particle *tu*', in E. O. Aboh, E. van der Linden, J. Quer and P. Sleeman (eds), *Romance Languages and Linguistic Theory*, 201–22, Amsterdam: Benjamins.

Munaro, N. (2011), 'Free Relatives as Defective Wh-Elements. Evidence from the North-Western Italian Dialects', in Y. D' Hulst, J. Rooryck and J. Schroten (eds), *Romance Languages and Linguistic Theory*, 281–306, Amsterdam: Benjamins.

Munaro, N. and C. Poletto (2002), 'La tipologia dei wh in situ nelle varietà alto-italiane', *Quaderni Patavini Di Linguistica*, 18: 79–91.

Munaro, N. and J. Y. Pollock (2005), 'Qu'est-Ce Que (Qu')-Est-Ce Que? A Case Study in Comparative Romance Interrogative Syntax', in G. Cinque and R. Kayne (eds), *Handbook of Comparative Syntax*, 542–606, Oxford: Oxford University Press.

Noonan, M. B. (1992), 'Case and Syntactic Geometry', PhD diss., McGill University, Montreal, Québec.

Obenauer, H. G. (1976), *Etudes de syntaxe interrogative du français: quoi, combien et le complémenteur*, Tübingen: Niemeyer.

O'Grady, W. (1997), *Syntactic Development*, Chicago, IL: University of Chicago Press.

Phillips, C. (2011), 'Some Arguments and Non-Arguments for Reductionist Accounts of Syntactic Phenomena', *Language and Cognitive Processes*, 26: 1–32.

Picard, M. (1991), 'Clitics, Affixes, and the Evolution of the Question Marker 'tu' in Canadian French', *French Language Studies*, 1: 179–87.

Picard, M. (1992), 'Aspects synchroniques et diachroniques du tu interrogatif en québécois', *Revue québécoise de linguistique*, 21 (2): 65–75.

Rizzi, L. (1990), *Relativized Minimality*, Cambridge, MA: MIT Press.

Rooryck, J. (1992), 'Negative and Factive Islands Revisited', *Journal of Linguistics*, 28 (2): 343–74.

Ross, J. R. (1967), *Constraints on Variables in Syntax*, PhD diss., MIT, Cambridge, MA. (Published as (1986), *Infinite Syntax!*, Norwood, NJ: Ablex.)

Rouveret, A. (1980), 'Sur la notion de proposition finie: gouvernement et inversion', *Languages*, 60: 61–88.

Rowlett, P. (2007), *The Syntax of French*, Cambridge, UK: Cambridge University Press.

Rudin, C. (1988), 'On Multiple Questions and Multiple Wh-Fronting', *Natural Language & Linguistic Theory*, 6: 445–501.

Shlonsky, U. (2012), 'Notes on Wh in Situ in French', MS, University of Geneva. Available online: www.researchgate.net/publication/242698219_Notes_on_Wh_In_Situ_in_French.

Starke, M. (2001), 'Move Dissolves into Merge: A Theory of Locality', MS, University of Tromso. Available online: https://pdfs.semanticscholar.org/6dff/93e834a7f3dceb0fc41dc3047ac6731fe166.pdf

Stepanov, A. (2007), 'The End of CED? Minimalism and Extraction Domains', *Syntax*, 10 (1): 80–126.

Szabolcsi, A. (2006), 'Weak and Strong Islands', in M. Everaert and H. van Riemsdjk (eds), *The Blackwell Companion to Syntax*, 479–531, Oxford: Blackwell.

Takahashi, D. (1994), 'Minimality of Movement', PhD diss., University of Connecticut, Storrs. CT.

Uriagereka, J. (1999), 'Multiple Spell-Out', in S. D. Epstein and N. Hornstein (eds), *Working Minimalism*, 251–82. Cambridge, MA: MIT Press.

Vinet, M-T. (2001), *D'un français à l'autre: La syntaxe de la microvariation*, Montréal: Fides.

Vlachos, C. (2014), 'Wh-Inquiries into Modern Greek and their Theoretical Import(ance)', *Journal of Greek Linguistics*, 14: 212–47.

10

Wh-questions at the syntax-discourse interface: German–Swedish contrasts

Valéria Molnár

The chapter investigates information-eliciting *wh*-questions at the syntax-discourse interface by comparing two closely related Germanic languages, German and Swedish. These languages show considerable differences in the syntactic realization of *wh*-questions and in their mapping to discourse strategies. In the contrastive analysis of Swedish and German *wh*-questions, the discourse-semantic properties of clefts and the restrictions on their use deserve special attention. Whereas clefts are often used in Swedish *wh*-questions to indicate the need for referential specification of the *wh*-element, they are extremely marked in German. In German, modal particles seem to be the most important structural devices for marking different discourse-semantic aspects of *wh*-questions. Our analysis of different strategies used in Swedish and German is also supported by empirical evidence, provided by the comparison of relevant examples taken from Sjövall and Wahlöö's detective novels and their translations into German by Eckehard Schulz.[1]

1 Introduction

Questions are an important linguistic means for structuring discourse by creating a link between the communicative situation and the further development of the discourse. During the last decades, much attention has been paid to the relevance of questions for human communication in discourse-semantic theories. The *Speech Act Theory*, focusing on speaker-controlled strategies of interaction, and the *Questions-under-Discussion* (QUD)-approach, which emphasizes the decisive role of questions in selecting and structuring information in the text, have been especially influential. The latter theory put forward the claim that *discourse can be understood as being structured according to explicit or implicit questions* under discussion (Beaver 2012; Roberts 1996).

In a discourse-semantic approach two relevant research questions arise concerning the relation of questions and discourse:

1. In what way does the discourse influence the structure and the discourse properties of questions?
2. In what way do questions influence the development of the discourse?

In order to answer the above questions, it is necessary to investigate the discourse-semantic properties of questions and to pay special attention to the relation between their syntactic structure and the communicative context. The chapter will focus on different types of *wh*-questions at the syntax-discourse interface, comparing two closely related Germanic languages, German and Swedish. These languages show considerable differences in the syntactic realization of *wh*-questions and in their mapping to discourse strategies.

As illustrated by examples (1) and (2), *wh*-questions are different in German and Swedish with respect to their acceptability. In a context after a phone call where a discourse participant would like to know who called, no special syntactic marking is required in German (1-G), but Swedish seems to be different. The structure of the corresponding Swedish question (1-S) is grammatical, but seems not to be appropriate in the given context. (In the contrastive analysis of the languages the German examples will be marked by *G* and the Swedish ones by *S*.)

(1-G)   *Wer* hat angerufen?
         who has called
         'Who called?'

(1-S)   ? *Vem* ringde?
         who called
         'Who called?'

The preferred choice in Swedish is the cleft structure (2-S) in these contexts. In contrast, clefted *wh*-questions are strongly marked in German (2-G). (In the English translations of clefted sentences capitals will be used for marking focus on the *wh*-word or on the corresponding noun phrase.)

(2-S)   *Vem var det* som ringde?
         who was it   that called
         'WHO has called?'

(2-G)   ? *Wer war es,* der angerufen hat?
         who was it   that called   has
         'WHO has called?'

Clefts are, however, possible in both languages (cf. Huber 2002), not only in declarative clauses but also in questions. This is illustrated by examples (3-G), (3-S) and (4-G), (4-S) below:

(3-G)   *Peter* hat angerufen.   →   *Es ist Peter,* der angerufen hat.
         Peter has called   it is Peter that called   has
         'Peter has called.'   'PETER has called.'

(3-S) *Peter* ringde.   →   *Det är Peter* som ringde.
       Peter called   it   is Peter that called
       'Peter has called.'   'PETER has called.'

(4-G) *Wer* hat angerufen?   →   *Wer ist es,* der angerufen hat?
       'Who called?'   'WHO called?'

(4-S) *Vem* ringde?   →   *Vem var det* som ringde?
       'Who called?   'WHO called?'

Attested examples (5-S) and (6-S) from Sjöwall and Wahlöö's decalogy *Roman om ett brott* (*The Story of a Crime*) also show that the use of *wh*-questions is different in Swedish and German. The clefted questions are translated into German without the use of clefts:

(5-S) [CONTEXT: Mystiskt,   sa Rönn...]
                mysterious said Rönn
                'Mysterious, said Rönn.'
       Vad är det som är mystiskt?
       what is it   that is mysterious
       'WHAT is mysterious?'

(5-G) [CONTEXT: Hört sich geheimnisvoll an,   meinte Rönn.]
                hears REFL mysterious   PART, thought Rönn
                'It sounds mysterious, thought Rönn.'
       Was ist geheimnisvoll?
       what is mysterious
       'What is mysterious?'

(6-S) [CONTEXT: Ja, just det, man måste leta   tills man hittar det sa   Rönn...]
                yes, just it   one must search until one finds it   said Rönn
                'Exactly, one must continue looking for it until one finds it, said R.'
       Vad är det som har försvunnit?
       what is it   that has disappeared
       'WHAT has disappeared?'

(6-G) [CONTEXT: Eben, dann muß man suchen, bis   man es findet, sagte Rönn]
                just, then must one search until one it finds, said Rönn
                'Exactly, one must continue looking for it until one finds it, said R.'
       Was ist *denn*   verschwunden?
       what is MOD PART disappeared
       'What has disappeared?'

The contrastive analysis of *wh*-questions will address the following questions:

1. How can it be explained that clefts in German *wh*-questions are avoided, as opposed to Swedish – where this construction is frequently used in certain contexts?

2. Which instances of clefts are in Swedish *wh*-questions appropriate – and why?
3. Which formal means are used in German *wh*-questions in those contexts where clefts are preferred in Swedish?

The clarification of the differences in the form and distribution of *wh*-questions in language comparison requires the discussion of relevant theoretical issues. Special attention will be paid to the relation between the syntactic structure and different discourse-semantic dimensions of questions. These include the *information structural properties* of questions and their specific *communicative effects*. We will take a closer look at the basic notions of information structure like 'focus' versus 'background' and 'presupposition', as well as the distinction of different types of questions – like 'information-eliciting questions' versus questions with special functions (e.g. 'rhetorical questions').

The problem is that linguistic research has concentrated on the information structure of the answers and the information structure of questions has been left in the background. Questions have primarily been used as tools for the elicitation of focus in declarative sentences, which were regarded as answers to questions (partly present in the discourse, partly created by linguists based on the requirements of the context). The claim is that the *wh*-word corresponds to the *focus* of the answer. Consider (7)b as an answer to (7)a where the focus is *his girlfriend*, corresponding to the *wh*-word *whom*:

(7) a. *Whom* did Peter visit in London?
     b. [Peter visited]$_{\text{BACKGROUND}}$ [*his girlfriend*]$_{\text{FOCUS}}$

Questions are, however, always integrated into a context that has an impact both on their structure and their discourse-semantic properties. The main aim of this chapter is to account for the discourse-semantics of various types of *wh*-questions and its relation to the grammatical structure in different languages.

The chapter is structured as follows: After a definition of questions is provided in Section 2 the relation of *wh*-questions and focusing will be discussed in more detail in Section 3. Section 4 will be devoted to the discussion of the complementary notion of focus in *wh*-questions, by evaluating different proposals of research. The categorization of *wh*-questions in Swedish proposed by Brandtler (2010, 2012) is presented in Section 5, followed by the comparison of Swedish *wh*-questions with their German equivalents in Section 6. The contrastive analysis will be extended with the results of an empirical investigation in Section 7. The main results of the study will be summarized in Section 8.[2]

2 Definition of questions

Reis and Rosengren (1991: 6) ask in their paper *what it means to ask a question* and answer this research question in the following way: 'Obviously, the general purpose of the question is to point out a knowledge gap on the part of the speaker which normally can and should be closed by a linguistic action.'[3] Thus, according to their claim there are two constitutive, closely related dimensions in questions:

1. The *cognitive* dimension: presence of a 'knowledge gap'
2. The *interactive* dimension: the relevance of 'closing a gap.'

It is a controversial issue in linguistic research whether the cognitive or the interactive dimension should be regarded as decisive in the discourse-semantic analysis and in the evaluation of the illocutionary force of *wh*-questions. In influential theories the definition of questions is provided with respect to their semantics. According to Hamblin (1973), questions denote the set of all *possible* answers, whereas Karttunen (1977) argues that questions denote the set of all their *true* answers. However, the full range of the discourse-semantics of questions cannot be accounted for by reference to their semantic meaning; hence the clarification of the functional load of questions requires the inclusion of the interactional aspect. From the pragmatic perspective special attention has been paid to the illocutionary force of questions. They were originally regarded as *directives* (e.g. Searle 1971, 1975), but their analysis as *assertives* has also been suggested (see Brandt et al. 1991). According to other approaches they should receive a special 'intermediate' position in the system of speech acts (Wunderlich 1976; Sökeland 1980; Zaefferer 1984; Meibauer 1986).

Importantly, the illocutionary force of questions is closely related to the cognitive dimension. If the speaker has a real knowledge gap, he is interested in the reaction of the hearer and expects an answer to the question. Besides these 'real', information-eliciting questions, there are also *wh*-questions that do not require an answer. In these cases, the hearer already knows how the cognitive gap should be filled, either being aware of the fact that the set corresponding to the *wh*-word is empty or having information about the referents belonging to this set. These types of questions are used for rhetorical purposes and generally express the speaker's attitude to the propositional content.

Consequently, an important theoretical aspect of the analysis of *wh*-questions at the syntax-discourse interface is related to the cognitive gap, that is, the type and the range of *alternatives* that are evoked by the *wh*-word. Various options can be structurally indicated in *wh*-questions; marking the expectations of the speaker with respect to the operation on the cognitive gap influences the type of interaction between speaker and hearer. Evoking an empty set is, for example, typical for rhetorical questions; in the German example (8-G) the empty set can be unambiguously indicated by the modal particle *schon*. In contrast, evoking a non-empty set and/or signalling of the expected 'referential filling of the gap' can be guaranteed by a cleft in example (9-S):

(8-G)   *Wer schon*   hat das gewollt?
          who MOD PART has that wanted
          'Who wanted it?'

(9-S)   *Vem är det* som knackar på dörren?
          who is it   that knocks on door-the
          'WHO is knocking on the door?'

This distinction between 'real', information-eliciting questions and rhetorical questions is, however, not always marked in an unambiguous way by structural means.[4] *Wh-*questions in German and Swedish like (10-G) and (11-S) are often ambiguous with respect to the properties of the set and/or the need of referential specification. In these cases, additional formal marking or contextual clues are needed for the choice of interpretation in a specific context:

(10-G)   *Wer* ist für die Wiedervereinigung?   (Meibauer 1986)
        who is for the reunification
        'Who is for the reunification?'

(11-S)   *Vem* kan acceptera förslaget?
        who can accept   proposal-the
        'Who can accept the proposal?'

As we have shown, marking the presence of alternatives in *wh-*questions can be achieved by the use of a *wh-*element. However, the type and range of alternatives in *wh-*questions is dependent on further structural devices, for example, modal particles and clefts.

3 Focus in questions

In *wh-*questions, the *wh-*word has central relevance for evoking alternatives and consequently also for the elicitation of focus in answers. Interestingly, the *wh-*word is also regarded as the focus of the question in semantic approaches. However, this claim is not unproblematic from a discourse perspective since the *wh-*word does not specify any new information. The highlighted, informative element corresponding to the *wh-*word is given in the answer.

The solution of the problem is only possible if two different dimensions of *focus* are taken into consideration (see É. Kiss 1998). Focus is a semantic (set-theoretical) notion, operating on alternatives (as also suggested in *Alternative Semantics*, see Rooth 1985, 2016). Focus is at the same time a pragmatic (context-dependent) notion, specifying the relevant, 'at issue' part of the utterance (cf. Beaver 2012).

The semantic definition of focus covers both the *wh-*word in the question (with the function of set creation) and the focus in the answer, with the specification of the relevant alternatives, illustrated in (12)a and (12)b:

(12)   a. λx (Peter visited x) [his mother, his sister, his girlfriend...]
       (i.e. Whom did Peter visit? His mother, his sister, or his girlfriend...?)
   b. Peter visited [his girlfriend]$_{\text{FOCUS}}$

The *wh-*word – marked λx in (12)a – is the set of all those persons whom *Peter* visited. The corresponding constituent *his girlfriend* in the answer (12)b specifies the contextually relevant alternative(s).

Focus defined as a pragmatic notion related to the 'at issue' part of the information is, however, dependent on the context. It can – but does not need to – correspond to the semantically anchored focus. The 'at issue' part of information provided in (13)b can thus be narrowed down to the *wh*-word:

(13) a. Peter did not work yesterday, he made a visit in London.
      b. [Whom]$_{\text{FOCUS}}$ [did he visit in London?]$_{\text{BACKGROUND}}$

However, the 'at issue' information can have a larger extension as in example (14)b, where the domain of focus is 'broad' and incudes the whole question in the specified context:

(14) a. It's time to make plans for vacation.
      b. [Where should we go]$_{\text{FOCUS}}$?

The 'at issue' information of the question can also be related to a further 'narrow' constituent in marked cases like in (15)b:

(15) a. Peter visited his friends in England.
      b. Whom did he visit [in London]$_{\text{FOCUS}}$?

We can conclude that 'the pragmatically defined focus' and 'the semantic focus' are defined by different criteria. They can overlap in certain contexts, but this is not necessarily the case. The pragmatic focus of *wh*-questions can only be specified in relation to the previous context and can be related to different parts of the question. In contrast, the semantic focus is set-related, is obligatorily marked by the *wh*-word in *wh*-questions and has crucial influence on the development of discourse.

4 Focus and its complementary notion in questions

The distinction between the semantic and pragmatic dimension seems also to be relevant for the specification of further discourse-semantic properties of *wh*-questions. In this section we will discuss the impact of structurally and contextually anchored factors on the utterance by concentrating on the domain complementing the *wh*-word.

According to an influential proposal (see Stechow 1989) concerning the division of *wh*-questions in German, the complementary notion of 'focus' is 'background'. This claim is correct for the analysis of those cases where the part of the question following the *wh*-word is already contextually given (as in example (13)b). However, the complementary part of the *wh*-word can also belong to the new informative part of the question (see example (14)b) and the division of the *wh*-question in focus and background is not motivated in these cases. It is also obvious in example (16) that a general information-seeking question in discourse-initial position cannot contain a background part:

(16) [What]$_{\text{FOCUS???}}$ [happened]$_{\text{BACKGROUND???}}$?

Consequently, the specification of the status of the complementary part of the *wh*-element in questions requires the distinction of several discourse-semantic aspects and references to different notions (see Jacobs 1991). As we will argue, besides the context-dependent notion of *background* defined as *given* information, the notions *presupposition* and *implicature* seem to be relevant for the discussion. Presupposition can be regarded as an 'assertion' with an established positive truth value supported by lexical or structural devices. Conversational implicatures are less 'stable' than presuppositions; as weaker inferences, they are cancellable and do not guarantee contextual givenness.

In linguistic research, questions are often regarded as 'presuppositional' structures (cf. Katz and Postal 1964). It could be argued that the part of the question after the *wh*-word standing in square brackets in example (17)a is a presupposition (marked by the double arrow):

(17) a. Why [did Peter go to London]?   >>
     b. Peter went to London.

A standard diagnostic for presuppositions is the negation test and the claim is that presuppositions show constancy under negation. Thus (17)b is true independent of the positive or negative character of the answer to the *wh*-question (17)a. Consider (18)a and (18)b below containing a positive and a negative answer to (17)a:

(18) a. He visited his girlfriend.
     b. He had no special reasons.

However, the presuppositional character of the question (19)a is problematic in the following case:

(19) a. Who went to London?   >>
     b. Someone went to London.

The assumption of an 'existential presupposition' in example (19)a seems not to be correct, since (19)c would also be a potential appropriate answer to (19)a:

(19) c. Nobody went to London.

As argued by several researchers (see Karttunen 1977; Rosengren 1990; Brandtler 2010, 2012), the cancellability of the inference in cases like (19)a can be accounted for by the assumption of 'implication of existence' in the sense of a (generalized) conversational implicature.

We can thus conclude that the discourse-semantics of *wh*-questions requires a more nuanced analysis where different structural factors and contextual properties should be taken into consideration. In the following sections, we will argue for the following claims:

1. The presence of an 'implicature' or 'presupposition' in *wh*-questions complementing the *wh*-word is dependent on the question type which makes the differentiation of questions necessary.

2. Languages can differ with respect to the relevance of certain structural properties. As argued below, German and Swedish show interesting language-specific differences with respect to the triggering of presuppositions and marking implicatures. These differences also influence the behaviour of *wh*-questions in discourse, leading to contrasts in the preferred and appropriate marking of 'backgrounding' in German and Swedish.

5 The categorization of *wh*-questions

The starting point of our analysis is the proposal made by Brandtler (2010, 2012) for Swedish *wh*-questions. Brandtler distinguishes three types of *wh*-questions, paying special attention to their discourse-semantic structure and the presence of implicatures versus presuppositions. He points out that clefts are decisive for triggering presuppositions in *wh*-questions; however, other grammatical means like definiteness of the noun phrases, choice of tense forms and modality markers play an important role too. Interestingly, he also argues that the function of clefts is dependent on the question type.

The distinction of three categories – 'argument *wh*-questions', 'framing *wh*-questions' and 'propositional *wh*-questions' – is based on different 'degrees of factivity'. Brandtler (2012: 172) claims that argument *wh*-questions starting with *who, what, which* 'give rise to an implication of existence' and 'request the identification of an unspecified syntactic argument [...] selected for by the verb'. These questions allow the cancellation of the existential inference (being in this case an implicature). Consider example (20-S):

(20-S) a. *Vad åt du till lunch igår?*
             what ate you to lunch yesterday
             'What did you eat yesterday?'

        b. *Ingenting.*
             nothing
             'Nothing.'

The so-called 'framing *wh*-questions' of the second category (with *wh*-words like *when, where*) are 'semi-factive'; 'The function of these questions is to request specification of a spatiotemporal anchor to the event under discussion' (Brandtler 2012: 171). Whereas example (22-S)a contains a presupposition (22-S)b, motivated by the definiteness of the noun phrase *concert*, the implicature is cancellable in (21-S)a with an indefinite noun phrase:

(21-S) a. *När är koncerten   på Palladium?*   >>
             when is concert-the at Palladium
             'When will the concert at the Palladium be held?'
        b. There is a concert being held at the Palladium.

(22-S)　a.　*När*　är det　en koncert på Palladium? ~ >>
　　　　　　when　is there a　concert at　Palladium
　　　　　　'When will a concert be held at the Palladium?'
　　　　b.　There is a concert being held at the Palladium.

'Propositional questions' with *why, how* are subsumed by Brandtler (2012: 171) into the third category: 'This class of *wh*-questions requests the specification of e.g. the reasons for, the consequences of or the explication of the expressed proposition. Such information is extra-propositional, since it lies outside the structural domain of the sentence.' According to Brandtler, these *wh*-questions are 'true factive', where different definiteness and tense options do not influence the presuppositional character of the proposition:

(23-S)　a.　*Varför* hålls　　/ hölls　　en konsert / konserten　på Palladium? >>
　　　　　　why　hold REFL / held REFL a　concert / concert-the at　Palladium
　　　　　　'Why will be / was held a /the concert at the Palladium?'
　　　　b.　There is a concert being held at the Palladium.

The use of clefts in Swedish has, however, crucial importance for the discourse-semantics of *wh*-questions. 'Argument *wh*-questions' with clefts (introduced by *who, what, which*) are always factive. (24-S)b is thus not a felicitous answer to (24-S)a:

(24-S)　a.　*Vad　var det* (som) du　åt　till lunch igår?
　　　　　　what was it　that　you ate to　lunch yesterday
　　　　　　'WHAT did you eat for lunch yesterday?'

　　　　b.　# *Ingenting.*
　　　　　　nothing
　　　　　　'Nothing.'

Importantly, the two other categories of *wh*-questions – (certain types of) the 'framing *wh*-questions' and all 'propositional *wh*-questions' – carry a presupposition. Brandtler (2012: 175) claims that the use of clefts has a special effect in these cases: '[They are] primarily used to request re-activation of information that for some reason is unavailable to the speaker at the time of the utterance.' These *wh*-questions indicate a kind of backgrounding – with marking of the speaker's attitude to the proposition:

(25-S)　a.　*Vart　var det* du　skulle åka på semester (nu　igen)?
　　　　　　where was it　you would go　on vacation (now again)
　　　　　　'WHERE would you go on vacation (again)?'

　　　　b.　Det har　jag ju　redan　sagt – till Florida!
　　　　　　it　have I PART already said　to　Florida
　　　　　　'I have already said – to Florida!'

(26-S) a. *Varför var det* (som) du skulle åka till Israel (nu   igen)?
            why   was it   that you would go to Israel (now again)
            'WHY would you go to Israel (again)?'

    b. Det har jag ju   redan   sagt – för en konferens.
            it   have I   PART already said   for a   conference
            'I have already said – for a conference.'

We can thus conclude that clefts in Swedish are idiomatic and preferred in argument questions and have the function of indicating an existential presupposition, that is, for signalling a non-empty set. In contrast, clefts in framing and propositional questions generally have special effects and are marked structures.

6 Different types of *wh*-questions – from a contrastive perspective

German *wh*-questions can also be categorized according to Brandtler's proposal. 'Argument questions' (27-G)a are 'only' related to implicatures, whereas 'framing *wh*-questions' (28-G)a can and 'propositional *wh*-questions' (29-G)a must be related to presuppositions:

(27-G) a. *Wer* ist nach London gefahren?
            who is to   London gone
            'Who went to London?'

    b. *Niemand.* / Jemand.   / Peter.
            Nobody / someone / Peter
            'Nobody. / Someone. / Peter'.

(28-G) a. *Wann* ist Peter nach London gefahren?   >>
            when is Peter to   London gone
            'When did Peter go to London?'

    b. Peter ist nach London gefahren.
            Peter is to   London gone
            'Peter has gone to London?'

(29-G) a. *Warum* ist Peter nach London gefahren?   >>
            why   is Peter to   London gone
            'Why has Peter gone to London?'

    b. Peter ist nach London gefahren.
            Peter is to   London gone
            'Peter has gone to London?'

However, there are relevant differences between German and Swedish with respect to the use of clefted and non-clefted variants: in argument *wh*-questions (even in case of non-empty sets) the use of clefts in German is possible, but marked and not frequent; in 'framing *wh*-questions' and 'propositional *wh*-questions', clefts seem to be ungrammatical in most cases in German. Our evidence is based on informal grammaticality judgements and attested corpus examples taken from Sjöwall and Wahlöö's novels.

According to Brandtler (2012) clefts in argument *wh*-questions are appropriately used in contexts clearly indicating a non-empty set like in (30-S). The corresponding structure in German (30-G) is, however, problematic:

(30-S)   *Vem är det* som står   där   borta?
          who is it   that stands there away
          'WHO is standing there?'

(30-G)   ? *Wer ist es,* der da   drüben steht?
          who is it   that there over   stands
          'WHO is standing there?'

Framing *wh*-questions are possible with clefts in Swedish, even if they require special discourse contexts and trigger special effects. Their German equivalents are strongly marked:

(31-S)   *Var   var det* som du   åt   lunch?
          where was it   that you ate lunch
          'WHERE did you eat lunch?'

(31-G)   ?/* *Wo   war es,* dass du   zu Mittag gegessen hast?
          where was it   that you to lunch   eaten   have
          'WHERE did you eat lunch?'

(32-S)   *När   var det* du   var   i   Berlin?
          when was it   you were in Berlin
          'WHEN were you in Berlin?'

(33-G)   ?/* *Wann war es,* dass du   in Berlin warst?
          when was it   that you in Berlin were
          'WHEN were you in Berlin?'

Propositional *wh*-questions are also possible with clefts in Swedish with special effects. Clefts seem, however, not to be grammatical in these cases in German:

(34-S)   *Varför var det* (som) du ville   åka   till Berlin?
          why   was it   that you wanted to go to Berlin
          'WHY did you want to go to Berlin?'

(34-G)   * *Warum war es,* dass du   nach Berlin fahren wolltest?
          why   was it that you to   Berlin go   wanted
          'WHY did you want to go to Berlin?'

The differences between the two languages of our study can probably be traced back to two relevant structural reasons: First, clefts are often used in Swedish, even in the assertive cases (see Huber 2002). They are less marked structures than clefts in German and can more easily be used in *wh*-questions. Secondly, the use of clefts in Swedish is not only unmarked; clefts are quite relevant in argument *wh*-questions for disambiguation, that is, for indicating the necessity of referential specification. This is, however, not the case in German.

In German, modal particles seem to be the most important structural devices for the discourse-semantic partition of *wh*-questions. Interestingly, these additional tools are preferred for marking an empty set especially in rhetorical questions. Consider the use of the modal particles *schon, denn, überhaupt* in rhetorical questions (35-G)– (37-G) (cf. also Meibauer 1991):

(35 G) Wer will   *denn*   das?
        who wants MOD PART that
        'Who wants that?'

(36-G) Wer *überhaupt* will   das?
        who MOD PART wants that
        'Who wants that?'

(37-G) Wer will   *schon*   das?
        who wants MOD PART that
        'Who wants that?'

In 'normal' argument *wh*-questions (without modal particles), the tendency in German is stronger than in Swedish not to choose the rhetorical, but rather the information-eliciting interpretation. In Swedish, the empty set (typical for rhetorical questions) is not necessarily marked (38-S), but marking is possible by the use of the negation particle (39-S) and by negative polarity items (40-S) (cf. Brandtler 2012; SAG 1999):

(38-S) *Vem   väntar vi   på?*
        whom wait   we   on
        'Whom are we waiting for?'

(39-S) Vem vill   *inte* det?
        who wants not that
        'Who wouldn't want that?'

(40-S) Vem vill   *någonsin* stiga upp när   det är måndag?
        who wants ever   get up   when it is Monday
        'Who ever wants get up on a Monday?'

Even if 'normal' argument *wh*-questions are often ambiguous both in Swedish and German and can be interpreted as information-eliciting and/or rhetorical questions, the rhetorical interpretation (indicating an empty set for the *wh*-word) is more easily accessible in Swedish than in German. In Swedish, the special indication of a non-empty set by clefts is often required for the disambiguation of the question interpretation.

7 Language-specific differences – empirical evidence

The analysis presented of the Swedish and German *wh*-questions and the different use of clefts and modal particles was also verified by the translation of *wh*-questions found in Sjöwall and Wahlöö's novels collectively titled *Roman om ett brott* (*The Story of a Crime*).[5] The two relevant results of the empirical investigation are the following:

1. Clefts are only attested in Swedish *wh*-questions and the identified twelve instances are all argument *wh*-questions.
2. In the German translations of the Swedish clefted argument *wh*-questions, other strategies are used for rendering equivalent meanings.

The German translations appear without special devices for marking of the referential specification in examples (41-G) and (42-G):

(41-S) *Vad är det* du vill   veta?   (*What?*)
         what is it   you want to know
         'WHAT would you like to know about him?'

(41-G) *Was* willst du über ihn wissen?
         what want you about him know
         'What would you like to know about him?'

(42-S) *Vad   är det* som är mystiskt?   (*What?*)
         what is it   that is mysterious
         'WHAT is mysterious?'

(42-G) *Was* ist geheimnisvoll?
         what is mysterious
         'What is mysterious?'

In most cases, different modal particles (*denn, nun, da eben*) are used for referential specification in examples like (43-G)–(47-G):

(43-S) *Vem är det* som garvar?   (*Who?*)
         who is it   that laughs
         'WHO is laughing so loudly?'

(43-G) Wer lacht *denn*   so laut?
         who laughs MOD PART so loudly
         'Who is laughing so loudly?'

(44-S)   *Vem var det* som ville   ha   honom skuggad?   (*Who?*)
         who is   it   that wants have him   shadowed
         'WHO wanted to have him shadowed?'

(44-G)   Welche Dienststelle wollte   der *denn*   überwacht haben?
         which   position   wanted he MOD PART shadowed have
         'Which position did he want to shadow?'

(45-S)   *Vad   är det* som har försvunnit?   (*What?*)
         what is   it   that has disappeared
         'WHAT has disappeared?'

(45-G)   Was   ist *denn*   verschwunden?
         what is MOD PART disappeared
         'What has disappeared?'

(46-S)   *Vad   är det* som har hänt   egentligen?   (*What?*)
         what is   it   that has happened MOD PART
         'WHAT happened?'

(46-G)   Was   ist *nun*   *eigentlich* passiert?
         what is MOD PART MOD PART happened
         'What happened?'

(47-S)   *Vad   är det* Rönn pratar om?   (*What?*)
         what is   it   Rönn talks   about
         'WHAT is Rönn talking about?'

(47-G)   Was   erzählt mir   Rönn *da*   *eben*?
         what tells   me.DAT Rönn MOD PART MOD PART
         'What is Rönn talking about?'

8 Conclusion

Concluding the analysis of *wh*-questions at the interface between grammar and discourse we would like to draw attention to the following results:

According to our theoretical claim, an adequate account for the structure and discourse strategies of *wh*-questions requires the distinction of different discourse-semantic levels. Focusing in *wh*-questions is related to the semantic dimension by the *wh*-word inducing alternatives on the one hand; on the other, focusing is a pragmatic matter since focus as a context-dependent concept specifies the 'at issue' information in a given context. We have also argued that the 'remainder domain' (the complementary part of the *wh*-word, the semantic focus) in *wh*-questions should also be evaluated on different levels of discourse-semantics: 'background' is to be defined in relation to the context, whereas 'presupposition' and 'implicature' are structurally anchored. The structural anchoring of presupposition versus implicature is, however, dependent on the type of the *wh*-question (belonging to the category of argument, framing or propositional questions), the use of clefts and other grammatical means like (in)definiteness of noun phrases, tense forms and modality markers.

The contrastive analysis has shown that there are relevant differences between German and Swedish with respect to the structural devices used for triggering existential presuppositions in *wh*-questions (and the unambiguous marking of the expectation of referential specification versus empty set in the answers). In Swedish – as opposed to German – the marking of a 'non-empty set' is preferred by the use of clefts in argument questions. Here clefts can guarantee not only the existential presupposition but often the anchoring of the question in the previous context. Clefts are also possible in framing questions and propositional questions; however, they induce special effects in these cases. In contrast, the most important structural means for the discourse-semantic partition of *wh*-questions in German are the modal particles. They can be used for indicating the expectation of an 'empty set' in rhetorical questions. However, they are also relevant for structuring the information in *wh*-questions in other cases, especially for the marking of the background part in information-eliciting *wh*-questions.

Notes

1 The following four novels of the decalogy with their German translations were investigated in the study:

- 1968. *Den skrattande polisen*, 1971. *Endstation für neun* (*The Laughing Policeman*),
- 1969. *Brandbilen som försvann*, 1972. *Alarm in Sköldgatan* (*The Fire Engine that Disappeared*),
- 1971. *Den vedervärdige mannen aus Säffle*, 1973. *Das Ekel aus Säffle* (*The Abominable Man*),
- 1974. *Polismördaren*, 1976. *Der Polizistenmörder* (*Cop Killer*).

2 See also Molnár (2013).
3 Translated from German by VM: 'Es ist offensichtlich die allgemeine Aufgabe der Frage, auf eine Wissenslücke des Sprechers und Hörers hinzuweisen, die im Normalfall mit einer sprachlichen Handlung geschlossen werden kann und soll.'
4 See also Molnár and Winkler (forthcoming).
5 The decalogy of the Swedish authors Maj Sjöwall and Per Wahlöö *Roman om ett brott* (*The Story of a Crime*) was published between 1965 and 1975 in Stockholm (by Piratförlaget). The decalogy was translated into German by Eckehard Schulz and was published with the title *Roman über ein Verbrechen* in Reinbek bei Hamburg (by Rowohlt).

References

Beaver, J. (2012), 'IT Constructions', Talk given at GLOW, Potsdam, 30 March 2012.
Brandt, M., M. Reis, I. Rosengren and I. Zimmermann (1991), 'Satztyp, Satzmodus und Illokution', in I. Rosengren (ed.), *Satz und Illokution, Linguistische Arbeiten* 278, 1–90, Tübingen: Niemeyer.

Brandtler, J. (2010), 'The Evaluability Hypothesis', PhD diss., Lunds Universitet, Lund, Sweden.

Brandtler, J. (2012), *The Evaluability Hypothesis: The Syntax, Semantics, and Pragmatics of Polarity Item Licensing*, Amsterdam: Benjamins.

Kiss, K. É. (1998), 'Identificational Focus versus Information Focus', *Language*, 74 (2): 245–73.

Hamblin, C. L. (1973), 'Questions in Montague English', *Foundations of Language*, 10: 41–53.

Huber, S. (2002), *Es-Clefts und det-Clefts*, PhD diss., Lunder germanistische Forschungen 64, Lunds Universitet, Lund, Sweden.

Jacobs, J. (1991), 'Implikaturen und "alte Information" in Fragen', in M. Reis and I. Rosengren (eds), *Fragesätze und Fragen, Linguistische Arbeiten* 257, 201–22, Tübingen: Niemeyer.

Karttunen, L. (1977), 'Syntax and Semantics of Questions', *Linguistics and Philosophy*, 1: 1–44.

Katz, J. J., and P. Postal (1964), *An Integrated Theory of Linguistic Descriptions*, Cambridge, MA: The MIT Press.

Meibauer, J. (1986), *Rhetorische Fragen, Linguistische Arbeiten* 167, Tübingen: Niemeyer.

Meibauer, J. (1991), 'Existenzimplikaturen bei rhetorischen *w*-Fragen', in M. Reis and I. Rosengren (eds), *Fragesätze und Fragen, Linguistische Arbeiten* 257, 223–42, Tübingen: Niemeyer.

Molnár, V. (2013), 'Fragen im Fokus – Fokus in Fragen', in M. Grote, K. Berg Henjum, E. Ingebrigtsen and J. P. Pietzuch (eds), *Perspektiven. Das IX. Nordisch-Baltische Germantistentreffen, Stockholmer Germanistische Forschungen* 78, 45–62, Stockholm: Stockholm University Library.

Molnár, V. and S. Winkler (forthcoming), 'Strategic Functions of Questions and Ambiguity', in M. Bauer and A. Zirker (eds), *Strategies of Ambiguity*, London: Routledge.

Reis, M. and I. Rosengren (eds) (1991), *Fragesätze und Fragen, Linguistische Arbeiten* 257, Tübingen: Niemeyer.

Roberts, C. (1996), 'Information Structure in Discourse. Towards an Integrated Formal Theory of Pragmatics', in J. H. Yoon and A. Kathol (eds), *Ohio State University, Working Papers of Linguistics*, 49: 91–136.

Rooth, M. (1985), 'Association with Focus', PhD diss., University of Massachusetts, Amherst, MA.

Rooth, M. (2016), 'Alternative Semantics', in C. Féry and S. Ishihara (eds), *Oxford Handbook of Information Structure*, 128–46, Oxford: Oxford University Press.

Rosengren, I. (1990), 'W-Interrogativsatz, Skopus und Fokus', *Sprache und Pragmatik*, 16: 29–71.

Searle, J. R. (1971), *Sprechakte. Ein philosophischer Essay*, Frankfurt am Main: Suhrkamp.

Searle, J. R. (1975), 'Indirect Speech Acts', in P. Cole and J. L. Morgan (eds), *Speech Acts. Syntax and Semantics* 3, 59–82, New York: Academic Press.

Sökeland, W. (1980), *Indirektheit von Sprachhandlungen, Reihe Germanistische Linguistik* 26, Tübingen: Niemeyer.

Stechow, A. von (1989), 'Focusing and Backgrounding Operators', *Fachgruppe Sprachwissenschaft*, Arbeitspapier Nr. 6, Universität Konstanz, Germany.

Teleman, U., S. Hellberg and E. Andersson (1999), *Svenska Akademins Grammatik*, Stockholm: Norstedts Ordbok. (cited as SAG 1999)

Wunderlich, D. (1976), *Studien zur Sprechakttheorie*, Frankfurt am Main: Suhrkamp.

Zaefferer, D. (1984), *Fragen und Frageausdrücke im Deutschen*, München: Fink.

11

Focus types: A crosslinguistic study of clause and information structure

Michalis Georgiafentis and Angeliki Tsokoglou

In this chapter we comparatively examine the clause and information structure of English, German, Spanish, Italian and Greek, drawing our attention to focus types (information focus and contrastive focus) and the various word order patterns that result from them. The study aims at tracing the similarities and the differences of the aforementioned languages, with respect to focus types, on the one hand, and specific characteristics of the languages, on the other.

The findings of this study shed light on the issue of word order variation in relation to focus types and the mechanisms employed in its crosslinguistic realization. More specifically, the morpho-syntactic properties of the languages affect clause structure and the syntactic operations involved. Since information structure is not a purely syntactic phenomenon, intonation also plays a crucial role. It appears that, in the axis of the languages under investigation, we have two poles, namely a very restricted one with respect to morpho-syntactic properties, that is, English, where focus is regulated by prosody, and an almost unrestricted one, that is, Greek, which allows for both prosodic and syntactic operations. In between stands German with a restricted clause structure, where *in situ* stressing is possible, whereas Spanish and Italian with restricted prosodic properties (lack of *in situ* stress) employ movement mechanisms.

1 Introduction

The study of word order has always been one of the most important factors in the investigation of clause structure, associated with information structure (topic-comment, topic-focus) in various frameworks (e.g. in Systemic Functional Grammar, but also in Generative Grammar).

Within these studies, Comparative Linguistics plays a key role, aiming at either the typological categorization of languages (see e.g. Greenberg 1963) or the identification of a universal clause structure, as well as the common mechanisms involved in the derivation of the various patterns.

In this chapter we comparatively examine the clause and information structure of English (see e.g. Guéron 1980; Birner and Ward 1998), German (see e.g. Fanselow 1988, 2008, Abraham and Molnárfi 2002; Frey 2005; Krifka 2007; Fanselow and Lenertová 2011), Spanish (see e.g. Zubizarreta 1998; Ordóñez 1998, 2000; Zagona 2002; Ortega-Santos 2016), Italian (see e.g. Rizzi 1997; Cardinaletti 2001; Belletti 1999, 2001, 2004; Bocci 2013) and Greek (see e.g. Philippaki-Warburton 1985; Tsimpli 1990, 1995, 1998; Lascaratou 1998; Georgiafentis 2004; Skopeteas 2016), paying attention to focus types and the various word order patterns that result from them. The choice of these languages is based on the specific characteristics that each of them has with respect to: (a) language family, (b) basic clause structure, (c) the possibility of subject pronoun omission (pro-drop), (d) word order flexibility and (e) the inflectional (verbal and nominal) system.

The aim of this chapter is to identify the similarities and the differences of the languages under investigation with respect to focus types, namely, information and contrastive focus on the one hand, and specific characteristics of the languages on the other.

This chapter is organized as follows: In Section 2 we roughly sketch some basic notions of information structure and in Section 3 we briefly present the characteristics of the languages under investigation. In Section 4 we refer to the mechanisms of realization of information and contrastive focus in each language and in Section 5 we make some remarks that result from the comparison of the languages. Section 6 concludes the discussion.

2 Information structure – focus: Types and mechanisms of its realization

The term 'information structure', first introduced by Halliday (1967), describes in general the way in which information is formally packaged within a sentence and has been investigated by different linguistic frameworks. In particular, it has been pointed out that information structure involves the interaction of different linguistic levels.[1]

The complex notion of Focus has thus been examined from a syntactic, semantic, and prosodic, as well as a pragmatic, point of view.[2] The literature on focus comprises a number of terms used to describe different categories, functions and interpretative properties of focus. The most frequently used are 'broad' versus 'narrow' focus (first presented in Ladd 1980), on the one hand, and 'information' versus 'contrastive' focus, on the other.

Broad focus is typically associated with utterances in 'out-of-the-blue' contexts, as in (1), in which all information introduced is new.

(1)   What happened?
        Georgia bought a house.

On the other hand, narrow focus requires the hearer to partition the utterance into presupposed and asserted parts, and provides them with unambiguous cues as to which constituent is the focus of the utterance, as in (2):

(2) Who bought a house?
     Georgia[3] bought a house.

Narrow focus allows for two versions: information focus, which may simply convey new information, as in (2) above, or contrastive focus, which may express identification/contrast by selecting the member of a subset that makes the assertion of the sentence true,[4] as in (3):

(3) So, Alexandra bought a house?
     No, PETER bought a house.

In the present study we concentrate on information focus and contrastive focus, but we do not ignore the fact that the interpretations and the names attributed to the two focus notions have not been exactly the same.[5]

The main mechanisms[6] that languages employ in order to mark focus elements can be summarized as follows:

1. Phonological rules: The focused element has the main stress/accent, which is realized by applying rules such as: (a) the Nuclear Stress Rule (Chomsky and Halle 1968) as revised by Cinque (1993) and Zubizarreta (1998), according to which the most embedded constituent receives the main stress of the sentence/phrase in neutral/unmarked structures or (b) the rule 'assign stress to the focus constituents' (Erteschik-Shir 2007: 31), which covers also stressing elsewhere.
2. Syntactic mechanisms, in which word order plays a crucial role, involving the position of a constituent in the base structure or in a derived structure, either through movement of the focused constituent to a (potential) focus position or through movement of other constituents.

Given the information structure notions roughly sketched, our aim is to examine to what extent prosodic and syntactic properties interact with respect to clause structure, taking into account the characteristics of each language under investigation. Therefore, we concentrate on some of the standard cases, following generally accepted assumptions, although we are aware of the fact that some cases have received various and often contradicting analyses.

3 Characteristics of the languages under investigation

In Table 11.1 we present the main characteristics and properties of the languages under investigation. We will make use of them as we proceed with the presentation of each language.

Table 11.1 Characteristics and Properties of the Languages

Characteristics of the languages	ENGLISH	GERMAN	SPANISH	ITALIAN	GREEK
language family	Germanic	Germanic	Romance	Romance	Greek
basic word order	S-V-O	S-O-V, but also S-V-O (V2 language)	S-V-O[7]	S-V-O	S-V-O and V-S-O[8]
inflectional system	poor inflection in both verbal and nominal systems	rich verbal and nominal system	rich verbal / less rich nominal system	rich verbal / less rich nominal system	very rich verbal and nominal system
pro-drop	no	no[9]	yes	yes	yes
word order flexibility	no	yes (with fixed positions for the verb)	yes	yes	yes (all variants are possible)
other characteristics	no left periphery	V→T→C, no rich left periphery, scrambling	V→T, post verbal subjects, left dislocated topic (left periphery), scrambling/ p-movement	V→T and Subject→ Spec-TP, rich left periphery (topics and focus in the C-domain), movement in the VP/ IP-domain	V→T, post verbal subjects, rich left periphery (topics and focus in the C-domain)

4 Mechanisms of realization of information and contrastive focus in English, German, Spanish, Italian and Greek

We begin with a common characteristic for all languages: The Nuclear Stress Rule (NSR) applies to the most embedded constituent of the sentence. In out-of-the-blue contexts, all languages behave similarly, as illustrated in examples (4)–(8):

(4) What happened?   (English)
     John sold *the car*.

(5) Was ist passiert?   (German)
     Hans hat *sein Auto* verkauft. (S-V-O)[10]
     'Hans has sold his car.'

(6) ¿Qué pasó?   (Spanish)
     José fue *a casa*. (S-V-O)
     'What happened?'
     'José went home.'

(7) Che succede?   (Italian)
     Giovanni sta rimproverando *Maria*. (S-V-O)
     What is happening?'
     'Giovanni is scolding Maria.'

(8) Τα 'μαθες τα νέα;   (Greek)
     a. Ο Γιάννης παντρεύτηκε *τη Μαρία*. (S-V-O)
     b. Παντρεύτηκε ο Γιάννης *τη Μαρία*. (V-S-O)
        'Have you heard the news?'
        'Janis married Maria.'

4.1 Information focus

English is a strictly S-V-O language, in which information focus is marked via the NSR for the object (9) and by stressing *in situ* for the subject (10) or the verb (11):

(9) What did John sell?
     He sold *the car*. (S-V-O)

(10) Who sold the car?
     John sold it. (S-V-O)

(11) What did John do with his car?
     He *sold* it. (S-V-O)

German, on the other hand, is an S-O-V language with respect to its base structure[11] and the structure of subordinate clauses and a V2-language with respect to main clauses. This means that VP and TP are head-final, while CP is head-initial. Furthermore, in main clauses the finite verb obligatorily moves to C and an XP must obligatorily move to SpecCP. Another relevant characteristic is that it allows scrambling (movement) to higher projections below C.[12]

Information focus is marked in neutral sentences via the NSR, which means that the DO carries the main stress in transitive or ditransitive constructions in both subordinate and main clauses (12). Since German is an S-O-V language and thus left branching with respect to VP, main prominence is on the left (see Cinque 1993).

(12) a. …, dass Hans dem Lehrer *das Buch* gegeben hat. (S-IO-*DO*-V)
      b. Hans hat dem Lehrer *das Buch* gegeben. (S-V-IO-*DO*)
         'Hans has given the teacher the book.'

Focus is also marked *in situ*, by stressing the focused element (13) (Krifka 2000, referring to Paul 1880):

(13) Karl ist gestern nach Berlin gefahren.
      a. A: Wer ist gestern nach Berlin gefahren?
         B: *Karl* ist gestern nach Berlin gefahren.

      b. A: Wohin ist Karl gestern gefahren?
         B: Karl ist gestern *nach Berlin* gefahren.

      c. A: Wie ist Paul gestern nach Berlin gereist?
         B: Karl ist gestern nach Berlin *gefahren*.
            'Karl drove to Berlin yesterday.'

In marked sentences, scrambling of constituents leaves one constituent as the most embedded.[13] Scrambling applies in German on both subordinate (14) and main clauses (15) in the same way:[14]

(14) a. …, dass Hans das Buch *dem Lehrer* gegeben hat. (S-DO-*IO*-V)
      b. …, dass dem Lehrer das Buch *Hans* gegeben hat. (IO-DO-*S*-V)
         '… that Hans has given the teacher the book.'

(15) a. Gestern hat Hans das Buch *dem Lehrer* gegeben. (XP-V-S-DO-*IO*)
      b. Gestern hat dem Lehrer das Buch *Hans* gegeben. (XP-V-IO-DO-*S*)
         'Hans gave the teacher the book yesterday.'

Regardless of how scrambling is analysed, as A- or A-bar movement[15] or movement within vP/VP (via adjunction)[16] or in the IP area, it is assumed that scrambled elements target topic-positions (see Fanselow 1988; Haftka 1995: 863–5; Meinunger 2000; cf. Struckmeier 2017 for a different view)[17] or stand outside the focus domain (see Rosengren 1993).

In wh-questions, information focus is also realized by topicalizing the DO, that is, moving it to SpecCP, leaving the subject in SpecTP or vP-internal, where it gets the main stress (16), or by fronting the focused constituent to SpecCP (17):[18]

(16) Wer hat gestern den Chef getroffen?
Den Chef hat gestern *Hans* getroffen. (O-V-*S*)
'Who met the boss yesterday?'
'Hans met the boss yesterday.'

(17) Wen hat Hans gestern getroffen?
Den Chef hat er getroffen. (*O*-V-S)
'Whom did Hans meet yesterday?'
'He met the boss yesterday.'

Spanish is an S-V-O language (but see endnote 7), in which information focus is marked: (a) by applying the NSR for the object, as in (18) (Zagona 2002: 209), and (b) by moving other elements through scrambling (Ordóñez 1998, 2000) or p-movement (Zubizarreta 1998), leaving the focused constituent as most embedded, as in (19) and (20) for the subject (Zagona 2002: 210–11 and Zubizarreta 1998):[19]

(18) ¿Adónde fue José?
José fue *a casa*. (S-V-*O*)
'Where did José go?'
'José went home.'

(19) ¿Quién fue a casa?
Fue a casa *José*. (V-O-*S*)
*José fue a casa.
'Who went home?'
'José went home.'

(20) Comió una manzana *Juan*. (V-O-*S*)
'Juan ate an apple.'

Italian is also an S-V-O language, in which information focus is realized through the NSR for the object (21):

(21) Chi ama Giovanni?
Giovanni ama *Maria*. (S-V-*O*)
'Whom does Giovanni love?'
'Giovanni loves Maria.'

The NSR applies to the final position, that is, either the verb, as in (22)a, or the subject becomes the focused constituent, as shown in (22)b (from Cinque 1993: 260), which means *in situ* stressing is not available (22)c:

(22) a. Truman è *morto*. (S-*V*)
'Truman died.'

b. È morto *Johnson*. (V-*S*)
'Johnson died.'

c. **Johnson* è morto.

As Cardinaletti (2001) mentions, in the V-O-S order, the subject can be an information focus, as the most embedded constituent in the clause, and be assigned main prominence via the NSR, as illustrated in (23):

(23)   Chi porterà la macchina?
         Porterà la macchina *Mara*. (V-O-S)
         'Who will drive the car?'
         'Mara will drive the car.'

Whereas Cardinaletti assumes that in this case the subject remains vP/VP-internal, Belletti (1999, 2001, 2004) argues that the VO sequence constitutes the given part of the information provided by the sentence, so that the subject has moved to a clause internal SpecFocusP and the given constituent (object) moves to a SpecTopicP, which is located right above the clause internal FocusP.

It is crucial to point out here, that contrary to Spanish, Italian lacks V-S-O (24) (see Zubizarreta 1998: 118, 123):

(24)   *Ieri ha dato Gianni un libro a Maria.
         'Yesterday, Gianni gave a book to Maria.'

Zubizarreta (1998: 123) claims that the subject in Italian checks nominative case in SpecTP, while it does not in Spanish; it can remain vP/VP-internal, where SpecTP is a syncretic position.

Greek exhibits great flexibility with respect to word order, so that every possible pattern yields a grammatical sentence, as (25) shows:

(25)   a. Ο μαθητής ρώτησε τον δάσκαλο. (S-V-O)
         b. Ρώτησε ο μαθητής τον δάσκαλο. (V-S-O)
         c. Ρώτησε τον δάσκαλο ο μαθητής. (V-O-S)
         d. Τον δάσκαλο ρώτησε ο μαθητής. (O-V-S)
         e. Ο μαθητής τον δάσκαλο ρώτησε. (S-O-V)
         f. Τον δάσκαλο ο μαθητής ρώτησε. (O-S-V)
             'The pupil asked the teacher.'

With respect to the basic order, Greek has been traditionally classified as an S-V-O language. Within the generative framework the analyses are divided. In particular, it has been claimed that Greek is: (a) a V-S-O language, since it has obligatory movement V to T; the subject then in S-V-O is analysed as a topic in a peripheral position (SpecCP or TopicP) (Philippaki-Warburton 1982, 1987, 1990 and Tsimpli 1990; Alexiadou 1997, 1999; Alexiadou and Anagnostopoulou 1998; Spyropoulos and Philippaki-Warburton 2001; Kotzoglou 2013) or (b) an S-V-O, with the subject not interpreted as a topic (Horrocks 1994; Drachman and Klidi 1992; Roussou and Tsimpli 2006; Spyropoulos and Revithiadou 2009).

As far as information focus is concerned, regardless of the basic word order adopted, in the S-V-O order the object, as the most embedded constituent in the clause, is assigned main prominence via the NSR, as in (26):

(26) Τι έφαγε ο Γιάννης;
     Ο Γιάννης έφαγε *την τούρτα*. (S-V-*O*)
     'What did Janis eat?'
     'Janis ate the cake.'

However, alongside (26) above, we may find S-V-O patterns in Greek, where the subject carries main prominence; that is, it is informationally focused (27). In this case, it can be claimed that information focus is realized *in situ*.[20]

(27) Ποιος έφαγε την τούρτα;
     Ο Γιάννης έφαγε την τούρτα.[21] (*S*-V-O)
     'Who ate the cake?'
     'Janis ate the cake.'

It is worth pointing out here that, unlike Spanish and Italian, where the V-O-S pattern is the only preferred option as an answer to a 'who-question', in Greek the preferred patterns are either S-V-O or O-cl-V-S (see the experimental data in Georgiafentis and Sfakianaki 2004, cf. also Keller and Alexopoulou 2001; Georgakopoulos and Skopeteas 2010). This means that Greek appears not to need scrambling or movement, so that the NSR can apply for information focusing, but the subject can be stressed *in situ*. This is not an option in Spanish or Italian, where an S-V-O pattern with an informationally focused subject does not exist, unlike Greek. Consider the relevant data (in (28)–(29)), which show that in such cases the V-O-S pattern arises.

(28) Comió una manzana *Juan*. (Spanish V-O-*S*)
     'Juan ate an apple.'

(29) Porterà la macchina *Mara*. (Italian V-O-*S*)
     'Mara will drive the car.'

4.2 Contrastive focus

In English, contrastive focus is realized by stressing the constituent *in situ*, as in (30) and (31) for the subject and the object, respectively:

(30) JOHN bought the book, not Peter. (*S*-V-O)
(31) John bought A BOOK, not a magazine. (S-V-*O*)

Marginally, English allows fronting of the DO, in SpecCP or as an IP adjunction, where it takes emphatic stress, as in (32) (Birner and Ward 1998); otherwise, it is interpreted as a topic (33):

(32) RED wine I prefer, not white. / COFFEE I drink / NATURE I like.
(33) Red wine, I like. / That kind of thing, I don't think I'd ever do.

Alternatively, it is realized as a cleft sentence, such as (34):

(34) It was John that bought the book.

In German, contrastive focus is realized: (a) by stressing *in situ* (35), (b) by fronting the focused constituent to SpecCP and the verb to C (36), (c) by topicalizing or scrambling other constituents – since scrambled constituents target topic-positions – as in (37), or (d) by paraphrasing (38):

(35) a. HANS hat den Chef getroffen, nicht Peter. (S-V-O)
      b. Hans hat DEN CHEF getroffen, nicht den Koch. (S-V-O)
          'HANS has met the boss, not Peter.'
          'Hans has met the BOSS, not the cook.'

(36) DEN CHEF hat Hans getroffen. (O-V-S)
      'Hans has met THE BOSS.'

(37) Karl hat den Gästen die Wahrheit gesagt.
      Nein, die Wahrheit hat den Gästen (wohl) HANS gesagt. (DO-V-IO-S)
      'Karl said the truth to the guests. / No, (part.) HANS said the truth
      to the guests.'

(38) Es war HANS, der dem Lehrer das Buch gegeben hat.
      'It was Hans who gave the teacher the book.'

In Spanish, it is generally assumed that contrastive focus involves movement to a fronted position, possibly SpecFocusP, for both the subject (39) (Zagona 2002: 248, 254), and the object (40) (Domínguez 2004: 177):[22]

(39) MARÍA compró esos tomates en el mercado, no José. (S-V-O)
      'It was Maria who bought the tomatoes at the market, not José.'

(40) LA MESA ha roto Javi. (O-V-S)
      'It's the table that Javi has broken.'

As for contrastive focus *in situ*, such as V-O in (41), Domínguez (2004: 174) proposes that it involves covert movement at LF:

(41) Ha roto LA MESA. (Domínguez 2004: 177)
      'It's the table that he has broken.'

What is crucial is that Spanish allows V-S-O, with an XP occupying the preverbal position (42a),[23] it allows for more than one topic (42b) (see Zubizarreta 1998: 100–2),[24] Emphatic-V and Focus-V are possible (43), while Emphatic-XP-V or Focus-XP-V are excluded (44) (see Zubizarreta 1998: 103–4).

(42)   a.   Todos los dias compra Juan el diario. (XP-V-S-O)
           'Juan buys the newspaper every day.'

       b.   Todos los dias, Juan compra el diario. (XP-S-V-O)
           'Every day, Juan buys the newspaper.'

(43)   (Estoy segura que) Pedro, LAS ESPINACAS trajo (y no las papas).
       '(I'm sure that) Pedro, it is the spinach that he brought (and not the potatoes).'

(44)   *LAS ESPINACAS, Pedro trajo (y no las papas).

This means, according to Zubizarreta's (1998) analysis of contrastive focus, that no focus phrase is assumed in the CP domain, but rather focused phrases, wh-phrases, topics, subjects and emphatics make up syncretic categories when combined with the feature 'T(ense)'. In particular, Zubizarreta (1998: 117) assumes that the 'focus' feature makes up a syncretic category with T, and SpecTP is a position where focused elements check their 'focus' feature.

   In Italian, it is generally assumed that contrastive focus involves movement. As far as subjects are concerned, it appears that contrastively focused preverbal and postverbal subjects must necessarily move to FocusP at the left periphery (Belletti 1999, 2001, 2004), as in (45):

(45)   GIANNI ha capito il problema (non tutta la classe). (S-V-O, S in FocusP)
       'It is Gianni that understood the problem, not the whole class.'

A low contrastive focus, as in (46), involves – according to Belletti (1999, 2001, 2004) – overt movement of the subject to the Spec of the high FocusP, and subsequent remnant movement of the IP[25] to the Spec of a higher TopicP, which makes the subject postverbal:

(46)   Ha capito il problema GIANNI (non tutta la classe). (V-O-S, S in FocusP)
       'It is Gianni that understood the problem, not the whole class.'

The same operation holds also for the object (Belletti 2004; Bocci 2013: 12), as in (47):

(47)   a.   – A: Mi hanno detto che hai incontrato Lucia Domenica. Come l'hai
           trovata?
           'They told me that you met Lucia on Sunday. How did you find her?'

       b.   – B: VERONICA ho incontrato Domenica (, non Lucia)! (O-V, O in
           FocusP)
           'VERONICA I met on Sunday (, not Lucia)!'

Alternatively (Bocci 2013: 12), a direct object can undergo a purely prosodic focalization strategy; that is, it can be contrastively stressed *in situ* (48):

(48)   Ho incontrato VERONICA Domenica (, non Lucia)! (V-O, O in situ)
       'I met VERONICA on Sunday (, not Lucia)!'

For contrastive focus in Greek, Tsimpli (1998) considers the possibility of postulating two distinct focusing strategies, namely *in situ* focusing and overt focus-raising (to FocusP). She claims that it is possible for the *in situ* focus to be interpreted contrastively in the appropriate context, without invoking a [focus] feature. This means that an *in situ* focused XP can be ambiguous between a presentational (i.e. information) (as in (27) above) and a contrastive reading (as in (51) below), whereas a preposed focused XP cannot be construed as information focus.[26] Thus, in (49) the object has moved to SpecFocusP (see Tsimpli 1990, 1995; Roussou 2000; Georgiafentis 2004, among others).

(49)   ΤΗΝ ΤΟΥΡΤΑ έφαγε ο Γιάννης (όχι τον μπακλαβά). *O-V-S*
       'It is the cake that Janis ate (not the baklava).'

Movement is also involved in the V-O-S order, as in (50), where the subject appears in a clause-final position. Following Belletti's analysis (see Georgiafentis 2004 for Greek), this structure can be analysed as overt movement of the subject to the Spec of the high FocusP, and subsequent remnant movement of the IP to the Spec of a higher TopicP.

(50)   Έλυσε την άσκηση Ο ΓΙΑΝΝΗΣ (κανείς άλλος). (*V-O-S*)
       'It is Janis who solved the problem (nobody else).'

In (51), on the other hand, one could claim that the object receives emphatic prominence *in situ* (cf. Tsimpli 1998 for Greek; Bocci 2003 for Italian):[27]

(51)   Ο Γιάννης έφαγε ΤΗΝ ΤΟΥΡΤΑ (όχι τον μπακλαβά). (*S-V-O*)
       'It is the cake that Janis ate (not the baklava).'

5 Comparative remarks

In Table 11.2 we summarize how the languages under investigation behave with respect to the mechanisms of focus realization for both focus types.

Taking the above properties into consideration and associating them with the special characteristics of each language, the following picture emerges with respect to their clause and information structure as far as focus types are concerned.

Table 11.2 Focus Types and Mechanisms of Realization

| | | LANGUAGE | | | | |
TYPE OF FOCUS	MECHANISM	English	German	Spanish	Italian	Greek
Information focus	NSR	√	√	√	√	√
	Stress in situ	√	√	X	X	√
Contrastive Focus	FocusP	X	X	√/X	√	√
	Stress in situ	√	√	X	X	√

English, which is a Germanic language, has poor inflection in both verbal and nominal systems. This fact disallows pro-drop, limits word order variation (to S-V-O) and restricts the left periphery. Thus, it only allows for NSR and *in situ* focus for both focus types. Furthermore, English appears to have very restricted movement for contrastive focus or for topics (SpecCP or IP adjunction). This means that the existence of FocusP or TopicP is thus questionable.

German, which is also a Germanic language, has a very rich verbal and nominal inflectional system but it is non pro-drop, and crucially both an S-O-V and a V2-language, which results in relative flexibility in word order variation. More specifically, V2 restricts the left periphery, but the fact that SpecCP is available for any constituent (Focus/Topic), and the existence of scrambling in the VP/IP area allows for reordering of the base structure. Focus is regulated by the NSR, *in situ*, topicalizing or scrambling of other constituents and fronting of the focused element to SpecCP, while it has a very restricted left periphery; that is, TopicP exists only for left dislocated and hanging topics. Thus, the existence of FocusP is again questionable.

Spanish and Italian, which are two Romance languages, have rich verbal and less rich nominal inflectional systems and allow for pro-drop and for word order flexibility. It seems that the NSR is very powerful and that both languages lack *in situ* stressing. This is mainly the reason why the languages employ movement (scrambling/p-movement) within the VP/IP area in order for the NSR to apply. What is crucial for the difference between Spanish and Italian is that, while Spanish permits vP/VP-internal subjects, Italian subjects move to SpecTP. For Italian, on the one hand, this means that the subject reaches a high clausal position, which makes it necessary to have a larger IP area for movement (as Belletti 2004 suggests), as well as a richer left periphery (as Rizzi 1997 suggests), supported by the existence of clitics. For Spanish, on the other hand, the low subject position limits this necessity (as Zubizarreta 1998 claims).

Finally, Greek, which has a very rich verbal and nominal inflectional system, allows for pro-drop, has a great freedom in word order variation and a rich left periphery (see Roussou 2000 adapting Rizzi's 1997 system), supported by the existence of clitics, as in Italian. In the case of information focus, the NSR seems to function but in many cases its operation can be superseded by stressing *in situ*, unlike Spanish and Italian, where the NSR has a primary function and crucially determines word order variation via scrambling operations. With respect to contrastive focus, movement of the focused XP to SpecFocusP exists. However, in this case, alongside this mechanism, it appears that *in situ* focusing (via an emphatic/contrastive stress) is possible as well.

6 Conclusion

In the present study we comparatively examined the clause and information structure of English, German, Spanish, Italian and Greek, in relation to focus types (i.e. information and contrastive focus) and the various word order patterns that result from them. As we observed, the morpho-syntactic characteristics of the languages affect clause structure and the syntactic mechanisms (i.e. movement) involved. Given that information structure, which comprises Focus, is not a purely syntactic phenomenon, the role of intonation is equally important. In the axis of the languages we considered, it appears that there are two poles, namely a very restricted one with respect to morpho-syntactic properties, that is, English, where focus is regulated by prosody, and an almost unrestricted one, that is, Greek, where both prosodic and syntactic operations are allowed. In between stands German with a restricted clause structure, where *in situ* stressing is available, whereas Spanish and Italian with restricted prosodic properties (absence of *in situ* stress) opt for movement mechanisms.

Notes

1 See Molnár and Winkler (2006) for an overview of the interaction between focus and the linguistic levels.
2 Although prosody is important in the realization of focus, the point of view adopted in the present study primarily involves syntax.
3 The use of italics denotes information focus, while capitalization signifies contrastive focus.
4 In numerous analyses there is no distinction between information focus that comes as an answer to wh-questions and contrastive focus; both are interpreted as excluding alternatives (Krifka 2007). Cf. also Molnár (2006) on different types of focus and Skopeteas and Fanselow (2011) on the relation between exhaustivity and focus-fronting in Hungarian, German, Spanish, and Greek.
5 This distinction has been present in linguistic literature for a long time (see Halliday 1967; Chomsky 1972; Guéron 1980; Rooth 1985; Rochemont 1986; Cohan 2000, among others).
6 Along with these mechanisms, there are also discourse-semantic principles, according to which, in neutral or Topic-Comment structures, old/given information (topic) precedes new information (focus), which tends to appear in sentence final position (see also Molnár 2012).
7 According to Leonetti (2014), V-S-O is also very common in Spanish.
8 V-S-O is also information neutral.
9 German allows pro-drop in very limited constructions, that is, passives under restrictions.
10 In examples from languages other than English, glosses are not provided; we just provide the relevant translation. This is because these examples typically illustrate the order of constituents, which is clearly noted at the end of each of them; thus, glosses are not relevant to what we are examining and are avoided to save space and reduce any unnecessary burden for the reader.
11 The analysis goes back to Koster (1975).
12 For a detailed presentation of the relation between clause structure and information structure see also Tsokoglou (2007).
13 Fanselow (1988) and Haftka (1995: 863–5) point out that elements enter a topic domain, when they scramble and Webelhuth (1992: 193–205) that focused elements do not move. Abraham and Molnárfi (2002) claim that the VP-domain is focal.
14 See Grewendorf (1995) for an overview of scrambling as an adjunction to VP and IP in both main and subordinate clauses.
15 For an analysis of scrambling as A-movement see Fanselow (1988, 1990) and as A-bar movement see Webelhuth (1992).

16 See Haider and Rosengren (2003) for an analysis of scrambling as VP-Adjunction.
17 Grewendorf and Sabel (1996) and Grewendorf (2002: 53–66) argue that scrambled constituents move to AgrPs in the functional IP-domain and Meinunger (2000) associates the AgrPs with a [+topic] feature.
18 Since German is a V2-language, it is not clear whether it possesses a FocusP; on the contrary a new Phrase is created in the left periphery for Left Dislocation (*Dem Jungen*, dem hat er die Geschichte erzählt. [=The boy, *him* has he the story told]).
19 V-O-S is derived via scrambling of the object (Ordóñez 1998, 2000) or p-movement of VP_2 (Zubizarreta 1998). Ordóñez (1998, 2000) observes that in the V-O-S order the subject receives main stress and can be the only understood focus of the sentence. According to Zubizarreta (1998), the end product of p-movement in Spanish is the generation of the V-O-S order with a narrow focus interpretation on the subject, as in (20).
20 See Georgiafentis (2004: 261–2) for a possible explanation, according to which the non-focused part/backgrounded material of (27) undergoes ellipsis; the subject is thus found in the lowest node and is assigned main stress via the NSR.
21 Note that in Greek this pattern is clearly distinct from an S-V-O pattern with a contrastively focused subject. Consider the following example: *Ο ΓΙΑΝΝΗΣ έφαγε την τούρτα, όχι ο Θανάσης.* 'It is Janis who ate the cake, not Thanasis.' See Keller and Alexopoulou (2001) and Georgiafentis (2004) for the relevant experimental data and theoretical discussion.
22 But cf. Zubizarreta's (1998) analysis of contrastive focus under which no focus phrase is assumed and SpecTP is the position where focused elements check their 'focus' feature.
23 According to Leonetti (2014), V-S-O in Spanish does not necessarily require a preverbal XP. For example: *Ha ganado el Madrid la final.* 'Real Madrid has won the final.'
24 Zubizarreta claims that in this case the adverbial XP occupies SpecTP.
25 It should be pointed out here that Belletti (1999: 26–7, 2001: 71–2) refers to 'the remnant XP/VP'. It is only in Belletti (2004) that one finds that the topicalization involves the IP. We cannot see how the V-O-S order would be produced by topicalization of the VP given that V has already moved to I. In our opinion, the proposed analysis only works with remnant movement of IP, which contains the verb, the object and the trace of the subject, as in Belletti (2004).
26 It is worth mentioning here that this also holds for German, which allows for focus *in situ*. In particular, *in situ* focus is only possible when no other constituent moves (except for grammatical reasons).
27 Alternatively, it has been argued (see Georgiafentis 2004: 264–5) that such a pattern involves movement of the object *tin turta* to the left periphery, that is, to SpecFocP and subsequent remnant movement of the rest of the clause to the specifier of a higher TopicP. Cf. Belletti (2004) on remnant movement for Italian.

References

Abraham, W. and L. Molnárfi (2002), 'German Clause Structure under Discourse Functional Weight: Focus and Antifocus', in W. Abraham and J. W. Zwart (eds), *Issues in Formal German(ic) Typology*, Linguistik Aktuell 45, 1–43, Amsterdam: Benjamins.
Alexiadou, A. (1997), *Adverb Placement: A Case Study in Antisymmetric Syntax*, Amsterdam: Benjamins.

Alexiadou, A. (1999), 'Greek Word Order Patterns', in A. Alexiadou, G. Horrocks and M. Stavrou (eds), *Studies in Greek Syntax*, 45–65, Dordrecht, The Netherlands: Kluwer.

Alexiadou, A. and E. Anagnostopoulou (1998), 'Parametrizing Agr: Word Order, V-Movement and EPP Checking', *Natural Language and Linguistic Theory*, 16: 491–539.

Belletti, A. (1999), '"Inversion" as Focalization and Related Questions', *Catalan Working Papers in Linguistics*, 7: 9–45.

Belletti, A. (2001), '"Inversion" as Focalization', in A. C. J. Hulk and J. Y. Pollock (eds), *Subject Inversion in Romance and the Theory of Universal Grammar*, 60–90, Oxford: Oxford University Press.

Belletti, A. (2004), 'Aspects of the Low IP Area', in L. Rizzi (ed.), *The Structure of IP and CP: The Cartography of Syntactic Structures* 2, 16–51, Oxford: Oxford University Press.

Birner, B. and G. Ward (1998), *Information Status and Noncanonical Word Order in English*, Amsterdam: Benjamins.

Bocci, G. (2013), *The Syntax-Prosody Interface: A Cartographic Perspective with Evidence from Italian*, Amsterdam: Benjamins.

Cardinaletti, A. (2001), 'A Second Thought on *Emarginazione*: Destressing vs. "Right Dislocation"', in G. Cinque and G. Salvi (eds), *Current Studies in Italian Syntax: Essays Offered to Lorenzo Renzi*, 117–35, Amsterdam: Elsevier.

Chomsky, N. (1972), 'Deep Structure, Surface Structure and Semantic Interpretation', in N. Chomsky (ed.), *Studies on Semantics in Generative Grammar*, 62–119, The Hague: Mouton.

Chomsky, N. and M. Halle (1968), *The Sound Pattern of English*, New York: Harper & Row.

Cinque, G. (1993), 'A Null Theory of Phrase and Compound Stress', *Linguistic Inquiry*, 24: 239–97.

Cohan, J. B. (2000), 'The Realization and Function of Focus in Spoken English', PhD diss., University of Texas at Austin, Austin, TX.

Domínguez, L. (2004), 'Mapping Focus: The Syntax and Prosody of Focus in Spanish', PhD diss., Boston University, Boston, MA.

Drachman, G. and S. Klidi (1992), 'The Proper Treatment of Adverbial Questions in Greek: The Extended Minimal Structure Hypothesis', *Studies in Greek Linguistics*, 13: 371–90.

Erteschik-Shir, N. (2007), *Information Structure: The Syntax-Discourse Interface*, New York: Oxford University Press.

Fanselow, G. (1988), 'German Word Order and Universal Grammar', in U. Reyle and C. Rohrer (eds), *Natural Language Parsing and Linguistic Theories*, 317–55, Dordrecht, The Netherlands: Kluwer.

Fanselow, G. (1990), 'Scrambling as NP-Movement', in G. Grewendorf and W. Sternefeld (eds), *Scrambling and Barriers*, 113–40, Amsterdam: Benjamins.

Fanselow, G. (2008), 'In Need of Mediation: The Relation between Syntax and Information Structure', *Acta Linguistica Hungarica*, 55: 1–17.

Fanselow, G. and D. Lenertová (2011), 'Left Peripheral Focus: Mismatches between Syntax and Information Structure', *Natural Language and Linguistic Theory*, 29: 169–209.

Frey, W. (2005), 'Pragmatic Properties of Certain German and English Left Peripheral Constructions', *Linguistics*, 43: 89–129.

Georgakopoulos, Th. and S. Skopeteas (2010), 'Projective vs. Interpretational Properties of Nuclear Accents and the Phonology of Contrastive Focus in Greek', *The Linguistic Review*, 27: 319–46.

Georgiafentis, M. (2004), 'Focus and Word Order Variation in Greek', PhD diss., The University of Reading, Reading, UK.

Georgiafentis, M. and A. Sfakianaki (2004), 'Syntax Interacts with Prosody: The VOS Order in Greek', *Lingua*, 114: 935–61.

Greenberg, J. H. (1963), 'Some Universals of Grammar with Particular Reference to the Order of Meaningful Elements', in J. H. Greenberg (ed.), *Universals of Language*, 73–113, Cambridge, MA: MIT Press.

Grewendorf, G. (1995), 'Syntaktische Skizzen: German', in J. Jacobs, A. von Stechow, W. Sternefeld and T. Vennemann (eds), *Syntax. Ein internationales Handbuch zeitgenössischer Forschung*, Bd. 2, 1288–319, Berlin: de Gruyter.

Grewendorf, G. (2002), *Minimalistische Syntax*, Tübingen: Franke.

Grewendorf, G. and J. Sabel (1996), 'Multiple Specifiers and the Theory of Adjunction: On Scrambling in German and Japanese', *Sprachwissenschaft in Frankfurt* 16, Frankfurt/M: Johann Wolfgang Goethe Universität.

Guéron, J. (1980), 'On the Syntax and Semantics of PP extraposition', *Linguistic Inquiry*, 11: 637–78.

Haftka, B. (1995), 'Topologische Felder und Versetzungsphänomene', in J. Jacobs, A. von Stechow, W. Sternefeld and T. Vennemann (eds), *Syntax. Ein internationales Handbuch zeitgenössischer Forschung*, Bd. 1, 846–67, Berlin: de Gruyter.

Haider, H. and I. Rosengren (2003), 'Scrambling – Non Triggered Chain Formation in OV-Languages', *Journal of Germanic Linguistics*, 15 (3): 203–67.

Halliday, M. A. K. (1967), 'Notes on Transitivity and Theme in English', Part 2, *Journal of Linguistics*, 3: 199–244.

Horrocks, G. (1994), 'Subjects and Configurationality', *Journal of Linguistics*, 30: 81–109.

Keller, F. and T. Alexopoulou (2001), 'Phonology Competes with Syntax: Experimental Evidence for the Interaction of Word Order and Accent Placement in the Realization of Information Structure', *Cognition*, 79: 301–72.

Krifka, M. (2000), *Dimensionen grammatischer Variation – Ein sprachtypologischer Überblick*, Institut für deutsche Sprache und Linguistik, MS, Universität zu Berlin, Berlin: Germany.

Krifka, M. (2007), 'Basic Notions of Information Structure', in C. Féry, G. Fanselow and M. Krifka (eds), *Working Papers of the SFB632*, Interdisciplinary Studies on Information Structure (ISIS) 6, 13–56, Potsdam: Universitätsverlag Potsdam.

Koster J. (1975), 'Dutch as an SOV Language', *Linguistic Analysis*, 1: 111–36.

Kotzoglou, G. (2013), 'On the Unmarked Position for Greek Subjects: Problematic Issues and Implications for Constituent Order', *Journal of Greek Linguistics*, 13: 203–38.

Ladd, D. R. (1980), *The Structure of Intonational Meaning: Evidence from English*, Bloomington, IN: Indiana University Press.

Lascaratou, C. (1998), 'Basic Characteristics of Modern Greek Word Order', in A. Siewierska (ed.), *Constituent Order in the Languages of Europe*, 151–71, Berlin: Mouton de Gruyter.

Leonetti, M. (2014), 'Spanish VSX', in K. Lahousse and S. Marzo (eds), *Romance Languages and Linguistic Theory*, 37–63, Amsterdam: Benjamins.

Meinunger, A. (2000), *Syntactic Aspects of Topic and Comment*, Amsterdam: Benjamins.

Molnár, V. (2006), 'On Different Kinds of Contrast', in V. Molnár and S. Winker (eds), *The Architecture of Focus*, 197–233, Berlin: Mouton de Gruyter.

Molnár, V. (2012), 'Zur Relevanz der linken Peripherie für die Strukturierung der Information – kontrastive und typologische Überlegungen', in L. Gunkel and G. Zifonun (eds), *Jahrbuch des Instituts für Deutsche Sprache 2011*, 383–416, Berlin: de Gruyter.

Molnár, V. and S. Winker (2006), 'Exploring the Architecture of Focus in Grammar', in V. Molnár and S. Winker (eds), *The Architecture of Focus*, 1–29, Berlin: Mouton de Gruyter.

Ordóñez, F. (1998), 'Post-verbal Asymmetries in Spanish', *Natural Language and Linguistic Theory*, 16: 313–46.

Ordóñez, F. (2000), *The Clausal Structure of Spanish: A Comparative Study*, New York: Garland Publishing Inc.

Ortega-Santos, I. (2016), *Focus-related Operations at the Right Edge in Spanish: Subjects and Ellipsis*, Amsterdam: Benjamins.

Philippaki-Warburton, I. (1982), 'Η Σημασία της Σειράς Ρήμα Υποκείμενο Αντικείμενο στα Νέα Ελληνικά' ('The Significance of the Verb Subject Object Order in Modern Greek') [in Greek], *Studies in Greek Linguistics*, 3: 135–58.

Philippaki-Warburton, I. (1985), 'Word Order in Modern Greek', *Transactions of the Philological Society*, 83: 113–43.

Philippaki-Warburton, I. (1987), 'The Theory of Empty Categories and the pro-drop Parameter in Modern Greek', *Journal of Linguistics*, 23: 289–318.

Philippaki-Warburton, I. (1990), 'Η Ανάλυση του Ρηματικού Συνόλου στα Νέα Ελληνικά' ('The Analysis of the Verbal Group in Modern Greek') [in Greek], *Studies in Greek Linguistics*, 11: 119–38.

Rizzi, L. (1997), 'The Fine Structure of the Left Periphery', in L. Haegeman (ed.), *Elements of Grammar: Handbook in Generative Syntax*, 281–337, Dordrecht, The Netherlands: Kluwer.

Rochemont, M. S. (1986), *Focus in Generative Grammar*, Amsterdam: Benjamins.

Rooth, M. (1985), 'Association with Focus', PhD diss., GLSA, University of Massachusetts, Amherst, MA.

Rosengren, I. (1993), 'Wahlfreiheit mit Konsequenzen', in M. Reis (ed.), *Wortstellung und Informationsstruktur*, 252–312, Tübingen: Niemeyer.

Roussou, A. (2000), 'On the Left Periphery: Modal Particles and Complementisers', *Journal of Greek Linguistics*, 1: 65–94.

Roussou, A. and I. M. Tsimpli (2006), 'On Greek VSO Again!', *Journal of Linguistics*, 42: 317–54.

Skopeteas, S. (2016), 'Information Structure in Modern Greek', in C. Féry and S. Ishinhara (eds), *The Oxford Handbook of Information Structure*, 686–708, Oxford: Oxford University Press.

Skopeteas, S. and G. Fanselow (2011), 'Focus and the Exclusion of Alternatives: On the Interaction of Syntactic Structure with Pragmatic Inference', *Lingua*, 121: 1693–706.

Spyropoulos, V. and I. Philippaki-Warburton (2001), '"Subject" and EPP in Greek: The Discontinuous Subject Hypothesis', *Journal of Greek Linguistics*, 2: 149–86.

Spyropoulos, V. and A. Revithiadou (2009), 'Subject Chains in Greek and PF Processing', *MIT Working Papers in Linguistics*, 57: 293–309.

Struckmeier, V. (2017), 'Against Information Structure Heads: A Relational Analysis of German Scrambling', *Glossa*, 2 (1): 1–29.

Tsimpli, I. M. (1990), 'The Clause Structure and Word Order in Modern Greek', *UCL Working Papers in Linguistics*, 2: 226–55.

Tsimpli, I. M. (1995), 'Focusing in Modern Greek', in K. É. Kiss (ed.), *Discourse Configurational Languages*, 176–206, Oxford: Oxford University Press.

Tsimpli, I. M. (1998), 'Individual and Functional Readings for Focus, Wh- and Negative Operators: Evidence from Greek', in B. Joseph, G. Horrocks and I. Philippaki-Warburton (eds), *Themes in Greek Linguistics II*, 197–227, Amsterdam: Benjamins.

Tsokoglou, A. (2007), *Η Δομή της Πρότασης και η Σειρά των Όρων στη Γερμανική Γλώσσα. (Clause Structure and Word Order in German)* [in Greek], Parousia Monograph Series 72, University of Athens.

Webelhuth, G. (1992), *Principles and Parameters of Syntactic Saturation*, Oxford: Oxford University Press.

Zagona, K. (2002), *The Syntax of Spanish*, Cambridge, UK: Cambridge University Press.

Zubizarreta, M. L. (1998), *Prosody, Focus and Word Order*, Cambridge, MA: MIT Press.

12

Strong pronouns as postverbal subjects in Spanish and Italian[1]

Manuel Leonetti and Victoria Escandell-Vidal

Although Spanish and Italian share a remarkable number of grammatical properties, some unexpected asymmetries show up in the behaviour of strong pronouns as postverbal subjects. In this chapter we aim to describe these facts and suggest a plausible unified explanation based on the constraints that each language puts on the mapping between syntax and information structure. We consider three sets of data: overt pronouns as postverbal subjects in syntactically induced inversion, overt pronouns as subjects in free inversion, and the special case of polite pronominal forms. In the three cases Italian behaves like a more restrictive language than Spanish; whereas Spanish allows for pronouns to occur inside larger informational units without being interpreted as topics or as narrow foci, Italian requires that overt pronouns be singled out as topics or as narrow foci, that is, they must be pushed out from a larger informational constituent through some kind of split (*topic/comment* or *focus/background*).

1 Preliminaries

Spanish and Italian, as Romance languages, share a significant number of grammatical properties:

1. Both are consistent null-subject languages.
2. Both have the same kind of pronominal system, with a series of strong pronouns opposed to a series of clitic pronouns.
3. Both are SVO languages.
4. In both cases strong pronouns as subjects are in competition with null subjects: null subjects represent the basic, default option, and strong pronouns – either preverbal or postverbal – are used only when certain specific Information Structure factors justify them (either because referent identification requires it or in order to express contrast or emphasis).

Strong pronouns are used to communicate what null subjects cannot convey, and the competition between a marked and an unmarked option results in a balanced division of labour (cf. for Spanish, Luján 1999; Fernández Soriano 1999: §19.3; RAE 2009; Mayol 2010; Leonetti 2014a; for Italian, Cordin and Calabrese 1988; Benincà 1988; Bocci and Pozzan 2014; Belletti and Guasti 2015). Thus, the behaviour of strong pronouns as subjects can be expected to be almost identical in the two languages. However, there are some intriguing differences, which have received little attention so far. A selection of the most relevant facts is given in the examples in (1)–(4).

(1) a. ¿Qué habéis   comido vosotros?   Sp.
       what have.PRS.2PL   eaten you.PL?
       'What did you eat?'

    b. Cosa avete   mangiato {*voi / ᴼᴷ ,voi}?   It.
       what have.PRS.2PL   eaten   you.PL?

(2) a. Estaba   ella muy nerviosa.   Sp.
       be.PST.3SG   she very nervous
       'She was very nervous.'

    b. Era   (*lei) molto nervosa.   It.
       be.PST.3SG   she   very nervous

(3) a. Es   mejor así,   creo   yo.   Sp.
       be.PRS.3SG   better this-way, think.PRS.1SG I
       'It's better this way, I think.'

    b. È   meglio così,   credo   (*io).   It.
       be.PRS.3SG better this-way, think.PRS.1SG I

(4) a. Dígame   usted.   ¿En qué puedo   ayudarle?   Sp.
       tell.SBJV.3SG-I.DAT you.FRML. In what can.PRS.1SG help.INF-you.FRML.ACC
       'Tell me. Can I help you?'

    b. Mi   dica   (*Lei).   Posso   aiutarLa?   It.
       I.DAT tell.SBJV.3SG you.FRML. Can.PRS.1SG help.INF-you.FRML.ACC

The examples show four different environments where a subject strong pronoun in postverbal position is grammatical in Spanish, but not in Italian, namely wh-interrogatives, sentences with VSX order, parenthetical clauses and imperative clauses with polite pronominal forms. This is a surprising fact, given the number of important grammatical properties that the two languages share. At this point, two generalizations emerge:

1. The observed asymmetries in the distribution of strong pronouns as subjects concern postverbal positions exclusively. There are no noticeable differences in the preverbal subject position.[2]
2. Spanish looks like a less restrictive language than Italian: in the examples, the Spanish versions are always acceptable, whereas the Italian versions are excluded.

Our goal in this chapter is to describe the facts and to provide a unified account for them, including the generalizations in (1) and (2). In doing this, we assume that the differences are not to be located in the semantic features of pronouns, which are the same in Spanish and Italian, but elsewhere. More precisely, we intend, on the one hand, to argue for a more fine-grained account of the relations between the postverbal position of a strong pronoun and its informational status. On the other hand, we would like to provide further support for the idea that *new information* and *contrast* are independent notions.

In the following section, three sets of data will be analysed and discussed. The first group concerns grammatical contexts where subjects are obligatorily postverbal, that is, basically wh-interrogatives and contrastive focalization. The second group covers contexts of 'free' subject inversion (VS, VOS, VSO). Finally, the third group represents the special case of the polite pronominal forms *usted* 'you, formal' and *Lei* 'you, formal'. Section 3 offers an account of the facts based on the articulation between grammar and Information Structure (IS). Section 4 briefly presents our conclusions.

2 Three sets of data

In order to obtain an adequate view of the behaviour of postverbal subjects in Romance languages, it is useful to start by making a basic distinction between subjects appearing in a postverbal slot by virtue of a general syntactic constraint, on the one hand, and subjects that appear in postverbal position because the speaker freely makes that choice, thus discarding an alternative option with a preverbal subject that would be perfectly grammatical, on the other (cf. Leonetti 2018). This distinction has interesting consequences for the mapping between syntax and Information Structure (IS), and it will turn out to be a crucial piece for a contrastive approach to the occurrence of strong pronouns. Briefly, this distinction, combined with some simple assumptions on the competition between grammatical options, leads us towards a principled account of the contribution of word order to Focus structure: when subject inversion is obligatory – that is, if it is imposed by some syntactic constraint – it does not compete with other possible options anymore (for instance, with the preverbal position in a SVO pattern), and, as a consequence, it is not significant, in the sense that it has no interpretive import. In contrast, when subject inversion is optional – that is, 'free', as in the usual term *free inversion* – and competes with other possibilities, it must have some interpretive effect. The main interpretive effect of inversion is marking the subject as focal information. This explains why, at least in Romance, postverbal subjects are not information foci when their position is determined by a syntactic constraint, whereas they are focal when their position is the result of the speaker's choice.[3] With this in mind, we can review the main data corresponding to the two situations just introduced.

2.1 Syntactically induced VS order

In this section, we want to describe the behaviour of subject pronouns in contexts where the VS order is syntactically induced, such as wh-interrogatives and focus fronting (Torrego 1984, for Spanish). The VS pattern for Spanish is illustrated in (5) and (6).

(5) ¿Qué (*vosotros) habéis   (*vosotros) comido (vosotros)?
    what (*you.PL) have.PRS.2PL   (*you.PL) eaten   (you.PL)?
    'What did you eat?'

(6) PASta (*yo) he   (*yo) comido (yo)   (, no pizza).
    PASta (*I) have.PST.1SG (*I) eaten (I)   (, not pizza)
    'I ate PASta (, not pizza)'.

As preverbal subjects are banned from the contexts in (5) and (6), the only grammatical options remaining are null subjects and postverbal explicit subjects. There is a feature of subject pronouns in (5) and (6) that is particularly significant for a comparison with Italian, as we will see: the pronouns *vosotros* and *yo* occur in the same intonational phrase as the verb. In (5') the pronoun heads the intonational phrase and carries the Nuclear Pitch Accent.

```
{                               *    }ᵥ
[                               *    ]ᵢ
(    *) (                 * )(    *    )ᵩ
```

(5') ¿Qué habéis   comido vosotros?
     what have.PRS.2PL   eaten you.PL?

A reasonable question arises at this point: given that subject inversion is syntactically induced here (and hence inversion lacks any interpretive effect), and given that subject pronouns compete with their null counterparts, but in (5) the subject is not interpreted as a narrow focus,[4] why does the subject appear at all? A reasonable answer should be based on the natural assumption that strong pronouns in competition with null subjects must convey some kind of meaning that their null counterparts are unable to express. With this idea in mind, it is worth having a look at the contextual conditions for a felicitous use of strong pronouns. Analysing the contrast between (7) and (8) provides a valuable clue: an interrogative sentence like (5) fits in well with the linguistic context in (7), but sounds odd in (8).

(7) Yo he   comido tallarines. ¿Qué habéis   comido #(vosotros)?
    I have.PRS.1SG eaten tagliatelle. What have.PRS.2PL eaten   #(you.PL)?
    'I have eaten tagliatelle. What did YOU eat?'

(8) ¡Qué rápido habéis   vuelto! ¿Qué habéis   comido (#vosotros)?
    How quick   have.PRS.2PL returned! What have.PRS.2PL eaten (#you.PL)?
    'You are back so early! What did you eat?'

In (7) the strong pronoun is needed to establish a contrast between the first person subject in the previous sentence (*Yo he comido tallarines*) and the new subject (*vosotros*) in the wh-interrogative. The occurrence of the strong pronoun triggers the retrieval of a contextually determined set of alternative referents: *yo* 'I', *nosotros* 'we', *vosotros* 'you$_{PL}$', *ellos* 'they'. Since one of these alternative referents is already present in the context in which the wh-interrogative is processed, the contrast is easily obtained. The situation in (8) is clearly different: in the two sentences, the subject refers to the addressees, so there is no contrast involved, but continuity. Therefore, the strong pronoun *vosotros* is inadequate in the wh-interrogative; only a null subject is felicitous. The same explanation goes for examples involving subject inversion triggered by focus fronting, as illustrated in (6).

This suggests, then, that it is precisely contrast that justifies resorting to an overt pronoun here. This conforms to the basic assumption we rely on: null subjects are unable to convey contrast, and hence strong pronouns are used whenever there is contrast. This is why strong pronouns in competition with null pronouns are typically contrastive, as pointed out by most descriptive grammars.

It is important to draw attention to the fact that in (5) contrast is independent from focus, since the subject pronoun has a contrastive reading without being in focus. The same happens in the default interpretation of strong pronouns as preverbal subjects in Spanish, when contrast is associated with topicality, but not with focus. This supports the idea that contrast must be considered as an independent notion of IS, one that can be combined with either focus or topic, as proposed in Neeleman and Vermeulen (2012).

To sum up, the main points that result from an analysis of subject pronouns in syntactically induced inversion in Spanish are the following:

1. The subject pronoun is a part of the same intonational phrase where the verb occurs.
2. It is not in focus.
3. It is licensed by contrast with other alternative referents in the context.
4. Contrastive readings are independent from focus.

In Italian, in contrast, we find a slightly different situation. In wh-interrogatives[5] with fronted bare wh-elements (*cosa* 'what', *quando* 'when', *dove* 'where' …) subjects are obligatorily postverbal, like in Spanish. However, preverbal subjects are allowed with *perchè* 'why' and *come mai* 'how come',[6] and with D-linked and complex wh-expressions (Benincà 1988; Rizzi 2001; Cardinaletti 2007; Bocci and Pozzan 2014). Here we consider only those cases where the subjects must be postverbal. Now, as in Spanish, such postverbal subjects cannot be narrow foci:[7] in Belletti's (2004) terms, the activation of a left peripheral Focus position with fronted wh-words is incompatible with the activation of a low Focus position for the subject. Again, as in Spanish, overt, strong pronouns involve contrast, and hence the choice of a pronoun instead of its silent counterpart triggers the search for a contextually relevant set of alternative referents. Italian, however, differs from Spanish in a specific aspect of the grammar of wh-interrogatives, illustrated in the contrast between (9) and (10):

(9) Io ho　　　　mangiato　tagliatelle. Cosa avete　　　　mangiato, voi?
　　I have.PRS.1SG eaten　　　tagliatelle. What have.PRS.2PL eaten,　　you.PL?
　　'I have eaten tagliatelle. What did YOU eat?'

(10)　Io ho　　　　mangiato tagliatelle. *Cosa avete　　　mangiato voi?
　　　I have.PRS.1SG　eaten tagliatelle. What have.PRS.2PL eaten　you.PL?

In Italian the postverbal subject – this holds for pronouns as well as for most lexical DPs – must be pronounced as an independent intonational phrase;[8] it cannot remain inside the same intonational phrase as the main verb. This condition is obeyed in (9), but not in (10), which, on the other hand, would be acceptable in Spanish (cf. (5')). For Italian, only the prosodic phrasing in (9') is acceptable:

$$
\begin{array}{lllll}
\{ & & ^* & & \}_\upsilon \\
[& & ^*\ ]_\iota & [\ ^*\ ]_\iota \\
(\,^*\,)(& & ^*\ )_\varphi & (\ ^*\ )_\varphi \\
\end{array}
$$

(9')　Io ho　　　　mangiato tagliatelle. Cosa avete　　　mangiato, voi?
　　　I have.PRS.1SG eaten　　tagliatelle. What have.PRS.2PL　eaten,　you.PL?

The difference concerning intonational phrases reveals, thus, a crucial grammatical asymmetry: in Italian, but not in Spanish, a postverbal subject in a VS wh-question must be either right-dislocated[9] or destressed *in situ* (Cardinaletti 2001, 2007). Notice that Italian subject pronouns retain their contrastive value when right-dislocated or destressed. Italian behaves, with respect to the behaviour of this type of subjects, exactly like Catalan, as shown in Villalba (2011) and Planas-Morales and Villalba (2013): Catalan makes a pervasive use of right-dislocation for marking background material in interrogatives, whereas Spanish tends to resort to the realization of background material in canonical position (or, alternatively, to ellipsis).

2.2 Subject inversion (VS, VOS, VSO)

In this section we consider data of so-called *free inversion* with strong pronouns as postverbal subjects; this kind of inversion gives rise to verb-initial orders like VS, VOS and VSO. It is well known that subject inversion is more productive in Spanish than in Italian (Lobo and Martins 2017; Leonetti 2017). This is essentially due to the constraints that Italian places on inversion with transitive verbs. On the one hand, VOS is mostly used in Italian with narrow focus – possibly contrastive – on the final subject, whereas it can also be used with wide focus readings in Spanish – though narrow focus on the subject remains the preferred interpretation. On the other hand, the VSO pattern is usually excluded in Italian, as it is in French and Catalan, but is quite common in Spanish, European Portuguese and Romanian (Leonetti 2014b). In VSO order, the subject must be focal, but it does not receive a narrow focus interpretation (unless the object is right-dislocated; we consider only Spanish sequences with no intonational breaks, i.e. without dislocations): VSO is associated to an interpretation that lacks informational Focus/background articulation, typically a wide focus reading.

　　Significant differences between Spanish and Italian show up when the postverbal subject pronoun is within the focal domain without being a narrow focus. The VSO pattern is usually acceptable in Spanish, but not in Italian, as shown in the contrasts in (11)–(13).

(11) a. Estaba   ella muy nerviosa.   Sp.
   be.PST.3SG she very nervous

  b. Era   (*lei) molto nervosa.   It.
   be.PST.3SG she   very   nervous
   'She was very nervous.'

(12) a. No le veo   yo la gracia.   Sp.
   not CL see.PRS.1SG I   the humour

  b. Non ci vedo   (*io) niente di divertente.   It.
   not CL see.PRS.1SG I   nothing of funny
   'I can't see the humour in it. (That's not funny)'.

(13) a. ¡Vete   tú a saber!^{10} Sp.
   go.IMPRT.2SG.CL you to know

  b. Vai   (*tu) a sapere! (cf. dialectal *Vatte a sapè!*)   It.
   go.IMPRT.2SG you   to know
   'You figure it out/Who knows!'

The presence of overt subject pronouns in Spanish VSO raises an interesting question: why do they appear there? They may well contribute to solving possible ambiguities in some cases, when verbal inflection is not explicit enough (Fernández Soriano 1999: §19.3.6), and may also give rise to mild emphatic and contrastive effects in other cases (Fernández Soriano 1999: §19.3.7), but such factors cannot definitely explain all uses, because in many examples the pronoun is neither emphatic nor contrastive (for instance, in (11)a and (13)a). Thus, it is not clear why in VSO an overt pronoun is chosen instead of a null subject.

We suggest that the main reason for inserting an overt pronoun is making the VSO pattern 'recognizable' for the addressee (Escandell-Vidal and Leonetti 2017), with all its interpretive consequences. Resorting to an overt pronoun is justified because with a null subject the sentence would be interpreted as (S)VO; null subjects typically refer to given antecedents and count as topics in the informational articulation of the clause, so that speakers would not recognize the VSO order with its wide focus reading if the subject were null. This is, therefore, the basic motivation for the use of overt subject pronouns in (11)–(13).

At first sight, the relevance of the data in (11)–(13) might seem scarce, given that the examples simply show the effects of a ban against VSO in Italian, and not a specific feature of the behaviour of postverbal pronouns. However, we think they deserve some attention, for different reasons. First, we intend to connect them with the facts we described in the previous section, so as to treat all of them as manifestations of a more general phenomenon (see Section 3). Second, the contrasts involving subject pronouns

in inversion are not limited to VSO. In (14) we reproduce a contrast that is found
in parenthetical expressions[11] with verbs like *creer/credere* 'think'. As in the preceding
cases, inversion is fully acceptable in Spanish, but not in Italian.

(14) a. Es   mejor así,   creo   yo.   Sp.
          be.PRS.3SG better this-way,   think.PRS.1SG I

      b. È   meglio così,   credo   (#io).   It.
          be.PRS.3SG better   this-way, think.PRS.1SG I
          'It's better this way, I think.'

Though this seems to be a case of focal inversion, the subject pronoun is not interpreted
as narrow focus in Spanish: rather, it is integrated into the parenthetical predication
from both a prosodic and an informational point of view. As in several previous
examples, the pronoun evokes a set of contextual alternatives, and its occurrence is
justified as a means for expressing contrast.

The situation is thus the same in the two sets of contexts reviewed so far, namely,
syntactically induced inversion and 'free inversion'. In Spanish subject pronouns
in postverbal position always involve contrast – or some other interpretive effect –
independent of their informational status: they may be integrated in the background
(the case of wh-interrogatives) or in the focal domain (the case of subject inversion),
and no other condition has to be satisfied. In Italian, subject pronouns in postverbal
position must indicate contrast, but they must also obey a further specific condition: they
need to be singled out, either as topics – when right-dislocated in wh-interrogatives –
or as narrow foci – in inversion.[12] Italian examples in (11)–(14) are ruled out because
this second condition is not satisfied, the pronouns being simply integrated in the
background or the focal domain. Before reviewing the whole issue in Section 3, we
would like to introduce some additional evidence for our comparative generalization,
based on the behaviour of polite pronominal forms.

2.3 Use of respect forms – *usted* versus *lei*

Both Spanish and Italian resort to a third person pronominal form – *usted* in Spanish,
Lei in Italian – to convey deference and respect for the addressee. Both languages belong
to the category of so-called T/V (*tu/vous*) languages, that is, those having a pronominal
system that makes a distinction between two forms to refer to the addressee, a pronoun
of familiarity and solidarity, and another one for respect and distance.

Sánchez López (1993), building on previous observations by Fernández Ramírez
(1986), shows that *usted* displays some peculiar properties, with respect to the rest of
pronominal forms. The most significant one is that it appears as subject, without any
contrastive value, in postverbal positions where other pronouns are excluded, as in the
contrast between *usted* and *vosotros* in (15).

(15) a. Tendrán   ustedes   que hacer-lo.
          have.FUT.3PL you.PL.FRML that do.INF-it.ACC

b. #Tendréis   vosotros que hacerlo
   have.FUT.2PL you.PL   that do.INF-it.ACC
   'You will have to do it.'

The distribution of *usted* could be accounted for in strictly syntactic terms, but it seems simpler to assume that it is the set of special features of this form what actually brings about these contrasts. First, its presence can disambiguate between third person readings and polite second person readings, since *usted* shows third person agreement features. In addition, the fact that it always conveys deference and respect – which the rest of forms cannot express – could work as a licensing factor for this form. In sum, its use can be motivated on different grounds, independently of focus structure and contrastivity, which makes *usted* a special, marked form in the Spanish pronominal system.

Now, the point we want to stress here has to do with the subtle contrast between Spanish *usted* and Italian *Lei* that shows up in contexts like the ones in (16) and (17):

(16) a. Díga-me   usted.   ¿En qué puedo   ayudar-le?   Sp.
          tell.SBJV.3SG-I.DAT you.FRML. In   what can.PRS.1SG help.inf-you.FRML.ACC

      b. Mi dica   (Lei).   Posso   aiutar-La?   It.
          I.DAT tell.SBJV.3SG you.FRML. Can.PRS.1SG help.INF-you.FRML.ACC
          'Tell me. Can I help you?'

(17) a. Pues, mire   usted…   Sp.
          well, look.SBJV.3SG   you.FRML

      b. Beh, guardi   (#Lei)…   It.
          well, look.SBJV.3SG   you.FRML
          'Well, look…'

The essential difference lies in the fact that Spanish *usted* can occur without bearing narrow focus – that is, integrated in the focal domain in (16)–(17) – and without any contrastive value, whereas Italian *Lei* requires either a narrow focus reading or a topic reading (through right-dislocation). A postverbal *Lei* is excluded whenever it is not singled out from an informational point of view. A clear contrast derived from this condition emerges in (18), where *Lei* needs to be right-dislocated.

(18) a. No se preocupe   usted.   Sp.
          no   CL worry.SBJV.3SG you.FRML

      b. Non si preoccupi,   Lei.   / *Non si preoccupi Lei.   It.
          no   CL worry.SBJV.3SG you.FRML
          'Don't worry.'

The data thus confirm that respect pronominal forms follow the same pattern as the rest of the strong pronouns. This calls for a unified account of the three sets of facts we describe.

3 Strong pronouns and information-structure articulation

At this point, we need to draw a general picture that encompasses our two original generalizations together with the kind of evidence found for a systematic difference between Spanish and Italian in the occurrence of subject pronouns in postverbal position. More specifically, we seek to explain the facts by treating them as particular cases of a basic, more general asymmetry between the two languages. In what follows, we first give a sketch of the mentioned asymmetry and then try to derive the generalizations from it.

Spanish and Italian, despite their evident shared properties, differ in the constraints they put on the mapping between syntax and IS, as discussed in Leonetti (2014b, 2017). Italian, Catalan and French impose a neat informational articulation[13] (*topic/ comment* or *focus/background*) on marked orders – therefore, on inversion patterns – especially when certain factors such as aspect, definiteness or thematic prominence conspire to favour such division. Italian makes pervasive use of syntactic devices such as dislocation, focus fronting and clefting to avoid the formation of complex strings without informational articulation. As a result, wide focus readings in inversion are severely constrained, and non-focal constituents included in the background in interrogative sentences are typically detached. This makes Italian a restrictive language, with a strikingly transparent mapping between syntax and IS (cf. Calabrese 1992 for some ground-breaking observations). In contrast, Spanish, together with Romanian and European Portuguese, shows the opposite tendency: it is less restrictive, and allows for marked orders without internal informational articulation quite naturally. In Spanish, wide focus readings in subject inversion are common, and non-focal constituents in interrogatives do not need to be detached from the core clause, which explains the low frequency of dislocation with respect to central Romance languages. This means that the mapping between syntax and IS is less straightforward, and this language shows low sensitivity to the factors determining informational chunking.

What are the consequences for subject pronouns? We should bear in mind that

1. subjects, in the constructions under examination, correspond to external arguments, and thus are maximally prominent from a thematic perspective; and
2. personal pronouns are definite and deictic/anaphoric, mostly referential expressions and strongly context-dependent.

If this is the case, then it is reasonable to conclude that, due to these factors, subject pronouns are especially suited to being informationally singled out by means of prosodic or syntactic strategies. Their prominence hinders their integration into wider informational units, at least in languages that are highly sensitive to prominence factors. This, combined with the distinction between restrictive and less restrictive languages, provides us with the essential ingredients for an account of the data.

Our first generalization stated that differences between Spanish and Italian are only found in postverbal subjects. This is expected, since the differences follow from conditions on marked orders: Italian needs to create two distinct informational regions in these cases (in particular, when prominence factors favour them), whereas Spanish can do without them. In preverbal position, subjects are usually singled out as topics.[14]

The second generalization characterizes the asymmetry as one between a more restrictive language and a less restrictive one. Let's review each of the three contexts.

In wh-interrogatives the subject pronoun is a part of the background. In a restrictive language, its referential/discourse prominence forces its overt marking as a singled-out constituent; in fact, in Italian it is detached, or at least destressed, keeping its background nature. In a less restrictive language like Spanish, the subject pronoun stays *in situ*, inside the informational unit that corresponds to the background.

In subject inversion, the subject pronoun is focal – narrow focus, or part of wide focus. VOS is usually associated with a narrow focus reading for the subject, and does not give rise to noticeable differences between Spanish and Italian (except for the fact that Spanish allows wide focus readings much more easily). VSO, instead, together with certain contexts for VS (cf. examples in (14)), is the source of major differences, because it is fully acceptable in Spanish, but not in Italian: as the VSO pattern includes a focal subject that is a part of wide focus and cannot be singled out as narrow focus, only a non-restrictive language is able to accept it. A restrictive language, in contrast, needs to single the subject pronoun out, and that is incompatible with the informational nature of VSO.

One could reasonably raise the doubt that here we are dealing with a general constraint on the position of subjects in Italian, but not with a specific restriction on overt pronouns. However, as our data include not only examples of VSO but also instances of VS with familiarity and respect pronouns, we can safely conclude that the empirical facts are not limited to VSO orders. Moreover – and this is the main point – the account works similarly for non-focal pronouns and focal pronouns: in both cases, Italian forces interpreting the subject pronoun as a singled-out constituent in IS (either through dislocation/destressing or through narrow focus prosodic marking), whereas Spanish allows for the pronoun to be interpreted as part of a larger informational unit. Contrast, as the first licensing factor for strong pronouns, seems to be parasitic on establishing informational units in Italian, not in Spanish. This is just an indirect effect of the basic difference between the two languages, which affects the interplay of syntax and IS.

4 Conclusions

Our aim in this chapter was to give a unified account of the differences between Spanish and Italian in the distribution of postverbal subject pronouns. We put forward three sets of data, which could be actually reduced to two contexts: syntactically induced inversion and 'free' inversion (with either 'unmarked' pronouns or special, respect pronouns). The analysis showed that the contrasts follow a systematic pattern, by which Spanish strong pronouns may occur in positions where Italian pronouns are excluded.

We have come to two main conclusions:

1. Italian subject pronouns in postverbal positions must obey stricter conditions than their Spanish counterparts: they need to be marked either as narrow foci or as topics (by detachment or destressing). Spanish pronouns do not have to

obey such a constraint. This is the result of a basic difference in the mapping from syntax to IS. Languages like Italian are characterized by a strong tendency to make overt the information structure articulation, especially on marked orders. Languages like Spanish, on the other hand, are less restrictive, and do not need to single out phrases that are discourse prominent: such phrases may be integrated into larger informational units.

2. The contrastive value of subject pronouns is independent of other aspects of IS (informational focus, rheme). Contrast is contextually inferred on the basis of the competition between overt pronouns and null subjects, following general pragmatic principles.

The major advantage of this perspective is that the distribution of postverbal subject pronouns follows from the same principles that explain other additional differences between Spanish and Italian (cf. Leonetti 2014b, 2017): the productivity of subject inversion patterns, the use of Clitic Right Dislocation, and the use of clefting in interrogative clauses. The way IS is expressed in syntax and prosody is the crucial factor behind all these phenomena.

Notes

1 The investigation presented in this chapter is included in the research project 'The Semantics-Pragmatics Interface and the Resolution of Interpretive Mismatches' (SPIRIM), funded by the Spanish *Ministerio de Economía y Competitividad* (FFI2015-63497-P). A previous version was presented at the 8th International Contrastive Linguistics Conference (National and Kapodistrian University of Athens, May 2017). We are very grateful to the audience for stimulating discussion and to two anonymous reviewers for their suggestions. Our gratitude goes also to Aoife Ahern for checking the English.

2 The relevant facts in the preverbal position have to do with the alternation between strong pronouns and null subjects. Though Spanish and Italian belong to the same kind of null-subject languages, it is actually true that certain subtle differences in speakers' preferences for explicit versus implicit subjects have been observed in recent research (cf. Filiaci 2011; Filiaci, Sorace and Carreiras 2014). Thus, the scope of the generalization in (a) might be in need of a revision. However, it is not entirely clear to us whether such differences should be explained by means of the same reasoning that we follow for asymmetries with postverbal pronouns. We cannot deal with this issue here.

3 Notice that we assume that IS is only partially encoded in syntax; hence, postverbal subjects occur *in situ* in both cases: being focal or not is not tied to specific positions in VP or vP.

4 A focal reading of the subject pronoun is, of course, possible, but then the subject has to carry emphatic stress. We are not considering this option here. The default pronunciation of (5) needs neither emphasis nor focalization of the pronoun.

5 Subject inversion does not have the same status in Italian and Spanish focus fronting; in Italian, it is not actually obligatory. This point deserves a detailed comparative analysis that we cannot develop here. Our general conclusions, however, are not seriously affected by this particular case.

6 This can be observed also in Spanish.

7 For different possibilities in *yes-no* questions, see Bocci and Pozzan (2014).

8 As shown by the occurrence of typical preboundary processes, such as lengthening of both the stressed vowel and the final vowel.

9 We are not relying on a specific analysis for right dislocation, apart from the basic assumption that the right-dislocated phrase is external to the clause.

10 The example in (13)a is an illustration of the widespread use of VSO in emphatic and ironic exclamations in colloquial Spanish (cf. Escandell-Vidal and Leonetti 2014).

11 Some of the relevant parenthetical expressions are becoming formulaic, but we believe that this does not affect the role of the facts in the overall argumentation. A detailed analysis of this context for inversion and the way it differs from so-called Quotative Inversion is left for future research.

12 It is not strictly true that postverbal subjects in inversion contexts must always be interpreted as narrow foci in Italian: inversion with unaccusative predicates, as in *È arrivata lei* 'She arrived', is mostly associated with wide focus readings. This is a general property of unaccusative and presentative constructions, and does not undermine our generalization. We assume that in such contexts, factors like aspect and thematic structure override the natural prominence of subject pronouns. See Bentley (2006: Chapter 8) for an insightful discussion.

13 The notion of informational articulation or partition may require some clarification, as our reviewers pointed out. The basic idea is that the two fundamental distinctions in IS – *topic/comment, focus/background* – involve a splitting of a syntactic string into two or more parts. This splitting into informational units is crucial for determining the way a clause fits in a context and can be observed in any language. Under certain conditions, strings can be interpreted as single informational units: this is what happens in thetic, all-focus sentences, when information focus extends all over the predication, with no overt constituent singled out as topic. However, the more structurally complex a string is, the more it needs informational articulation in order to be processed, in particular if its internal constituents, due to their intrinsic properties, resist integration into a larger informational unit. If some sort of internal articulation is needed, it is obtained by singling some constituents out either as topics or as narrow foci. Languages differ in their degree of resistance to having large, compact non-split informational units, especially in marked orders (cf. Leonetti 2014b, 2017 for details). This is why we distinguish between *restrictive* and *non-restrictive* languages. As we understand it, the distinction cannot be reduced to specific syntactic rules or to the encoding of discourse-related features in certain positions. We are not assuming a cartographic approach; we would rather favour a model in which IS is viewed as an independent level of representation that evaluates well-formed syntactic structures, thus acting like a filter.

14 We acknowledge the possibility of having thetic, all-focus readings with preverbal subjects too (in both languages), but we will not deal here with eventual differences in the availability of such readings.

References

Belletti, A. (2004), 'Aspects of the Low IP Area', in A. Belletti (ed.), *Structures and Strategies*, 161–91, New York: Routledge.

Belletti, A. and M. T. Guasti (2015), 'The Acquisition of the Syntax and Interpretation of Subjects', in A. Belletti and M. T. Guasti (eds), *The Acquisition of Italian: Morphosyntax and Its Interfaces in Different Modes of Acquisition*, 231–62, Amsterdam: Benjamins.

Benincà, P. (1988), 'L'ordine degli elementi della frase e le costruzioni marcate', in L. Renzi (ed.), *Grande grammatica italiana di consultazione*, vol. I, 129–208, Bologna: Il Mulino.

Bentley, D. (2006), *Split Intransitivity in Italian*, Berlin: Mouton De Gruyter.

Bocci, G. and L. Pozzan (2014), 'Questions (and Experimental Answers) about Italian Subjects. Subject Positions in Main and Indirect Questions in L1 and Attrition', in C. Contemori and L. Dal Pozzo (eds), *Inquiries into Linguistic Theory and Language Acquisition: Papers Offered to Adriana Belletti*, 28–44, Siena: CISCL Press.

Calabrese, A. (1992), 'Some Remarks on Focus and Logical Structures in Italian', *Harvard Working Papers in Linguistics*, 1: 91–127.

Cardinaletti, A. (2001), 'A Second Thought on *Emarginazione*: Destressing vs "Right Dislocation"', in G. Cinque and G. Salvi (eds), *Current Studies in Italian Syntax: Essays Offered to Lorenzo Renzi*, 117–35, Amsterdam: Elsevier.

Cardinaletti, A. (2007), 'Subjects and Wh-questions: Some New Generalizations', in J. Camacho et al. (eds), *Romance Linguistics 2006: Selected Papers from the 36th Linguistic Symposium on Romance Languages (LSRL)*, 57–79, Amsterdam: Benjamins.

Cordin, P. and A. Calabrese (1988), 'I pronomi personali', in L. Renzi (ed.), *Grande grammatica italiana di consultazione*, vol. I, 535–92, Bologna: Il Mulino.

Escandell-Vidal, V. and M. Leonetti (2014), 'Fronting and Irony in Spanish', in A. Dufter and A. Octavio de Toledo (eds), *Left Sentence Peripheries in Spanish: Diachronic, Variationist and Typological Perspectives*, 309–42, Amsterdam: Benjamins.

Escandell-Vidal, V. and M. Leonetti (2017), 'Pronombres sujeto posverbales no focales', paper presented at *XXI Congreso de la Asociación Alemana de Hispanistas*, Ludwig-Maximilians Universität München, March 2017.

Fernández Ramírez, S. (1986), *Gramática española. El verbo y la oración*, Madrid: Arco Libros.

Fernández Soriano, O. (1999), 'El pronombre personal', in I. Bosque and V. Demonte (eds), *Gramática descriptiva de la lengua española*, vol. I, 1209–73, Madrid: Espasa-Calpe.

Filiaci, F. (2011), 'Anaphoric Preferences of Null and Overt Subjects in Italian and Spanish: A Cross-Linguistic Comparison', PhD diss., University of Edinburgh, Edinburgh UK.

Filiaci, F., A. Sorace and M. Carreiras (2014), 'Anaphoric Biases of Null and Overt Subjects in Italian and Spanish: A Cross-Linguistic Comparison', *Language, Cognition and Neuroscience*, 29 (7): 825–43.

Leonetti, M. (2014a), 'On Contrastive Readings in the Interpretation of NPs/DPs', in S. Chiriacescu (ed.), *Proceedings of the VI NEREUS Workshop 'Theoretical Implications at the Syntax / Semantics Interface in Romance'*, Arbeitspapier 127, 99–116, Fachbereich Sprachwissenschaft Universität Konstanz.

Leonetti, M. (2014b), 'Spanish VSX', in K. Lahousse and S. Marzo (eds), *Romance Languages and Linguistic Theory 2012*, 37–63, Amsterdam: Benjamins.

Leonetti, M. (2017), 'Basic Constituent Orders', in A. Dufter and E. Stark (eds), *Manual of Romance Morphosyntax and Syntax*, 885–930, Berlin: Mouton de Gruyter.

Leonetti, M. (2018), 'Two Types of Postverbal Subject', *Italian Journal of Linguistics*, 30(2) 11–36.

Lobo, M. and A. M. Martins (2017), 'Subjects', in A. Dufter and E. Stark (eds), *Manual of Romance Morphosyntax and Syntax*, 27–88, Berlin: Mouton de Gruyter.

Luján, M. (1999), 'Expresión y omisión del pronombre personal', in I. Bosque and V. Demonte (eds), *Gramática descriptiva de la lengua española*, vol. I, 1275–315, Madrid: Espasa-Calpe.

Mayol, L. (2010), 'Contrastive Pronouns in Null Subject Romance Languages', *Lingua*, 120 (10): 2497–514.

Neeleman, A. and R. Vermeulen, eds (2012), *The Syntax of Topic, Focus and Contrast: An Interface-Based Approach*, Berlin: Mouton de Gruyter.

Planas-Morales, S. and X. Villalba (2013), 'The Right Periphery of Interrogatives in Catalan and Spanish: Syntax/Prosody Interactions', *Catalan Journal of Linguistics*, 12: 193–217.

RAE (2009), *Nueva Gramática de la Lengua Española*, Madrid: Espasa.

Rizzi, L. (2001), 'On the Position Int(errogative) in the Left Periphery of the Clause', in G. Cinque and G. Salvi (eds), *Current Studies in Italian Syntax: Essays Offered to Lorenzo Renzi*, 287–96, Amsterdam: Elsevier.

Sánchez López, C. (1993), 'Una anomalía del sistema pronominal español', *Dicenda*, 11: 259–84.

Torrego, E. (1984), 'On Inversion in Spanish and Some of Its Effects', *Linguistic Inquiry*, 15: 103–29.

Villalba, X. (2011), 'A Quantitative Comparative Study of Right-Dislocation in Catalan and Spanish', *Journal of Pragmatics*, 43 (7): 1946–61.

13

Cliticization patterns in Greek: A comparative examination with crosslinguistic remarks

Anthi Revithiadou and Vassilios Spyropoulos

Greek exhibits dialectal and diachronic variation in the cliticization pattern of weak pronouns. In Standard Modern Greek, clitics are strictly preverbal with finite non-imperative verb forms, whereas in the southeastern dialects, as well as in Byzantine and Medieval Greek, clitics seem to obey a second position requirement, since they are preverbal when a function word precedes the verb and postverbal otherwise. A comparison with the adverbal Romance cliticization system and the second position cliticization system of Slavic languages reveals that Greek clitics are neither C- nor v*-related elements and cliticization involves clitic movement to the T-layer. We further argue that the attested variation results from the ways PF (Phonetic Form) processes the syntactic output of this movement. Finally, we show that the two systems are diachronically related to each other by means of a prosodic reanalysis that resulted in the evolution of the non-second position system of Standard Modern Greek from the second position system of Medieval Greek.

1 Introduction

The position of Greek weak pronomimal objects (henceforth *clitics*) in the clause exhibits an interesting pattern of variation, which cuts across synchrony (dialectal split) and diachrony (see Pappas 2005; Revithiadou and Spyropoulos 2006, 2008, for an overview). More specifically, in Standard Modern Greek (SMG) and most of Modern Greek (MG) dialects, clitics are strictly preverbal and proclitic on finite non-imperative verb forms in all environments. They are, however, postverbal and enclitic only with the imperative verb forms and the gerund. On the other hand, in Cypriot and the rest of the southeastern dialects, clitics are preverbal when a particle or a complementizer (collectively referred to here with the cover term *function word* and abbreviated as *fnc*) precedes the verb form and postverbal when nothing occurs before the verb. Because the clitic in question looks like occupying the second position of the clause, this pattern is commonly known as 'second position cliticization' (2P) (Janse 1994; Pappas 2001, 2004a,b, 2005; Condoravdi and Kiparsky 2001; Revithiadou and Spyropoulos 2008;

among others). Interestingly, this pattern was also attested in Byzantine and Medieval Greek (BMG; fifth to fifteenth century), which entails that the evolutionary path in Greek cliticization involved the transition from 2P to non-2P.

The comparative examination of these two cliticization patterns provides some significant typological insights, since they appear to be very similar to the cliticization structures of other languages. In particular, the non-second position system is very similar to the cliticization system of Romance languages, whereas the 2P system shares similarities with the 2P systems of Slavic languages (e.g. Serbian-Croatian) and the encliticization system of European Portuguese. Given that there is a considerable body of research on the properties and the derivation of these constructions in the aforementioned languages, their comparative examination with Greek clitics will offer significant insights into the typology of the systems and their derivation, and it will provide valuable, new information on the place of Greek in this typology.

In addition, the described pattern of variation offers an excellent ground for a comparative analysis within the same language that addresses issues of both dialectal variation and diachronic evolution and raises the following pivotal questions: Is this variation the result of deeper underlying differences in the syntactic derivation? Can the evolution of cliticization shed light on the nature of this variation and vice versa?

2 The non-2P system

In SMG and the majority of MG dialects, clitics are strictly preverbal with finite non-imperative verb forms and postverbal with imperative verb forms and gerunds. Some representative examples are given in (1) and (2), respectively. (The sign '=' denotes the direction of clitic attachment.)

(1) a. (o   jánis)   ton=   éðese   (ton   kómbo)
      The   John-NOM   CL3-M.SG.ACC AUG-tie-PST.3SG   the   knot-ACC
      'John tied it (the knot).'

   b. o   jánis   ðé   θa   ton=   ðési
      the   John-NOM   NEG   EM   CL3-M.SG.ACC tie-3SG
      'John will not tie it.'

   c. mu=   ípan   óti   ti=   fílise
      CL1-SG.GEN   say-PST.3PL   that   CL3-F.SG.ACC kiss-PST.3SG
      'They told me that s/he has kissed her.'

   d. ti   maría,   ti=   fílise   o   jánis
      the   Maria-ACC   CL3-F.SG.ACC   kiss-PST.3SG   the   John-NOM
      'As for Maria, John kissed her.'

   e. O   jÁNIS   ti=   fílise
      the   John_FOC-NOM   CL3-F.SG.ACC   kiss-PST.3SG
      'JOHN kissed her.'

(2) a. fílisé   =tin   (< fílise =tin)
       kiss-IMP.2SG   CL3-F.SG.ACC
       'Kiss her!'

    b. ðénondás   =ton   (< ðénondas =ton)
       tie-GER   CL3-M.SG.ACC
       'by tying it'

As evident from these data, the verb form standardly serves as the clitic host. At the prosodic level, the clitic adjoins at the left side of the *phonological word* (PW) of the verb form forming a recursive PW, that is, $[cl \, [V]_{PW}]_{PW}$, as shown in (3). For instance, although resyllabification between the /s/ of the clitic *tus* and the onset of the following word is blocked, *s*-voicing obligatorily takes place between the clitic and the PW of the verb form. This rule is obligatory within the PW, (e.g. /pinas-ménos/ → $[pinazménos]_{PW}$ 'hungry') but optional across different PWs (e.g. /éxis maɣirépsi/ → $[éçis/z]_{PW}$ $[majirépsi]_{PW}$). This prosodic behaviour indicates that the clitic does not incorporate into the PW of the verb but rather adjoins to it into an extended PW.

(3) clitic V → $[cl \, [V]_{PW}]_{PW}$
    Mas   tuz.   majirévi   (/mas tus maɣirévi/)
    CL1-PL.ACC   CL3-PL.GEN   cook-3SG
    'S/he cooks them for us.'

The direction of attachment and the attested prosodic structure do not change when a function word precedes the [clitic V] string. Thus, if the function word is stressed (*fnć*), it forms itself an independent PW, whereas the clitic adjoins to the PW of the verb form as usual: $[fnć]_{PW} \, [cl \, [V]_{PW}]_{PW}$.

(4) fnć clitic V → $[fnć]_{PW} \, [cl \, [V]_{PW}]_{PW}$
    prín   maz.   majirépsi   (/prín mas maɣirépsi/)
    Before   CL1-PL.ACC   cook-3SG

When the preceding function word is unstressed, both the *fnc* and the clitic adjoin to the PW of the verb form in the same fashion as the clitic alone: $[fnc \, cl \, [V]_{PW}]_{PW}$.

(5) fnc clitic V → $[fnc \, cl \, [V]_{PW}]_{PW}$
    θa   maz.   majirépsi   (/θa mas maɣirépsi/)
    EM   CL1-PL.ACC   cook-3SG

Thus, in the non-2P pattern the position and the directionality of attachment is not prosodically conditioned and the clitic always attaches to the verb form either as a proclitic or as an enclitic depending on the grammatical make-up of the verb form. This means that the position of the clitic is syntactically determined, as a result of the derivation of the relevant structure.

SMG cliticization is very similar to the cliticization patterns found in Romance languages (see Cardinaletti 1999 for an overview). For instance, in Spanish the clitic appears always attached to the verb form and it is proclitic with non-imperative forms and enclitic with imperative and non-finite forms (Zagona 2001):

(6) a. (María) lo= escribió   ayer
       (Maria) CL.DO write-PST.3SG yesterday
       'Maria/she wrote it yesterday.'

   b. (María) no   lo= escribió   ayer
       (Maria) NEG CL.DO write-PST.3SG yesterday
       'Maria/she didn't write it yesterday.'

   c. Pedro   dijo   que   lo=   escribió   ayer
       Pedro   say-pst.3sg   COMP   CL.DO write-PST.3SG   yesterday
       'Pedro said that he wrote it yesterday.'

   d. La   respuesta,   (Susana) la=   sabe
       the   answer,   (Susana) CL.DO know-3SG
       'The answer, Susana/she knows it.'

(7) a. Haz=lo   ahora!
       Do.IMP=CL.DO   now
       'Do it now!'

   b. Intentó   mandár=me=lo
       try-PST.3SG   send-INF=CL.IO=CL.DO
       'S/he tried to send it to me.'

   c. Estaba   cantándolo
       be-IMPFV.3SG   sing.PRTC=CL.DO
       'S/he was singing it.'

In order to account for these facts, a movement analysis of cliticization has been put forward in the literature (Kayne 1975, 1989, Emonds 1975; Quicoli 1976). According to this analysis, the clitic is base generated at the relevant argument position in the VP and it moves to its surface position in order to attach to the verb form. Roberts (2010) proposes that this movement is a kind of an incorporation process, which is triggered by the defective status of clitics as goals in an Agree situation. More specifically, based on Cardinaletti and Starke (1999), Roberts (2010) argues that in Romance the clitic is not a proper $D^{min/max}$, but rather a $\phi^{min/max}$, that is, a bundle of ϕ-features, which crucially lacks the case feature. As such, it is a defective goal for the Agree operation triggered by the relevant ϕ-features of the v^* phasal head, and it is forced to incorporate to this head, forming a complex verbal head $[_{v^*} \text{cl} [_{v^*} \text{Root } v^*]]$. Given that Romance exhibits overt V-to-T movement, this complex head moves to T and creates the complex clitic–verb form: $[_T [_{v^*} \text{cl} [_{v^*} \text{Root } v^*]] \text{ T }]$.

Although we adhere to the movement analysis for MG non-2P cliticization, there seem to exist some very interesting differences from its Romance equivalent, which point towards the conclusion that Greek clitics do not incorporate to the v^* head (contra Mavrogiorgos 2010), but, rather, move as full $D^{min/max}$ to the T-layer. More specifically, Greek clitics carry overt case morphology, which is the same as in other nominal categories. For instance, third-person singular accusative clitics carry the characteristic accusative marker -*n*, which is found in articles (e.g. *ton* 'the-M.SG.ACC'), demonstratives (e.g. *aftón* 'this-M.SG.ACC'), wh-words (e.g. *pçón* 'who-M.SG.ACC', *ópçon* 'whoever-M.SG.ACC') and quantifiers (*kápçon* 'somebody-M.SG.ACC') and genitive singular clitics carry the characteristic genitive marker -*u* found in all the nominal subsystems. Based on these morphological facts, we infer that in Greek, clitics carry case features. Therefore, they are not defective goals for the Agree operation triggered by the φ-features of the v^* phasal head and they do not incorporate to the v^* head. The latter conclusion is also supported by certain morphophonological facts that indicate that the clitic attaches to its verb host after the full M(orphological)-Word of the verb is formed, that is, after the verb head has moved to the relevant functional projections that provide its inflection.[1] First, the clitic appears outside the augment prefix of the past tense:

(8) a. ton=   fern-i
       CL3-M.SG.ACC   bring- 3SG
       'He is bringing him.'

    b. ton=   é-fern-e
       CL3-M.SG.ACC   AUG-bring-PST.3SG
       'He was bringing him.'

Given that the augment is a morphological exponent of T[+past] (Spyropoulos and Revithiadou 2009), the appearance of the clitic before it indicates that the clitic attaches to the verb form after the latter has moved to the T head. If the clitic incorporated in the v^* head, then the augment wouldn't be able to appear after the clitic.

Second, in encliticization situations, the clitic occurs outside the imperative subject agreement and gerund suffixes, which have been argued to be the exponents of a Mood (or a C) head above T to which the verb head moves overtly (Rivero 1994; Philippaki-Warburton 1998; Philippaki-Warburton and Spyropoulos 1999; Roussou 2000; Tsimpli 2000). In other words, the clitic attaches to these verb forms after the formation of their M-Words, that is, after the verb head has reached all the relevant functional projections. This is also evident from the fact that when the clitic is postverbal and the trisyllabic window for the positioning of stress is violated, the original stress of the verb form is respected, but a secondary stress pattern arises (9)a, in contrast with ordinary morphological affixation, which causes a stress shift (9)b:

(9) a. fílis-e   →   fílis-é   =tin / *filís-e =tin
       kiss-IMP.2SG   kiss-IMP.2SG CL3-F.SG.ACC
       versus

b. máθima   →   maθímat-os / *máθimátos
    lesson.NOM/ACC.SG   lesson-GEN.SG

All these facts indicate that in the MG non-2P pattern the clitic is not a $\phi^{min/max}$ and, therefore, it does not incorporate in the v* head and carried over by the verb head in its movement to the relevant functional projections which derive its inflectional make-up. On the contrary, we conclude that the clitic is a full $D^{min/max}$, which moves independently of the verb movement and cliticizes onto the M-Word of the verb postsyntactically by means of a merging operation (Marantz 1988; Embick and Noyer 2001; Embick 2007).

3 The 2P system

The 2P system appears in BMG and in the southeastern Modern Greek dialects, which include Cypriot, the dialects spoken in the Dodecanese (Karpathiot, Rhodian, Symiot, etc.), Cappadocian and other Asia Minor Greek varieties, as well as Cretan. Currently, it is best preserved in Cypriot and in some Dodecanese dialects (Karpathiot and Symiot), although even in these varieties, interference from the SMG non-2P patterns has become increasingly strong. In this system, the clitic is preverbal when the verb form is preceded by a (stressed/unstressed) function word and postverbal otherwise:[2]

(10) a. *Cypriot*
      i.   ém   mu   eθcávasen   (/én mu eθkjávasen/)
           NEG   CL1-SG.GEN AUG-read-PST.3SG
           'S/he didn't read for me.'
      ii. pos   to   θcávasen (/pos tu eθkjávasen/)
           COMP   CL3-SG.ACC AUG-read-PST.3SG
           'that s/he read for him'

   b. *Karpathiot*
       sat   to   poxtísasin   (/san to apoxtísasin/)
       as   CL3-N.SG.ACC get-3PL.PAST'
       'as they got it'   (Minas 2002: 189)

   c. *Cappadocian*
       án   da   skotóit
       if   CL3-PL.ACC kill-3SG
       'if he kills them'   (Ulaghatsh, D380)

   d. *Medieval*
       píos   sas   tin   éðoke
       'who-NOM   CL2-PL.GEN CL3-F.SG.ACC give-PST.3SG
       'Who gave you this?'   (Chroniko tu Moreos, 3759)

(11) a. *Cypriot*
     Ípez   mu   (/ípes mu/)
     tell-PST.2SG   CL1-SG.GEN
     'You told me.'

    b. *Karpathiot*
       íkusá   tu
       hear-PST.1SG   CL3-M.SG.GEN   (Minas 2002: 186)
       'I heard him.'

    c. *Cappadocian*
       ðínis   me   to
       give-2SG   CL1-PL.ACC   CL3-SG.ACC   (Potamia, D458)
       'You give it to me.'

    d. *Medieval*
       ðíðo   su   to   loɣári   mu
       give-1SG   CL2-SG.GEN the   treasure-ACC   CL1-SG.GEN
       'I give you my treasure.'   (Digenis Akritis E, 995)

As Revithiadou (2006, 2008) has shown, the directionality of attachment is prosodically determined, creating a number of variable prosodic patterns. More specifically, when there is a preceding stressed *fnć*, the clitic is preverbal, but it attaches prosodically to the *fnć* rather than to the verb form, that is, $[fnć=cl]_{PW} [V]_{PW}$. For instance, the prosodic organization of the string in (10ai) is $[ém=mu]_{PW} [eθcávasen]_{PW}$, because consonant assimilation takes place between the function word and the clitic and coalescence between the /u/ of the clitic and the /e/ of the verb form into [o] is blocked ($*[ém]_{PW}$ $[moθcávasen]_{PW}$; cf. $[poθcávasen]_{PW}$ < /pu eθkjávasen/ 'that s/he read'). Crucially, however, with a preceding unstressed *fnc* (10aii) fusion applies between the clitic and the verb form (/tu eθkjávasen/ → toθcávasen), offering empirical support for a recursive prosodization of the relevant elements to their verbal host: $[fnc=cl=[V]_{PW}]_{PW}$. An extended PW is also the attested pattern in Karpathiot, as suggested by examples such as (10)b. Here, vowel deletion is enforced between the clitic and the verb form in order for hiatus to be resolved. When there is no preceding function word in the string, the clitic is always postverbal and enclitic (11). In conclusion, the 2P pattern predominantly involves enclisis, since the clitic cannot surface as the first element in its prosodic constituent.

    Crucially, the Medieval and Modern Greek 2P system is not a real 2P system like the one exemplified by languages such as Serbian-Croatian (Progovac 1996; Dimitrova-Vulchanova 1999; Franks and King 2000) or Ancient Greek (Revithiadou 2014; Goldstein 2015). In such languages, the clitic cannot appear in a clause initial position and it always follows a syntactic or a prosodic constituent:

(12) *Serbian-Croatian* (examples from Franks and King 2000)
    a. Olga   nam   nešto   dovikuje
       Olga   CL1.PL.DAT   something   shout-out.3SG
       'Olga is shouting something out to us.'

b. Jesam   mu   predstavio   Mariju
   AUX.PST.1SG   CL3.DAT   introduce   Maria
   'I introduced Maria to him.'

c. Sutra   ga   deca   neće   videti
   tomorrow   CL3.ACC   children NEG-FUT.3SG   see-INF
   'The children will not see him tomorrow.'

d. Dade   mi   ga   Nena
   give.PST-3SG   CL1.DAT   CL3.ACC Nena
   'Nena gave it to me.'

e. da   me   je   Ivan   vidio
   COMP   CL1.ACC AUX.3SG   Ivan   see.PST.3SG
   'that Ivan saw me'

f. koliko   im   ki   daje?
   how-many   CL3.PL.DAT   who   give.PST.3SG
   'Who gave them how many?'

As evident from the examples above, the clitic can appear away from the verb form. Moreover, in order to achieve the target second position, it can even split the first phrase of the clause:

(13) Anina   im   sestra   nudi   čokoladu
     Ana-GEN   CL3.PL.DAT   sister   offer.3SG chocolate
     'Ana's sister is offering them chocolate.'

The 2P clitics have been considered to be C-related elements and the relevant cliticization pattern has been analysed as involving movement of the clitic to C or to some specialized functional head in the C-domain (Ćavar and Wilder 1994; Progovac 1996; Rivero 1997; Dimitrova-Vulchanova 1999). Crucially, the Medieval and Modern Greek 2P pattern lacks two very important properties of this type of cliticization. First, the clitic does not appear as the second word in the clause by breaking up the first constituent. Thus, constructions like the one in (13) are not attested. Second, and more importantly, the clitic is strictly adverbal, which entails that a head X^0 or a phrasal XP can never intervene between the clitic and the verb form, even when the clitic is not prosodically attached to it:

(14) *[fnć=cl]$_{PW}$ X^0/XP [V]$_{PW}$

The 2P phenomena in Medieval Greek and Modern Greek dialects are more similar to the encliticization pattern found in European Portuguese and some other Romance varieties, including Medieval Romance. This pattern has been analysed as involving further movement of V from T to some other functional projection over the clitics (Martins 1994; Uriagereka 1995; Galves 2000; Raposo 2000). A similar syntactic approach for Medieval and Modern Greek 2P patterns has been proposed by Terzi

(1999a, 1999b) and Agouraki (2001), according to which the encliticization pattern of Cypriot Greek is the result of verb movement from T to the higher Mood or C heads over the clitics. Revithiadou (2006) shows that these approaches fail to explain the whole range of facts regarding the positioning of the clitic in these dialects, especially situations in which variation is attested with other C-related elements (e.g. complementizers and wh-phrases). In addition, from a theoretical point of view, the verb-movement approach to encliticization has the shortcoming that there is no independent evidence that the verb moves away from T in non-imperative contexts; the postulation of such movement looks like an ad hoc operation to derive the attested pattern.

A closer examination of the Greek 2P system indicates that the positioning and the directionality of the attachment of the clitic are prosodically determined. The clitic seems to be an enclitic that has to encliticize on a host within a given prosodic constituent. This conclusion is supported by the fact that when a syntactic phrase precedes the verb form, the position of the clitic varies, depending on the status of this preceding XP. When the XP is a topic, the clitic follows the verb, whereas, when it is a fronted emphatic element, it precedes the verb (Condoravdi and Kiparsky 2001 2004; Pappas 2005; Revithiadou and Spyropoulos 2008; Soltic 2012, 2013a, 2013b):

(15) *topic XP*

    a. *Cypriot*

        eɣjó,   tus   vasiljáðes,   voúme   tus

        I-NOM the   king-PL.ACC   fear-1SG CL3-PL.ACC

        'As for the kings, I fear them.'   (Aceras Anthropophorum)

    b. *Cappadocian*

        ta   tría   güzélja,   ívra   ta

        the   three-PL.ACC   Fair One-PL.ACC   find-PST.1SG CL3-PL.ACC

        'As for the three Fair Ones, I found them.'   (Delmesos, D310)

    c. *Medieval*

        tus   kóntus   ke   kavalaríus,

        the   count-PL.ACC   and   horseman-PL.ACC

        apoxerétisén   tus

        say goodbye-PST.3SG   CL3-M.PL.ACC

        'As for the counts and horsemen, he sent them off.'

                            (Chroniko tu Moreos, 8610)

(16) *fronted emphatic XP*

    a. *Cappadocian*

        eséna   PÁL$_{FOC}$ se   sálsan

        you-ACC   again$_{FOC}$ CL2-SG send-PST.3PL

        s   éna   batáx   tópos

        to   one   slippery place

        'They have sent you AGAIN to a slippery place.'   (Delmesos, D322)

b. *Medieval*

POLÁ	ðÁKRIA	se	γémisen
many	tear-PL.ACC$_{FOC}$	CL2-SG.ACC	fill-PST.3SG

'With many tears she has filled you…'   (Ptochoprodromika, IV260)

We suggest that clitic placement in such structures depends on the prosodic properties of the preceding XP and the prosodification of the utterance. Topicalized phrases have a higher prosodic constituent boundary (*phonological phrase*/PPh or *intonational phrase*/IPh) at their right edge (Baltazani 2002), so that the clitic cannot appear first in the subsequent prosodic constituent:

(17) ta tría güzélja]$_{PPh/IPh}$ [ívra ta   (=15b)

On the other hand, fronted emphatic phrases are focalized. As expected, focus causes deaccentuation of post-focal elements (see Baltazani and Jun 1999 for Greek), deleting the relevant prosodic boundaries and allowing for the clitic to occur preverbally ((16) a, b).

That clitic positioning is prosodically determined is also evident by the fact that in medieval texts it may obviate the expected pattern due to rhythmic requirements. Thus, in (18), although there is a preceding emphatic element (*timitiká* 'honorably'), the clitic appears after and not before the verb as would have been expected, because the metrical caesura falls after the adverb and creates a prosodic boundary. As a result, the clitic cannot appear in the first position of the immediately following prosodic constituent:

(18) ke	o	vasiléfs	TIMITIKÁ |	apoxeretisén	tus
and	the	king-NOM	honourably$_{FOC}$	say goodbye-PST.3SG	CL3-M.PL.ACC

'and the king honourably sent them off'   (Velisarios ρ, 954)

Before moving to the analysis we propose to account for these patterns, it should be noted that European Portuguese also exhibits the same enclisis versus proclisis pattern with preverbal topic and focal elements, which has led Frota and Vigário (1996) and Barbosa (2000) to argue that cliticization patterns are subject to prosodic conditioning (see also Duarte and Matos 2000). In order to account for these facts, Raposo and Uriagereka (2005) have proposed a variant of the verb-movement approach, according to which clitics move to an F head over T and enclisis derives from overt movement of the verb to the F projection over the clitic. This movement is a last resort operation motivated by certain PF requirements and conditions on the directionality of clitic attachment. However, such an analysis requires too many stipulations about (a) the nature and the content of the special F projection that attracts the clitic and the verb and (b) the nature and the trigger of the extra verb movement to F, in order to account for the preverbal versus postverbal placement of clitics in the various contexts. Furthermore, this account implies that the postverbal positioning derives from a structure with preverbal positioning. In her study of the acquisition of Cypriot Greek cliticization, Neokleous (2015) has shown that postverbal clitic placement is the first stage in acquisition and preverbal placement appears later. Thus, postverbal placement cannot be the result of a more complex derivation (see also Duarte and Matos 2000 for a similar argumentation about European Portuguese).

4 Relating the two systems: The proposed analysis

The syntactic conditioning on clitic placement in Greek non-2P systems points towards a movement analysis of cliticization, according to which, the clitic moves to the T-layer (Philippaki-Warburton 1994; Philippaki-Warburton and Spyropoulos 1999; Philippaki-Warburton et al. 2004). This movement creates the preverbal pattern in finite non-imperative verb forms, given that the verb moves to T in Greek. In imperative forms, the verb moves further to the Mood functional head, leaving behind the clitic in the T-layer and resulting in postverbal placement:

(19)		Mood	Neg	EM	cl	T-Agr[2sg]...	[$_{vP}$	$\sqrt{}$-v	cl]
	a. indicative:	Ø	(ðén)	(θa)	tin	filísis		~~fil-~~	~~tin~~
	b. subjunctive:	na/as	(mín)		tin	filísis		~~fil-~~	~~tin~~
	c. imperative:	fílise			tin	~~filis-~~		~~fil-~~	~~tin~~
								KISS	her

In the 2P system, we showed that, although the positioning and the directionality of the attachment of the clitic is prosodically determined, it also obeys a crucial syntactic restriction; that is, the clitic is strictly adverbal even in the cases in which it does not prosodify with the verb form. Such facts indicate that in the 2P system the clitic has a fixed position in the syntactic structure, which must be adjacent to the one occupied by the verb form. Thus, both 2P and non-2P systems share the same syntactic representation and differ in the phonological processing of this syntactic output.

To account for this observation, we propose that there is a single syntactic derivation of cliticization for all systems in Greek. This derivation involves clitic movement from its theta position inside the vP to the T-layer (through the intermediate functional or phasal projections), which creates a chain of copies. We assume that the linearization of this chain of copies, that is, which copy will be pronounced, is a matter of the PF-interface (see Bošković 1995, 2000, 2001; Franks 2000). Thus, the two systems described above derive from the different ways this chain of clitic copies is linearized at PF: When PF imposes no requirements, the highest clitic copy is pronounced as the default strategy; the result is the non-2P clitic system. However, when the clitic copies are evaluated and selected for pronunciation by prosodic alignment constraints (McCarthy and Prince 1993) that may suppress the 'blind' pronunciation of the highest copy (Bošković 1995, 2001; Franks 2000), the 2P system emerges. These prosodic constraints are the ones that also determine the particular prosodic structure that 2P clitics participate in with their hosts. Clitics prefer to be prosodized together with a stressed *fnć*, so that the left edge alignment of the PW of the verb form is respected (i.e. M-Words should begin and end with a PW boundary; see Revithiadou 2006, 2008 for details and a constraint-based analysis). If the *fnc* is unstressed, it cannot support a PW. In this case, the [*fnc* clitic] cluster adjoins to the PW of the verb form into a recursive PW. A structure where the *fnc* surfaces at the left edge of the verb and the clitic surfaces at the right (due to pronunciation of the lower copy) and, thus, both elements adjoin at either side of the verb; that is, [fnc [V]$_{PW}$ cl]$_{PW}$ is less optimal than the one attested in the data. This is because a recursive PW, which has compromised the crispness of both edges of the [V]$_{PW}$, is always less optimal than a recursive PW with prosodic adjuncts at only one side. When there is no *fnc*, the lower copy of the clitic will be opted by the prosodic constraints to surface, because the right edge of the PW is cross-linguistically more prone to incorporating material compared to the left edge (Bye and de Lacy 2000).

The proposed approach can also explain in a natural way the distribution of clitic placement in constructions with a preceding XP. As illustrated in examples (20)a, b – repeated from (15) and (16) respectively – the clitic follows the verb, when the XP is a topic, but precedes it, when it is a fronted emphatic element:

(20) *Cappadocian*

    a. *topic XP*

ta	tría	güzélja,	ívra	ta
the	three-PL.ACC	Fair One-PL.ACC	find-PST.1SG	CL3-PL.ACC

        'As for the three Fair Ones, I found them.'   (Delmesos, D310)

    b. *fronted emphatic XP*

eséna	PÁL$_{FOC}$	se	sálsan
you-ACC	again$_{FOC}$	CL2-SG	send-PST.3PL
s	éna	batáx	tópos
to	one	slippery	place

        'They have sent you AGAIN to a slippery place.'   (Delmesos, D322)

Given that topic phrases end in a right PPh or IPh boundary, there is no other option for the clitic but to prosodify with the verb. Pronunciation of the lower copy is the most optimal solution because, as explained above, the right edge of the PW is more likely to prosodically incorporate the clitic, giving rise to encliticization:

(21) ta tría güzélja]$_{PPh/IPh}$ [ta ívra ta   (=15b/17/20a)

On the other hand, when the XP is a fronted emphatic phrase, focus causes deaccentuation of all post-focal elements, destroying any chance the clitic copy has to create a prosodically optional prosodic structure with its host. This gives the opportunity to the elsewhere selection mechanism, which promotes pronunciation of the highest copy, to take effect, resulting in preverbal placement of the clitic.

5 Prosodic reanalysis and the transition from 2P to non-2P

The analysis presented above gains further support from the diachronic development of cliticization in Greek. As described above, BMG exhibited a 2P system in which clitics were preverbal with function words and fronted emphatic elements, and postverbal otherwise. From the middle medieval period onwards the grammaticalization of the mood, epistemic modality and negation particles reaches the final stages as they lose their stress and attach to the verb form by incorporating into its PW (Philippaki-Warburton and Spyropoulos 2004; Roberts and Roussou 2003; Horrocks 2010):

(22) a. *subjunctive particle*
        ína → iná → ná → na=

     b. *epistemic modality/future particle*[3]
        θélo (ína) → θená / θelá / θalá → θena / θela / θala= → θa=

(23) *Constructions with weakened particles*
     a. $[\text{fnć}]_{PW} [V]_{PW} \to [\text{fnc} [V]_{PW}]_{PW}$
     b. $[\text{fnć=cl}]_{PW} [V]_{PW} [V]_{PW} \to [\text{fnc=cl=}[V]_{PW}]_{PW}$

The weakening of stressed function words and the loss of their independent prosodic status led to their recursive adjunction to the left edge of the verb form (23)a. Since clitics occupied a position in between, they also attached to the left edge of the verb form (23)b, resulting in a proliferation of structures with proclitics. This development triggered a prosodic reanalysis, according to which clitics were reanalysed as proclitics to the PW of the verb form:

(24) … $=\text{cl}]_{PW} [V]_{PW} \to$ … $\text{cl=}[V]_{PW}]_{PW}$

The prosodic reanalysis was further facilitated by the [XP clitic V] constructions with a fronted emphatic XP, in which the clitic was preverbal. Crucially, the clitic in these constructions was prosodically stray and not encliticized to the fronted element. In example (25), the absence of the accent symbol on the penultimate of the adverb *síndoma*, which would have marked rhythmic stress as a result of encliticization, suggests that the preverbal clitic is not enclitic to the preceding element (Pappas 2001: 77):

(25) síndoma   ton   etíflose   (*síndomá =ton)
      quickly_FOC CL3-MSC.SG.ACC blind-PST.3SG
      'Quickly, he blinded him…'   (*Velisarios* χ, 350)

Under the pressure of such extended PWs, the constructions with preceding functional elements that didn't lose their stress (e.g. complementizers) were reanalysed as follows:

(26) $[\text{fnć cl}]_{PW} [V]_{PW} \to [\text{fnć}]_{PW} [\text{cl} [V]_{PW}]_{PW}$

The prosodic reanalysis from enclisis to proclisis resulted in the emergence of the non-2P system by means of an actualization process by which all non-imperative verb forms, even the ones not introduced by a function word, were associated with proclitic pronouns. The immediate consequence of this development was the relaxation of the prosodic constraints that regulated which copy would be pronounced; from the moment the left edge of the PW of the verb form was willing to host constituents, the transparency restriction of this edge was unavoidably weakened. Thus, PF ceased to control selection of copy and the higher copy was pronounced by default.

6 Conclusions

The comparative examination of the two cliticization systems of Greek with the corresponding adverbal Romance cliticization and the C-related 2P cliticization of Slavic languages led us to the conclusion that Greek clitics are not defective $\phi^{min/max}$ goals, but rather full $D^{min/max}$ elements, which are neither C-related nor do they incorporate in the verb form at the v^* phase level. Instead, we claimed that Greek clitics are T-related elements, in the sense that they move to the T-layer and cliticize to the verb form after the latter has formed its M-Word. We proposed that this syntactic derivation lies behind the core property of Greek cliticization, namely that the clitic must be always adverbal regardless the directionality of its attachment and its prosodification. In this respect, cliticization in Greek is uniform as far as its syntactic derivation is concerned and the two different systems, that is, 2P and non-2P, derive from a set of PF conditions that linearize the output of syntactic movement. When these conditions are inert in a grammar, the highest copy of the clitic chain is pronounced by default and the non-2P system emerges. When, however, they are in effect, they select the optimal clitic in the copy chain to be pronounced, yielding 2P effects in the respective grammar.

A welcome result of the proposed account is that it treats the observed patterns of variation in Greek cliticization as a result of the workings of the PF-interface on the syntactic output. Furthermore, it straightforwardly relates the observed patterns of variation both synchronically and diachronically. If the change from the 2P system to the non-2P system in Greek was caused by a prosodic reanalysis from enclisis to proclisis, which led to the suspension of the effect of the prosodic constraints, then the nature of this diachronic change reveals the source of variation in clitic placement in Greek in general, which is the different ways the PF-component chooses to process the syntactic output of clitic movement.

Notes

1   We follow Embick (2007: 307) in defining M-Word as a potential complex head not dominated by further head projection. Notice that incorporation of the clitic in v^* brings the clitic inside the M-Word of the verb.

2   For more information see Dawkins (1916), Mackridge (1993, 1995), Janse (1993, 1994, 1998, 2008), Condoravdi and Kiparsky (2001, 2004), Terzi (1999a,b), Pappas (2001, 2004a,b, 2005, 2006, 2011), Agouraki (2001), Minas (2002), Revithiadou (2006, 2008), Chatzikyriakidis (2010, 2012), Soltic (2012, 2013a,b,c).

3   See Pappas and Joseph (2001), Joseph and Pappas (2002), Markopoulos (2009) on the evolution of the particle *θa* from the various constructions with the verb *θélo* 'I want'.

Abbreviations

2P	second position
ACC	accusative
AUG	augment
AUX	auxiliary
BMG	Byzantine and Medieval Greek
C/COMP	Complementizer
CL	clitic
D	Determiner
DO	direct object
EM	epistemic modality
F	feminine
fnc	function word
FOC	focus
FUT	future
GEN	genitive
GER	gerund
IMP	imperative
IMPFV	imperfective
INF	infinitive
IO	indirect object
IPh	Intonational Phrase
M	masculine
M-Word	Morphological Word
MG	Modern Greek
N	neuter
NEG	negation
NOM	nominative
PFV	perfective
PL	plural
PST	past
PPh	Phonological Phrase
PW	Phonological Word
SG	singular
SMG	Standard Modern Greek
PRTC	participle
T	Tense

Sources

Cappadocian

Abbreviated as D: Dawkins, R. M. (1916), *Modern Greek in Asia Minor: A Study of the Dialects of Silly, Cappadocia and Pharasa with Grammar, Texts, Translations and Glossary*, Cambridge, UK: Cambridge University Press.

Cypriot

Aceras Anthropophorum: Blog in Cypriot Greek (http://acerasanthropophorum.blogspot.gr/)

Medieval Greek

1. Digenis Akritis E. An 11th century epic from the Escorial manuscript
   Jeffreys, E. (1998), *Digenis Akritis. The Grottaferatta and Escorial Versions*, Cambridge, UK: Cambridge University Press.

2. Chroniko tu Moreos. A 14th century text
   Kalonaros, P. (1940), *Το Χρονικόν του Μορέως [The Chronicle of Moreas]*, Athens, Dimitrakou.

3. Ptochoprodromika. A collection of poems from the 12th century
   Hesseling, D. C. and H. Pernot (1910), *Poèmes Prodromiques en Grec Vulgaire*, Amsterdam: Müller.

4. Velisarios ρ. A 15th century text (the ρ version)
   Bakker, W. F. and A. F. van Gemert (1988), *Η Ιστορία του Βελισαρίου [The Story of Velisarios]*, Athens: National Bank of Greece Cultural Foundation.

References

Agouraki, Y. (2001), 'The Position of Clitics in Cypriot Greek', in A. Ralli, B. Joseph and M. Janse (eds), *Proceedings of the First International Conference on Modern Greek Dialects and Linguistic Theory (Patras, Greece, 12–14 October 2000)*, 1–18, Patras, Greece: University of Patras.

Baltazani, M. (2002), 'Quantifier Scope and the Role of Intonation in Greek', PhD diss., UCLA, Los Angeles, CA.

Baltazani, M. and S. A. Jun (1999), 'Focus and Topic Intonation in Greek', *Proceedings of the XIVth International Congress of Phonetic Sciences*, 2: 1305–8.

Barbosa, P. (2000), 'Clitics: A Window to the Null-Subject Property', in J. Costa (ed.), *Portuguese Syntax: New Comparative Studies*, 31–93, Oxford: Oxford University Press.

Bošković, Ž. (1995), 'Particle Movement and Second Position Cliticization in Serbo-Croatian', *Lingua*, 96: 245–66.

Bošković, Ž. (2000), 'Second Position Cliticization: Syntax and/or Phonology?', in F. Beukema and M. den Dikken (eds), *Clitic Phenomena in European Languages*, 71–119, Amsterdam: Benjamins.

Bošković, Ž. (2001), *On the Nature of the Syntax-Phonology Interface: Cliticization and Related Phenomena*, Amsterdam: Elsevier.

Bye, P. and P. de Lacy (2000), 'Edge Asymmetries in Phonology and Morphology', in M. Hirotani, A. Coetzee, N. Hall and J. Y. Kim (eds), *Proceedings of NELS 30*, vol. 1, 121–35, Amherst, MA: GLSA.

Cardinaletti, A. (1999), 'Pronouns in Germanic and Romance Languages: An Overview', in H. van Riemsdijk (ed.), *Clitics in the Languages of Europe*, 33–82, Berlin: Mouton de Gruyter.

Cardinaletti, A. and M. Starke (1999), 'The Typology of Structural Deficiency: A Case Study of the Three Classes of Pronouns', in H. van Riemsdijk (ed.), *Clitics in the Languages of Europe*, 145–233, Berlin: Mouton de Gruyter.

Ćavar, D. and C. Wilder (1994), 'Long Head Movement? Verb-Movement and Cliticization in Croatian', *Lingua*, 93: 1–58.

Chatzikyriakidis, S. (2010), 'Clitics in Four Dialects of Modern Greek: A Dynamic Account', PhD diss., King's College, University of London, London, UK.

Chatzikyriakidis, S. (2012), 'A Dynamic Account of the Cypriot Greek Clitic Positioning System', *Lingua*, 122: 642–72.

Condoravdi, C. and P. Kiparsky (2001), 'Clitics and Clause Structure', *Journal of Greek Linguistics*, 2: 1–40.

Condoravdi, C. and P. Kiparsky (2004), 'Clitics and Clause Structure: The Late Medieval System', *Journal of Greek Linguistics*, 5: 159–83.

Dawkins, R. M. (1916), *Modern Greek in Asia Minor: A Study of the Dialects of Silly, Cappadocia and Pharasa with Grammar, Texts, Translations and Glossary*, Cambridge, UK: Cambridge University Press.

Dimitrova-Vulchanova, M. (1999), 'Clitics in the Slavic Languages', in H. van Riemsdijk (ed.), *Clitics in the Languages of Europe*, 83–142, Berlin: Mouton de Gruyter.

Duarte, I. and G. Matos (2000), 'Romance Clitics and the Minimalist Program', in J. Costa (ed.), *Portuguese Syntax: New Comparative Studies*, 116–42, Oxford: Oxford University Press.

Embick, D. (2007), 'Linearization and Local Dislocation: Derivational Mechanics and Interactions', *Linguistic Analysis*, 33: 303–36.

Embick, D. and R. Noyer (2001), 'Movement Operations after Syntax', *Linguistic Inquiry*, 32: 555–95.

Emonds, J. (1975), 'A Transformational Analysis of French Clitics without Positive Output Constraints', *Linguistic Analysis*, 1: 1–32.

Franks, S. (2000), 'Clitics at the Interface: An Introduction to Clitic Phenomena in European Languages', in F. Beukema and M. den Dikken (eds), *Clitic Phenomena in European Languages*, 1–46, Amsterdam: Benjamins.

Franks, S. and T. H. King (2000), *A Handbook of Slavic Clitics*, Oxford: Oxford University Press.

Frota, S. and M. Vigario (1996), 'On Weight Effects in European Portuguese', Paper presented at the 19th GLOW Workshop *Weight Effects* (10 April 1996, Athens).

Galves, Ch. (2000), 'Agreement, Predication and Pronouns in the History of Portuguese', in J. Costa (ed.), *Portuguese Syntax: New Comparative Studies*, 143–68, Oxford: Oxford University Press.

Goldstein, D. (2015), *Classical Greek Syntax: Wackernagel's Law in Herodotus*, Leiden: Brill.

Horrocks, G. (2010), *Greek: A History of the Language and its Speakers*, 2nd edn, Oxford: Wiley-Blackwell.

Janse, M. (1993), 'La position des pronoms personnels enclitiques en grec néo-testamentaire à la lumière des dialectes néo-helléniques', in C. Brixhe (ed.), *La koiné Grecque Antique*, vol. I, 83–121, Nancy: Presses Universitaires de Nancy.

Janse, M. (1994), 'Son of Wackernagel. The Distribution of Object Clitic Pronouns in Cappadocian', in I. Philippaki-Warburton, K. Nicolaidis and M. Sifianou (eds), *Themes in Greek Linguistics*, 435–42, Amsterdam: Benjamins.

Janse, M. (1998), 'Cappadocian Clitics and the Syntax-Morphology Interface', in B. Joseph, G. Horrocks and I. Philippaki-Warburton (eds), *Themes in Greek Linguistics II*, 257–81, Amsterdam: Benjamins.

Janse, M. (2008), 'Clitic Doubling from Ancient to Asia Minor Greek', in D. Kallulli and L. Tasmowski (eds), *Clitic Doubling in the Balkan Languages*, 165–202, Amsterdam: Benjamins.

Joseph, B. and P. Pappas (2002), 'On Some Recent Views Concerning the Development of the Greek Future System', *Byzantine and Modern Greek Studies*, 26: 247–73.

Kayne, R. (1975), *French Syntax*, Cambridge, MA: MIT Press.

Kayne, R. (1989), 'Null-Subjects and Clitic Climbing', in O. Jaeggli and K. Safir (eds), *The Null Subject Parameter*, 239–61, Dordrecht, The Netherlands: Kluwer.

Mackridge, P. (1993), 'An Editorial Problem in Medieval Greek Texts. The Position of the Object Clitic Pronoun in the Escorial Digenes Akrites', in N. Panayotakis (ed.), *Origini della Literatura Neogreca I*, 325–42, Venezia: Instituto Ellenico di Studi Bizantini e Postbizantini di Venezia.

Mackridge, P. (1995), 'On the Placement of the Weak Personal Pronoun in Medieval Greek Vernacular', *Studies in Greek Linguistics*, 15: 906–29.

Marantz, A. (1988), 'Clitics, Morphological Merger, and the Mapping to Phonological Structure', in M. Hammond and M. Noonan (eds), *Theoretical Morphology: Approaches in Modern Linguistics*, 253–70, San Diego, CA: Academic Press.

Markopoulos, Th. (2009), *The Future in Greek: From Ancient to Medieval*, Oxford: Oxford University Press.

Martins, A. (1994), *Focco e Cliticosno Português Europeu*, PhD diss., University of Lisbon.

Mavrogiorgos, M. (2010), *Clitics in Greek: A Minimalist Account of Proclisis and Enclisis*, Amsterdam: Benjamins.

McCarthy, J. J. and A. Prince (1993), 'Generalized Alignment', in G. Booij and J. van Marle (eds), *Yearbook of Morphology 1993*, 79–153, Dordrecht, The Netherlands: Kluwer.

Minas, K. (2002), *Τα Γλωσσικά Ιδιώματα της Καρπάθου (The Varieties of Karpathos)* [in Greek], Rhodes, Greece: Prefecture of Dodecanese.

Neokleous, Th. (2015), 'The L1 Acquisition of Clitic Placement in Cypriot Greek', *Lingua*, 161: 27–47.

Pappas, P. (2001), *Weak Object Pronoun Placement in Later Medieval and Early Modern Greek*, PhD diss., The Ohio State University, Columbus, OH.

Pappas, P. (2004a), 'Medieval Greek Weak Object Pronouns and Analogical Change: A Response to Condoravdi and Kiparsky (2001)', *Journal of Greek Linguistics*, 5: 127–58.

Pappas, P. (2004b), *Variation and Morphosyntactic Change in Greek: From Clitics to Affixes*, New York: Palgrave McMillan.

Pappas, P. (2005), 'Pronominal Clitics in Greek', MS, Simon Fraser University, British Columbia, Canada.

Pappas, P. (2006), 'Object Clitic Placement in the Dialects of Medieval Greek', in M. Janse, B. Joseph and A. Ralli (eds), *Proceedings of the Second International Conference of Modern Greek Dialects and Linguistic Theory (Mytilene Greece, September 30–October 3 2004)*, 314–28, Patras, Greece: University of Patras.

Pappas, P. (2011), 'An Empirical Perspective on Cypriot Clitics', *Νεοελληνική Διαλεκτολογία (Modern Greek Dialectology)*, 6: 391–413.

Pappas, P. and B. Joseph (2001), 'The Development of the Greek Future System: Setting the Record Straight', in Greek *Linguistics 1999: Proceedings of the 4th International Conference on Greek Linguistics, Nicosia, September 1999*, 354–9. Thessaloniki, Greece: University Studio Press.

Philippaki-Warburton, I. (1994), 'Verb Movement and the Distribution of Clitic Pronouns', in I. Philippaki-Warburton, K. Nikolaidis and M. Sifianou (eds), *Themes in Greek Linguistics*, 53–60, Amsterdam: Benjamins.

Philippaki-Warburton, I. (1998), 'Functional Categories and Modern Greek Syntax', *The Linguistic Review*, 15: 158–86.

Philippaki-Warburton, I. and V. Spyropoulos (1999), 'On the Boundaries of Inflection and Syntax: Greek Pronominal Clitics and Particles', in G. Booij and J. van Marle (eds), *The Yearbook of Morphology 1998*, 45–72, Dordrecht, The Netherlands: Kluwer.

Philippaki-Warburton, I. and V. Spyropoulos (2004), 'A Change of Mood: The Development of the Greek Mood System', *Linguistics*, 42: 523–49.

Philippaki-Warburton, I., S. Varlokosta, M. Georgiafentis and G. Kotzoglou (2004), 'Moving from Theta-Positions: Pronominal Clitic Doubling in Greek', *Lingua*, 114: 963–89.

Progovac, Lj. (1996), 'Clitics in Serbian/Croatian: Comp as the Second Position', in A. Halpern and A. Zwicky (eds), *Approaching Second: Second Position Clitics and Related Phenomena*, 411–28, Stanford, CA: CSLI Publications.

Quicoli, C. (1976), 'Conditions on Clitic Movement in Portuguese', *Linguistic Analysis*, 2: 199–223.

Raposo, E. (2000), 'Clitic Positions and Verb Movement', in J. Costa (ed.), *Portuguese Syntax: New Comparative Studies*, 266–97, Oxford: Oxford University Press.

Raposo, E. and J. Uriagereka (2005), 'Clitic Placement in Western Iberian: A Minimalist View', in G. Cinque and R. Kayne (eds), *The Oxford Handbook of Comparative Syntax*, 639–97, Oxford: Oxford University Press.

Revithiadou, A. (2006), 'Prosodic Filters on Syntax: An Interface Account of Second Position Clitics', *Lingua*, 116: 79–111.

Revithiadou, A. (2008), 'A Cross-dialectal Study of Cliticization in Greek', *Lingua*, 118: 1393–415.

Revithiadou, A. (2014), 'Clitic Group', in G. Giannakis (ed.), *The Encyclopedia of Ancient Greek Language and Linguistics*, 296–300, Leiden: Brill.

Revithiadou, A. and V. Spyropoulos (2006), 'A Typology of Greek Clitics with Special Reference to their Diachronic Development', MS, University of the Aegean, Rhodes, Greece. lingBuzz/000496

Revithiadou, A. and V. Spyropoulos (2008), 'Greek Object Clitic Pronouns: A Typological Survey of their Grammatical Properties', *STUF – Language Typology and Universals*, 61: 39–53.

Rivero, M. L. (1994), 'Clause Structure and V-movement in the Languages of the Balkans', *Natural Language and Linguistic Theory*, 12: 63–120.

Rivero, M. L. (1997), 'On Two Positions for Complement Clitic Pronouns: Serbo-Croatian, Bulgarian and Old Spanish', in A. van Kemenade and N. Vincent (eds), *Parameters of Morphosyntactic Change*, 170–206, Cambridge, UK: Cambridge University Press.

Roberts, I. (2010), *Agreement and Head Movement: Clitics, Incorporation and Defective Goals*, Cambridge, MA: MIT Press.

Roberts, I. and A. Roussou (2003), *Syntactic Change: Grammaticalization in the Minimalist Program*, Cambridge, UK: Cambridge University Press.

Roussou, A. (2000), 'On the Left Periphery: Modal Particles and Complementizers', *Journal of Greek Linguistics*, 1: 65–94.

Soltic, J. (2012), 'Distribution of the Object Clitic Pronouns in the Grottaferrata Manuscript of the Digenis Akritis', *Byzantine and Modern Greek Studies*, 36: 178–97.

Soltic, J. (2013a), 'The Πολιτικός Στίχος Poetry as Reliable Evidence for Certain Linguistic Phenomena. Case-study: The position of Object Clitic Pronouns in the Chronicle of Morea', *Byzantinische Zeitschrift*, 106: 811–42.

Soltic, J. (2013b), 'A Defence of the Focus Hypothesis Concerning Late Medieval Greek Object Clitic Pronouns: A Case Study of Light Verbs in the Chronicle of Morea', *Journal of Historical Pragmatics*, 14: 185–209.

Soltic, J. (2013c), 'Clitic Doubling in Vernacular Medieval Greek', *Transactions of the Philological Society*, 111: 379–405.

Spyropoulos, V. and A. Revithiadou (2009), 'The Morphology of PAST in Greek', *Studies in Greek Linguistics*, 29: 108–22.

Terzi, A. (1999a), 'Cypriot Greek Clitics and their Positioning Restrictions', in A. Alexiadou, G. Horrocks and M. Stavrou (eds), *Studies in Greek Syntax*, 227–40, Dordrecht, The Netherlands: Kluwer.

Terzi, A. (1999b), 'Clitic Combinations, their Hosts and their Ordering', *Natural Language and Linguistic Theory*, 17: 85–121.

Tsimpli, I.-M. (2000), 'Gerunds in Greek', *Journal of Greek Linguistics*, 1: 131–69.

Uriagereka, J. (1995), 'Aspects of the Syntax of Clitic Placement in Western Romance', *Linguistic Inquiry*, 26: 79–124.

Zagona, K. (2001), *The Syntax of Spanish*, Cambridge, UK: Cambridge University Press.

14

Towards a formal model of transfer under contact: Contrasting Asia Minor Greek to mainland Greek and Turkish in search of syntactic borrowings

Dimitris Michelioudakis and Ioanna Sitaridou

We contrast Asia Minor Greek to older and contemporary mainland Greek and the dominant language of the area, Turkish, in relation to constructions which appear to be vulnerable in contact situations. We treat all relevant diachronic and cross-dialectal differences as the result of parametric changes and discuss their implications for a constrained theory of syntactic transfer under contact.

1 Introduction

In this chapter, we investigate suspected contact phenomena in Asia Minor Greek (AMG), a dialectal group which has been subjected to intense contact with Turkish (and also other languages of the Black Sea, such as Laz and Armenian). The three AMG varieties considered here are Romeyka, Cappadocian and Pharasiot. The Romeyka data come from speakers still living in Çaykara, near Trabzon (see Sitaridou 2013, 2014a, b, 2016, see also: www.romeyka.org), while the Cappadocian and Pharasiot data come from speakers currently living in Northern Greece as reported in Bağriacik (2017). These varieties are nearly unique within the Greek-speaking world in exhibiting extensive (at least surface) head-finality, both in the clausal and the nominal domain. Related to this is the pervasive fronting of XPs as the only available strategy for various discourse-related purposes (see Sitaridou and Kaltsa 2014). These same discourse requirements can be fulfilled either via focus-movement or *in situ* in all other Greek varieties, including Standard Modern Greek (SMG).

For the purposes of this chapter, we focus on (i) multiple fronting of *wh*-phrases in multiple questions, establishing that multiple movement of *wh*-phrases also exists in Turkish, while it is not to be found in non-Asia Minor contemporary varieties of Greek (e.g. Italiot Greek), and on (ii) aspects of noun-finality in AMG, namely the ban on postnominal adjectives, the unmarked prenominal genitive and the emergence of prenominal relatives, that is, properties which are all apparently shared with Turkish and are not to be found anywhere else in present-day Greek.

We suggest that the two competing approaches to syntactic change in contact situations, that is, explanations based on transfer and accounts based on language-internal dynamics, can and should be reconciled. Syntactic changes that look like borrowings could not have happened if the target language did not already have certain properties at some level of its grammar. At the same time, of all varieties that meet the relevant preconditions, only varieties exposed to contact will end up developing what looks like a borrowed pattern. We build on the assumption that, in order for a parameter to change its value under contact with a language L, some core manifestations of the borrowed value (or, more generally, a value due to the influence of L) must already be allowed by the grammar prior to contact with L (see Guardiano et al.'s 2016 'Resistance Principle', as well as Sitaridou 2014a: 52; Neocleous and Sitaridou 2018; Donabedian and Sitaridou, forthcoming). In this study, by means of a contrastive analysis, we concretize this claim by putting forward some precise hypotheses as to how we can determine which subsets/classes of manifestations are of this type, that is, manifestations which do not suffice to trigger the new value by themselves but are necessary for contact (i.e. exposure to patterns that do constitute sufficient cues) to trigger such a parametric change.

2 A contrastive analysis of multiple *wh*-questions

Multiple *wh*-questions in most varieties of Modern Greek involve fronting to the left periphery of just one *wh*-phrase (1). Typically, it is the thematically higher *wh*-phrase that gets attracted, obeying Superiority (see also Sinopoulou 2008). Any other *wh*-phrase(s) may only appear lower (2). Superiority is suspended in cases of D-linking (3), as observed by Anagnostopoulou (2003).

(1) a. Pços   efere   ti?   (SMG)
       who.NOM brought.3SG what.ACC
       'Who brought what?'

   b. *Pços   ti   efere?
       who.NOM what.ACC brought.3SG

(2) Context: A murder happened last night.
    *pçon   skotose   pços?
    who.ACC killed.3SG who.NOM
    'Who killed whom?'

(3) Context: Mary, Jane and Bill were asked to cook one dish each for a dinner party. So, we ended up having lasagne, moussaka and Beijing duck. Everything was great, but I am wondering:
    a. pços   majirepse ti?
       who.NOM cooked. 3SG what.ACC

    b. ti   majirepse pços?
       what.ACC cooked.3SG who.NOM

However, in the Asia Minor Greek group, all *wh*-phrases are obligatorily fronted (see Michelioudakis and Sitaridou 2012, 2016 for a detailed account of multiple *wh*-fronting (MWF) in two Pontic Greek varieties, namely Romeyka of the Black Sea and Pontic of Northern Greece, as well as Bağriacik (2017) for a presentation of the same patterns in Cappadocian and Pharasiot Greek). *Wh*-phrases may only appear in the left periphery, even when echoic, next to one another; that is, they can neither be coordinated nor separated by anything, for example, a verb form or any non-*wh* elements (4). Fronting is strictly order-preserving, except when at least one *wh*-phrase is D-linked (5)–(6). The latter is reminiscent of the Standard Modern Greek (in fact, non-Asia Minor Greek) pattern illustrated in (2)–(3): *wh*-fronting obeys Superiority, with the exception of D-linked phrases, which may in fact be targeting a different (type of) position.

(4) Tinan   (doɣna) eŋdže   (*doɣna)?   (Romeyka)
     who.ACC.HUM what.ACC brought.2SG what.ACC

(5) Context: I heard a rumour about some boy kissing some girl.
    a. Pios   tinan   efilise?
       who.NOM who.ACC.HUM kissed.3SG
       'Who kissed whom?'

    b. *Tinan pios efilise?

(6) Context: Each girl brought a different book.
    Eɣo tši ksero   pion   kitapin pion patši   eŋdže.
    I.NOM NEG know.1SG what.ACC book.ACC which girl.NOM brought.3SG
    'I don't know which girl brought which book.'
                          (Michelioudakis and Sitaridou 2016: 12)

As we will see later on, constructions with contiguous/adjacent *wh*-phrases in left-peripheral positions may not sound familiar in most contemporary Greek varieties; they were, however, possible in earlier stages of Greek, for example, in Classical and Hellenistic Greek. Moreover, strings of this type are also possible in Turkish. Therefore, we are faced with a situation such as the one sketched in Section 1: AMG varieties exposed to contact exhibit strings which are possible in the dominant language of the area, namely Turkish, and which are, crucially, absent in other related Greek varieties, yet, at the same time, there is no diachronically stable property of the language that categorically excludes such strings in the absence of contact, given earlier attestations of what looks like the same phenomenon. As argued by Sitaridou (2016), most cases of change in AMG and Romeyka, in particular, fall into this category: it is hard to distinguish whether we are dealing with an inherited feature or back-mutation (see for instance, the same problem with the development of null objects in Romeyka in Sitaridou 2016: 4). It is therefore of paramount importance to look into all these constructions in as much detail as needed in order to establish whether the underlying syntax of the superficially similar patterns in question is indeed the same and whether one can indeed treat the AMG pattern as a curious case of continuity from Hellenistic Greek, despite the fact that there are no attestations of the ancient pattern in medieval texts,[1] or whether all of it has to be traced to more recent influences, namely exposure to strings with contiguous *wh*-phrases in Turkish. Crucially, these (non)homoplastic puzzles cannot be solved unless such detailed contrastive analysis takes place (for more on this approach, see Sitaridou 2016; Donabedian and Sitaridou, forthcoming).

Michelioudakis and Sitaridou (2016) analyse the SMG-AMG pair as a previously unknown but possible type in the typology of *wh*-movement proposed by Bošković (2002). Bošković distinguishes different types on the basis of the availability of Attract-1 heads in CP, that is, A'-heads that only attract the highest *wh*-phrase. Each type (i. no Attract-1 C_{Wh}, ii. all C_{Wh} heads are Attract-1, iii. C_{Wh} is Attract-1 only in certain configurations) can have either an MWF or a non-MWF version. In non-MWF languages in this typology, *wh*-phrases not attracted by an Attract-1 head, that is, any *wh*-phrases below the highest stay low. When there is no Attact-1 head, *wh*-phrases stay *in situ*. This derives three possible non-MWF types, i. languages with *wh*-fronting obeying Superiority always, ii. languages with *wh*-fronting in some contexts and *wh*-in-situ in others, iii. languages with *wh*-in situ always. By contrast, in MWF languages, in multiple questions, *wh*-phrases not attracted by C_{Wh}, that is, *wh*-phrases first-merged below the highest one, are attracted by Attract-all Focus heads. Such heads can host *wh*-phrases in multiple specifiers in any order. Parameterizing this with respect to the availability of Attract-1 C_{Wh}, we get three types again: i. languages with MWF obeying Superiority always, ii. languages with MWF obeying Superiority sometimes, iii. MWF languages not subject to Superiority at all. Michelioudakis and Sitaridou suggest that this typology be expanded by allowing for Attract-1 heads other than $C_{[+wh]}$, namely Focus and Topic heads.

Both AMG and SMG have an Attract-1 Focus head in the CP-periphery. The motivation for postulating a Focus head rather than $C_{[+wh]}$ comes from the fact that in both languages multiple *wh*-questions also allow for single-pair answers. According to Hagstrom's (1998) semantics of questions, as adopted and adapted by Bošković (2007), single-pair readings are only possible when the two relevant *wh*-phrases are in the scope of a Q morpheme, which is an existential quantifier over choice functions. This morpheme is always merged below C, either at a fixed head position in the CP domain (7)a or directly with the *wh*-phrase (7)b. Movement of a *wh*-phrase to Spec-C across Q gives rise to a Relativized Minimality violation (7)c.

(7) a. C_{+wh} Q   Wh1   Wh2
    b. Wh1 C_{+wh} t_{Wh1} [Wh2+Q]
    c. *Wh1   C   Q t_{Wh1} Wh2

When Q forms a constituent with the *wh*-word, only that one *wh*-phrase is in its scope and only pair list readings are available. Therefore, in AMG and SMG multiple questions with single-pair readings, both *wh*-phrases have to be lower than C, that is, in the scope of Q. We conclude that they can be at most as high as CP-peripheral Focus, which can be assumed to be below Q. At the same time, even in the presence of single-pair interpretations, Superiority is strictly obeyed. Therefore, the (Focus) head attracting the highest *wh*-phrase has to be an Attract-1 head (8). The difference between SMG and AMG is the same as the difference between any other pair of languages that fall under the same type: AMG also has an (additional) Focus head in its CP-periphery which can host foci and *wh*-phrases, while SMG does not have such a head.

(8) $[_{CP} \ C_{[+wh]} \ [_{FocusP} \ Foc^0_{Attract-1} \ [_{FocusP} \ Foc^0 \ ...$ (AMG)

Michelioudakis and Sitaridou (2016) identify this head as New Information Focus⁰. Indeed, AMG systematically features preverbal new information foci, while in SMG such foci can only appear postverbally (but see Gryllia 2009). Nevertheless, as Sinopoulou (2008) shows, in SMG too, non-fronted *wh*-phrases are in fact not *in situ* and occupy a low peripheral position, preceding all vP-internal material. This position is also available to low, narrow information foci.

(9) a. Pote ayorase   (?*o Janis)   ti   (o Janis)? (SMG)
       when bought.3SG the Janis.NOM what.ACC the Janis.NOM
       'When did Janis buy what?'

    b. Ayorase   to vivlio   o Janis.
       bought.3SG the book.ACC the Janis.NOM
       'John bought the book.' (as an answer to the question: 'What did John buy?')

In other words, there is a New Information Focus⁰ for informationally focused XPs and *wh*-phrases alike, in the low/vP-periphery in SMG. Therefore, the difference between SMG and AMG is, in fact, microparametric: both grammars have a dedicated projection for this type of foci, but they differ with respect to whether it is activated in the low (10) or the left periphery of the clause (11). Furthermore, the availability of such an additional focus projection may also be the reason why the higher Focus projection does not have to be Attract-all, unlike for example, in the Slavic languages.

(10) $[_{CP} \ C_{[+wh]} \ [_{FocusP} \ Foc^0_{Attract-1} \ [_{TP} \ T \ [_{FocusP} \ Foc_{New \ Info}^0 \ [_{vP} \ ...$ (SMG)

(11) $[_{CP} \ C_{[+wh]} \ [_{FocusP} \ Foc^0_{Attract-1} \ [_{FocusP} \ Foc_{New \ Info}^0 \ [_{TP} \ T \ ...$ (AMG)

Assuming that focus-driven MWF in AMG is the result of some sort of transmission, either historical or horizontal/geographic, rather than a spontaneous development, a natural question is whether the key pattern stems from the availability of linearly similar constructions in the source language (Hellenistic Greek) or the contact language (Turkish) or some deeper formal property. Given the analysis of MWF above, we take the most irreducible relevant property to be the possibility of having two or more *wh*-phrases targeting CP-peripheral positions, higher than any A-position. The mere existence of 'wh1 wh2 V' strings is thus not a sufficient cue in this sense. Such strings can in principle be generated even without both (or in fact any of the) *wh*-phrases being in the CP-periphery. For instance, in a strictly V-final language (such as Turkish), all *wh*-phrases would have to precede the verb, whether or not any *wh*-

phrases actually reach the left periphery. In other words, the syntax of multiple *wh*-questions looks like MWF but it is epiphenomenal to the OV property of the language. Similarly, a predominantly VO language with object shift or object fronting below the canonical subject position, such as Hellenistic Greek (see Kirk 2012), would also be compatible with non-peripheral *wh*-phrases preceding the verb, but not necessarily constitute MWF in the left periphery.

We can then safely establish that more than one peripheral position is available for *wh*-phrases if there are cases in which the lowest (preverbal) *wh*-phrase is not adjacent to V and at least one (non-topicalized) XP can intervene. However, note that (i) SOV in Hellenistic Greek does not involve unmarked objects/non-subject XPs in preverbal position (see Kirk 2012), (ii) the co-occurrence of 2 *wh*-phrases and another focalized XP in the same (left) periphery is unlikely, and (iii) both direct and indirect questions favour verb-subject inversion and, as a result, the subject cannot appear between a *wh*-phrase and V either. Given these facts, it is no surprise that no 'wh1 wh2 XP V' are attested in Hellenistic Greek, even though the New Testament does feature some (admittedly few) 'wh1 wh2 V' orders (12). Therefore, on the basis of this diagnostic, we cannot really exclude the possibility that Hellenistic Greek had multiple (residual or restricted) *wh*-fronting into the left periphery.

(12) Ballontes kle:ron ep'   auta tis   ti are:i   (Mark 15.24)
      casting   lots on them who what takes.SUBJ
      '... casting lots on them to decide who should take what'

Nevertheless, multiple *wh*-phrases preceding the verb were significantly more common in Classical Greek (Dag Haug, p.c.), where OV was also more productive and unmarked (see Taylor 1994). Therefore, in the earlier stages of Greek (apparent or real) MWF does correlate with OV (unmarked/productive or residual). In AMG, on the other hand, in which OV is more marked than in Classical Greek and VO is the unmarked order (see Sitaridou and Kaltsa 2014), MWF is fully productive. Also, crucially, contemporary AMG does not force subject-verb inversion in questions, so the abovementioned diagnostic is applicable and, indeed, 'wh1 wh2 Subject V' orders are possible (13). This clearly indicates that all *wh*-phrases are in the CP-periphery.

(13) Tinan   (*esi)   *doxna*   (esi)   endžes? (Romeyka)
      who.ACC.HUM you.NOM what.ACC you.NOM brought.2SG
      'What did you bring to whom?'

Let us now turn our attention to Turkish. It is commonly analysed as a wh-*in situ* language (Özsoy 2009) with optional scrambling of *wh*-phrases. Note that, being strictly V-final, Turkish linearizes *wh*-in situ as 'wh1 wh2 V' (14). Therefore, multiple *wh*-phrases preceding the verb could be just a deceptive case of MWF; in fact, it can just be an artefact of OV, coupled with free PF (Phonetic Form) scrambling.

(14) Tamer   ne-yi   nere-ye   koy-du?   (Turkish)
      Tamer.NOM what-ACC where-DAT put-PAST.3SG
      'What did Tamer put where?'

However, Özsoy (2009) shows convincingly that movement of *wh*-phrases higher than the canonical subject position is not just PF scrambling. Firstly, local movement of an object *wh*-phrase above the subject can repair a Weak Crossover effect (15) and, secondly, long-distance multiple movement of *wh*-phrases from within different clauses strictly obeys Superiority (16).

(15) a. *[$_{\text{TP}}$ pro$_i$ Anne-si$_i$ [$_{\text{VP}}$ kim$_i$-i   ara-dı]]?
              mother-3POSS who-ACC call-PAST

  b. [$_{\text{TP}}$ Kim-i$_i$ [$_{\text{IP}}$ pro$_i$ anne-si$_i$ [ara-dı]]]?
        who-ACC   mother-3POSS call-PAST
        'Who$_i$ did his$_i$ mother call?'

(16) a. [Kim-e$_i$ Aylin t_i [Zeynep-in kim-i   gör-düğ-ü-nü]   sor-du]?
        who-DAT Aylin-NOM Zeynep-GEN who-ACC see-NOM-3POSS-ACC ask-PAST
        'Who did Aylin ask whom Zeynep saw?'

  b. *[Kim-i$_i$ Aylin   kim-e   [Zeynep-in t_i gör-düğ-ü]-nü   sor-du?
        Who-ACC Aylin-NOM who-DAT Zeynep-GEN see-NOM-3POSS-ACC ask-PAST

Therefore, fronting of *wh*-phrases higher than their first-merged positions takes place in narrow syntax and, at least sometimes, fronted *wh*-phrases in multiple questions can all target left-peripheral positions and in fact an Attract-1 position, given the presence of Superiority in some contexts. In other words, the minimal ingredient we identified above as an irreducible requirement for the development of MWF is also present in Turkish.

To sum up, the main syntactic ingredients of MWF in AMG are as follows: (a) *wh*-fronting as focus-movement, (b) attraction of the highest *wh*-phrase by an Attract-1 head, hence Superiority, (c) obligatory attraction of any *wh*-phrase(s) below the highest one by a Focus head, (d) activation of all relevant Focus heads in the CP-periphery. Of these ingredients, (a) and (b) are clearly present in SMG and, as Sinopoulou (2008, 2011), (c) is also true of SMG multiple *wh*-questions, as no *wh*-phrases really stay *in situ*. As for (d), it can be broken down into two sub-features: (d1) the head attracting *wh*-phrases below the highest is a New Information Focus head; (d2) New Information Focus is in the CP-periphery. Following Sinopoulou, again, (d1) is also the case in SMG, as low new information foci and low *wh*-phrases have the same distribution.

Therefore, the only shift that happened in AMG was from a system with a Focus head in the vP-periphery for *wh*-phrases to a system with such a projection in the CP-periphery only (d2). Turkish then urged AMG to associate *wh*-phrases in multiple questions beyond the highest with a Focus head in the left periphery, which would make the shift in question a case of back-mutation. Recall that in Turkish this type of fronting is only optional, the other option being to leave *wh*-phrases *in situ*. However, given (c) above, a Greek grammar that undergoes this shift has to make this fronting obligatory. Also, given the SMG state of affairs, it was natural for AMG too to associate low *wh*-phrases with New Information Focus[0]. In SMG and Cypriot Greek, among others, new information foci are predominantly postverbal (while Gryllia (2008:

Table 14.1 The Syntactic Ingredients of Multiple *Wh*-Questions in SMG, Turkish and AMG

	SMG	Turkish	AMG
Focus-fronting of wh-	+	+	+
Attract-1 for the highest wh-	+	+	+
Focus-movement of low wh-phrases	+	+	+
Wh- can stay in situ	-	+	-
Focus heads (for wh) are only left-peripheral	-	+	+

11–12) also discusses contexts in which they can be preverbal too; on focus in SMG, see also Georgiafentis 2004). Table 14.1 above summarizes the relevant properties.

All in all, the (micro-)parameter regulating the height at which the focus projection for *wh*-phrases is activated has indeed been reset due to Turkish influence. Nonetheless, which type of projection is to be used for *wh*-phrases was probably predetermined, as the link between new information focus and low *wh*-phrases is common to all contemporary Greek varieties. Contact must then have played a role in activating New Information Focus[0] exclusively in the left periphery. Yet again, Greek grammars in general are compatible with various types of Focus in the left periphery. This is a key point which the rest of this chapter will also highlight: a new parameter setting due to contact is often such that the new grammar generates (as the unmarked option now) strings which were previously generated as a marked option (in our case: left-peripheral new information foci; for the same claim regarding final-auxiliaries in AMG, see Neocleous and Sitaridou 2018). At the same time, what looks like a totally novel and previously unattested pattern (MWF in our case), only to be found in the contact language, does not signal a parameter change *per se*. Instead, it is a necessary manifestation of a previously existing parameter setting (namely 'Low *wh* = New Information Focus') which now interacts with a parameter (in our case: the position of New Information Focus) whose value changed through contact.

3 N-finality in Asia Minor

Head-finality in the AMG DP mainly concerns (a) the position of genitive adnominal arguments, (b) adjective placement and (c) the position of relative clauses. In contemporary AMG, adjectives are exclusively prenominal, genitives are also prenominal with some AMG-internal variation as to their surface positions, and relatives are predominantly prenominal with some varieties allowing for extraposed relatives.

With regard to genitives, as Michelioudakis et al. (2016, 2017) show, all AMG varieties have exclusively prenominal genitives. Nonetheless, there appears to be a continuum as to the flexibility of genitive placement within the prenominal field: Cappadocian Greek appears to be the least flexible (see also Bağriacik 2017), as genitives may only occur to the right of any adjectives (17), while Romeyka is the most flexible, with genitives also being able to precede adjectives (18). However, orders with postadjectival genitives are still judged as the most natural and unmarked.

(17) a. du-šímirnu Ø-papajiú   du krúšima   (Cappadocian)
        the-today's the-priest.GEN the hitting

     b. * Ø-papajiú   du-šímirnu du krúšima
        'today's hitting of the priest'

(18) (t=Ali)   t=askemon (t-Ali) to muxteron (Romeyka)
     the=Ali.GEN   the=ugly the=Ali.GEN the animal.NOM
     'Ali's ugly animal'

This seems to correlate perfectly with the extent to which a structurally lower adjective can surface to the left of a structurally higher adjective when emphatic. In Romeyka, emphatic fronting of APs is readily available (19)a, while in Cappadocian it is prohibited (19)b. Therefore, the preadjectival position of genitives is also a discourse-related position in the left periphery of the DP (see also Mathieu and Sitaridou 2005).

(19) a. (to-tranon) t=emon (to-tranon) t=arapa   (Romeyka)
        the-big   the=my   the-big the=car
        'my big car'

     b. (*du-kalon) to-mo (du-kalon) du-peškír   (Cappadocian)
        the-good   the-my the-good the-towel
        'my good towel'

At this point a comment is in order regarding the fact that, in definite DPs, genitive arguments always precede what looks like the definite article. This is due to the fact that AMG has developed definiteness agreement, namely every [+N] constituent has to bear its own agreement morpheme (see Guardiano et al. 2016). Such agreement morphemes bear full *phi*-specification, that is, number, gender and person, which is spelt out by the same morpheme that realizes the definite article (as well as third-person pronominal clitics in SMG). Thus, while in SMG the order [Def X Def N] necessarily signals fronting of X over D, in AMG a definiteness affix before the noun does not necessarily signal a DP boundary. A non-fronted genitive still precedes Def as NPs too have to bear their own agreement morpheme.

Turkish too has exclusively prenominal genitives (20). Also, like both AMG and SMG, it only allows one genitive DP per head noun. Unlike both, though, Turkish exhibits head marking, whereby the head noun is marked with the phi-features of the genitive argument. Also, importantly, genitive DPs in Turkish strictly precede any/all adjectives, as the ungrammaticality of (21) shows.

(20) (Ada-nın) şirin oyuncağ-ı (*Ada-nın)   (Turkish)
     Ada-GEN nice toy-3SG   Ada-GEN
     'Ada's nice toy'

(21) *şirin Ada-nın oyuncağ-ı

Crosslinguistically (see e.g. Longobardi and Silvestri 2013), there seem to be just two functional projections in the extended projection of the nominal for non-iterable genitive arguments (22): one preceding the base position of all direct modification adjectives (which we will conventionally call Gen1^0) and one following the base position of all direct modification adjectives (Gen2^0).

(22) [D... [Gen1^0 [(A*) ... [Gen2^0 [$_{nP}$ ...

Placement of the genitive with respect to the head noun is orthogonal to this distinction. The genitive in either position may end up preceding or following the N depending on whether N and/or projections containing N move higher than either of the two positions. Thus, Turkish and AMG are similar in lacking any N(P)-movement over either of the two positions. However, they differ with respect to which position each language activates for its unique genitive DPs. AMG genitives are hosted in the Spec of Gen2^0, while Turkish genitives are in Spec-Gen1. Note that all other contemporary varieties of Greek also activate just the postadjectival position for genitives, that is, Gen2. The difference is that in mainland and Cypriot Greek, the head noun precedes the genitive (while in Italiot Greek nouns have to precede some adjectives as well). This difference can be formalized in terms of an N(P)-movement parameter over Gen2^0 (cf. Guardiano 2011) with AMG having a negative value and all other contemporary varieties having a positive value (see Michelioudakis et al. 2016, 2017).

With respect to the syntax of adjectives, AMG (23) is like Turkish (24), which lacks any postnominal adjectives, and unlike any other Greek variety (see Guardiano et al. 2016).

(23) (to tranon) (t-askemon) to muxteron (*to tranon) (*t-askemon)   (Romeyka)
      'the big ugly animal'

(24) (şirin)   oyuncak (*şirin)   (Turkish)
      nice   toy   nice
      'a/the nice toy'

Mainland Greek freely allows typically prenominal adjectives to occur postnominally in indefinite DPs (25)a, while in definite DPs postnominal APs have to carry their own definiteness marker (25b), thus giving rise to what is known as 'polydefiniteness' (see Alexiadou 2014 and references therein).

(25) a. ena zoo megalo/omorfo   tis   Afrikis   (SMG)
          an animal big/beautiful   the.GEN Africa.GEN
          'a big/beautiful animal from Africa'

      b. to zoo   to   megalo/to omorfo tis   Afrikis
          the animal the   big/the beautiful   the.GEN Africa.GEN
          'Africa's big/beautiful animal'

Italiot Greek takes a step further and in fact has adjectives of certain classes, which can only occur postnominally; that is, it has developed obligatory NP-movement over certain adjectival projections (26).

(26) Meletisa ton   (*rodino) libbro   (rodino)   (Italiot Greek)
      read.1SG the   red   book   red
      'I read the red book.'

                                                            (Guardiano and Stavrou 2014: 132)

In mainland Greek, the source of postnominal adjectives preceding genitives can be argued to be a small-clause-like structure that takes the NP as the subject of the predication and the postnominal AP as its predicate (see Campos and Stavrou 2011; Stavrou 2012). Like in clausal predication, a copula-like head, which Campos and Stavrou call $Pred^0$, mediates the relation between the two elements and carries all relevant agreement features, namely number, gender and (third) person (27).

(27) $[_{DP}\ D\ [_{RP}\ NP_i\ R\ [_{PredP}\ t_i\ Pred^0_{[+phi]}\ AP]]]$

As already mentioned, a bundle of such features is spelled out as the definite article in definite DPs. In indefinite DPs, since third person is not spelled out in D, $Pred^0$ remains phonologically null. In AMG, having become a prefix, the definiteness morpheme can only be parsed as part of the AP, therefore it can no longer realize $Pred^0$. Thus, this source of postnominal adjectives was lost. At the same time, the Turkish input also lacks postnominal APs altogether, so it was impossible for AMG to keep postnominal adjectives and reanalyse them as occupying projections obligatorily crossed by a moving nominal constituent. A change of this sort indeed took place in Italiot Greek, after a similar procedure that led to the loss of polydefiniteness (Guardiano and Stavrou 2017), under the pressure of heavily N-over-Adj nominal structures in the local Romance varieties.

Finally, the syntax of relative clauses in AMG is quite unique in involving patterns which are not possible in the rest of the Greek diasystem, even as marked orders. For instance, while adjectival and genitival placement in AMG involves orders which are otherwise derivable in at least some of the other Greek varieties, at least as informationally marked orders, pre-DP relatives have never been possible in any diatopic or diachronic variety of Greek outside AMG. More specifically, all three contemporary varieties of AMG allow relative clauses DP-initially. In Cappadocian, relatives are now exclusively DP-initial (28) (see Bağriacik and Danckaert 2016). Contemporary Pharasiot also allows some extraposition of relatives to the right of DPs (29) (ibid.), while Romeyka allows relative extraposition to the right of DPs (30). Notably, older/more conservative speakers of Romeyka still only allow postnominal relatives thus indicating that DP-initial relatives must have been absent prior to any contact with Turkish which has exclusively prenominal/pre-D relatives (31).

(28) [du rántsa šímiru] du peškír   (Cappadocian)
      the saw.1SG today   the towel
      'the towel that I saw today'

(29)　(tu íða　　zapá:na)　　　to peškíri (tu íða　　zapá:na)　　(Pharasiot)
　　　that saw.1SG in the morning the towel that saw.1SG in the morning
　　　'the towel I saw in the morning'

(30)　a.　psomin　　d=endʒen　　　o peðas　　　　　　　(Romeyka)
　　　　　bread.ACC that=brought.3SG the boy.NOM
　　　　　'the boy that brought bread'

　　　b.　t=aʎi　　　tin iɲeka opse　　eɣnorisa　　　p=epire
　　　　　the=Ali.GEN the wife yesterday met.1SG　　that=took.3SG
　　　　　'yesterday I met Ali's wife that he took/married'

(31)　[aǧırla-dıǧ-ım]　　　　　bir misafir　　　　　　　(Turkish)
　　　host-NON.SUBJ.REL-1SG a　　guest
　　　'a guest that I am hosting/host/have hosted'

Arguably, all three changes that AMG has undergone, namely a shift to (i) (exclusively) pre-N placement of genitives, (ii) exclusively pre-N placement of adjectives and (iii) (predominantly) pre-N placement or relatives, are all facets of the prevalence of head-finality in the nominal domain. Nevertheless, in the case of genitives, at least, what we observe is not a wholesale import of the Turkish pattern. The licensing position of genitive DPs on the nominal functional spine in AMG is still the same employed as in every other historical and diatopic Greek variety, at least since Hellenistic Greek, namely Gen2. Moreover, obligatory definiteness agreement/spread gives rise to surface orders such as [Def Gen Def N]. Such orders are perfectly grammatical in contemporary (at least mainland) Greek too, though they are only felicitous if the genitive argument is contrastively focused or topicalized. In other words, in this case too, we are faced with the generalization/grammaticalization of a construction which was already derivable by the pre-existing grammar.

　　Exact emulation of the Turkish pattern in the syntax of genitives would give rise to [Def Gen Def AP Def N] orders, which are also possible in mainland Greek, as the result of fronting of the genitive argument to a DP-peripheral position, coupled with polydefiniteness. Nevertheless, despite the availability of such strings, the pattern is not generalized and does not become unmarked in AMG; that is, it does not reflect the licensing position of genitive DPs. This suggests that we are dealing with an impossible parametric change, namely the rise of a Gen1 position in a Greek variety, and that indeed syntactic borrowings are only possible if they constitute possible parametric changes. Crosslinguistically, realization of the genitive DP in Gen1 correlates either with definiteness inheritance effects (like e.g. Saxon genitives in English) or with obligatory phi-agreement between the genitive and the head noun (see Longobardi 1996, among others). These seem to be core and necessary manifestations of parameters that have Gen1 placement as its reflex. Neither of the two, however, could possibly emerge in an AMG-like grammar. Since definiteness is already obligatorily and multiply marked, that is, it also has to appear on the NP after the genitive; AMG cannot develop an English-like system whereby definiteness of the overall DP is determined on the basis of the genitive, thus blocking definite articles (cf. *(the) John's bike*). As for agreeing

Table 14.2 Attachment Height and Movement Parameters in the DP in Greek and Turkish

	Hellenistic/ Modern Greek	AMG	Turkish
Gen1^0	-	-	+
Gen2^0	+	+	-
NP-over-Gen2	+	-	-
NP-movement over direct modification As	-	-	-
NP-movement over indirect modification (including relatives)	+	-	-

head marking, which also seems to result in Gen1 placement crosslinguistically, AMG resists it due to deeper typological reasons, namely the presence of fusional rather than agglutinating morphology of the sort attested in head-marking languages.

All in all, while innovative, the changed syntax of genitives in AMG is both an instance of a successful syntactic borrowing and of a failed one. A negative setting for N(P)-over-Gen2 indeed arose under contact, but the core strings manifesting this setting were already possible. What contact did was to reduce the input that would trigger a positive setting. At the same time, the parameter setting that gives rise to Gen1 placement in Turkish could not be transferred, because the core strings triggering it were not independently possible.

As for adjectives, contact did the same as above; that is, it made the input contain a radically reduced percentage of postnominal APs which could have given rise to a positive N(P)-over-A parametric setting, after the independently triggered loss of DP-internal Pred^0. Crucially, the syntax of adjectives must also be a core and sufficient manifestation, and therefore a trigger, for a broader parameter regarding the presence/absence of N(P)-movement over modifiers. Recall also the commonly held assumption that at least indirect modification adjectives have the same source/first-merged position as relative clauses (see Cinque 2010, among others). In Asia Minor Greek, adjectives with the interpretive effects (e.g. stage-level readings) that Cinque (2010) associates with reduced relative clauses all appear prenominally only (like e.g. in English, though in English a postnominal position is also available under certain conditions). Thus, by eliminating NP-movement over both direct and indirect modification adjectives, AMG forced loss of obligatory NP-placement before relatives too. In Table 14.2 we summarize our findings regarding nominal syntax in AMG.

4 Towards a model of syntactic borrowing: some foundational principles and conclusions

If one considers all the cases discussed in the previous sections, there are some recurrent themes and generalizations to be drawn. First, as already noted in previous research, a parameter value can only be borrowed if part of the strings it generates were already possible (even if analysed differently) in the pre-existing grammar. In the light of the observations above, we can now be more precise regarding the kind of overlap that does trigger a borrowing:

1. If the parameter in question regulates base-generated orders (e.g. the external merge position of functional heads) or orders resulting from the application of non-discourse-related movement rules (e.g. A-movement, agreement-triggered movement or head-movement), these orders should already be generated by the pre-existing grammar, at least as an artefact of/through the application of discourse-related rules.

This is why in many of the cases discussed above emergent unmarked patterns are also attested in the rest of the diasystem as marked orders.

Second, although language acquisition obtains on the basis of positive evidence, in language contact situations often involving L2 (adult) data, negative evidence may also play a role:

2. Even though the input from the dominant language is not enough to trigger a new value, unless the respective strings are attested in the L1 input, the absence from the L2 input of strings that trigger the opposite value can indeed change the balance in favour of the borrowed value.

So, for instance, the systematic absence of postnominal material in Turkish did play a significant role in the shift to head-final settings for most functional heads in the AMG DP.

Third, a more general conclusion is this:

3. All contact-induced syntactic change is necessarily parametric change even if it is of the micro-/nano- type.

A pattern cannot be borrowed if it is only a peripheral manifestation of a deeper parametric setting, whose core properties are resisted by the target language. At the same time, if the interaction of (I) and (II) suffices for the emergence of a new parametric setting (including potentially macro-parametric changes), then any other manifestations following from the new value are immediately made possible, even if previously completely unavailable (cf. Lightfoot's (1979) 'cascade effect'). An example of this effect is the totally innovative syntax of relatives in AMG, as part of the resetting of ±N-over-indirect-modifiers, as well as the emergence of MWF as a result of activating all Focus projections in the CP-periphery.

Notes

1   We base this observation on our knowledge of the medieval record. To the best of our knowledge, no such study exists.

Abbreviations

-F	agglutinated morpheme
.F	fusional morpheme
=F	morpheme with elided unstressed vowel
1/2/3	1st/2nd/3rd person
A	adjective
A-movement	movement to argument (e.g. subject) position
A'-movement	movement to non-argument/peripheral positions
A'-head	head of projection hosting A'-moved constituents
ACC	accusative
AMG	Asia Minor Greek
AP	adjectival phrase
CP	complementizer phrase
C_{Wh}	interrogative complementizer
D	determiner
D-linked	discourse-linked
DAT	dative
Def	definiteness morpheme
DP	determiner phrase
GEN	genitive
HUM	human
L1	first/native language
L2	second language
N	noun
NEG	negation
NOM	nominative
NON.SUBJ.REL	non-subject relativizer
NP	noun phrase
nP	light noun phrase
OV	object-verb order
PAST	past
phi	phi-feature bundle (person, number, gender)
POSS	possessive
Pred	predication
PredP	predication phrase
pro	null pronoun
R	relator
RP	relator phrase
SG	singular
SMG	Standard Modern Greek
SUBJ	subjunctive
T	Tense
t_i	movement trace (co-referential with expressions with index i)
V	verb
VO	verb-object order
vP	light verb phrase
XP	maximal projection/phrase

References

Alexiadou, A. (2014), *Multiple Determiners and the Structure of DPs*, vol. 211, Amsterdam: Benjamins.

Anagnostopoulou, E. (2003), *The Syntax of Ditransitives: Evidence from Clitics*, vol. 54, Berlin: Walter de Gruyter.

Bağrıacık, M. (2017), 'Pharasiot Greek: Word Order and Clause Structure,' PhD diss., University of Ghent, Ghent, Belgium.

Bağrıacık, M., and Danckaert, L. (2016), 'On the Emergence of Prenominal and Postnominal Relative Clauses in Pharasiot Greek,' Paper presented at DiGS 18, University of Ghent, 1 July 2016.

Bošković, Ž. (2002), 'On Multiple Wh-fronting.' *Linguistic Inquiry*, 33 (3): 351–83.

Bošković, Ž. (2007), 'A Note on Wh-typology', in P. Kosta and L. Schürcks (eds), *Linguistic Investigations into Formal Description of Slavic Languages: Contributions of the Sixth European Conference held at Potsdam University*, 159–70, Frankfurt am Main: Peter Lang.

Campos, H. and M. Stavrou (2011), 'Definiteness Effects in Spanish and Greek (Appositive) Nominals', Talk given at the Colloquium on Generative Grammar (CGG), Seville, 7–9 April 2011.

Cinque, G. (2010), *The Syntax of Adjectives: A Comparative Study*, vol. 57, Cambridge, MA: MIT Press.

Donabedian, A. and I. Sitaridou (forthcoming), 'Language Contact in Anatolia', in E. Adamou and Y. Matras (eds), *Handbook of Language Contact*, London: Routledge.

Georgiafentis, M. (2004), 'Focus and Word Order Variation in Greek', PhD diss., University of Reading, Reading, UK.

Gryllia, S. (2009), *On the Nature of Preverbal Focus in Greek: A Theoretical and Experimental Approach*, PhD diss., Utrecht: Netherlands Graduate School of Linguistics (LOT).

Guardiano, C. (2011), 'Genitives in the Greek Nominal Domain: Parametric Considerations,' *Studies in Modern Greek Dialects and Linguistic Theory*, 123–34, Nicosia, Cyprus: Research Center of Kykkos Monastery.

Guardiano, C. and M. Stavrou (2014), 'Greek and Romance in Southern Italy: History and Contact in Nominal Structures', *L' Italia dialettale*, LXXV: 121–47.

Guardiano, C. and M. Stavrou (2017), 'On the Loss of Polydefiniteness in Italiot Greek', Paper presented at CIDSM12, July 2017, Cambridge, UK.

Guardiano, C., D. Michelioudakis, A. Ceolin, M.-A. Irimia, G. Longobardi, N. Radkevich, G. Silvestri and I. Sitaridou (2016), 'South by South East: A Syntactic Approach to Greek and Romance Microvariation', *L'Italia dialettale*, LXXVII: 96–166.

Hagstrom, P. A. (1998), 'Decomposing Questions', PhD diss., Massachusetts Institute of Technology, Cambridge, MA.

Kirk, A. (2012), *Word Order and Information Structure in New Testament Greek*, PhD diss., Netherlands Graduate School of Linguistics (LOT), Utrecht, The Netherlands.

Lightfoot, D. (1979), *Principles of Diachronic Syntax*, Cambridge, UK: Cambridge University Press.

Longobardi, G. (1996), 'On the Typological Unity of Indo-European and Semitic Genitive Case', MS, University of Trieste, Trieste, Italy.

Longobardi, G. and G. Silvestri (2013), 'The Structure of Noun Phrases: Some Insights on Case, Empty Categories and Poverty of the Stimulus', *The Bloomsbury Companion to Syntax*. Continuum Companion, 88–117, London: Bloomsbury.

Mathieu, E. and I. Sitaridou (2005), 'Split Wh-constructions in Classical and Modern Greek: A Diachronic Perspective', *Grammaticalization and Parametric Variation*, 236–50, Oxford: Oxford University Press.

Michelioudakis, D. and I. Sitaridou (2012), 'Syntactic Microvariation: Dative Constructions in Greek', in B. Fernandez and R. Etxeparre (eds), *Variation in Datives: A Microcomparative Perspective*, 212–55, Oxford: Oxford University Press.

Michelioudakis, D. and I. Sitaridou (2016), 'Recasting the Typology of Multiple Wh-fronting: Evidence from Pontic Greek', *Glossa*, 1 (1): 1–40.

Michelioudakis, D., M. Bağriacik, C. Guardiano, G. Longobardi, I. Sitaridou and M. Stavrou (2016), 'Diagnosing Syntactic Effects of Language Contact and Historical Transmission: Asia Minor Greek as a Case Study', Paper presented at the *1st International Conference on Language Contact in the Balkans and Asia Minor*, 3–5 November 2016, Thessaloniki, Greece.

Michelioudakis, D., I. Sitaridou, M. Stavrou, M. Bağriacik, C. Guardiano and G. Longobardi (2017), 'When Greek Meets Other Languages: Diagnosing Structural Borrowing in Asia Minor and Southern Italy', Paper presented at the *International Conference on Greek Linguistics (ICGL 13)*, 7–9 September 2017, University of Westminster, London, UK.

Neocleous, N. and I. Sitaridou (2018). 'Never Just Contact: The Rise of Final Auxiliaries in Asia Minor Greek', MS, University of Cambridge, Cambridge, UK.

Özsoy, A. S. (2009), 'Turkish as a (Non)-wh-in-situ Language', *Turcological Letters to Bernt Brendemoen*, The Institute for Comparative Research in Human Culture, 221–32, Oslo: Novus Press.

Sinopoulou, O. (2008), 'Multiple Questions and Apparent Wh-in situ: Evidence from Greek', in S. Blaho, C. Constantinescu and E. Schoorlemmer (eds), *Proceedings of ConSOLE*, XV: 223–46.

Sinopoulou, O. (2011), 'Wh & Wh-questions in Greek: Monoclausal or Biclausal?', *Linguistic Analysis*, 37 (1): 189–229.

Sitaridou, I. (2013), 'Greek-speaking Enclaves in Pontus Today: The Documentation and Revitalization of Romeyka', in M. C. Jones and S. Ogilvie (eds), *Keeping Languages Alive. Language Endangerment: Documentation, Pedagogy and Revitalization*, 98–112, Cambridge, UK: Cambridge University Press.

Sitaridou, I. (2014a), 'The Romeyka Infinitive: Continuity, Contact and Change in the Hellenic Varieties of Pontus', *Diachronica*, 31 (1): 23–73.

Sitaridou, I. (2014b), 'Modality, Antiveridicality, and Complementation: The Romeyka Infinitive as a Negative Polarity Item', *Lingua*, 148: 118–46.

Sitaridou, I. (2016), 'Reframing the Phylogeny of Asia Minor Greek: The View from Pontic Greek', *CHS Research Bulletin*, Center for Hellenic Studies, Harvard University, 4 (1): 1–17.

Sitaridou, I. and M. Kaltsa (2014), 'Contrastivity in Pontic Greek', *Lingua*, 146: 1–27.

Stavrou, M. (2012), 'Postnominal Adjectives in Greek Indefinite Noun Phrases', in L. Brugé, A. Cardinaletti, G. Giusti, N. Munaro and C. Poletto (eds), *Functional Heads*, 379–94, Oxford: Oxford University Press.

Taylor, A. (1994), 'The Change from SOV to SVO in Ancient Greek', *Language Variation and Change*, 6 (1): 1–37.

15

Goal prevalence and situation types:
An empirical analysis of differences in Greek
and German motion event descriptions

Thanasis Georgakopoulos and Holden Härtl

The aim of the current study is to investigate crosslinguistic differences in the encoding of motion events and the distribution of their constituent parts, that is, the manner as well as the path focusing mainly on the Goal component. In the abundant literature on the effect of the lexicalization pattern of a language (Satellite- versus Verb-framed), only a few studies have systematically taken into account the specific properties of the situation underlying a verbalization. With a focus on German and Greek, we analyse verbal descriptions of motion events presented in video clips and link the linguistic characteristics of the different verbalizations to the salience of the Goal point. We find that in situations containing highly evident Goals towards which the motion is targeted, German speakers tend to realize Goals more often than Greek speakers. This finding is complemented with a crosslinguistic examination of the inventory for expressing manner and path of motion as well as by an analysis of the type of information expressed in the verbalizations. We discuss both in the context of the continuum between Satellite- and Verb-framed languages.

1 Introduction

Crosslinguistic differences are a central aspect in cognitively oriented analyses of the encoding of motion events, as well as their conceptualization. A broad spectrum of factors is discussed ranging from the lexicalization pattern of a language and the distribution of path and manner expressions across languages (see e.g. Slobin 1997, 2004; Talmy 2000, among many others) to grammatical viewpoint aspect (see e.g. Athanasopoulos and Bylund 2013; von Stutterheim and Nüse 2003; von Stutterheim et al. 2012; von Stutterheim, Bouhaous and Carroll 2017) as well as the interplay between these factors (see Georgakopoulos, Härtl and Sioupi 2019). In this context, the linguistic realization of motion Goals is of particular interest as it represents a primary conceptual notion, which is reflected, for example, in the bias to encode Goals of motion in comparison to Sources (see e.g. Ikegami 1987; Landau and Zukowski 2003; Lakusta and Landau 2005; Papafragou 2010; Kopecka and Narasimhan 2012; Luraghi, Nikitina and Zanchi 2017; Georgakopoulos 2018).

So far, however, only a few studies, among them von Stutterheim, Bouhaous, and Carroll (2017), have implemented as variables the specific properties of the situation underlying a verbal description. This is a gap our study aims to fill from a comparative point of view by systematically linking the linguistic realization of Goals with types of situations, instantiated as video clips and the corresponding motion verbs. With a focus on Modern Greek (henceforth Greek) and German, we aim at a fine-grained empirical analysis of the linguistic options the two languages can use when expressing Goals, with the intention to contribute to the definition of the locus of these languages on the continuum between Satellite- and Verb-framed languages (henceforth S-framed and V-framed languages, respectively).

We will start from the assumption that the lexicalization pattern of a language is a stronger predictor for the inclusion of a Goal expression in descriptions of motion events than the presence of grammatical viewpoint aspect. This insight is based on results from an experimental study, in which we compared auditory verbalizations of motion events accumulated for English, Greek and German on the basis of video clips (see Georgakopoulos, Härtl and Sioupi 2019). In this chapter, thus, we now exclude grammatical viewpoint aspect as a variable and concentrate on Greek and German for our comparative analysis of the collected data. Drawing on von Stutterheim, Bouhaous, and Carroll (2017), we follow a tripartite subdivision of the clips based on the visual salience of the Goal region. We hypothesize that visual salience of the Goal is a factor that influences attention to details of motion events. We complement our endeavour with a crosslinguistic examination of the inventory used to express manner and path of motion, as well as the distribution of peripheral elements used to express the path in light of the different lexicalization patterns Greek and German exhibit.

The structure of this chapter is as follows: In Section 2, we consider aspects of the prominence of Goals in connection to the different lexicalization patterns German and Greek display and in Section 3, we briefly report on data from an experimental study we previously conducted. In Section 4, the clips used in the study are then classified according to the visual salience of the Goal of the motion event. An analysis of (a) the inventory used for realizing the different meaning components involved in motion events and (b) the distribution of the different meaning components involved in a motion event across the clause complements our investigation. Section 5 concludes.

2 Goal prominence and the lexicalization pattern

Talmy (2000) suggested a two-way typology of motion event constructions according to which the world's languages are divided into S- and V-framed languages (cf. Slobin 2004). Talmy's dichotomy relates to where the information about the path of motion is encoded in a sentence. In S-framed languages, such as Dutch, English or Russian, path is systematically expressed outside the verb root, that is, in satellites, usually by means of prefixes, prepositional phrases or adverbs. Manner of motion is usually encoded in the verb in this type of languages. This is illustrated in (1) from English.

(1) A man   is walking   into   a church.
     Figure   manner   path   Ground

On the other hand, in V-framed languages, such as French, Spanish or Turkish, path is typically encoded in the verb and manner either is omitted (example (2)) or appears elsewhere in the sentence (example (3)). These two possibilities are exemplified in (2)–(3) from Greek.

(2) Ένα λεωφορείο   διασχίζει   το δρόμο.
     A bus   cross:PRS.3SG   the street
     Figure   path   Ground
     'A bus crosses the street.'

(3) Ένας σκύλος   μπαίνει   σε ένα κτίριο   τρέχοντας.
     A dog   enter:PRS.3SG   at/to a building   run:PTCP
     Figure   path   Ground   manner
     Lit. 'A dog is entering a building by running.'

Research in spatial semantics in the last fifteen years has highlighted the fact that S-framed and V-framed constructions can co-exist in a language (see e.g. Slobin 2004; Beavers, Levin and Tham 2010; Croft et al. 2010). This does not mean that the Talmian dichotomy is necessarily wrong; rather it suggests that there is within-type variation in both S-framed and V-framed languages. This variability may be better described as a continuum (see Montero-Melis et al. 2017: 54 and references therein). It also moves the focus from the question of whether categorical differences exist to the question of which encoding options are preferred by the speakers of a particular language and in which situations.

In Greek, both S-framed and V-framed constructions are available, as exemplified in (4), in which one can find the manner being expressed in the verb (cf. example (3)).

(4) Ένας σκύλος   έτρεξε   μέσα   στο κτίριο.
     A dog   ran.PFV.3SG   inside   at/to the building
     Figure   manner   path   Ground
     'A dog ran into the building.'

Despite the availability of both constructional types, Greek is usually listed as an example of a V-framed language, because it shows a preference for V-framed encoding options (see e.g. Papafragou, Massey and Gleitman 2006; Selimis 2007; Papafragou and Selimis 2010; Selimis and Katis 2010; cf. Talmy 2000: 66–7; Soroli 2012; Soroli and Verkerk 2017). Conversely, German motion events are typically encoded by S-framed constructions and, thus, German is categorized as S-framed language (see e.g. Berthele 2006).

What is important for the purpose of the current study, is that S- and V-framed languages have been reported to differ in the degree of the Goal prominence as Goal expressions, namely peripheral elements that occur outside the verb and encode the endpoint of motion, are included in motion descriptions more often in the former than in the latter. More specifically, some studies have reported a general path bias in S-framed languages,[1] which results from the tendency of speakers of those languages to express path information outside the verb as compared to speakers of V-framed languages, who are more prone to encode the path in the verb root (see Slobin 1996; Johanson and Papafragou 2010). These studies have shown that in S-framed languages, Goal information prevails as well a prevalence which is seen as an epiphenomenon of the path bias. Another study by Georgakopoulos and Sioupi (2015), which has focused on Change of Possession events, has demonstrated that German manifests a more robust Goal bias compared to Greek. In this case, the endpoint is favoured independently of the general path bias.

3 The empirical study: The old design

In the literature on crosslinguistic differences in the conceptualization of motion events and their verbalization, an additional factor – beyond the specific lexicalization a language exhibits – that has been discussed as relevant to have an impact on the inclusion of Goal expressions, is the presence of grammatical viewpoint aspect (see Athanasopoulos and Bylund 2013; Schmiedtová, von Stutterheim and Carroll 2011). To test the strength of the two factors, namely of the lexicalization pattern and of the grammatical viewpoint aspect, and investigate their interdependency, in Georgakopoulos, Härtl and Sioupi (2019) we conducted an experimental study, in which we collected event descriptions from German, English and Greek, three languages that differ from each other with respect to at least one property that has been reported to influence the mentioning of Goals (English: aspect and S-framed language; German: non-aspect and S-framed language; Greek: aspect and V-framed language). We repeat here the most basic information concerning the methodology used as well as the most relevant results for the purpose of this chapter.

Sixty native speakers of English, German and Greek participated in the study. Following the protocol designed by von Stutterheim et al. (2012), the stimulus material was divided into two major types, a GOAL NOT REACHED type and a GOAL REACHED type. The former showed a figure moving along a trajectory and towards a goal. These were the critical clips (*N*=10). The latter consisted of motion events in which the figure actually reaches a goal. These were used as controls (*N*=10). Ten clips depicting dynamic, though non-motion events were used as fillers. Items from the two conditions were presented in a between-subjects design; that is, participants from the different language groups were exclusively presented either with the critical clips or with the controls.

In the GOAL REACHED group, participants were asked to briefly describe the events they were about to watch after the end of each video and after the speaker symbol (introduced to them in the instruction) appeared on the screen. In the GOAL NOT REACHED group, participants were asked to describe the event shown right after the beginning of each video.

All verbalizations were digitally recorded, transcribed and encoded for the inclusion of Goal expressions. The statistical analysis for the differences in all verbalizations (*N*=586) across the group means revealed a significant main effect for CONDITION such that, across the three languages tested, more Goals were mentioned in the GOAL REACHED condition (*N*=250) than in the GOAL NOT REACHED condition (*N*=94). Furthermore, an effect of LANGUAGE was observed such that, with the two conditions again taken together, more Goals were included in the descriptions in German (*N*=134) than in Greek (*N*=98). The difference between German and English did not reach the conventional level of significance nor did the difference between Greek and English. A significant interaction between LANGUAGE and CONDITION was observed. Planned pairwise comparisons for the critical condition indicated a significant difference between German and Greek as well as English and Greek, with more Goal expressions noted in English (*N*=39) and German (*N*=42) than in Greek (*N*=12). No significant difference was observed between the two S-framed languages.

Our finding is compatible with a view that holds that the lexicalization pattern of a language has a stronger impact on the realization of Goals. This is reflected in the grouping of English and German versus Greek. Our results do not indicate a systematic effect of the presence of aspect on the inclusion of Goals in the event descriptions we elicited. Consequently, in the following, we ignore aspect as a variable. Instead, we concentrate on the lexicalization pattern and, in particular, on the differences between S-framed and V-framed languages. For the crosslinguistic comparison, we choose Greek and German, excluding English, given the non-difference between English and German (the choice between the two S-framed languages being random).

4 The empirical study: A new analysis

As mentioned in Section 3, in Georgakopoulos, Härtl and Sioupi (2019), we followed the bipartite distinction of the stimulus material – found in von Stutterheim et al. (2012) – into a GOAL NOT REACHED type and a GOAL REACHED type. However, within the GOAL NOT REACHED condition, the clips included goal points with varying salience, a factor that we assume to further affect the explicit expression of the realization of goals of motion in linguistic descriptions. Thus, we hypothesize that the visual salience of the goal would influence attention to details of motion events and, possibly, would be reflected in default verbalization of the languages under discussion.

Table 15.1 Classification of the Displayed Situations

Event type	Situation type
a. WOMAN TOWARDS CHURCH	Type A
b. WOMAN TOWARDS STOP	Type A
c. WOMAN TOWARDS BOOTH	Type A
d. WOMAN TOWARDS BENCH	Type A
e. MAN TOWARDS CAR	Type A
f. MAN TOWARDS BUILDING	Type A
g. CAR TOWARDS VILLAGE	Type B
h. CAR TOWARDS CHURCH	Type B
i. COUPLE TOWARDS VILLAGE	Type B
j. BUS TOWARDS VILLAGE	Type B
k. MAN INTO CHURCH	Type C
l. HORSE INTO STALL	Type C
m. CAR INTO GARAGE	Type C
n. VAN INTO YARD	Type C
o. KID INTO PLAYGROUND	Type C
p. CAT INTO ROOM	Type C
q. WOMAN INTO SHOP	Type C
r. WOMAN INTO STATION	Type C
s. HORSEMAN INTO STALL	Type C
t. DOG INTO HOUSE	Type C

Event types appear in small capitals. All examples reported in the paper will make reference to the situation type to which they belong as well as to the event type they represent (e.g. [Type A/a] for a description of a clip showing a woman walking towards a church).

To test the impact of this additional factor, we subdivided the clips belonging to the first condition to two types. In doing so, we relied on von Stutterheim, Bouhaous and Carroll (2017), who distinguish between events that show a figure 'moving along a short trajectory [...] towards a highly evident goal point marked by an object' (Type A) and events in which a figure moves 'along an extended trajectory with a potential, but not an evident goal point' (Type B). The GOAL REACHED condition will be henceforth referred to as Type C. Table 15.1 shows the result of this classification: six clips belong to Type A situations, four to Type B and ten to Type C. Figure 15.1 illustrates the three different types with examples of stills from the stimuli, split into three different phases, a beginning, an intermediate and a final phase. The first clip shows a woman moving towards a church (a highly evident goal point). The second clip depicts a couple walking down a road towards a village (a potential, not evident goal). Finally, the third clip shows a man walking into a church (boundary crossing).[2]

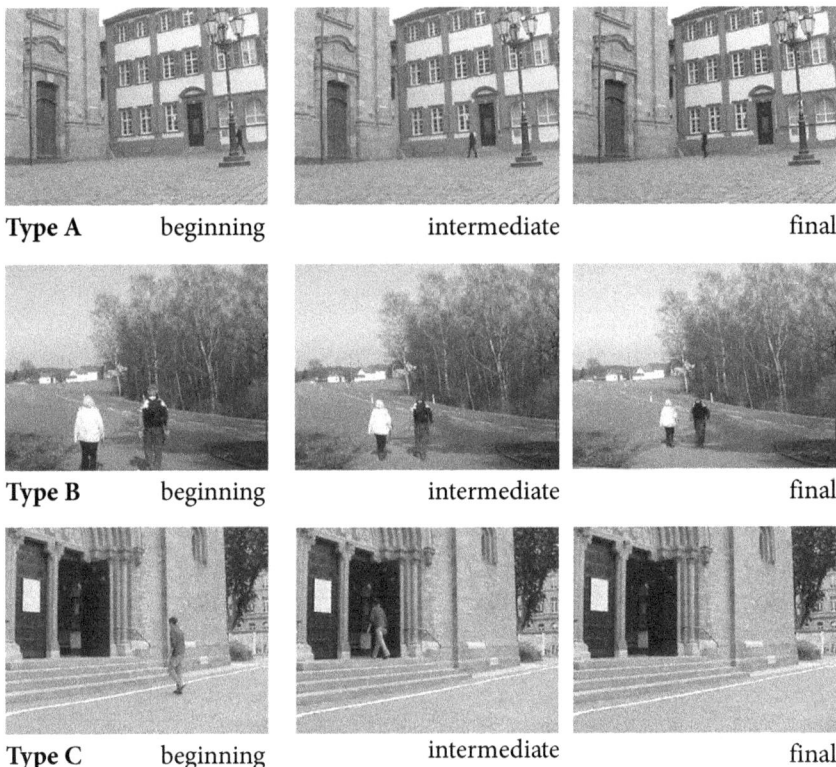

Figure 15.1 The three types of motion events.

4.1 Results

4.1.1 Goal realization in Greek and German

Table 15.2 lists the numbers of verbalizations from both German and Greek speakers that included reference to an endpoint – for each motion event as well as each type separately. Note that in some cases the participants failed to provide a description that involved a motion event. For that reason, we also give the number of valid tokens for each clip individually (e.g. 9/10 GER means that 9 out of 10 descriptions given by German speakers were valid; conversely, all descriptions by Greek speakers were valid).

Three main observations can be drawn from the data reported in Table 15.2. First, in almost all clips in which there is a difference in Goal mentions, the difference is in favour of the German group. Second, one can observe that within Type A situations there is variation in Goal preference. On the one hand, in most motion events (four out of six) German speakers mention more often the Goal than Greek speakers. On the other hand, there are some cases (two out of six) in which the two groups exhibit the same endpoint frequencies. For example, in the event in which a woman is walking towards a church, both groups generally omit the Goal. The omission of the Goal

Table 15.2 Mentions of Endpoints for Greek and German per Motion Event

Motion events	Situation type	Valid	Greek Goal	German Goal
a. WOMAN TOWARDS CHURCH	Type A	10	2	2
b. WOMAN TOWARDS STOP	Type A	10	0	9
c. WOMAN TOWARDS BOOTH	Type A	9/10 GER	4	8
d. WOMAN TOWARDS BENCH	Type A	10	0	6
e. MAN TOWARDS CAR	Type A	10	1	6
f. MAN TOWARDS BUILDING	Type A	10	5	6
g. CAR TOWARDS VILLAGE	Type B	7/10 GR	0	2
h. CAR TOWARDS CHURCH	Type B	9/10 GR	0	1
i. COUPLE TOWARDS VILLAGE	Type B	10	0	1
j. BUS TOWARDS VILLAGE	Type B	7/10 GR	0	1
k. MAN INTO CHURCH	Type C	10	9	9
l. HORSE INTO STALL	Type C	10	9	10
m. CAR INTO GARAGE	Type C	10	9	10
n. VAN INTO YARD	Type C	10	10	9
o. KID INTO PLAYGROUND	Type C	10	9	10
p. CAT INTO ROOM	Type C	10	5	9
q. WOMAN INTO SHOP	Type C	10	9	9
r. WOMAN INTO STATION	Type C	10	8	9
s. HORSEMAN INTO STALL	Type C	10	8	8
t. DOG INTO HOUSE	Type C	10	10	9

When we don't report the N of the valid tokens in a language, it means that all responses are valid. For example, in [Type A/c] situations there were 10 valid tokens in Greek and 9 in German.

might be the result of the fact that, in this case, it is not so obvious that the motion will end up at the targeted Ground, that is, the church. The whole clip highlights the woman's crossing of the square. Consider the following answers from the two groups:

(5) Eine Frau   geht   über einen Platz.
A woman   walk:PRS.3SG   across a square
'A woman is walking across a square.' *(Type A/a)*

(6) Eine Frau   läuft   durch die Straße.
A woman   walk:PRS.3SG   through the street
'A woman is walking through the street.' *(Type A/a)*

(7) Μια γυναίκα   περπατάει.
A woman   walk:PRS.3SG
'A woman is walking.' *(Type A/a)*

(8) Μια γυναίκα   περπατάει   σε ένα δρόμο.
A woman   walk:PRS.3SG   at/to a road
'A woman is walking on a road.' *(Type A/a)*

Conversely, in the clip showing a man heading towards a building, both groups generally express the Goal of motion. This situation is closer to a Type C situation: the final phase of the clip shows a man climbing up the stairs, thus increasing the probability that he will ultimately enter the building. This is evidenced by the fact that some speakers construed the situation as a cross-boundary one.

(9) Ein Mann   läuft   in ein Haus   rein.
     A man   walk:PRS.3SG   into a house   PRN-in
     'A man is walking into a house.' *(Type A/f)*

(10) Ein Mann   geht   in ein Gebäude.
     A man   walk:PRS.3SG   into a building
     'A man is walking into a building.' *(Type A/f)*

(11) Εδώ είναι   ένας κύριος   ο οποίος   ανεβαίνει   μια σκάλα.
     here is   a man   who   ascend:PRS.3SG   a staircase

     για να   μπει   σε ένα κτίριο.
     in order   enter:PRS.SUBJ.3SG   at/to a building
     'There is a man climbing up the stairs to enter a building.' *(Type A/f)*

Third, the data in Table 15.2 suggest that both language groups behave homogenously in Type B and Type C situations. More specifically, in Type B, speakers chose not to explicitly express the Goal of motion (see examples (12)–(13)), whereas in Type C they generally included the endpoint of motion in their descriptions (see examples (14)–(15)).

(12) Ein   Auto   fährt   eine Straße   entlang.
     A   car   drive:PRS.3SG   a street   along
     'A car is driving along a road.' *(Type B/g)*

(13) Ένα αυτοκίνητο   διασχίζει   ένα χιονισμένο δρόμο.
     A car   cross:PRS.3SG   a snowy road
     'A car crosses a snowy road.' *(Type B/g)*

(14) Ein Kind   geht   auf den Spielplatz.
     A child   go:PRS.3SG   on the playground
     'A child goes to a playground.' *(Type C/o)*

(15) Ένα παιδάκι   μπήκε   στην παιδική χαρά.
     A little.child   entered:PFV.3SG   at/to the playground
     'A child goes into the playground.' *(Type C/o)*

Table 15.3 Mentions of Endpoints per Situation Type

Situation Type	Greek	German
Type A	12 (20%)	37 (62.7%)
Type B	0 (0%)	5 (12.5%)
Type C	86 (86%)	92 (92%)

In both groups, the differences between the two languages are not significant (Type B: $\chi^2(1)=.059$, *n.s.*;[3] Type C: $\chi^2(1)=1.83$, *n.s.*). This means that the overall difference between the two languages reported in Section 3 was dependent on Type A situations ($\chi^2(1)=22.4$, *p*< .01). This is shown in Table 15.3, which sums the values for each situation type collectively.

In Georgakopoulos, Härtl and Sioupi (2019: 302), we suggested that the observed difference between German and Greek 'could be attributed to certain properties of the languages' lexicalization patterns and, in particular, to the different coding strategies that each language allows'. Given the result obtained by the new categorization of the situations, what we can add to this claim is that the realization of Goals in motion event descriptions is sensitive to the salience of the goal point towards which the motion is targeted. When the goal point is not evident (Type B), both groups ignore the Goal. When there is a boundary crossing (Type C), both groups express the Goal. But when the goal point is highly evident (Type A), German speakers are more prone to express the Goal than Greek speakers.

We should repeat at this point that by goals of motion, we mean the peripheral elements that occur outside the verb and encode the endpoint of motion (and not the verbs that can profile the endpoint of motion, such as *arrive* and *reach*). This clarification is important because it comes with a cost when comparing S-framed languages to V-framed ones: the former have an advantage over the latter when it comes to Goal realization, because S-framed languages typically express path information – and as a consequence Goal – in other-than-the-verb elements, whereas V-framed generally in the verb (see also Section 2).

In most cases, German speakers produce semantically more dense descriptions in that they include both the manner and the path throughout their verbalizations more often than Greek speakers. In the critical clips (i.e. in Type A situations), German speakers almost consistently chose to describe the motion events by means of S-framed constructions, using a rigid subject-verb schema involving indefinite NPs, as in *Ein Auto fährt in eine Garage* ('A car is driving into a garage'; *Type C/m*), and the present tense form of the verb. V-framed strategies were only sporadically used by German speakers, cf. *Ein Mann betritt eine Kirche* ('A man is entering a church'; *Type C/k*). In contrast, Greek speakers employ many different strategies. They use: (a) bare manner verbs; (see example (7)); (b) manner verbs together with relators that express general localization (example (8)); (c) manner verbs together with dynamic relators denoting the Goal (example (16)); (d) paths verbs without any relators (example (17)); (e) path verbs with relators that express general localization (example (18)); (f) path verbs with dynamic relators denoting the Goal (example (19)); (g) a main path verb together with another path verb as a subordinate element (see example (11)).

(16) Βλέπω   μια γυναίκα   να περπατάει
     See:PRS.1SG   a woman   to walk:PRS.3SG

     προς έναν τηλεφωνικό θάλαμο.
     towards a phone booth
     'I see a woman walking towards a phone booth.' *(Type A/c)*

(17) Ο κύριος   ανεβαίνει   τις σκάλες.
     The man   ascend:PRS.3SG   the stairs
     'The man is climbing up the stairs.' *(Type A/f)*

(18) Ένας άνδρας   προχωράει   στο δρόμο.
     A man   advance:PRS.3SG   at/to the road
     'A man is moving on a road.' *(Type A/e)*

(19) Μια κυρία   που κατευθύνεται   προς ένα σπίτι.
     A lady   that head:PRS.3SG   towards a house
     'A woman that is heading towards a house.' *(Type A/c)*

4.1.2 Inventories of verbs and peripheral elements

Table 15.4 and 15.5 below list the different verbs uttered by the Greek and German participants during the verbalization task in both conditions. These are categorized in two types, *path* and *manner* verbs:

The most striking difference between the two language groups is in the number of path verbs used. Greek speakers were found to produce more path verbs (N_{GR}=11) in their motion event descriptions than German speakers (N_{GER}=1). This is consistent with what we know about motion event descriptions in Greek and German (see Papafragou, Massey, and Gleitman 2006; Papafragou and Selimis 2010; Verkerk 2013, among others). In contrast, both groups contain a high proportion of manner verbs (N_{GR}=10 versus N_{GER}=11), which is unexpected given the different systems of the two languages (cf. Papafragou, Massey and Gleitman 2006: B85 for the distribution of manner verbs in English and Greek). However, as has been shown in previous research, 'cross-linguistic differences in speech habits are more likely when measured in tokens of expressions – above all, verbs – relative to types' (Selimis and Katis 2010: 70). Indeed, to anticipate

Table 15.4 Types of Verbs Used in Greek

Manner	Path
καβαλάω 'ride'	προχωρώ 'advance'
ιππεύω 'ride'	κατευθύνομαι 'head for'
οδηγώ 'drive'	εισέρχομαι 'enter'
περπατώ 'walk'	πάω 'go'
στρίβω 'turn'	διασχίζω 'cross'
τρέχω 'run'	κινούμαι 'move'
παρκάρω 'park'	περνώ 'pass'
περιφέρομαι 'roam around'	μπαίνω 'enter'
περιτριγυρίζω 'move around'	ανεβαίνω 'ascend'
βαδίζω 'walk'	βγαίνω 'exit'

The list does not include periphrases such as *πάω μια διαδρομή* ('I am doing (lit. going) a route.') or *πάω περίπατο* ('I am going for a walk.').

Table 15.5 Types of Verbs Used in German

Manner	Path
fahren 'drive'	*betreten* 'enter'
laufen 'walk'	
gehen 'go'	
spazieren 'walk'	
wandern 'wander'	
steigen 'climb'	
schreiten 'step'	
rennen 'run'	
eilen 'rush'	
reiten 'ride'	
parken 'park'	

Table 15.6 List of Goal Elements Accompanying the Motion Verbs of the Study

Category	Language	
	German	**Greek**
Adpositions *(simple or complex)*	*in NP* 'into NP' *auf NP* 'to NP' *in Richtung NP* 'towards NP' *zu NP* 'towards NP'	*προς NP* 'towards NP' *σε NP* 'at/to NP' *μέσα σε NP* 'in + at/to NP'
Adverbs	*hinauf* 'up' *hinein* 'in' *rein* 'in' *hoch* 'up'	
Particles	*zu* 'to' *ein* 'in'	

the results in Section 4.1.3, the type frequency of manner verbs differs significantly between German and Greek (see also Georgakopoulos, Härtl and Sioupi 2019).

There are dissimilarities between the two languages also with regard to the peripheral elements used to express the path (more specifically the Goal of motion). Table 15.6 shows that Greek speakers use fewer elements than German speakers (see Johanson and Papafragou 2010, among others, for the difference between English and Greek; cf. Aske 1989 for English versus Spanish path satellites). Additionally, the latter group employs more strategies for the expression of Goal (or other portions of the Source-Medial-Goal schema), since they rely on adpositions (e.g. *zu* + NP), adverbs that encode the general path of the event (e.g. *hinein*), or other particles that can be attached to the verb (e.g. *ein*).

4.1.3 The type of information expressed in the verbalizations

In Section 4.1.1, we correlated situation types with Goal realizations in the two languages. In this Section, we will analyse the verbalization data with respect to the distribution of the different meaning components involved in a motion event across the clause. For this purpose, all data were coded according to whether the description included: only the manner of motion (M); only the path (P); both manner and path in a single clause (MP); both manner and path in more than one clauses which were either juxtaposed or coordinated (M/P); some other information not related to a motion event (∅) (see Fagard, Stosic and Cerruti 2017; Soroli and Verkerk 2017). Following Fagard, Stosic and Cerruti (2017: 649), we hypothesize that German being a S-framed language will bundle manner and path in a single sentence ([MP] type), while Greek as a V-framed language will either omit manner or path ([M] and [P] types or will distribute the information on manner and path over different clauses.

Table 15.7 presents the overall result stemming from the above categorization. The displayed differences are significant ($\chi^2(1)$ = 287.3, p < .001) and the data reveal that the bundling of manner and path in one clause is significantly higher in German than in Greek. Additionally, Greek speakers tend to produce either path-only or manner-only sentences (N_{GR}=166 versus N_{GER}=14, $\chi^2(1)$ = 231.6 p < .001). Both results confirm Fagard, Stosic and Cerruti's (2017) hypothesis. Finally, when Greek speakers express both manner and path, they use two strategies equally frequently: either they encode both in one clause (see example (16)) or they split the two types of information into two clauses (see example (11)). The former finding shows that S-framed constructions are indeed available for Greek, as has been shown in the relevant literature (see e.g. Selimis and Katis 2010; Soroli 2011, 2012; Soroli and Verkerk 2017), whereas the second finding is in accord with the V-framed lexicalization pattern.

Table 15.8 breaks down this result across situation Types. German speakers are consistent across all three groups in producing semantically dense [MP] descriptions. Greek speakers are also consistent in that they mention only one type of information, be it either path or manner. At a closer look, we can see that there is a substantial difference among the three types in Greek: in Type A there is a bias towards manner descriptions; in Type B manner-only and path-only descriptions are equally represented and; in Type C there is a bias towards path descriptions.

Note that the preference of Greek speakers for only manner verbalizations in Type A situations is not entirely atypical for V-framed languages. What is relevant in this

Table 15.7 Proportion of [MP] versus [M] versus [P] versus [M/P] Descriptions for Greek and German

Language	Category				
	P	M	MP	M/P	∅
German	6 (3%)	8 (4%)	180 (91%)	1 (0.5%)	3 (1.5%)
Greek	96 (48%)	70 (35%)	12 (6%)	11 (5.5%)	11 (5.5%)

Note that if a description includes more than one path verb, we considered this description as including one single path.

Table 15.8 Proportion of [MP] versus [M] versus [P] versus [M/P] Descriptions for Greek and German per Situation Type

Type A

Language	Category				
	P	M	MP	M/P	∅
German	0 (0%)	2 (3.3%)	56 (93.3%)	0 (0%)	2 (3.3%)
Greek	13 (22%)	38 (64.4%)	2 (3.4%)	6 (10.2%)	0 (0%)

Type B

Language	Category				
	P	M	MP	M/P	∅
German	0 (0%)	4 (10.3%)	35 (89.7%)	0 (0%)	0 (0%)
Greek	14 (35.9%)	15 (38.5%)	0 (0%)	0 (0%)	10 (25.6%)

Type C

Language	Category				
	P	M	MP	M/P	∅
German	6 (6%)	2 (2%)	89 (89.9%)	1 (1%)	1 (1%)
Greek	69 (68.3%)	17 (16.8%)	10 (9.9%)	4 (3.96%)	1 (1%)

respect is that both S- and V-framed languages seem to have 'neutral everyday verbs' (see Slobin 1997: 459), to which they can resort on several occasions (e.g. when the scene to be described prompts the expression of manner). In all [M] type descriptions in Type A situations, Greek speakers use the translational equivalent of such a neutral everyday verb, that is, of *walk*. Additionally, they accompany very often these verbs with non-dynamic relators that express general localization (in 28/38 tokens; cf. Soroli and Verkerk 2017: 34). Finally, it is worthwhile to note that, although manner descriptions dominate within Type A, paths are also frequently included in the speakers' verbalizations (*N*=19).[4] Such descriptions are absent in the sentences produced by the German speakers.

5 Conclusions

This study demonstrates that differences in lexicalization patterns have certain ramifications for the linguistic choices made by speakers. In a previous study, we found that the lexicalization pattern is a stronger predictor than grammatical aspect for the realization of Goal expression in the description of a motion event. Our findings were based on the bipartite distinction into GOAL REACHED and GOAL NOT REACHED motion events. The current study shows that, although the differences between languages occur in GOAL NOT REACHED motion events, within this type of events there is structured variation. This internal variation is being captured by the new tripartite subdivision of the clips (Type A, B, and C), which splits the GOAL NOT REACHED condition into two different situation Types. This new subdivision is based on the visual salience of the Goal region towards which the motion is targeted (Type A: Goal salient versus Type B: Goal not salient).

Our findings reveal that both language groups behave homogenously in Type B and Type C situations and that the overall difference between the two languages comes from Type A situations. In the clips that contain a highly evident Goal, German speakers produce a higher proportion of Goals than Greek speakers. We attribute this difference to the advantage of the former over the latter as far as the realization of the Goals in peripheral elements is concerned, which is linked to the fact that S-framed languages typically express path information in satellites. Thus, we conclude that it is the typological distinction between S-framed and V-framed which gives us an answer as to why Goals are more prevalent in German. But the sensitivity to this typological distinction is activated under certain circumstances, which are determined by the salience of the Goal point towards which the motion is targeted.

In a second step, the question that arose concerned the distance in framing between German and Greek, as reflected in the responses of the participants in our experiment. Our data confirm prior evidence about the linguistic behaviour of S-framed and V-framed languages, suggesting that the two languages are quite distinct. As a matter of fact, adhering to S-framing, German speakers bundle manner and path in a single clause, whereas Greek speakers were found to produce a large number of path-only and manner-only utterances. Additionally, there was an imbalance in the lexico-grammatical elements used by the two language groups, with Greek speakers using fewer peripheral elements but more verbs for the expression of path than German speakers. The two groups show balance at the type level regarding the use of manner verbs. How far the crosslinguistic contrasts we observed are related to general cognitive differences between German and Greek speakers regarding the informational density of utterances and their underlying conceptual representations is a subject for further investigation.

Acknowledgements

We would like to thank the editors and two anonymous reviewers for their comments. Thanks are also due to Stathis Selimis and Athina Sioupi for commenting on drafts of the article and to Melina Heinrichs for the technical support. Early versions of this work were presented at the 'International Contrastive Linguistics Conference 8' which was held at the University of Athens (25–28 May 2017) and the 'Language Comparison and Typology: German and the Mediterranean languages' workshop, which was held at Humboldt University of Berlin (12 October 2018). We would like to thank the audiences of both meetings for their helpful comments.

Notes

1   For example, Slobin (1996: 199–201) shows that English speakers include ground objects more frequently than Spanish speakers when they describe scenes of downward motion, such as a scene showing an object falling in the water.

2   We wish to thank Christiane von Stutterheim for letting us use the material for the
    current study.
3   In Type B situations, we used Fisher's exact test, since the sample size was small.
4   This number includes both [p] and [m/p].

Abbreviations

PRN	Pronominal element
PRS	Present
PTCP	Participle
SUBJ	Subjunctive
PFV	Perfective aspect
3SG	3rd person singular

References

Aske, J. (1989), 'Path Predicates in English and Spanish: A Closer Look', *Annual Meeting of the Berkeley Linguistics Society*, 15 (1): 1–14.

Athanasopoulos, P. and E. Bylund (2013), 'Does Grammatical Aspect Affect Motion Event Cognition?: A Cross-linguistic Comparison of English and Swedish Speakers', *Cognitive Science*, 37: 286–309.

Beavers, J., B. Levin and W. S. Tham (2010), 'The Typology of Motion Expressions Revisited', *Linguistics*, 46: 331–77.

Berthele, R. (2006), *Ort und Weg: Die sprachliche Raumreferenz in Varietäten des Deutschen, Rätoromanischen und Französischen*, Berlin: de Gruyter.

Croft, W., J. Barðdal, W. Hollmann, V. Sotirova and C. Taoka (2010), 'Revising Talmy's Typological Classification of Complex Event Constructions', in H. C. Boas (ed.), *Contrastive Studies in Construction Grammar*, 201–35, Amsterdam: Benjamins. doi: 10.1075/cal.10.09cro

Fagard, B., D. Stosic and M. Cerruti (2017), 'Within-type Variation in Satellite-framed Languages: The Case of Serbian', *STUF*, 70 (4): 637–60.

Georgakopoulos, T. (2018), 'A Frame-based Approach to the Source-Goal Asymmetry: Synchronic and Diachronic Evidence from Ancient Greek', *Constructions and Frames*, 10 (1): 61–97. doi: 10.1075/cf.00011.geo

Georgakopoulos, T. and A. Sioupi (2015), 'Framing the Difference between Sources and Goals in Change of Possession Events: A Corpus-based Study in German and Modern Greek', *Yearbook of the German Cognitive Linguistics Association*, 3: 105–22.

Georgakopoulos, T., H. Härtl and A. Sioupi (2019), 'Goal Realization: An Empirically Based Comparison between English, German and Greek', *Languages in Contrast*, 19 (2): 280–309. doi.org/10.1075/lic.17010.geo

Ikegami, Y. (1987), '"Source" vs "Goal": A Case of Linguistic Dissymmetry', in R. Dirven and G. Radden (eds), *Concepts of Case*, 122–46, Tübingen: Narr.

Johanson, M. and A. Papafragou (2010), 'Universality and Language Specificity in the Acquisition of Path Vocabulary', in K. Franich, K. M. Iserman and L. L. Keil (eds), *Proceedings from the 34th Annual Boston University on Language Development*, 185–96, Somerville, MA: Cascadilla Press.

Kopecka, A. and B. Narasimhan, eds (2012), *Events of Putting and Taking: A Crosslinguistic Perspective*, Amsterdam: Benjamins. doi: 10.1075/tsl.100

Lakusta, L. and B. Landau (2005), 'Starting at the End: The Importance of Goals in Spatial Language', *Cognition*, 96 (1): 1–33. doi: 10.1016/j.cognition.2004.03.009

Landau, B. and A. Zukowski (2003), 'Objects, Motions and Paths: Spatial Language in Children with Williams Syndrome', *Developmental Neuropsychology*, 23: 107–39. doi: 10.1080/87565641.2003.9651889

Luraghi, S., T. Nikitina and C. Zanchi, eds (2017), *Space in Diachrony*, Amsterdam: Benjamins.

Montero-Melis, G., S. Eisenbeiss, B. Narasimhan, I. Ibarretxe-Antuñano, S. Kita, A. Kopecka, F. Lüpke, T. Nikitina, I. Tragel, T. F. Jaeger and J. Bohnemeyer (2017), 'Satellite- vs. Verb-Framing Underpredicts Nonverbal Motion Categorization: Insights from a Large Language Sample and Simulations', *Cognitive Semantics*, 3: 36–61.

Papafragou, A. (2010), 'Source-Goal Asymmetries in Motion Representation: Implications for Language Production and Comprehension', *Cognitive Science*, 34: 1064–92. https://doi.org/10.1111/j.1551-6709.2010.01107.x

Papafragou, A., C. Massey and L. Gleitman (2006), 'When English Proposes What Greek Presupposes: The Cross-linguistic Encoding of Motion Events', *Cognition*, 98: B75–B87.

Papafragou, A. and S. Selimis (2010), 'Event Categorisation and Language: A Cross-linguistic Study of Motion', *Language and Cognitive Processes*, 25: 224–60.

Selimis, S. (2007), *Γλωσσική Κωδικοποίηση του Εννοιολογικού Πεδίου της Κίνησης: Κυριολεξία και Μεταφορά στα Ελληνικά Παιδιών και Ενηλίκων* ('Linguistic Coding of the Concept of Motion: Literal and Metaphorical Expressions in Adult and Child Greek') [in Greek], PhD diss., National and Kapodistrian University of Athens, Athens, Greece.

Selimis, S. and D. Katis (2010), 'Motion Descriptions in English and Greek: A Cross-typological Developmental Study of Conversations and Narratives', *Linguistik Online*, 42: 57–76.

Slobin, I. D. (1996), 'Two Ways to Travel: Verbs of Motion in English and Spanish', in S. Thompson and M. Shibatani (eds), *Grammatical Constructions: Their Form and Meaning*, 195–219, Oxford: Clarendon Press.

Slobin, I. D. (1997), 'Mind, Code, and Text', in J. Bybee, J. Haiman and S. Thompson (eds), *Essays on Language Function and Language Type: Dedicated to T. Givón*, 437–67, Amsterdam: Benjamins.

Slobin, I. D. (2004), 'The Many Ways to Search for a Frog: Linguistic Typology and the Expression of Motion Events', in S. Strömqvist and L. Verhoeven (eds), *Relating Events in Narrative: Typological and Contextual Perspectives*, 219–57, Mahwah, NJ: Erlbaum.

Schmiedtová, B., C. V. Stutterheim and M. Carroll (2011), 'Implications of Language-specific Patterns in Event Construal of Advanced L2 Speakers', in A. Pavlenko (ed.), *Thinking and Speaking in Two Languages*, 66–107, Bristol: Multilingual Matters.

Soroli, E. (2011), 'Typology and Spatial Cognition in English, French and Greek: Evidence from Eye-tracking', in A. Botinis (ed.), *Proceedings of the ISCA Tutorial and Research Workshop on Experimental Linguistics*, 127–30, Paris: International Speech Communication Association and University of Athens.

Soroli, E. (2012), 'Variation in Spatial Language and Cognition: Exploring Visuo-spatial Thinking and Speaking Cross-linguistically', *Cognitive Processing*, 13: 333–7.

Soroli, E. and A. Verkerk (2017), 'Motion Events in Greek: Methodological and Typological Issues', *CogniTextes*, 6 (1): 1–53.

von Stutterheim, C., M. Andermann, M. Carroll, M. Flecken and B. Schmiedtová (2012), 'How Grammaticized Concepts Shape Event Conceptualization in Language

Production: Insights from Linguistic Analysis, Eye Tracking Data, and Memory Performance', *Linguistics*, 50 (4): 833–67.

von Stutterheim, C., A. Bouhaous and M. Carroll (2017), 'From Time to Space: The Impact of Aspectual Categories on the Construal of Motion Events: The Case of Tunisian Arabic and Modern Standard Arabic', *Linguistics*, 55 (1): 207–49.

von Stutterheim, C. and R. Nüse (2003), 'Processes of Conceptualization in Language Production', *Linguistics*, 41 (5): 851–81.

Talmy, L. (2000), *Toward a Cognitive Semantics, Vol. II: Typology and Process in Concept Structuring*, Cambridge, MA: MIT Press.

Verkerk, A. (2013), 'The Correlation between Motion Event Encoding and Manner Verb Lexicon Size in Indo-European', *Language Dynamics and Change*, 3: 169–217.

Index of subjects

active voice   16
adjective   64, 69, 74, 81–2, 86–7, 89,
    94–8, 123, 127, 252–7
    adjective position   252, 254–6
    modification adjective   254, 257
adverb   36, 85, 96, 123, 234, 237, 264, 273
    temporal adverbs   137–8, 141–9
affixation   81–2, 98, 130, 229
agency   19
agglutination   124
agree   64, 67, 228
    agreement features   164, 218, 255, 256
    definiteness agreement   253, 256
    gender agreement (*see* gender)
    subject agreement   142, 229
allomorphy   123
    allomorph   85
    allomorphic stem   11
analogy   111, 119
argument   40, 148, 162, 182, 219, 228,
    252
article   121, 143, 229
    definite article   22, 253, 255, 256
aspect   137, 138, 140–7
    semantic aspect   19

background   19, 20–1, 23, 29, 48, 177,
    180–3, 188–9, 210, 215, 217,
    219–20, 222 n.13
bilingualism   119, 121, 131
blending   109, 119–21, 129, 131–2
borrowing   45–6, 85, 245–6, 256–7
    structural borrowing   119, 129, 131–2
bound base   85, 87
bound morpheme   86
bound stem   127–9, 133

calque   129–33
calquing   119, 131–2
clause   14–15, 18, 22, 40–2, 89, 155–6,
    158, 159, 161–2, 164, 166, 169, 175,
    195–6, 198–9, 202, 216, 219, 225,
    232, 249, 251, 274, 276

clause structure   191–3, 195, 202–4
    imperative clause   211
    interrogative clause (*see* interrogatives)
    parenthetical clause   211
    relative clause (*see* relatives)
    subordinate clause   22, 40, 50, 51, 195
clefts   174–7, 179, 182–7, 189
    clefted questions (*see* questions)
    clefting   219, 221
cliticization   225–6, 228–9, 232, 234–6,
    238
    enclisis   231, 234, 237–8
    encliticization   226, 229, 232–3,
        236–7
    proclisis   234, 237–8
clitics   168, 203, 210, 225–38
    clitic attachment   226, 234
    clitic movement   225, 235, 238
    enclitic/postverbal   225, 227–8, 231,
        233–4, 237
    proclitic/preverbal   225, 227–8, 237
    pronominal clitics   253
Complementizer (C)   21, 155, 158–9,
    163–5, 169, 225, 233, 237
    C-domain   194, 232
    Complementizer Phrase (CP)   159,
        165–8, 194–6, 199–201, 203, 248–9
    CP-periphery   250–1, 258
    doubly-filled Comp   159
Complex NP Constraint (CNPC)   157,
    162
compound   13, 63–4, 69–71, 75–6, 86–7,
    102–16, 119–32
    adjectival compound   119–20, 124,
        126–7, 130–1
    attributive compound   124, 126
    coordinative compound   119–20,
        124–6, 130, 132
    (de)verbal compound   119–20,
        128–9, 133 n.12
    exocentric compound   126–7
    neoclassical compound   107, 115 n.5,
        133 n.13

nominal compound   69, 102, 104, 114
phrasal compound   122, 124, 127,
    133 n.5
verbal compound   129, 131–2
compounding   86, 102–4, 110–12,
    114–15, 119–21, 123–4, 127–32
compound marker   110, 112–14, 124–5,
    129
conditionality   51, 52
    conditional meaning   46
conditional protasis   46
congruence   81–3, 85, 91, 96
constructionalization   51
Construction Grammar   56
context   11–13, 16, 18, 23, 29, 37, 40, 53,
    76, 82, 143, 163, 164, 175–9, 181,
    185, 188–9, 192, 195, 202, 212–14,
    217–20, 233–4, 246–8, 251–2, 262
    contextualization   54
    contextualization cues   45, 46, 54–6,
    94
Contrastive Analysis   26, 27, 29, 37, 41,
    87, 98, 102–4, 114, 119–20, 155–6,
    170, 174–7, 189, 246, 248
    Contrastive Analysis Hypothesis   26
conventionalization   56
conversion   10, 124
copy   155, 235–6, 238
coreferentiality   39

definiteness   182–3, 189, 219, 253–6
    polydefiniteness   254–6
deixis   20, 23
demonstratives   20–3, 229
derivation   68, 88, 111, 191, 226–7, 235,
    238
    zero derivation   96
Determiner (D)   165–9, 253–5
    Determiner Phrase (DP)   165–8,
    252–3, 252–8
discourse   9, 18, 20–3, 174–5, 177,
    189–93, 220–1, 245
    discourse relations   51
    discourse-semantic properties   174,
    177, 188
    discourse strategies   174–5, 188
dislocation   156, 215, 217–21
D-linking/D-linked   214, 246–7
dropping   39, 40

ellipsis   215
endocentricity   126, 131
enthymemic thinking   10
equivalence   81–3, 88, 90, 92
ergative language/morphology   13, 17, 18
exocentricity   119–20

female marking   63, 66
figure   264–5, 267
focus   175, 177, 179, 180, 188, 191–6,
    200, 202–4, 210, 214–15, 219, 221,
    234, 236, 245, 248–9, 251–2, 258
    broad focus   180, 192
    contrastive focus   191–3, 195,
    199–203
    focal domain   215, 217, 218
    focalization   156, 201, 212
    focus fronting   212, 214, 219, 252
    FocusP   191–2, 198, 201–3, 249
    information focus   191, 193, 195–9,
    202–3, 249, 251–2
    in situ focus   196, 199, 200, 202–3
    narrow focus   192, 213, 215, 217–18,
    220
    wide focus   215–16, 219–20
foreign language   26, 27, 28, 41
    first foreign language   28
    second foreign language   41, 42
function word (fnc)   225, 227, 230–1,
    235–7

gender   63–80, 126, 253, 255
    gender agreement   63–4, 74–6
    gender marking   63–70
    grammatical gender   63, 64, 71
    lexical-gender word   63–4, 69, 75–6
    notional gender   63, 64
Generative Grammar   156, 191, 198
genitive   124, 229, 254–7
    genitive arguments   253–4
    genitive position   245, 252–3, 256
gerund   225–6, 229
global language   26, 28, 41, 42
goal   124, 262–3, 265–9, 271, 273,
    275–6
    goal of motion   266, 270, 271, 273
    goal realization   263, 266, 268, 271,
    274
    goal salience   262–3, 266, 271, 276

grammaticalization   14, 23, 113, 155, 237, 256
ground   264, 269

headedness   119–21, 126, 128, 130–2
heuristic approach   9, 10
heuristic levels   12, 18, 20, 23
    mental-representational level   9, 12
    social-interactive level   9, 20
    textual level   9, 13
hypotactical structures   56

imperative   49, 55, 211, 225–6, 228–9, 233, 235
imperfective   37–8, 42, 149
implicature   30, 181–2, 184, 188
incorporation   32, 147–9, 169, 227–30, 236–8
inflection   71, 123, 139, 164, 194, 229
    inflectional ending   70–2, 75
    inflectional morpheme   83
    nominal inflection   203
    verbal inflection   141–2, 146, 148, 203, 216
information   45, 52, 91, 102, 174, 178, 180–1, 183, 188–9, 192, 202, 262–3, 265, 271, 274
    given information   181, 198
    informational unit   219–21, 222 n.13
    information focus (*see* focus)
    information structure (IS)   177, 191–3, 202–3, 210, 212, 219–21
    new information   74, 179, 193, 212, 226
interrogatives   9, 51, 159, 165, 215, 219
    interrogative clauses   155, 221
    interrogative sentence   40, 213, 219
    polar interrogatives   51
    wh-interrogatives   211–14, 217, 220
intonation   191, 204
    intonational phrase (IPh)   213–15, 234
inversion   49, 122, 212–13, 215, 217, 219, 250
    AUX inversion   164
    focal inversion   217
    free inversion   210, 212, 215, 217, 220
    Subject Auxiliary Inversion (SAI)   45, 46, 49, 50–2, 56

    subject inversion   212–15, 219–21
    syntactically-induced inversion   210, 214, 217, 220
islands   156–7, 162

juxtaposition   70–4

labelling   165–9
language acquisition   26–7, 96, 157, 234–5, 258
language change   23, 113
language contact   119–21, 128, 131–2, 258
    transfer under contact   245–6, 257
layering   32
left periphery   155, 160, 194, 201, 203, 246–7, 249–53
lexical base   83
lexicalization process   124
linking element   102, 104, 110, 120, 124–5, 129, 133
loanword   69, 121

manner   262, 264, 271, 274–6
    manner of motion   262–4, 274
    manner verbs   271–3, 276
mapping   174–5, 210, 212, 219, 221
merging operation   230
metre   46, 48, 52, 54, 55
mood   143, 229, 233, 235, 237
morphologization   113–15
motion   262–6, 269–71, 273–4, 276
    conceptualization of motion   262, 265
    lexicalization patterns of
        motion   262–3, 265–6, 271, 274–5
    motion events   262–6, 268–9, 271–2, 274–5
    verbalization of motion   262–3, 265–6, 268, 271–2, 274–5
movement   155–6, 158–60, 162, 191, 193–4, 196, 199–204, 225, 228–31, 235, 238, 245, 254–5, 257–8
    clitic movement   225, 238
    p-movement   194, 197, 203
    remnant movement   201–3
    verb movement   233–4
    V-to-T movement   198, 228, 232
    wh-movement   155–60, 162, 245, 247–8, 248, 250–2

noun (N)-finality   245, 252
noun-verb nominalization   13
NP-movement   255, 257
Nuclear Pitch Accent   213
Nuclear Stress Rule (NSR)   193, 195–9,
        202–3
null-subject language   210

object   14–16, 20, 21, 26, 29, 32, 39, 40–2,
        67, 157–8, 195, 197–202, 215, 250
    intransitive object   13
    null object   247
    pronominal object   225
    transitive object   13
obviation   23
onomasiological approach   27
ontological domain   27
OV language   250

parameter   155–6, 159–60, 246, 252, 254,
        256–8
    parametric change   245–6, 256, 258
paremiology   46, 53, 56
    paremiological template   46, 48–9
particles   23, 143, 147, 163–4, 174,
        178–9, 186–7, 189, 225, 237, 273
passive voice   16, 17, 19
path   262–5, 271, 273–4, 276
    path of motion   262–3
    path verbs   271–4
perfective   37, 137, 139–42, 144–7, 149
phi-features/φ-features   228–9, 253
Phonetic Form (PF)   225, 234–5, 238,
        250–1
phonological phrase (PPh)   234
phonological word (PW)   124, 227
phraseology   45, 53, 56
political linguistics   55
pragmatic strategies   18, 19
prefix   16, 17, 86, 229, 255, 264
presupposition   177, 181–4, 188–9
pro-drop
    non-pro-drop language   39, 203
    pro-drop language   192, 194, 203
productivity   45, 48–9, 52, 56, 83,
        102, 105, 113, 114, 125, 126,
        128, 221
pronominal forms   157, 217
    polite pronominal form   210–12, 217

respect pronominal form   218
    weak pronomimal objects   225
        (*see* clitics)
pronoun   74, 163, 210, 213–20
    clitic pronouns   210 (*see also* clitics)
    familiarity pronoun   217, 220
    honorific pronoun   72, 75–6
    interrogative pronoun   41
    null pronoun   214
    overt pronoun   210, 214, 216, 220–1
    proclitic pronoun   237
    relative pronoun   21
    subject pronoun   40, 192, 211–17,
        219–21
    strong pronouns   210–14, 218–19
    weak pronouns   225 (*see* clitics)
prosody   191, 204, 217, 220–21, 227, 231
    prosodic constituent   231, 233–4
    prosodic constraints   235–6, 238
    prosodic properties   191, 193, 204, 234
    prosodic reanalysis   225, 236–8
    prosodic strategies   201, 219
    prosodic structure   227, 235
proverb   45–59
    proverbial-constructicon   45, 56
    proverbial-grammar   45, 56
    proverb templates   46, 54
proverbiality   45, 46, 54–6

quantifiers   229, 248
question   157, 158, 161, 163–6, 168–70,
        174–5, 177–84, 187, 189, 248, 250
    clefted questions   176
    information-eliciting questions   177,
        179, 186
    multiple questions   159, 245–6, 248,
        250–2
    rhetorical questions   177–9, 186, 189
    root questions   158, 161, 169
    wh-questions (*see* wh-questions)
    yes/no questions   159, 163–4

relatives/relative clause   40–1, 49, 155–6,
        162, 168–70, 246, 252, 255–8
    extraposed relatives   252
    free relatives   155, 165–7, 169
Relativized Minimality   248
rheme   221
rhyme   48, 53, 54, 55

Satellite-framed language (S-framed language) 262–6, 271, 274, 276
satellites 263, 273, 276
scrambling 194, 196–7, 199–200, 203, 250–1
semasiological approach 27
slogan 45–59
Social Construction Grammar 45, 46, 56
SOV language 194–6, 203
Sprachbund 10
    Balkan Sprachbund 119–21, 131
    Charlemagne Sprachbund 28
Standard Average European (SAE) 28
stress 22, 122–4, 193, 196, 199, 203, 229, 237
    in situ stress 191, 197, 202, 203–4
    rhythmic stress 237
    stress pattern 229
SVO language 16, 194–5, 197–8, 210
subject
    null subject 210, 213–14, 216, 221
    postverbal subject 201, 210, 212–15, 219–20
    preverbal subject 201, 211–14
    pronominal subject 41
    vP/VP-internal subject 223
subjectivity 33
suffix 64, 66–7, 69, 75–7, 81–3, 85–98, 105, 107, 111, 115, 127, 142, 229
    adjectival suffix 92, 127
    adjective-forming suffix 81–3, 85–8, 92–4, 96
    derivational closing suffix 111
    derivational suffix 83, 115
    diminutive suffix 66
    genitive suffix 104–5, 107, 116
    inflectional suffix 83, 104–6, 113, 115
    plural suffix 105, 107, 110–11, 113, 116
    semi-suffix 97
    suffixal derivative 66, 73, 77
suffixation 81–3, 85–6, 93, 98
    adjectival suffixation 81–2, 93
    adjective-forming suffixation 81, 83
suffixoid 97
superiority 246–9, 251
syllogistic thinking 10
syntax-discourse interface 174–5, 178
Systemic Functional Grammar 191

temporal-aspectual domain 26, 29
tense
    future progressive tense 30
    future tense 27, 29, 32, 148
    past tense 66, 137–41, 144–50, 229
    present progressive tense 18–19, 29–32, 137–8, 271
    present tense 30
    tense information 139, 147, 148
tenseless language 137–9, 143–4, 146–9
tense-rich language 138–9, 141, 146–9
theta position 235
topic 51, 191, 194, 196, 198–200, 203, 210, 214, 216–20, 233–4, 236, 248
    topicalization 156
    topicalized phrases 234, 250, 256
    topic-comment structure 51, 191, 210, 219, 222 n.13
    TopicP 198, 201–3
T/V (*tu/vous*) language 217
typology 10, 85, 87, 89, 141, 157, 226, 248, 263
    micro-typology 26, 27, 29, 37, 41
    pilot typology 27

universals of word order 10, 16

V1 verb-first 45–59
    V1-conditional 46, 48, 49–52
    V1-construction 45, 46, 49–51, 56
    V1-declarative 51
V2 verb-second (language) 51–2, 194–5, 203
variation
    diachronic variation 225
    dialectal variation 225–6
    lexico-semantic variation 48
    microvariation 155
    parameters of variation 155–6, 159–60
    syntactic variation 48
    word order variation 191, 203
verb
    agentive verb 32
    lexical verb 49, 51
    movement verb 32
    serial verb 13
    verb-initial 49, 51, 215

Verb-framed language (V-framed
    language)   262–6, 271, 274–6
V-final language   249–50
VO language   250
vP-periphery   249, 251
VSO language   18, 194, 198

weak crossover   251
wh-
    wh-constructions   156, 158
    wh-element   156–7, 159–63, 165–6,
        168–9, 174, 179, 214, 247
    wh-in situ   155, 158, 160–2, 250
    wh-in situ language   158, 248, 250
    wh-movement (*see* movement)
    wh-phrase   159, 166, 201, 233,
        245–52
    wh-questions (*see* wh-questions)
    wh-structures   165–6, 169
    wh-word   175, 177–82, 186, 188, 214,
        229, 248
wh-questions   155, 158–61, 163–5,
        174–89, 196, 215
    argument wh-question   182–7, 189

clefted wh-question   175
discourse-semantics of wh-questions
        23, 174, 177–8, 180–2, 186,
        188–9
    framing wh-question   182–5, 189
    multiple wh-questions   246, 248,
        251–2
    propositional wh-question   182–5,
        189
word class   81, 86–7, 89
word formation   66, 75, 81, 84, 87, 102,
        108, 110–12, 114, 141, 148
word order   16–18, 45, 55–6, 158, 191–4,
        198–9, 203, 212
    OSV   198
    OVS   197–8, 200, 202
    SOV   16, 194–5, 250
    SVO   16–18, 51, 56, 194–5, 197–202,
        212
    VOS   197–9, 201–2, 212, 215, 220
    VS   197, 212–13, 215, 220
    VSO   16–18, 195, 198, 200–1, 212,
        215–17, 220
    VSX   211

Index of languages

Albanian   119–33, 159
Algonquian languages   23
Amele   137–42, 146–50
Armenian   245
Austronesian language   140, 143, 149

Basque   13, 17
Bulgarian   159

Catalan   215, 219
Celtic languages   29
Chácobo   149
Chinese   137, 140–1, 144–9, 170
   Mandarin Chinese   137, 158
   Sino-Tibetan Chinese   141
Czech   74, 76, 159

Dagbani   13, 14
Dutch   28, 263

English   12–23, 26–42, 45–52, 56, 63–7,
   69–73, 75–8, 81–3, 85–98, 129, 138–9,
   141, 144, 147–9, 156–9, 165–7, 175,
   191–2, 194–5, 199, 202–4, 221,
   256–7, 263–6, 272–3, 276
   American English   21, 50, 63, 69
   Bangladesh English   70
   English as a bridge language   28, 29
   Indian English   70, 76–7
European languages   29, 107, 131, 133,
   137–9, 141, 145, 156

French   12, 15–16, 19, 132, 140, 160–4,
   169, 171, 215, 219
   Mainland French   164
   Québec French   163, 164
   Standard French   164

Ga   14
German   10, 13, 22, 28–37, 39–42, 45–9,
   51–6, 102–8, 110–14, 174–9, 184–7,
   189, 191–2, 196, 202, 204, 205,
   262–6, 268–76

Germanic languages   45, 51, 174, 175,
   194, 203
Greek   16, 71, 85–6, 102–4, 107–8, 110,
   113–15, 119–33, 191–2, 194–5,
   198–9, 202–5, 225–7, 229–37,
   238–9, 245–52, 254–7, 259, 262–6,
   268–76
   Ancient Greek   104, 115, 121, 123,
     133, 231
   Asia Minor Greek (AMG)   230, 245–61
   Byzantine and Medieval Greek (BMG)
     225, 226
   Cappadocian   230, 231, 233, 236, 245,
     247, 252–5
   Classical Greek   250
   Cretan   230
   Cypriot Greek   233, 234, 251, 254
   Hellenistic Greek   247, 248, 249,
     250, 256
   Italiot Greek   245, 254, 255
   Karpathiot   230, 231
   mainland Greek   245, 254–6
   Medieval Greek   225, 232
   Modern Greek (MG)   102, 115, 121,
     124, 128, 132, 133, 225, 226, 229,
     230–2, 239, 245–7, 259, 263
   Pharasiot   245, 247, 255–6
   Pontic Greek   247
   Rhodian   230
   Romeyka   245, 247, 250, 252–6
   Standard Modern Greek (SMG)
     225–49, 251–4
   Symiot   230

Indo-European languages   130
Italian   26, 29–42, 126, 128, 132, 160,
   167, 170–1, 191–2, 194–5, 197–9,
   201–5, 210–22
   Central varieties of Italian   37
   Florentine (dialect)   169
   Southern varieties of Italian   37

Japanese   92, 139, 144, 148

Kannada   158
Kobon   146

Laz   245

Malay   12, 16, 18, 19, 20
Ma Manda   137, 142, 148–50
Maybrat   149

Nguna   137, 140–1, 143–4, 146–9

Ojibwa   23
    Ottawa dialect of Ojibwa   23

Polish   63–78
Portuguese   169, 215
    European Portuguese   215, 219, 226,
        232, 234, 235

Romance languages   28, 131, 132,
        155–73, 203, 210, 212, 219,
        226, 228
    Medieval Romance   232
Romanian   215, 219
Russian   65, 67, 71, 74, 263

Serbian-Croatian   226, 231
Slavic languages   121, 225–6, 238
Spanish   81–3, 87–98, 128, 191–2, 195,
        197–200, 202–5, 210–22, 228, 264,
        273, 276
Swedish   174–90

Turkish   245–61, 264
Twi   14

Yagua   149

Ingram Content Group UK Ltd.
Milton Keynes UK
UKHW051458150623
423417UK00015B/179